WESTERN APACHE MATERIAL CULTURE

Western Apache Material Culture
The Goodwin and Guenther Collections

Alan Ferg
Editor

With contributions by
William B. Kessel
Morris E. Opler
Grenville Goodwin
Jan Bell

Photographs by
Helga Teiwes

Index by
Madelyn Cook

Published for

THE ARIZONA STATE MUSEUM
The University of Arizona
by
The University of Arizona Press

Third printing 1996

THE UNIVERSITY OF ARIZONA PRESS
Copyright © 1987
The Arizona Board of Regents
All Rights Reserved
Manufactured in the U.S.A.
∞ This book is printed on acid-free, archival-quality paper.

Publication of this book was assisted by grants from the University of Arizona Foundation, the Vice President for Research and Graduate Studies of the University of Arizona, and University of Arizona President Henry Koffler.

This book was composed in ITC Galliard and ITC Modern No. 216 Medium

Library of Congress Cataloging-in-Publication Data
Western Apache material culture.
Bibliography: p.
1. Apache Indians—Antiquities—Private collections—Catalogs. 2. Indians of North America—Southwest, New—Antiquities—Private collections—Catalogs. 3. Arizona State Museum—Ethnological collections—Catalogs. 4. Goodwin, Grenville, 1907–1940—Ethnological collections—Catalogs. 5. Guenther, Edgar—Ethnological collections—Catalogs. 6. Guenther, Minnie—Ethnological collections—Catalogs. I. Ferg, Alan. II. Kessel, William B. III. Arizona State Museum.
E99.A6W425   1987   979'.01   86-30806
ISBN 0-8165-1028-8 (alk. paper)

British Cataloguing-in-Publication Data
A catalogue record for this book is available from the British Library.

COVER: Western Apache dolls with 1880s clothing (ASM Neg. C–21673); see Figure 6.2.

Contents

Preface   vii

Chapter 1. The Collections   1
    Jan Bell and Alan Ferg

Chapter 2. Edgar and Minnie Guenther   9
    William B. Kessel

Chapter 3. Grenville Goodwin   27
    Morris E. Opler

Chapter 4. The Social Divisions and Economic Life of the Western Apache   41
    Grenville Goodwin (1935)

Chapter 5. Subsistence   49
    Alan Ferg and William B. Kessel

Chapter 6. Clothing   87
    Alan Ferg and William B. Kessel

Chapter 7. Ritual   109
    Alan Ferg and William B. Kessel

Chapter 8. Recreation   153
    Alan Ferg and William B. Kessel

Appendix A. The Southern Athapascans   165
    Grenville Goodwin (1938)

Appendix B. Common and Species Names of Materials used for Artifacts   175
    Alan Ferg

Appendix C. Inventory of the Collections   177
    Alan Ferg

References and Suggested Readings   197

Index   207

Contributors   222

Color Illustrations   following 86

to
THE WESTERN APACHE
who utilized their world so well

Preface

With the resurgence of interest in material culture studies, well-documented museum collections are becoming ever more valuable as basic resources. Public interest in the culture history of American Indians is strong, especially with regard to craft items, and some of the most important groups to gain from the greater availability of information on such collections are the Native Americans themselves. As an example, use has already been made of the Goodwin and Guenther Apache collections by Mr. Edgar Perry, Curator of the White Mountain Apache Culture Center in Fort Apache, and by members of the Payson Apache Community. Interest in their own cultural traditions, including material culture, is increasing among young Apaches; publishing information on these collections makes otherwise unknown material readily available.

The Arizona State Museum has served for many years as a major source for scholarly and student research on Apache culture. There are just over 1300 Apache objects in the Museum collections, with a large majority of them Western Apache. The items range in date from the mid-1800s to 1985. The single largest category of artifact represented is basketry, recognized as one of the finest craft accomplishments of Southwestern Indians. The unique aspect, and real strength, of the Arizona State Museum collection, however, is the wide diversity of lesser known materials, representing virtually every aspect of traditional and acculturated Western Apache life. This strength derives primarily from two major assemblages, the Goodwin and Guenther collections. Both were gathered essentially in the field by individuals who developed an intimate knowledge of Apache culture through years of close association. Goodwin's experience was as an anthropologist, the Guenthers' as resident missionaries. Both collections are systematic in their own distinct way, and both are well documented. Together these two collections give the scholar and the public a rare opportunity to examine the full range of Western Apache material culture and thereby gain a greater understanding of what was, and is, a many-faceted lifeway.

The Goodwin collection is a critically valuable body of data on pre-Reservation Western Apache culture, particularly when evaluated with respect to the extensive documentation that accompanies the items. Goodwin was guided in his collecting by a desire to document as precisely as possible what part these items played in the life of the Western Apache, and as Morris Opler states of Goodwin and his collections in Chapter 3, "It was their context and the interplay of the material and the ideological in human affairs that intrigued him. The material dimension expressed for him how well the people understood their natural surroundings and utilized their possibilities." This approach is extremely well reflected in the scope of his collection.

In 1931 Goodwin gave an Apache fiddle to the Arizona State Museum, and the following year he helped the Museum to purchase a set of *gaan* headdresses. In 1936 he placed his collection on loan at the Museum. These are the Western Apache materials that he had collected in conjunction with his field studies. In 1939 Goodwin loaned to the Museum many items he had secured specifically for a major Apache exhibit at the Museum. Goodwin's widow, Janice, ultimately donated most of the materials that had been on loan, and in 1971 she and her son, Neil, donated additional items collected by Goodwin. Materials from the Goodwin collection have remained the most important component of the ethnological exhibit in the Museum.

The Guenther collection has particular value in providing a diachronic view of the survival and modification of pre-Reservation traits in a twentieth-century, partially acculturated society. While the Goodwin collection focuses on utilitarian objects and emphasizes aboriginal subsistence technology, the Guenther collection contains an excellent representation of objects made specifically for sale to outsiders. It clearly shows the changes in native-made material culture that accompanied the transition from a subsistence to a cash economy. Although some of the items are duplicated in other museum collections, this particular assemblage has significance as a cohesive and well-documented reference source for Western Apache crafts made in one area over a seventy-year period.

For some time Mrs. Guenther and her family gave thought to the ultimate disposition of the Guenther collection. In the 1970s, Mrs. Guenther was approached by some members of her family regarding a bequest to the Arizona State Museum. Knowing the research value of the collection, she agreed to the bequest, but expressed her desire that the collection be available in some manner for anyone to look at and enjoy. Mrs. Guenther understood that the perpetual exhibit of the entire collection was not feasible, and she agreed to the publication of a catalogue that would provide a form of access to it by the general public. Work on that project started in 1980. Because of the extensive wealth of documentary information and the desirability of illustrating a large number of artifacts, the catalogue quickly grew beyond its original concept. Inasmuch as the Goodwin collection so neatly complemented the Guenther materials and the two combined formed a significant Apache resource, the scope of the publication was expanded further to cover both collections. While Apache basketry has received much attention in popular as well as scholarly publications, treatment of the broader range of other kinds of Apache materials, as represented so richly in these two collections, has been relatively neglected.

In assembling this volume we have tried to balance the presentation to appeal to the general public as well as to provide information of use to the professional community. Reprinting the two short articles by Grenville Goodwin in Chapter 4 and Appendix A serves to introduce the reader to the Western Apache. These articles have historical import for those interested in the development of ethnographic studies in the Southwest. The biographical sketches of Goodwin and of Edgar and Minnie Guenther are fascinating history in their own right, and they document the circumstances under which the collections were made. Both of these sketches are written by trained anthropologists who are thoroughly knowledgeable of their subjects, Kessel as a family member and Opler as a close friend. The inventory in Appendix C lists items by categories as presented in Chapters 5 through 8, subsistence, clothing, ritual, and recreation, and serves as an index to the material culture. Figure numbers are included and aid the interested reader in locating specific artifacts in the book.

Finally, Minnie was always concerned that people be able to enjoy the Guenther collection; the abundant photographs presented here are intended to make that enjoyment possible for all.

Preface

Grenville Goodwin was scrupulous in his attention to detail and the comparative method; the use of his notes in the captions, the liberal literature references, and the inventory take the work he began one step further.

Acknowledgments

The publication of this volume, at the most basic level, is possible because of the foresight of several individuals in collecting and preserving the materials and information presented here: Grenville Goodwin, Janice (Goodwin) Massy, Neil Goodwin, Minnie and Edgar Guenther, Frieda and Arnold Knoop, and William B. Kessel. Recognition also is given to the many Western Apache who befriended the Guenthers, the Knoops, and Goodwin, and shared their knowledge of things Apache. Goodwin's informants in particular must have had some understanding that through him they were preserving a good deal of their own history in a rapidly changing world.

Raymond H. Thompson, Director of the Arizona State Museum (ASM), has consistently supported the research and publication of the Goodwin materials. He and Bernard L. Fontana, Field Historian of the University of Arizona Library, arranged the publication of the Guenther materials with then University President John P. Schaefer. Funding for some of the research for this book and its publication came from the Office of the President, the University of Arizona Foundation, and the Arizona State Museum.

Many specialists generously gave of their time and expertise to help identify a wide range of objects and materials. Grenville Goodwin identified the materials in many of the artifacts in his collection. Walter H. Birkby (ASM) identified hair and blood specimens and provided X-rays of several items. Amadeo M. Rea (San Diego Natural History Museum) identified the feathers and bird parts. Charles H. Miksicek (Office of Arid Lands Studies, University of Arizona [UA]), Willard Van Asdall (ASM), Karen Adams (Herbarium, UA), Barney T. Burns (Native Seeds/SEARCH), Thomas H. Naylor (ASM), the late Charles W. Ferguson (Laboratory of Tree-Ring Research, UA) and Suzanne K. Fish (Office of Arid Lands Studies, UA) helped identify various plant materials. Stanley J. Olsen (ASM) and John W. Olsen (Department of Anthropology, UA) identified a number of hide and bone specimens. Stan Olsen, J. Duncan Campbell (Harrisburg, Pennsylvania), E. Wesley Jernigan (Department of Anthropology, UA), William Beaver (Sacred Mountain Trading Post, Arizona), and Robert M. Herskovitz (Arizona Historical Society) identified or commented on buttons and silverwork. Herskovitz, Nancy Odegaard (ASM), and Diane Dittemore (ASM) identified various pieces of clothing or materials. Dittemore and Odegaard also helped identify basketry materials. Ann L. Hedlund (Department of Anthropology, Arizona State University) examined the Zuni-Navajo blanket. Diana Pardue (Heard Museum, Phoenix) commented on the beadwork. Jonathan Batkin (Taylor Museum, Colorado Springs Fine Arts Center, Colorado Springs), Morris E. Opler (University of Oklahoma), Richard Conn (Denver Art Museum), and Richard A. Pohrt (Flint, Michigan) helped identify clothing and other buckskin items. Arthur W. Vokes (ASM) identified some of the marine shell items; Kenneth C. Rozen (ASM) and Bruce B. Huckell (ASM) commented on the various chipped stone items, and Rozen identified the rifle cartridges. Finally, Robert T. O'Haire (Arizona Bureau of Mines, UA) kindly provided identifications and spectroscopic analysis of the mineral specimens.

Appreciation is expressed to Barney T. Burns, who kindly contributed the detailed note at the end of Chapter 3. The recent attempt to locate Apache sites visited by Grenville Goodwin in the 1930s extends this historical record. Keith H. Basso (Yale University) and Wes Jernigan generously made available the extensive notes and illustrations they had compiled on Western Apache material culture. Dexter R. Schubert (Admissions and Records, UA) provided a transcript of Grenville Goodwin's university class records, Robert W. Rosaldo (Audio Productions, UA) enhanced some critical tape-recordings, and Anibal Rodriquez, Jr. (American Museum of Natural History) located some important Goddard specimens. Other people who provided information or assistance include Ruth Kessel, George Kessel, Arthur Guenther, Gloria Guenther, Dorothea Ferg, Karl Knoop, Fay Knoop, Neil Goodwin, Beth Rogan Ferg, Gloria Fenner, and Lester Oliver.

The Rev. Arthur A. Guenther kindly granted permission to use the many photographs from his collection taken by his father, the Rev. E. E. Guenther and by the Rev. Paul Mayerhoff. Neil Goodwin provided prints of photographs taken by and of his father, Grenville Goodwin, and permission to reproduce them. Martha Brace (Department of Anthropology, UA) watched for relevant materials while doing her own research and pointed out the good photograph of the crew at Turkey Hill Pueblo. Minnie Guenther, Waldo Wedel (Smithsonian Institution), Pamela Haas (American Museum of Natural History), Robert Euler (National Park Service), David M. Brugge (National Park Service), Steve Rogers (ASM), Gloria Guenther, Arthur Guenther, William Kessel, and Dorothea Ferg provided additional information on various photographs.

The fine artifact photographs that form the heart of this volume were taken by Helga Teiwes (ASM); her care and patience in producing them are much appreciated. Brigid Sullivan (National Park Service) drafted Figure 5.46 *(bottom)*. Charles Sternberg (ASM) drafted the maps in Figures 1.1, 1.2, 1.4, and 4.1. Ronald J. Beckwith (ASM) drafted or redrafted the other figures used.

All of the aforementioned individuals contributed in substantial ways. William B. Kessel and Morris E. Opler must be singled out, however, as having generously volunteered a great deal of their time in writing, editing, or contributing to the various sections of this book.

Often on a daily basis, sporadically for over five years, the staff of the Arizona State Museum has cheerfully borne the brunt of endless requests for access to collections, records, archives, photographs, exhibits, and more. These include: Helga Teiwes and Michael Barton of Photography; Diane Dittemore, Michael Jacobs, Steve Rogers, Jan Bell, and Rosemary Maddock of Collections; Kathy Hubenschmidt, Ellen Horn, and Pat Hollingshead of Photo Collections; Nancy Odegaard, Conservation; Hans Bart, Daphne Scott, Judy Reis, Jeanne Armstrong, and Madelyn Cook of the Library and Archives; Ernest E. Leavitt and Stuart (Skip) Meehan of Public Programs; Raymond H. Thompson, R. Gwinn Vivian, George Sample, and Dola Moore of Administration. The patience and help of all these people are greatly appreciated; they consistently exerted whatever extra effort was necessary to transform a good idea into a tangible book.

Gwinn Vivian continuously provided the administrative expertise and good suggestions to keep the work moving and on track. Jan Bell also helped with innumerable logistical matters, provided much-appreciated, sound advice, and those most valuable of commodities, quiet work space and quiet encouragement. Above all others, Jan and Gwinn must be credited with bringing this endeavor to a happy conclusion.

For the tedious task of typing and repeatedly changing the manuscript and especially her suggestions on certain organizational aspects of the book, thanks go to Rosemary Maddock.

Carol Gifford (Department of Anthropology, UA) was indispensable in editing the manuscript into a more readable form and exhibited an enviable attention to detail, so important in preparing an illustration-filled manuscript of this sort for publication. The professional organization and attractive appearance of this volume owe much to the staff of the University of Arizona Press, directed by Stephen F. Cox, and to the book designer, Al Whitehurst. Harrison Shaffer and John Bancroft supervised the production and printing process.

ALAN FERG

Chapter One
The Collections

Jan Bell and Alan Ferg

The Apache and Navajo are Athapaskan speakers, related to those of Alaska, western Canada, and the Northwest Coast. They arrived in what is now the southwestern United States probably during the sixteenth century. Compared with the long established Puebloan, Piman, and Yuman peoples, they are relative newcomers to the area. Exposed to a diversity of environments and cultural influences, the Southern Athapaskans split and developed into the distinct subgroups known in the historic period as the Jicarilla, Mescalero, Lipan, Kiowa-Apache, Chiricahua, Western Apache, and Navajo. The differences and similarities and the distinctive artifactual usages among these subgroups are described by Grenville Goodwin in Appendix A. His comparative discussion of the economic life, material culture, social organization, and religion of the Southern Athapaskans provides historical perspective for the inventory of items presented herein.

The term Western Apache was coined by Grenville Goodwin as a collective designation for the Southern Tonto, Northern Tonto, White Mountain, Cibecue, and San Carlos Apache, all of whom have more in common linguistically and culturally with each other than they do with the other Southern Athapaskans (Fig. 1.1). Once wide-ranging, the Western Apache now occupy the adjacent Fort Apache and San Carlos Indian Reservations in east-central Arizona and the Tonto Apache Indian Reservation near Payson. These groups remained relatively peaceful during the period of white encroachment into the Southwest, thereby avoiding most of the protracted war of attrition waged by the U.S. and Mexican military, relocation away from their homeland, and other pacification efforts that proved so devastating to the cultural survival of the closely related Chiricahua (Fig. 1.2).

The Western Apache have been in real contact with whites for only some 150 years, and their lifeway remained largely unchanged until the end of the last century. Since then, they have adapted rapidly to the changing conditions of reservation life and the outside world, especially in the economic sphere. Though the traditional native religion and belief system remain a viable force in Apache life, both Christian missionaries and Apache nativistic movements have had considerable impact. There has been loss and purposeful abandonment of many native cultural traits, especially in the realm of utilitarian and subsistence related material culture, during the past eighty years. Even the coiled basketry once so common, and now so coveted by collectors, has nearly ceased to be manufactured.

BOTTOM: Figure 1.1. Location of Western Apache groups.

OPPOSITE: Figure 1.2. Territories of tribes neighboring the Western Apache.

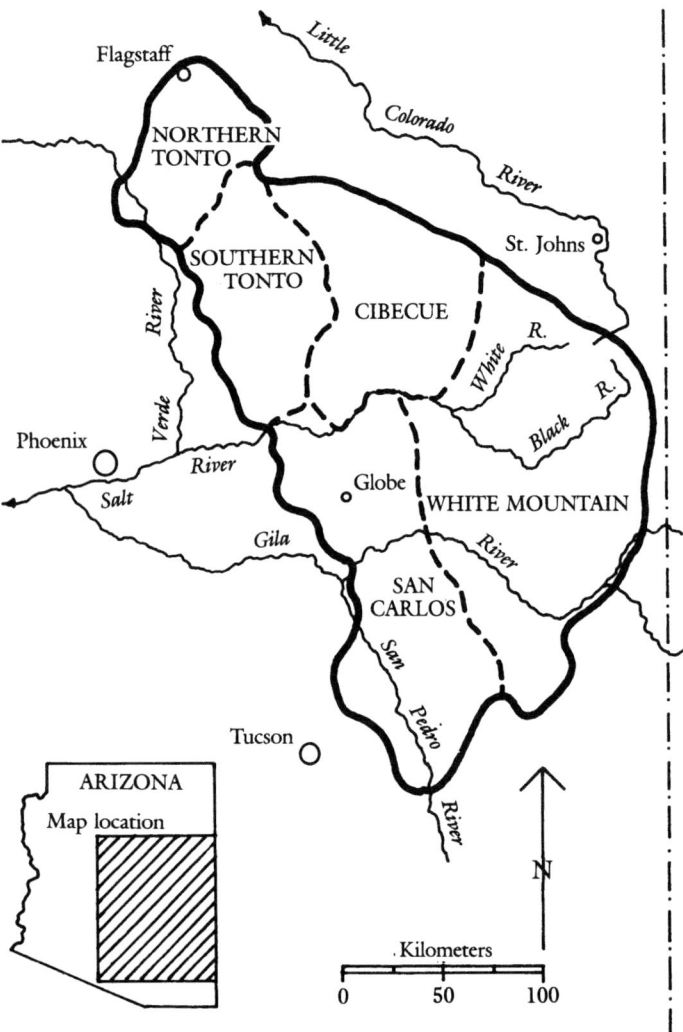

The Goodwin Collection

Despite the lack of formal academic training, Grenville Goodwin was a major contributor to Southwestern ethnology. He came to Arizona originally to attend a college preparatory school, and by his early twenties had chosen to immerse himself in a study of Western Apache culture that would be a primary focus of attention for the remainder of his short life. Though he did not pursue a college degree, he established contacts with colleagues at the University of Chicago and the University of Arizona that were to provide valuable direction to his studies. When Dr. Emil Haury became Director of the Arizona State Museum in 1938, he and Goodwin worked together in planning a major exhibit on the Apache. Its primary emphasis was on those indigenous to Arizona (the Chiricahua as well as the Western Apache), but the display also included selected comparative materials to illustrate differences and similarities with the other Southern Athapaskan groups (Fig. 1.3).

Goodwin's field work took place between 1929 and 1939, ultimately involving careful study of virtually all aspects of Apache culture. He had an intense interest in recording what was still known of the pre-Reservation period. Early in his studies he became interested in material culture and particularly in items related to past subsistence practices. Methodologically, Goodwin concentrated on documenting those artifacts no longer in use at the time of his field work and those that were rapidly becoming obsolete. He collected a number of extant examples of old artifact types. By requesting elderly Apaches to make items that were no longer available but that had been made and used by those individuals in their younger years, Goodwin was able to observe and record much about the physical details of construction and decoration of artifacts. He also documented taboos surrounding the manufacturing process as well as functional distinctions and other cultural associations known to the makers. Later he used some of the objects as an aid in eliciting additional information from other Apache informants. He also compared the objects with materials of other Southern Athapaskan groups

The Collections

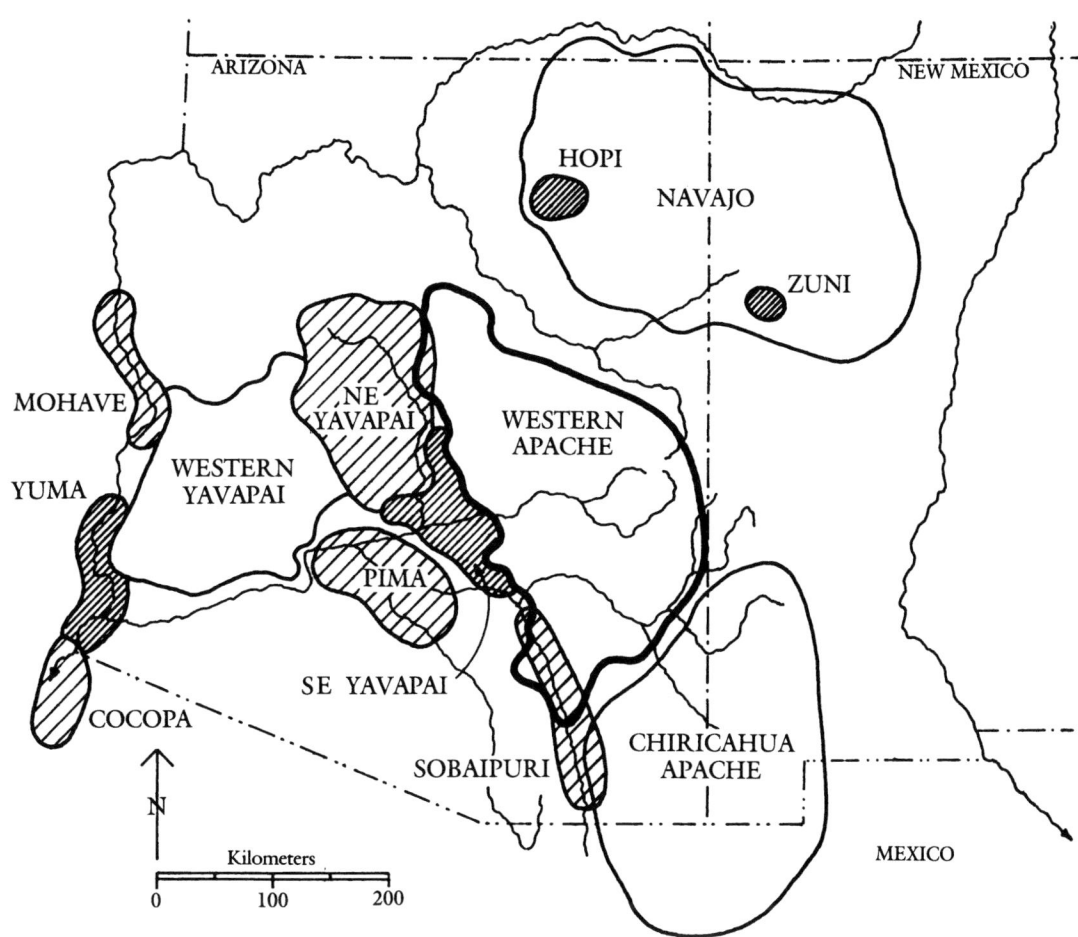

and collected some items with the goal of developing comparative museum exhibits.

In all, Goodwin collected nearly 300 objects. Contextual information about the use and derivation of material items was included in a personal catalogue as well as in his field notes, which number some 2,000 pages and cover essentially all areas of Apache culture. Additional notes contain linguistic data, biographies, and documentation of place names. He also produced 200 pages of meticulous watercolors and pen and ink sketches, and he took several dozen black-and-white photographs of Western Apache material culture, places, architecture, and people. All of these materials are in the Arizona State Museum. Appendix C contains a complete listing of all artifactual material that Goodwin collected, including materials at institutions other than the Arizona State Museum, and the References contain a listing of Goodwin's published articles and unpublished archival materials in the Arizona State Museum that are available to scholars.

Documentation of the Goodwin Collection

For the materials Grenville Goodwin collected, he recorded in his catalogue who had made the object, the band affiliation, when and where the object was made or collected, and occasionally

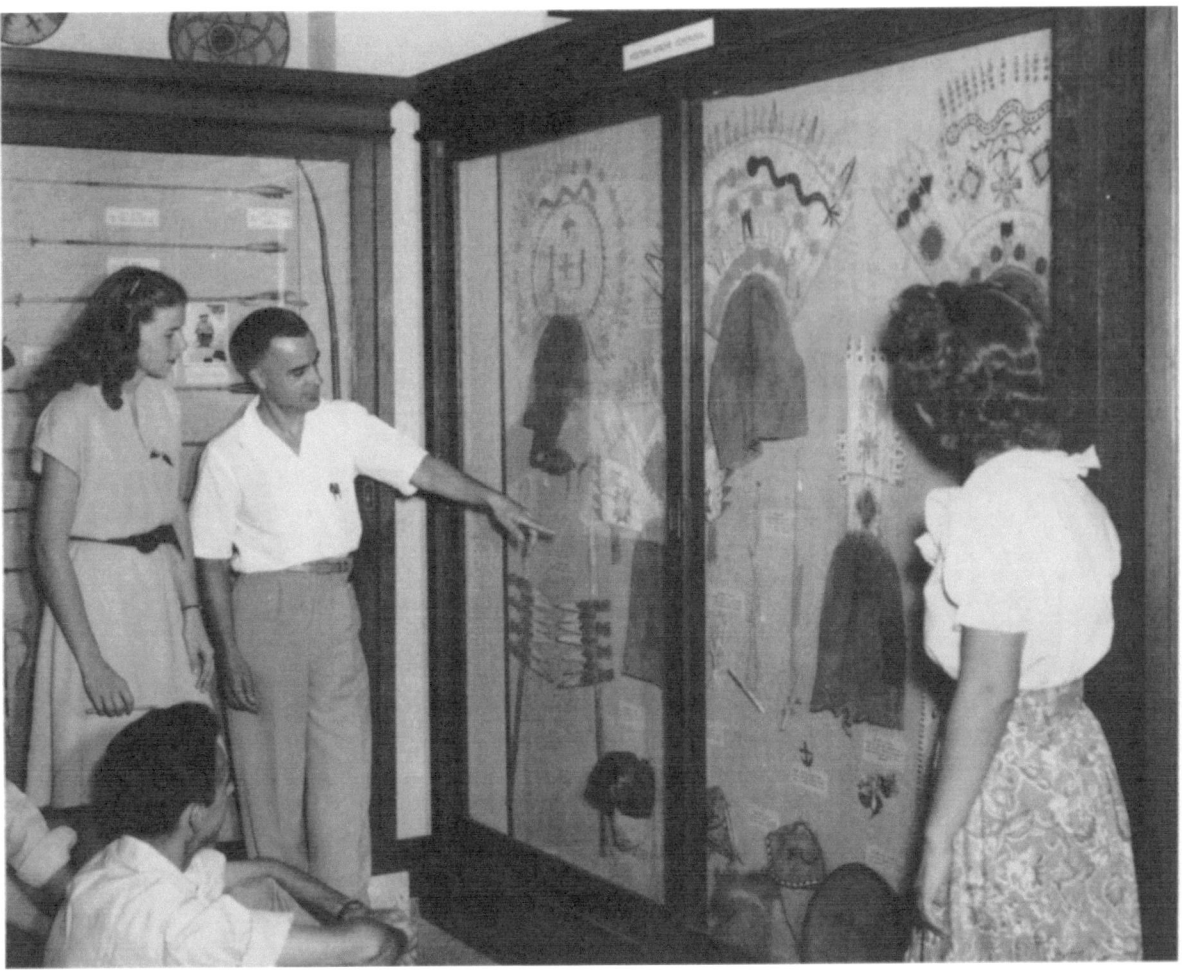

Figure 1.3. Prof. Harry Getty and a University of Arizona, Department of Anthropology class in the Arizona State Museum in 1946. Students are examining one of the cases that exhibited Western Apache materials collected by Grenville Goodwin. This case contains ceremonial paraphernalia, the one at left rear contains weapons, and at extreme right (not visible) is a comparative display of dolls (see Figs. AA.5–AA.7) collected by Goodwin from the various Southern Athapaskan tribes to illustrate pre-Reservation dress (photo by E. B. Sayles, ASM Neg. 1751).

particulars about details of construction, use, and decoration. By mischance, however, Goodwin's personal catalogue did not come to the Arizona State Museum with his other notes, and the documentation found on the Museum's catalogue cards was usually minimal. This undetailed information seemed out of character for a consistently meticulous note-taker, and incongruous with the fact the Goodwin had carefully numbered all the specimens he had loaned to the Museum. Suspecting the existence of a personal catalogue, Ferg contacted Grenville's son, Neil, in 1975 and was promptly supplied with a copy. It has now rejoined Grenville's other notes (Arizona State Museum Archive, Goodwin A–1087). Although many of the specimens that Goodwin collected have been illustrated repeatedly in books and articles on the

The Collections

Western Apache, much of the provenience information he recorded for them is published here for the first time, and incorporated into the Inventory presented in Appendix C.

In addition to increasing the study value of Goodwin's collection, his catalogue reveals interesting details of his relationship with his "informants." Goodwin commissioned and paid for many objects, but at other times, apparently when on camping trips with his informants or perhaps when discussing the old days, it appears that informants spontaneously made and gave him certain items. Some, such as a bundle of corn tied up the old way or a sample of the parts of yucca to be used for soap, probably had little value. Others, however, such as baskets and unfired clay toys and tobacco pipes, must have been small gifts given to a friend. These differences are noted because although perhaps remembered as an ethnologist, Goodwin, like the Guenthers, was often intimately involved in the lives of the Apaches he knew and was their friend, something the repeated use of the term "informant" in the following pages tends to obscure.

Extensive use has been made of Goodwin's field notes. How widely applicable some of the statements made by his informants may be is unclear, but his strongest body of information is from the Eastern and Western bands of the White Mountain group collected from Anna Price, her daughter Mrs. Jewett Wright, Mrs. Andrew Stanley, David Longstreet, Harvey Nashkine, John Rope, and Palmer Valor. Some of their classifications of items (like men's buckskin caps) or distinctions among items (like the two types of burden baskets) appear to be essentially new additions to the literature. Some of their statements directly contradict other such classifications and distinctions that are well embedded in the popular and anthropological literature, such as turkey feather caps being primarily for dress occasions rather than "war bonnets," and the round tabs on the front of moccasins being decorative rather than protective "toe guards." Whether or not such statements would be corroborated by members of other Western Apache groups and bands, the information used herein is applicable to the illustrated specimens.

The Guenther Collection

Edgar and Minnie Guenther spent the fifty years between 1911 and 1961 as Lutheran missionaries in the East Fork–Whiteriver area on the Fort Apache Indian Reservation (Figure 1.4). Rev. Guenther died in 1961, but Mrs. Guenther remained at Whiteriver an additional twenty-one years until the time of her death in 1982. During this seventy-year period the Guenthers maintained close ties with a large segment of the Fort Apache Reservation population and recorded their experiences and observations in a number of popular articles. Their collection began as an accumulation of gifts received from Apache friends. As the Guenthers' interest in and knowledge of Apache culture and crafts grew, they also selectively bought items. Mrs. Guenther purchased some objects as a means of providing income to needy Apache families and to encourage talented Apache craftspeople. The 275 objects bequeathed by Mrs. Guenther to the Arizona State Museum were collected during the entire seventy-year span of residence among the Apache.

Unlike the Goodwin assemblage, the focus of the Guenther collection was on contemporaneous material, items that were newly made at the time they were acquired. Some of the artifacts the Guenthers collected during the early decades of this century, however, were of types no longer made, used, or in some cases even remembered by the Apache by the time of Minnie Guenther's death in 1982. Thus, the decline of a number of older crafts as well as the evolution of new ones during much of the twentieth century is reflected in the collection.

The Guenther assemblage contains a wide range of artifacts, with emphasis on the "non-basketry" crafts such as beadwork, moccasins and other leatherwork, cradleboards, dolls, and a variety of toys. There are examples of recent craft innovations, including oil painting, carved *gaan* dancer figures, and the relatively recent use of *gaan* dancer motifs on secular items. Several outstanding nineteenth-century artifacts are included also, such as a beautifully preserved man's buckskin shirt and an elaborately painted war shield. In addition, there are a number of

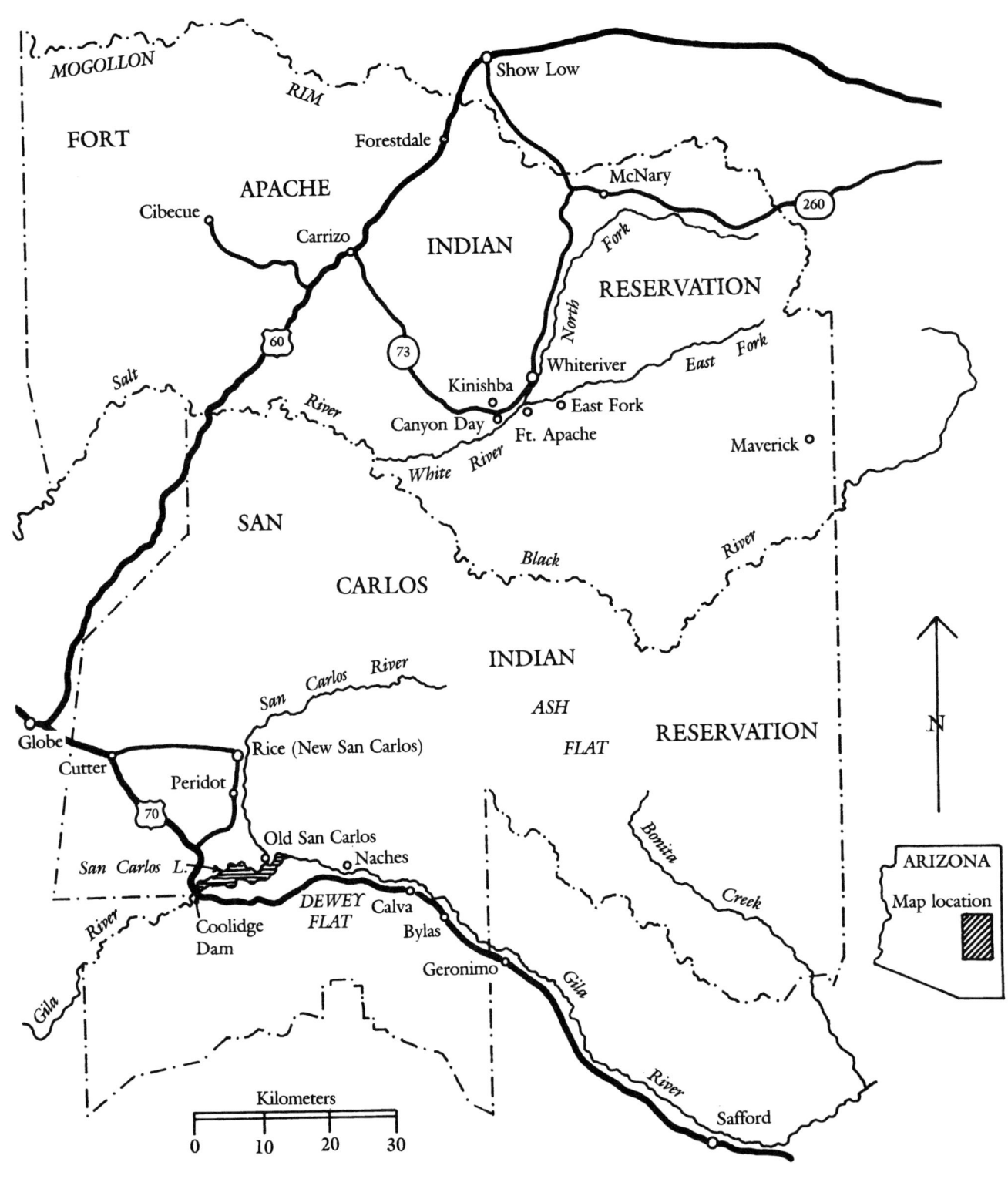

The Collections

OPPOSITE: Figure 1.4. The Fort Apache and San Carlos Indian reservations. Note: The original town of San Carlos (Old San Carlos) was located at the confluence of the San Carlos and Gila rivers. The town currently known as San Carlos (New San Carlos) was originally the town of Rice. With the construction of Coolidge Dam, Old San Carlos was abandoned, and was eventually submerged beneath the rising waters of San Carlos Lake. The Indian Agency and Post Office were moved to Rice in 1929 and 1930, and Rice was officially (and confusingly) renamed San Carlos on September 1, 1930. The boundaries of the reservations are shown as they exist today, but the route of U.S. 70 between Bylas and Cutter is shown as it was in the 1930s, going south around San Carlos Lake, by Coolidge Dam, with a secondary road connecting Peridot and New San Carlos.

rare artifacts from the Silas John religious movement, with which the Guenthers were closely involved. The Guenthers did not maintain full descriptive records on their collections, but the need for such documentation was recognized and remedied by two grandsons, William Kessel and Alan Ferg, both with degrees in anthropology. Over a span of ten years prior to Mrs. Guenther's death, they worked to fully document and catalogue the collection based on Mrs. Guenther's memory, family and church records, and the recollections of her children, all of whom grew up in Whiteriver. This documentation is a part of the Guenther collection at the Museum.

Documentation of the Guenther Collection

Documentation for the Guenther collection comes primarily from a tape-recorded interview by William Kessel with Mrs. Guenther in 1972, and from written notes compiled from interviews by Alan Ferg with Mrs. Guenther from 1979 to 1981. Many of the items in this collection are dated by a span of years (1911–1919, 1919–1924) because no catalogue was kept of these items as they were acquired, but Mrs. Guenther could bracket their age in relation to the dates of important events. The same is true of the articles acquired from her sister, Frieda Knoop. These often-used dates include:

1911–1919	Edgar and Minnie Guenther living at East Fork
1919–1923	Arnold and Frieda Knoop living at Carrizo Trading Post
1923–1924	Knoops living at East Fork Orphanage
1919	Guenthers move to Whiteriver to start building church
1922	Whiteriver church dedicated
1961	Edgar Guenther passes away

Most of the photographs used in this volume that were taken by Rev. E. E. Guenther are glass-plate negatives. A few are specifically dated, but most are not. He began taking glass-plate negatives at the time of his arrival in East Fork in 1911. The latest known date for one of these negatives is 1917, and it appears that he took few, if any, glass-plate photographs after moving to Whiteriver in 1919. Hence his undocumented photos are dated from 1911 to 1919. Glass-plate photos were taken also by Rev. Paul Mayerhoff, the Lutheran minister who preceded Guenther at East Fork. Mayerhoff's photos are assumed to have been taken in the vicinity of East Fork, and can only be dated as coeval with his stay there, from 1896 to 1903.

Organization of the Material Culture

The organization of the Western Apache objects in Chapters 5 through 8 follows the presentation used in *Navaho Material Culture*, authored by Clyde Kluckhohn, W. Hill, and Lucy Kluckhohn (1971). They clearly state the cultural and theoretical basis and justification for their organizational scheme in their opening pages and their reasoning is not repeated here. It is a convenient, already existing framework based on a closely related body of cultural material, and using it facilitates comparative studies between Navajo and Western Apache materials.

Even though the vast majority of portable artifacts made by the Western Apache are represented in either the Goodwin or Guenther collections, this volume is not an attempt to systematically cover all known items of Western Apache material culture. Trait numbers as in *Navaho Material Culture* have not been assigned, but the Apache materials have been divided into the major groupings of subsistence-related items, clothing, ritual-related items, and recreation-related items, corresponding to Chapters 1, 3, 4, and 5 in the *Navaho* book. Western Apache architecture is not considered, and the other topics treated in *Navaho* Chapter 2, Shelter, are included here under Subsistence, including items such as firedrills and cradleboards.

The exclusion by Kluckhohn, Hill, and Kluckhohn (1971: v, 3) of Navajo weaving, silversmithing, and sandpainting materials (because of their extensive treatment elsewhere in the literature) did not pose any real organization problems for this volume, because all three of these activities were much less important (or nonexistent) facets of Western Apache material culture than they were for the Navajo. Only a few pieces of silverwork are present in the Goodwin and Guenther collections. Although the Western Apache did make sandpaintings (Wyman 1983: 196–198), they are not represented in these collections. On the other hand, their exclusion of pottery, basketry, and "recent importations" in the *Navaho* book left unintegrated a host of Goodwin and Guenther items. Utilitarian pottery and basketry and artifacts related to their manufacture were placed under Subsistence, but pot drums, for example, are grouped with other musical instruments under Recreation, and baskets used in specific ritual contexts or religious movements are illustrated in the Ritual section. The text, or captions, in Chapters 5 through 8 specifically describe the illustrated pieces. The context of the various items within Western Apache culture is indicated, but the emphasis is definitely on the individual specimen. In addition to recognizing and appreciating the craftsmanship and resourcefulness of the Apache, the aim of this publication is to make this information widely available and to spark interest in the use of the collections by the general public, the Western Apache, and the professional anthropological community. As Kluckhohn remarked of the early versions of *Navaho Material Culture:*

> . . . it is intended primarily as a source book or reference work for comparative studies of various sorts. It presents an accumulation of details, often minute, upon obsolete or obsolescent objects and cultural habits and attitudes related thereto" (Kluckhohn, Hill, and Kluckhohn 1971: vi).

For convenience, plants and animals are referred to by their common names. Goodwin often recorded the materials from which his specimens were made, and many more items in both the Goodwin and Guenther collections were identified in the course of preparing this volume. Listed in Appendix B are the taxonomic names for the specifically identified plants and animals.

With the exception of a few words that have already entered the Anglo lexicon (*gaan, tus, na ih es),* Apache words are not used. The interested reader is directed to the *Western Apache Dictionary* by Perry and others (1972).

The present work presents a nearly complete assemblage of portable Western Apache material culture. The Guenther and Goodwin collections together represent Western Apache material culture in a diachronic and geographically complete manner. The two collections are complementary in terms of time (pre-Reservation and twentieth century), space (the San Carlos and Fort Apache areas), and type of subsistence base they represent (raiding, hunting, and gathering as opposed to wage labor and craft sale). As such, they comprise a significant resource for a variety of audiences, and their documentation in this publication is intended to expand public knowledge of the collections and increase their use.

Chapter Two
Edgar and Minnie Guenther

William B. Kessel

ne evening in late November, 1910, a senior in the Wisconsin Evangelical Lutheran Synod seminary at Wauwatosa, Wisconsin, was eating supper with his classmates. Someone asked for quiet and read a letter from the Executive of Indian Missions asking for a volunteer to fill a pastoral vacancy among the Apache Indians of Arizona Territory.

> Here was my call! I rushed over to Professor Schaller . . . [and] eagerly told him I was set to go to Arizona. The next day I went down to Pritzlaff's hardware store and purchased a cook stove and two guns: a 351 Winchester rifle for keeping distant enemies at bay and a 38 Colt Army pistol for close range encounters!

So wrote E. Edgar Guenther (1956: 65) in his autobiography.

Guenther never could have imagined that on the basis of this split-second decision he would be required to marry within a month and move to Arizona only weeks later. There he would embark on a life-long adventure in which he would establish a school and the first orphanage in the Southwest, risk his life on numerous occasions, become somewhat of a doctor, form a close friendship with a famous Apache chief, become the first white man to be adopted into the White Mountain Apache Tribe, and be responsible for no less than six mission congregations among the Indians. Meanwhile, his wife Minnie would raise their nine children and several Apaches, be church organist, nurse, school teacher, community leader, and one day be honored as the American Mother of the Year.

Edwin Edgar Guenther was born on 1 June 1885 near Rauville, South Dakota. There his parents, recently arrived from Germany, farmed a modest 160-acre homestead. As a child he developed a true appreciation of nature and carefully observed the growth of plants and behavior of animals. At the same time he imagined himself a Sioux Indian and fearless hunter.

These carefree days soon ended and young Guenther was enrolled in school. Outside of the classroom he served a stiff apprenticeship in farming. After graduating from the eighth grade and the Lutheran Church "Confirmation School," Guenther began thinking seriously about becoming a soldier. His aspirations were soon shattered, however, when his father decided that Edgar, as he was called, would go to Doctor

Martin Luther College in New Ulm, Minnesota. Reluctantly he attended. From there Guenther enrolled at Northwestern College in Watertown, Wisconsin, and later attended the Lutheran seminary in Wauwatosa. It was there, during his senior year, that Guenther was called to be a missionary among the Apache.

Before being allowed to leave for Arizona Territory, twenty-five-year-old Guenther was told he would first have to marry. It was felt that a single missionary would be too lonely in such a foreign setting. This presented somewhat of a problem. He was quiet, shy, and not yet engaged. Nevertheless, undaunted in his resolve to bring the Gospel to the Apaches, Edgar asked for two weeks to reconnoiter. Immediately he left for Arcadia, Wisconsin, to visit a young woman he had been dating for some time. Edgar arrived at her front door on Thanksgiving morning just as Miss Minnie Knoop was about to go to church. He knocked, she answered. Without any preliminaries whatsoever he asked, "I have a call to Arizona: will you go with me?" Her answer, which came as somewhat of a surprise, was simple and direct—"Sure" (E. Guenther 1956: 65).

Minnie Knoop was born in the little town of Neillsville, Wisconsin, on 12 July 1890. Her father was a cobbler who made shoes and boots to order and repaired anything made of leather. Meanwhile, her mother was completely occupied with the task of raising six children.

After young Minnie graduated from elementary school and "Confirmation School," her parents encouraged her to go to a local parochial school for one year. One day she made a grammatical mistake in German, and her teacher publicly ridiculed her and threatened her with corporal punishment. She turned and walked out of the class, never to return.

A few years later the Knoop family moved to Milwaukee where Minnie enrolled in the Cream City Business College. She financed her own education by dipping chocolates in a candy factory and tying bows and rosettes at a department store. Before long she accepted a job translating letters written in German into English for the Chicago, New York Electric Airline Railroad Company. From there she became the personal secretary to the president of the Thiery Piano Company.

By the time Minnie was twenty years old her parents had once again moved, this time to Arcadia, Wisconsin. Minnie went with them, and it was there that Edgar Guenther proposed marriage to her.

On 28 December 1910, Edgar and Minnie were married. Two weeks later they arrived in Globe, Arizona Territory. Although they were impatient to reach East Fork (see Fig. 1.4), they were delayed. Heavy snows in the Nantan Mountains rendered the roads impassable. Several weeks passed. The snow melted, but the run-off washed out the plank ferry at Black River Crossing (A. Guenther 1972: 30). Finally, the Guenthers took what little money remained in their "nest egg" and purchased train tickets that would take them around the problem. They traveled from Globe to Bowie, Arizona, then on to Deming and Albuquerque, New Mexico, and from there west to Holbrook, Arizona. While their detour had covered 700 miles they were still 90 miles from East Fork, not one mile closer than they had been in Globe. After a three-day trip on a freight wagon and a short journey on a buckboard pulled by mules, they reached their final destination (M. Guenther 1929: 142).

OPPOSITE: Figure 2.1. The Wisconsin Synod Lutheran parsonage at East Fork was the Guenthers' first home when they arrived in 1911; Minnie Guenther is seated on the porch (photo by E. E. Guenther).

Living at East Fork

Less than fifteen years earlier, in 1896, the first Lutheran missionary had arrived at East Fork. He was the Reverend Paul Mayerhoff, a reserved, although congenial young man who soon mastered the Apache language but never felt comfortable with the Apache people. Mayerhoff left Arizona in 1903, suffering poor health and no longer able to cope with the isolation of the reservation and his personal loneliness. Unlike Guenther, Mayerhoff had not been required to take a wife along with him to Arizona (Koehler 1970: 200–201). Over the next eight years two other missionaries served the mission station at East Fork for a while, then moved elsewhere. The Guenthers, however, had come to stay (Fig. 2.1).

The Apaches at this time (1911) generally were suspicious of "outsiders," and for good reason. In recent decades they had experienced the military might of the U.S. Army, seen their reservation shrink as great chunks of their land were deeded to Anglo miners and ranchers, and been victimized by killer epidemics first introduced by white men (Kessel 1976). Consequently, at first, the Guenthers were closely watched and were forced to earn the trust and respect of the Apaches.

Only days after arriving in East Fork, Pastor Guenther began his ministry preaching to a handful of people in the small chapel. The next week Guenther realized that if he was to serve his parish (which measured 50 miles wide by 100 miles long and included 2,500 Apaches), he needed reliable transportation. Thus, he let it be known that he was in the market for a horse.

One Sunday, while the worshipers were leaving the church, a white man rode up leading a horse. He beckoned to the Reverend and invited him to take the animal out for a test ride. As Guenther began to mount the horse, it began bucking wildly. Somehow Edgar, a self-professed "tenderfoot," stayed on until the horse quieted down. Guenther later wrote in his autobiography (1956: 91), "In spite of the ludicrous figure I must have presented to the congregation gathered around us, my reputation as a horseman was established: 'He sure stuck, he sure stuck!'" Needless to say, Guenther declined the offer to buy, but later purchased two fine horses from another dealer (Fig. 2.2).

One of Pastor Guenther's first "assignments" as a missionary was to reopen the mission school that had been closed for six years. There were, however, certain details he was expected to work out. For example, there were no furnishings, equipment, books, building, or money allocated for the project, and no students (E. Guenther 1949a: 293). To complicate matters, all older Apache children attended the government boarding school at Whiteriver and younger students were enrolled in a day school only a stone's throw from the mission. Furthermore, the day school provided clothing for the pupils and fed them a noon meal. Finally, the Guenthers spoke no Apache and the younger Indian children little or no English.

With reserved optimism Pastor Guenther decided to move forward, tackling one problem at a time. Initially he had to locate some students. One day he happened upon a large gathering of older Apache men playing the traditional "pole game." The missionary waited for an opportune moment and then began canvassing for students. Only one Apache responded, and then only with the advice, "Why don't you let us take more than one wife; then there will soon be plenty of children for your school" (E. Guenther 1956: 93). However, by September when the school was scheduled to open, sixteen students had been registered: one had tuberculosis and was not allowed to attend the government school, one was crippled and hence not required to go to school, two youths had been dismissed by the government educators after being labeled "hopeless cases," and a handful of children beyond school age were simply curious (Board of Education 1947: 85).

The Guenthers solved the problem of not having a school building by remodeling the church into a classroom. Not to be outdone by the government day school, they also decided to feed their students a noon meal. One of the four rooms in the parsonage was set aside as the school dining room, and Mrs. Guenther volunteered to be chief cook and dishwasher (M. Guenther 1929: 186).

There were still no furnishings for the school. The Guenthers borrowed a buckboard and drove it twenty miles to the nearest sawmill, where they were given a load of scrap lumber. Back home at East Fork, Edgar Guenther worked until the wee hours of the morning fashioning the rough lumber into desks and chairs, while Minnie sat at the Oliver typewriter and pounded out school lessons, being careful to use only examples and illustrations that were familiar to the Apache children.

The school opened in September and by Christmas the students could carry on simple English conversations and the Guenthers had learned the corresponding Apache. The school had proven to be an overwhelming success. Never again did the missionaries have to solicit students, for the Apache parents came to appreciate not only the education, but also the love their children were receiving.

In addition to conducting the worship service on Sunday and teaching school Monday through Friday, the Guenthers made time to visit the Apaches at their homes. They rode up the valleys or along the streams locating Apache camps and stopping to share their message with the people. Pastor Guenther was careful to present Christianity in a positive fashion and seldom mentioned the Apache religion or condemned Apache customs. Like his predecessor, Paul Mayerhoff, Guenther believed that his mission was to present Christ to the Apaches and the Holy Spirit would cause them to embrace Christianity (Kessel 1976: 119).

Within a couple years of their arrival, the Guenthers had won the confidence of most Apaches. However, if there were any remaining questions about their personal integrity or commitment to the Indians, they were answered during the winter of 1914 to 1915 when an

OPPOSITE: Figure 2.2. Edgar Guenther on Lois, Minnie Guenther on Ranger, and Heine, at East Fork in 1911 (photo by E. E. Guenther).

Edgar and Minnie Guenther

epidemic paralyzed the reservation. Edgar Guenther (1956: 112) later recalled that time.

> In the early days, with the breaking out of an epidemic disease our Apaches would pack up at twilight and head for the valleys in the foothills after dark to prevent the sickness from being able to follow them.
>
> Stepping out one snowy wintery morning, I noticed an absence of campfire smoke over the camps in our neighborhood. From this I judged something to be wrong, for our Indians are early risers. . . .
>
> When we rang the school bell on the aforesaid morning only a few children put in their appearance, and from them we learned that almost every family with children had moved to a hiding place in the foothills to escape whooping cough and pneumonia. Their fears were well founded for these maladies soon swept across the entire Reservation. My wife and I spent many weary days in the saddle from morning till dark trying to find our people so that we might minister to their children. We were led to many a temporary abode by smoke rising from camp fires; others we came upon merely by chance. Having no medicines of any kind I trapped skunks, rendered the fat and mixed it with turpentine and coal-oil. To give the concoction a pleasant odor my wife added some of her precious perfume. For containers we begged extract and other bottles from the Officers' wives at Ft.

Apache. For chest pads we cut up every spare piece of warm cloth on hand and when that was used up our long winter underwear was dedicated to the cause. Humanly speaking we saved the lives of many youngsters; everyone of our school children survived, but several hundred others died throughout the Reservation for lack of proper care. For weeks we were awakened almost every morning by a rifle shot announcing that another family had lost one of its little ones.

Shima

Of the hundreds of Apache friends the Guenthers made in their early years on the reservation, two were most memorable. The first was an Apache woman known by the identification number B–3, a Chiricahua Apache of Geronimo's band. She had been married to a man who enlisted in the Army as an Apache Scout. Together they had one child, a daughter. By 1911 her husband had died or left her, and her small daughter was dying. The Guenthers

OPPOSITE: Figure 2.3. Minnie Guenther, and Wenonah in the cradleboard made for her by Mrs. Jack Keyes, the wife of Rev. Guenther's first interpreter (see Fig. 5.42, Color Illustration 2); taken at East Fork in 1912 (photo by E. E. Guenther).

RIGHT: Figure 2.4. Wenonah on the porch of the East Fork parsonage, probably in 1913, wearing the tiny moccasins made for her by Shima; see Figure 6.9 and Color Illustration 8 (photo by E. E. Guenther).

learned of her tragic situation and began making regular visits to her camp. They concentrated most of their efforts on the little girl, with whom they shared their message of Jesus Christ. Meanwhile B–3 silently listened. Sometime that year the girl died (E. Guenther 1945: 608–609).

In February of 1912, Mrs. Guenther gave birth to a healthy daughter they named Wenonah. While Minnie would have preferred to stay at home and tend her daughter, she could not escape her responsibilities of teaching school, preparing and serving the students a noon meal, typing the daily lessons, teaching Sunday School, and playing the organ for church. Although not neglected, baby Wenonah was frequently strapped into an Apache cradleboard and set in a corner of the school room (Figs. 2.3, 5.42).

One day in September of 1912, B–3 walked into the school during class, picked up the cradleboard with its precious contents and walked out the door. She went over to the Guenthers' house, comforted the baby, and then proceeded to do the dishes, sweep the floor, and make the beds, the whole time muttering in Apache, scolding Minnie, in absentia, for leaving things such a mess (E. Guenther 1945: 608–609). From that time on this little scene was repeated almost daily.

B–3 had found a new daughter (Fig. 2.4). She even referred to Wenonah as "my daughter," and to Edgar and Minnie Guenther as "my children." Out of love and respect for B–3 the Guenthers called her "my mother" (*shi ma* in Apache). This then became her name. Shima virtually raised Wenonah and taught her how to speak fluent Apache; however, Shima never learned but a few words of English.

Over the next twenty years the Guenthers had eight more children, and Shima loved each of them. She particularly enjoyed helping the children build structures with blocks on the floor. Even after the Guenthers moved to Whiteriver, Shima frequently made the seven-mile walk just to visit (Fig. 2.5). She remained a true friend until her death in 1945 (M. Guenther 1935: 413–414; E. Guenther 1945: 608–609).

Chief Alchesay

The other great friendship the Guenthers made was with Chief Alchesay. As a youth Alchesay joined the U.S. Army as a scout. He so distinguished himself that General Crook once told him, "I am not above you; we are both of the same rank" (E. Guenther 1928a: 2). After hostilities between the Apaches and Anglos had subsided, Alchesay returned to civilian life and farmed his fields along the North Fork of the White River.

The Apaches along the North Fork respected Alchesay and acknowledged him to be their chief. The government agents and military personnel mistakenly hailed Alchesay as the chief of all the

Apaches. However, many Indians, especially those living near East Fork, recognized him only as violent and unpredictable, a troublemaker.

Thus, when the Guenthers arrived in East Fork in 1911 they heard conflicting opinions about Alchesay. Concluding that Alchesay had "very strong likes and dislikes, and to avoid getting off on the wrong foot with him," Pastor Guenther (1956: 58) had little contact with the man before the fateful winter of 1918–1919.

That was the coldest winter ever recorded (Kessel 1976: 145), but it is remembered for the flu epidemic that took so many lives. The epidemic was first felt on the San Carlos Apache

Reservation where it claimed over 200 lives. Then it spread north. The White Mountain Apaches fled to the hills but could not escape. Dozens died.

At the onset of the epidemic, the Guenthers closed their school and Edgar committed himself to helping the Apaches. Aware that he daily would come in contact with the infirm, and not wanting to spread the disease to his own family, Guenther kissed Minnie and their four children good-by, then moved to Whiteriver where he stayed with Dr. Fred Loe, the agency doctor. During the next three and one-half months Mrs. Guenther saw her husband only once. He completely wore out his trousers, and she brought him a new pair.

Day after day, week after week, Guenther and Loe rode on horseback searching for Apaches. When they found them, their procedure seldom varied. Guenther would greet the people and inquire about their health. He would then roll out several layers of building paper and insulate their beds from the dampness of the ground. Next, Dr. Loe would administer medicine. Before they left, Pastor Guenther would speak words of comfort and assurance, and offer up prayers. Then they rode off looking for another camp.

One day Dr. Loe decided to remain at home and give his horse a well-deserved rest. Guenther loaded his building paper, took some medicine, and alone set out searching for the camps of the sick and dying. His horse carried him about eight miles north of Whiteriver when Edgar noticed a small trail leading through the brush. He followed it a couple miles before turning up a side canyon. A short distance later he saw smoke curling its way through the tops of the pine trees. He had located Alchesay's camp. The chief had the flu and had retreated to this solitary place to die. Guenther rather matter-of-factly greeted Alchesay, insulated his pallet with paper, administered medicine, made some suggestions about food and drink, and after a short visit, rode on.

The next day Guenther remained in Whiteriver to give his horse a rest, and Dr. Loe rode out to visit Alchesay. No sooner had Loe dismounted than Alchesay inquired, "Why did you not bring that tall missionary with you?" (E. Guenther 1957: 16). The next day Guenther, the "tall missionary" (*inashoot ndezen* as the Apaches called him) revisited the chief. A lasting friendship had been established.

In the years that followed Alchesay frequently rode into Whiteriver and spent the night or several days with the Guenthers before reluctantly returning home. Like Shima, he was fond of the Guenther children and in 1923, when Minnie gave birth to her sixth child, Alchesay insisted that the baby boy be made his namesake. The child was duly named Alchesay Arthur, but because of a clerical mistake he was officially listed as Arthur Alchesay Guenther (Fig. 2.6). Alchesay showed his friendship for the Guenthers in many ways. Frequently he presented the family a gift of venison from one of his own successful hunting trips (E. Guenther 1928b: 7). Pastor Guenther and Chief Alchesay had become like brothers.

In 1928 when Alchesay lay dying, the Apaches tried to comfort him by saying he would recover. Pastor Guenther went to visit his old friend. He approached the chief's pallet and said his "good-bys." Alchesay responded:

> You are the only friend I have; these people are not my friends. They say that I am going to ride again; they are all lying to me. I am just like the cars passing by along the road; first they are new and shiny; then they get older and one part after another falls off and then you don't see them any more. I am falling apart just like that old car and know that I will never ride again. I know that I am going Home soon" (E. Guenther 1957: 43).

Alchesay died a few days later.

OPPOSITE, LEFT: Figure 2.5. Shima, the Guenthers' adoptive "mother" (photo by E. E. Guenther).

OPPOSITE, RIGHT: Figure 2.6. Chief Alchesay and his one year old namesake, Arthur Alchesay Guenther, in 1924 (photo by E. E. Guenther).

Living at Whiteriver

After the devastating flu epidemic of 1918 to 1919 was over, Pastor Guenther left the East Fork Mission under the care of an assistant pastor, M. Wehausen, and moved his family to Whiteriver. There he was determined to start a new mission. Whiteriver was rapidly becoming the largest community on the reservation. It was the site of the Indian Agency and a government boarding school that housed 400 students.

The "parsonage" in Whiteriver was a three-room shack (Fig. 2.7) formerly occupied by the agency blacksmith, but later abandoned (E. Guenther 1957: 14–15). It was to be "home" until a larger house was built two years later.

Once in Whiteriver, Guenther set himself to the task at hand. The following indicates a typical week. On Sunday he conducted Sunday School and worship services at the boarding school, often preaching to all 400 pupils. On Monday he spent some time in his office, writing sermons and preparing for Bible classes. On Tuesday he rode horseback or, if roads permitted, drove his newly acquired Model T Ford to Canyon Day. There he taught Bible history to the children of the day school. If Mrs. Guenther accompanied him, as she often did, she played her portable pump organ and led the children in song. After the lessons the Guenthers made camp calls on the Indians living in the vicinity, but by 5:00 P.M. were in Fort Apache for a short service with the scouts. Then the Guenthers returned to White-

Edgar and Minnie Guenther

river where Edgar held confirmation instruction class with sixty boarding school students (E. Guenther 1920). During the remainder of the week the minister spent his time calling on the Apaches living near Whiteriver and North Fork, trying to procure land for a parsonage and church, attempting to elicit money from his denomination, and supervising all the Lutheran pastors and missions on both reservations (in 1917 the Lutheran Mission Board had appointed him superintendent of missions on the San Carlos and Fort Apache reservations).

On Christmas Day, 1919, Pastor Guenther held the first general church service in Whiteriver. The agency carpentry shop had space for only 60, but 200 Apaches tried to fit into the temporary chapel.

Just weeks later another influenza epidemic seized the reservation. One-half of the 400 boarding school students contracted the disease. Because there was a shortage of medical personnel, Guenther volunteered for alternating day and night shifts caring for the infirm. One day he, too, became ill. He was confined to bed for six weeks. Near the end of his convalescence he received a report that one of his good friends was ill. Edgar got out of bed, dressed, and sneaked out on horseback to visit him. On the way home fording a river he became chilled and returned to bed for six weeks more (E. Guenther 1957: 15).

Frieda and Arnold Knoop

During the next several years sickness and death were commonplace everywhere on the reservation. The situation at Carrizo Creek was typical. In the fall of 1919, Mrs. Guenther's sister, Frieda, and her husband Arnold Knoop moved to Carrizo where they opened a trading post. Like the Guenthers, the Knoops developed a sincere love of the Apaches and a desire to help them. Within months the Indians had nicknamed Frieda "the good little woman who runs around like crazy," because she frequently visited the Apache camps, helping the sick and needy (Knoop 1981).

Frieda did not have far to look to find subjects for her volunteer social work. Many of the local Apaches were destitute, and for this reason the Knoops' trading post became an economic disaster. At first the Indians exchanged what money and trade items they had for food and supplies. When those ran out, Arnold granted them credit. Eventually the Knoops made a decision. They could not morally justify having a store full of goods when so many were going hungry. Thus they began giving away their inventory. While the Apaches never took advantage of the Knoops' generosity, nevertheless, the shelves were soon bare.

Meanwhile the Apaches reciprocated in the only way they could. From time to time individuals gave the Knoops Apache baskets, dolls, and personal items such as knife sheaths.

Little did Arnold and Frieda realize, at this time, the sentimental value attached to many of these possessions. The Apaches were still seminomadic and, consequently, could not amass large quantities of personal items. They owned only what was necessary for life and easily transportable. Thus, through practicality, the list of personal possessions was relatively small. When a person died all of his or her personal property (including clothes, moccasins, knives, sheaths, caps, guns, baskets, and dolls) were either burned or buried with the deceased (Goodwin 1942: 518–521; unidentified newspaper articles by Paul Mayerhoff, on file with William B. Kessel). Occasionally, if an Apache knew he was dying, he might give a prized possession to a relative and in so doing save it from mandatory destruction. Many of the gifts given to the Knoops were such prized heirlooms. Later the Knoops sold these artifacts to the Guenthers and they comprise the bulk of the Guenther Indian Collection.

OPPOSITE: Figure 2.7. The Guenthers' first home in Whiteriver, in 1919, down near the river. Mrs. Guenther is standing in the sleeping porch that she enclosed, with Wenonah on the step (photo by E. E. Guenther).

By the winter of 1922 to 1923, the Knoops had given away the last items in their trading post. They boarded up the windows and doors and moved to East Fork, where Arnold accepted a position teaching industrial arts in the mission school. Frieda was employed as the cook for the school and matron of the newly established orphanage (E. Guenther 1923: 8).

The Orphanage

The orphanage, which was the first such institution in the Southwest, grew out of the Lutheran missionaries' compassion for the suffering infants and children they saw around them. Years earlier Pastor Guenther learned that many Apache infants were killed or abandoned at birth. The Apaches believed that any baby born with a defect was "bad medicine" and the infant was eliminated. One day, for example, a small boy from the mission school knocked on Guenther's door and relayed the message: "You come quick." Edgar immediately responded by stepping into his slippers and following the youth. Together they jogged for about two miles until they reached an Apache camp. There, many relatives had gathered and were discussing the fate of a baby girl born with six fingers on each hand. The grandmother insisted she be killed immediately. Guenther, realizing the gravity of the situation, picked up a butcher knife, held it over the flames of the campfire, wiped it clean with his handkerchief, and then quickly cut off the infant's extra fingers. The parents immediately accepted the child as normal (M. Guenther 1956: 40).

Not only were the lives of deformed infants put in jeopardy but so were those of twins. An Apache woman who bore twins was considered an adultress, and to escape embarrassment she either smothered or discarded the weaker of the two (Mahoney 1954: 3; Wehausen 1923: 2).

The thought of infants being put to death greatly disturbed the Guenthers. They were concerned also for the children whose mothers had died in childbirth or from disease. Eventually, in spite of Edgar's meager salary and the small size of the parsonage, the Guenthers began receiving helpless Apache babies into their home. There they raised them alongside their own children. Meanwhile, in 1922 the missionary at East Fork, M. J. Wehausen, formally adopted an unfortunate Apache boy (Wehausen 1923: 1–2).

While the two missionaries acknowledged the need for an orphanage, they lacked the facilities. This situation soon changed, for in March of 1922 the Lutherans purchased the government school, residence, and pumping plant at East Fork (E. Guenther 1949b: 30). Immediately the two pastors turned the school building into an orphanage.

Initially six children were admitted to the facility. Three had been brought in after their mothers had died. One infant was committed because its mother was convalescing from a lingering illness and was unable to care for her child properly. One infant was born with a hair lip and cleft palate and was abandoned to die. The final baby was born the weaker one of twins and had been rescued from strangulation (Board of Education 1947: 87).

The original orphanage was woefully inadequate. The babies were put in wooden cracker, catsup, baking powder, and tomato boxes. Meanwhile, Arnold Knoop, recently arrived from Carrizo, went to work building cribs, beds, potty chairs, and other furniture. The first winter it was so cold in the orphanage that the Knoops moved all the babies into their own quarters. In time new buildings were constructed, and today the East Fork Lutheran Orphanage is a model facility.

Years of Mission Expansion

During the decade of the 1920s the Guenthers maintained their exhausting pace. In 1922 work was completed on the new church in Whiteriver. On April 30 it was dedicated. During that service Alchesay was baptized first, followed by a hundred Apaches (E. Guenther 1939: 87).

Meanwhile, the Guenthers expanded their activities at Fort Apache. There they began

Edgar and Minnie Guenther

holding regular instructional classes with the children of the government school.

In addition to conducting services at Whiteriver, Canyon Day, and Fort Apache, the Guenthers intensified their efforts to take the Gospel directly to the Apaches. The basic pattern for "camp calls" was set. The Guenthers arrived at a cluster of Apache dwellings and chatted with the Indians. Edgar then selected a suitable location for a service. There Minnie set up her portable pump organ and began playing and singing hymns. Once a crowd had gathered, the service began with spirited singing. Pastor Guenther followed with a short sermon or devotional message and prayer. The Guenthers dispersed any literature they had brought, bade the people farewell, and drove on to the next cluster of camps (Brown 1963: 107–108).

While Edgar truly enjoyed holding worship services and making camp calls, during the 1920s he was forced to spend much of his time as a church administrator. This he loathed (E. Guenther 1957: 38). In 1917 he had been appointed Superintendent of Apache Missions. His duties included writing lengthy reports on the status of the various mission stations, training and supervising the ever increasing number of new missionaries, and trying to solicit sufficient funds to keep the East Fork boarding school, orphanage, and various churches operating.

In 1923 Pastor Guenther began a newsletter called *The Apache Scout*. It contained illustrations, pictures, and items of interest to the Lutheran Apaches. He remained its editor, business manager, and primary author for three decades.

It was during this period of mission expansion that Pastor Guenther faced the greatest challenge to his authority and the religion he espoused. Opposition came in the person of Silas John Edwards. Silas was the son of a well-known and respected medicine man. When the Guenthers first arrived at East Fork in 1911 they were met by Silas, who made a very favorable first impression (M. Guenther 1911). Soon Silas, who was extremely intelligent, received religious instructions and was made the mission interpreter. A few years later he left the missionaries to pursue his own interests. In 1920 he emerged as a medicine man advocating a new Apache religion, which was a careful synthesis of the old Apache religion, Christianity, and his own unique doctrine and practice (Basso and Anderson 1973; Kessel 1976: 142–185). Immediately the impact of his new religion was felt on both reservations. Hundreds of Indians rallied around Silas to receive his blessing and to be cured from their diseases.

Prior to this time Guenther had carefully avoided publicly criticizing Apache medicine men. However, he felt obliged to speak out against Silas' new religion, which so threatened all the work done by the Lutherans. Active opposition between the two religious leaders persisted until 1933, when Silas was accused by the government of murdering his wife, pronounced guilty, and imprisoned (Gardner 1952).

The decade of the 1930s was a turbulent time on the Fort Apache Indian Reservation. Consistent pressure was placed on the Apaches to assimilate into the mainstream of Anglo culture. Concomitantly, the instances of public drunkenness and violence increased on the reservation. Although Guenther blamed the Anglos for stripping the Apaches of their dignity and traditions, he felt duty bound to speak out against the unwholesome behavior that had become so prevalent. His criticisms, while accepted by many, were not well received by others.

In 1936, longing for relief from paper work and somewhat discouraged, Pastor Guenther resigned as Superintendent of the Apache Mission. He wanted to spend more time calling on the Indian people. Later that year his spirits were lifted when the Lutheran Church honored him for his twenty-five years in the ministry. During the anniversary celebration it was noted that he had baptized over a thousand Apaches. In addition, during that quarter century the missionary force had grown from two missionaries to five, who, along with two men and two women teachers, served six preaching stations, two day schools, one boarding school, and the orphanage (Otto 1936: 486). Before the ceremony was over, several Apaches addressed the crowd of 400 and thanked Pastor Guenther for his love and devotion.

The anniversary celebration revived Edgar.

With renewed vigor he set about his task. However, the years of continuous labor were beginning to take their toll on the missionary. He became ill and his doctors instructed him to curtail some of his activities, to call an assistant, and to get more rest. He refused to heed their advice. In 1941 he helped remodel a building that became the Canyon Day church (Brown 1963: 112–113).

Meanwhile, the Second World War was raging. About 300 Apaches were called on to serve their country. While Edgar continued to preach and teach, Minnie faithfully corresponded with over a hundred of the soldiers (E. Guenther 1957: 41). In addition, she spent many hours a week at the Whiteriver Hospital, visiting with the older patients and reading Bible stories to the children.

Figure 2.8. Rev. Edgar Guenther holding the burden basket given to him at the time of his adoption into the White Mountain Apache Tribe of the Fort Apache Indian Reservation on May 18, 1950. To his left is Baha (son of Alchesay), and to his right is Nelson Lupe, Sr., then Tribal Chairman (photographer unknown, ASM Neg. 52505).

Edgar and Minnie Guenther

In 1942 the Guenthers began holding regular services in the lumbering town of McNary, some twenty-two miles north of Whiteriver. Although there had been a sawmill there for years, the advent of World War II saw an increased demand for lumber, and the town began to grow. For the next several years services during the summer months were held outside under the pines. The men of the congregation usually sat on a huge log, while the women and children leaned against it. In the winter months the worshipers gathered in an Apache's cabin. On several occasions Pastor Guenther asked his denomination for funds to build a chapel, but to no avail. Finally, Southwest Forest Industries donated enough lumber to erect a building. Friends of Edgar and Minnie contributed enough money to buy the windows and doors (E. Guenther 1957: 42).

In 1945 the Guenthers built the McNary church. Edgar fashioned the old log that had served as an outside pew into the pulpit and altar. While putting up the church rafters, however, he suffered a severe heart attack and was forced to rest for six months (Mahoney 1954: 4; 1956: 38). Meanwhile, Mrs. Guenther applied two coats of varnish to the interior of the church.

Scarcely two years later, the sixty-two-year-old missionary started yet another mission. This time he began holding outside services in the newly organized lumbering town of Maverick. This community was fifty-two miles east of Whiteriver and was situated at an altitude of 9,000 feet above sea level (E. Guenther 1949b: 36).

About this same time Pastor Guenther supervised the construction of a church in Cedar Creek. The Guenthers had begun holding camp services there years earlier.

By 1949 Pastor Guenther was exhausted and his health was failing. However, on 18 May 1950 an event occurred that brought him much satisfaction and happiness. The White Mountain Apache Indians officially adopted him into the tribe (Fig. 2.8). He was the only white man ever so honored. In addition to tribal membership he was given full Indian hunting and fishing privileges. His life had come full circle. When he was a small boy he imagined himself to be an Indian and great hunter. Now he literally had become an Indian and was recognized as one of the best turkey hunters in east-central Arizona.

Pastor Guenther decided it was time to step back and enjoy a slower pace of life. In November of 1950 Pastor Arthur Alchesay Guenther, Edgar and Minnie's son, was installed as the assistant pastor in Whiteriver. Soon Arthur was given the responsibility of caring for the Whiteriver, Fort Apache, and Maverick congregations. The senior Guenthers continued to serve the congregation of McNary.

At last the Guenthers had some leisure time. They purchased a Metro delivery truck and installed a bed, gas stove, sink, and cupboards. When their "camper" was completed, the Guenthers were at liberty to drive anywhere they desired and to stay as long as they liked. Mostly they chose to drive around the reservation, renewing old acquaintances, making new friends, and visiting sites that called to mind fond memories.

The Rev. Guenther never completely retired. When he was not serving the congregation in McNary or visiting friends on the reservation, he was in his study giving personal and spiritual advice and counsel to his Apache friends.

In the winter of 1960 Edgar became seriously ill. He was taken to Tucson where he could receive proper medical attention. While there, he became terribly homesick for the reservation and lonely for his fellow Apaches. One day in February, thirty Indians piled into five cars and made the 210-mile drive to Tucson simply to brighten his day (Fairchild 1961).

On 16 March 1961 Pastor Guenther was honored by the University of Arizona. He was given the Medallion of Merit as part of that institution's seventy-fifth anniversary celebration. The aging minister had always been partial to the University of Arizona and seven of his nine children had attended there.

Although he was dying, Edgar was allowed to return to his beloved reservation one final time. On a cold day in April a golden anniversary celebration was held in honor of the Guenthers. Over 1500 Apaches and Anglos gathered at the Whiteriver fairgrounds to be part of the festivities. The Guenthers had been on the Fort Apache Indian Reservation for fifty years. Edgar had been in the ministry for fifty years. Edgar and Minnie had been married for fifty years.

Figure 2.9. Minnie Guenther in her study at home in Whiteriver, January 1980 (photo by Helga Teiwes, ASM Neg. 52500).

Edgar and Minnie Guenther

After the celebration, the Guenthers returned to Tucson where Edgar was immediately admitted to the hospital. There he died on May 31, just hours before his seventy-sixth birthday.

Funeral services were held first in Tucson, then in Whiteriver. More than 600 Apaches turned out to mourn the passing of their brother and friend. He was buried in the Whiteriver cemetery.

As might be expected, Mrs. Guenther was almost overcome with grief and loneliness. Many of her children invited her to move in with them. Nevertheless, she refused to leave the reservation. A few months later Minnie's daughter Ruth and her family volunteered to move to Whiteriver and live with the seventy-one-year-old widow. They remained with her for the next eight years.

With her daughter Ruth right there and her son Arthur living next door, Mrs. Guenther overcame her grief. Soon she regained the enthusiasm and energy that had characterized her entire life. She remained active in community affairs and worked for the Whiteriver P.T.A., the Women's Club, and the Public Library that she helped to establish.

Children remained supremely important to Mrs. Guenther. She was painfully aware that many Apache children were being born with congenital hip deformities, and she decided to do something about it. With determination she campaigned single-handedly to show that these unfortunate children could be helped. She had several of the children with hip trouble X-rayed. Next she took a crippled child with a typical deformity to a bone specialist, who consented to operate. The surgery was a success, and Mrs. Guenther was able to prove to the Apache Tribal Council that many of these children need not remain handicapped. As a result of her crusade, scores of children underwent successful operations and are now living normal lives.

Mrs. Guenther also should be credited with vitalizing the Apache arts and crafts enterprise. Often Apache women would come to her home, look at the items displayed in her cabinets, and ask what they were. When she explained that these were articles made by the Apaches long ago, the young Indian women were fascinated. Frequently these women asked to buy various objects, since they did not know how to make them. Mrs. Guenther encouraged the Apache women to study her collection of Apache articles and to consult with the older women. She offered to buy the cradleboards, *tuses,* dolls, and other items that they made. During the decade of the 1960s, Mrs. Guenther watched many of her Apache friends turn into gifted craftsmen. Soon the Tribe and outside collectors were buying Apache art and crafts.

In 1967 Mrs. Guenther received her highest honor. Unbeknownst to her, the church Ladies' Aid Society submitted her name to the committee that was to elect the Arizona Mother of the Year. Mrs. Guenther was nominated and won the title. Then in May she went to New York City to compete against the other forty-nine state winners. Much to her surprise, she was named the American Mother of the Year for 1967. On her return trip home the airplane pilot announced over the intercom that they had the American Mother of the Year aboard and in her honor flew over the reservation so she could see her home. Mrs. Guenther was met at the airport in Phoenix by state officials and dignitaries, tribal chairman Ronnie Lupe, and the entire high school marching band from Whiteriver (*Fort Apache Scout* 1967). That same year the Greater Arizona Savings and Loan Association presented her with the Builders of a Greater Arizona award (*Glances at Greater Arizona* 1968).

Mrs. Guenther spent most of the next decade at her home in Whiteriver (Fig. 2.9), where she gave talks to civic groups, wrote articles for the local paper, and mingled with the Apaches. From time to time her health failed. She suffered several strokes from which she recovered. She had a massive heart attack, but with the help of a pacemaker was soon back on her feet.

During the fall of 1981 Minnie became deathly ill. Her doctors insisted that she be taken to Tucson for care. For months she waged a life and death struggle, but then partially recovered. While her physicians warned her against returning to the high elevation of Whiteriver, she went home anyway. There she died on 8 January 1982 at the age of ninety-one.

Funeral services were held in Whiteriver, in the church Mrs. Guenther helped to establish. Hundreds of Apaches jammed the church to pay their final respects. At the graveyard, in spite of a blizzard, several Apaches made long speeches–their way of honoring their own.

Pastor and Mrs. E. E. Guenther lived rich and full lives among the White Mountain Apache Indians. Their collection of Indian baskets, headdresses, war clubs and other objects constitutes an important chapter in Apache history. The legacy of Edgar and Minnie goes far beyond their Indian collection, however. They left a shining example of honesty, integrity, and selfless service to their fellow man. The Guenthers long will be remembered.

NOTE. Various dates concerning the Guenthers, particularly that of their arrival in Arizona and the founding of the East Fork orphanage, occasionally have been reported incorrectly. The dates presented here should be considered definitive. Brief biographical sketches of the Guenthers may also be found in Herbert and Herbert (1962) and Mails (1974: 183–185).

Chapter Three
Grenville Goodwin

Morris E. Opler

Grenville Goodwin was born on Long Island, New York, in 1907 and spent his early years in the eastern part of the country. Since he suffered from a respiratory ailment and the dry, sunny climate of Arizona was considered particularly salubrious for such a condition, he was sent to the Mesa Ranch School of south-central Arizona for college preparatory studies. This was the beginning of his affection for the Southwest and of his high regard and continuing interest in the American Indians of the region.

While he was a student at the Mesa Ranch School, Goodwin met Dean Byron Cummings of the University of Arizona, and the well-known archaeologist and the young student took an immediate liking to each other. From this point on Dr. Cummings provided Goodwin with friendship, professional guidance, and a model. It is to Dr. Cummings' great credit that he sensed his young friend's promise, and it is plain that the good Dean gave Goodwin much more than simple encouragement. Goodwin's practice of making meticulous drawings, keeping careful records, and preserving the material remains of the culture he sought to interpret owes much to the methods and example of the seasoned archaeologist.

It was Dr. Cummings' hope that Goodwin would continue his formal education and study anthropology at the University of Arizona.[1] Goodwin's health problem persisted, however, and dictated that he live a less confining life than the classroom and library allowed. Besides, he had an easy manner with people and a talent for eliciting information from them. Consequently, in seeking answers to the questions that perplexed him, he was drawn as readily to the human laboratory as to the library. This does not mean that Goodwin spurned books. He became well acquainted with the historical, archaeological, and ethnological literature of the Southwest, but his reading became increasingly selective, directed to the problems in which he was immediately involved.

Goodwin's first sustained contact with an American Indian group was with the Navajo. After several camping trips in Navajo country, which allowed little more than casual observation, he realized that the many questions he had in mind could be satisfied only by a longer and closer association. Therefore, in 1927, when he was twenty years of age, he took a position on the Navajo Reservation in the trader's store at Piñon, Arizona, west of Black Mountain. The situation proved admirable for his purposes.

The trading post was a convenient place for the Indians to meet and chat at length with their fellow tribesmen of the vicinity as well as to obtain provisions. Goodwin became friendly with many of his customers and visited them in their camps. Immersion in this Navajo-speaking setting had another important consequence. He discovered that he had a talent for learning the language and was soon making progress in understanding and speaking Navajo, an ability of considerable usefulness in his work at the trading post.

In August, 1927, while he was working at Piñon, Goodwin met Mr. Hoffman, the chief of police of the Navajo Reservation, who had formerly been sheriff at Columbus, a town close to the Mexican border in southwestern New Mexico. The region around Columbus, both north and south of the border, had been, until the subjugation of the Chiricahua, part of the range of these Apache, and Mr. Hoffman regaled Goodwin with stories about Chiricahua who had escaped both the American and Mexican military nets and who were still living in the rocky fastnesses of the Sierra Madre range in northern Mexico. Goodwin was intrigued with the idea of traveling to Mexico and investigating these tales. He knew that Navajo and Apache were related languages and mutually intelligible and that after some additional exposure to Navajo and practice in its use he would have a valuable tool with which to deal with any "wild" Apache whom he might encounter south of the border.

Once Goodwin was aware of the popular belief that Apache still roamed the eastern Sierra Madre of northern Mexico, he looked for references concerning them in the newspapers of the border towns. In 1928, 1929, and early 1930 he found articles in the newspapers of Douglas and Tucson that described the stealing of stock by these people, the discovery of their camp sites and storage caves by ranchers and travelers, the capture of one or two of their children by Mexicans, and the sighting of Sierra Madre Apache adults at a distance. In some of these accounts the names of Leslie Gatliffe, the chief of police at Douglas, Arizona, and of Bill Curtis, a man who made frequent visits to northern Mexico in connection with his ranching and business interests, were mentioned. By 1930 Goodwin had decided to learn more about the Apache and, with this in mind, got a job as assistant to the trader at Bylas, Arizona, on the San Carlos Apache Reservation. Perhaps this intensified interest in the Western Apache may have been stimulated by his ties with Dr. Cummings, who was preparing to begin his excavation of Kinishba, a large prehistoric pueblo in Western Apache country. Nevertheless, before settling down to the study of the reservation Indians, Goodwin was determined to learn as much as possible at first hand about the "wild" Apache of the Sierra Madre. He met with Leslie Gatliffe, who had journeyed through northern Mexico a number of times and who described to Goodwin the area in which he believed the Apache were still to be found. Bill Curtis, who had come upon a cave cache that he was sure had been left by Apache, promised to take Goodwin along and guide him to this Apache storage cave on one of his trips to Mexico.

Trips to Mexico

The opportunity to accompany Curtis on a trip to his Mexican ranch came in the late fall of 1930. On November 20, after several days of preparation, Goodwin and the Curtis party crossed the border at Douglas, passed through Agua Prieta, and reached Morelos, Sonora. The party followed a southeasterly course to the valley of the Rio Bavispe. The journey lasted a little more than a month, and by December 24 the travelers were back in Douglas. Goodwin saw no Apache, but he did explore the cave Curtis had discovered and satisfied himself that it and others of the vicinity did indeed show evidence of human habitation. They yielded items of material culture (arrows, beads, bits of cloth, a corncob, petroglyphs) that could have been the handiwork of Apache or some other nomadic people of northern Mexico.

In the fall of 1931 another opportunity arose for Goodwin to acompany Bill Curtis into northern Mexico. This trip lasted about six weeks, from September 22 to November 8. Goodwin was promised that on this journey he would be able to see abandoned Apache camps,

Grenville Goodwin

Figure 3.1. Bill Curtis *(left)* and Art Schraeder *(right)* at "House 6, at big corrals on ridge" in the Sierra Espuela, Chihuahua. Photo taken by Grenville Goodwin on 29 October 1931 (reproduced courtesy of Neil Goodwin).

and he did visit two sites attributed to the Apache. Both were in Chihuahua, one on the eastern slope of the Sierra Cochita Hueca and the other near the head of the Bola Canyon, on the eastern side of the Sierra Espuela (Figs. 3.1–3.4). Again no Apache were met or seen, and there is no certainty that the camps examined had been the homes of Chiricahua Apache. During this period there were fugitive remnants of a number of other tribes in northern Mexico, and the rectangular log cabins of the settlements to which he was led were a far cry from the Chiricahua wickiup.[2] Yet these expeditions are of great significance in assessing Goodwin's work. He kept a detailed account of his travels, complete with sketch maps, photographs, careful drawings of artifacts and petroglyphs, and records of conversations with anyone encountered who claimed to have information about the Sierra Madre Chiricahua. These extensive diaries are now in the possession of his son, Neil Goodwin. It was a harbinger of the solid research to come that a young man in his early twenties, with a minimum of formal training, would sense the value of such a complete record and, in spite of the rigors of travel in difficult country, extend himself to keep it on a daily basis.

Top: Figure 3.2. Looking up Bola Canyon in the Sierra Espuela, with the location of the main Apache camp and lookout indicated by the arrow (see also Fig. 3.3). Note the extremely rugged terrain. Photo taken by Grenville Goodwin on 29 October 1931 (reproduced courtesy of Neil Goodwin).

Bottom: Figure 3.3. Looking down Bola Canyon in the Sierra Espuela, from the Apache main camp-lookout indicated in Figure 3.2. Note the clear view of much of the canyon. Photo taken by Grenville Goodwin on 29 October 1931 (reproduced courtesy of Neil Goodwin).

These forays into Mexico may be considered a milestone in Goodwin's career in another sense. They raised more questions than they solved about the existence of Sierra Madre Apache, their numbers, and the possibility of contacting them. Too many of the accounts Goodwin gathered about these people on his journeys were contradictory or self-serving. Though he never lost his interest in any claims that Sierra Madre Apache had been sighted or his hope that any remnants of the group who were still alive might be rescued from a fugitive and precarious existence, he realized that a reliable and comprehensive account of Apache culture would have to be based on work with tribal members who were more accessible and cooperative. Upon his return to Bylas, Goodwin settled down to research tasks, which, though they were less romantic than responding to colorful frontier accounts of Apache in the wilds, were still quite as demanding.

Material Culture Studies

When Goodwin embarked on intensive work among the Western Apache, the first aspect of the culture about which he gathered abundant information was the material culture. There were a number of reasons for this. It is a subject area about which people are ordinarily willing to talk freely and in which inquiry does not arouse suspicion and resentment. Even the most seasoned of ethnologists usually finds it prudent to begin his study with an investigation of the material basis of life and the tool complex that supports it rather than with an inquiry into religion, family life, or some other sensitive topic. It should be remembered, too, that Goodwin's first contact with anthropologists was with archaeologists such as Byron Cummings and Emil Haury, scholars who had to depend heavily on the material remains of a culture to interpret the life of its carriers (Fig. 3.5). Consequently, he had a hearty respect for artifacts and what their study and associations could reveal. Moreover, while he had many scattered clues and bits of information about other aspects of the culture, he still lacked the training and direction to explore them systematically.

On the other hand, he was in an excellent position to build up an accurate and rounded picture of Western Apache material culture. There were still a reasonable number of excellent Western Apache craftsmen making tray baskets, burden baskets, water jars, buckskin, saddlebags, and other traditional objects. Other Apache friends, though they were no longer involved in manufacturing artifacts, were familiar with the materials and processes involved and could accurately describe them. Goodwin, who was an experienced camper and an outdoors enthusiast, was well acquainted with the flora and resources of the Southwest and was keenly interested in the manner in which the Apache utilized them for various purposes. Moreover, by the time Goodwin first immersed himself in sustained field work, he was aware of what was already known about Apache material culture and what gaps and problems remained. He had made a practice, when visiting relatives and friends in the East, of stopping off at major museums, studying their Apache collections, and making meticulous sketches, to scale and in color, of whatever he found (Fig. 3.6). This alerted him to the variety of objects to be sought on the reservation and also the need for determining tribal differences, for often something that seemed distinctive in design or shape was simply labeled "Apache." Goodwin several times consulted me in an attempt to obtain a more accurate designation for something that he felt was vaguely or erroneously labeled. This concern for accuracy guided him when he was building the collection that is being catalogued and pictured in these pages and gives us confidence in its authenticity.

In the 1930s, particularly the early 1930s, the times were propitious for the collector of Indian-made artifacts. No section of the population suffered more from the Great Depression than the American Indian, and the Western Apache endured their share of privation. Many Indians who had skills in crafts brought examples of their handiwork to the traders in an effort to exchange the pieces for credit or necessities. Goodwin, with his knowledge of Western Apache material culture, was in a favorable position to acquire the best-made and most authentic of these artifacts.

TOP: Figure 3.4. Apache artifacts from the Sierra Madre. Goodwin identified these items as Chiricahua Apache; all were found in 1927 in a camp in Bola Canyon, Sierra Espuela, Chihuahua, by Bill Curtis and were purchased from him by Goodwin. Goodwin visited this camp with Curtis in late 1931. At *left (a)* is a calfskin sack (E–35) made by skinning a calf over the head, rather than casing from the rear end or slitting down the belly; with the ends of the feet tied and the anus-vulva area patched with heavy commercial cloth and sinew stitching, a complete sack is produced, with the mouth area of the calf being the mouth of the bag. A tear in the belly was also patched. When found it still had the hair on and was full of acorns. From nose to end of the right rear leg it is 112 cm long. A similar type of sack made from a fawn deer, and also used for storing seeds for food, was described by a Western Apache informant (Goodwin A–71). At *right (a)* is a pair of horse saddlebags (E–58), 72 cm tall when folded in half. It is made of cowhide, stitched with sinew, and has spatters of blue paint on the outside. At *center (a)* is a coil of 4–ply rawhide rope (E–32) approximately 10 to 11 m long (30 to 35 feet). Two rawhide strips were plied together in a Z-twist and then plied with a second such strand, again in a Z-twist, to produce the final rope. Sitting in the rope and shown closeup at *right (b)* is a rawhide bottle (E–33), 8.5 cm tall. It is made from calf hide with the hair on, half brown, half white, and the two pieces stitched with heavy yellow commercial thread. It has a seven-armed decorative leather collar with a brass split-rivet at the end of each arm. There is no evidence of what type of cap or plug it may have had (*a*, ASM Neg. 64286; *b*, 64288).

OPPOSITE: Figure 3.5. Grenville Goodwin (standing, *right*) at Turkey Hill Pueblo near Flagstaff, during its excavation by Byron Cummings and the University of Arizona in the summer of 1929. Standing next to Goodwin is Waldo Wedel, seated at right is Carl F. Miller, and seated at left is Charles Wisdom. All four were students at the University of Arizona at this time; Wedel and Miller went on to work for the Smithsonian Institution, mainly on the Plains, and Wisdom to study the Chorti Indians of Guatemala. Standing second from the left is E. J. Hands, a prospector whom Cummings took to Mexico to help excavate Cuicuilco because of his expertise with dynamite and who subsequently assisted Cummings on a number of archaeological projects. At front center is Joseph Hubbard of Harvard, and at upper left is Charles McKee of Yale. Photographer unknown, but may have been Cummings (photo courtesy of the Arizona Historical Society, Neg. 73858).

Grenville Goodwin

Also, there were still fine old pieces of Apache manufacture in many households, and, during those grim times, some of them found their way to the trader's salesroom. Indeed, as I know from experience, during this period a sale was often pressed upon a person who visited the Indian camps. It was under these conditions that Grenville Goodwin brought together the nucleus of the collection his widow has so generously donated to the Arizona State Museum. In the course of his work, Goodwin learned about artifacts that were no longer made because they had been replaced by trade goods, or because, though they had been useful under aboriginal conditions, they were of little value in the altered circumstances of reservation life, or because they were considered too drab to interest the tourist trade. Nevertheless, so that the full round of aboriginal Western Apache material culture might be preserved, Goodwin engaged knowledgeable Indian friends to make representative specimens of them. Thus, there are a number of items that Goodwin included in the collection mainly for completeness and to bear witness to the ceaseless exertions for sustenance and survival that were once the lot of the Western Apache.

I am confident that Goodwin would not want those who view the artifacts he brought together to consider them apart from their use. Though he never failed to determine the substances of which artifacts were made and the precise manner in which they were made, he was much

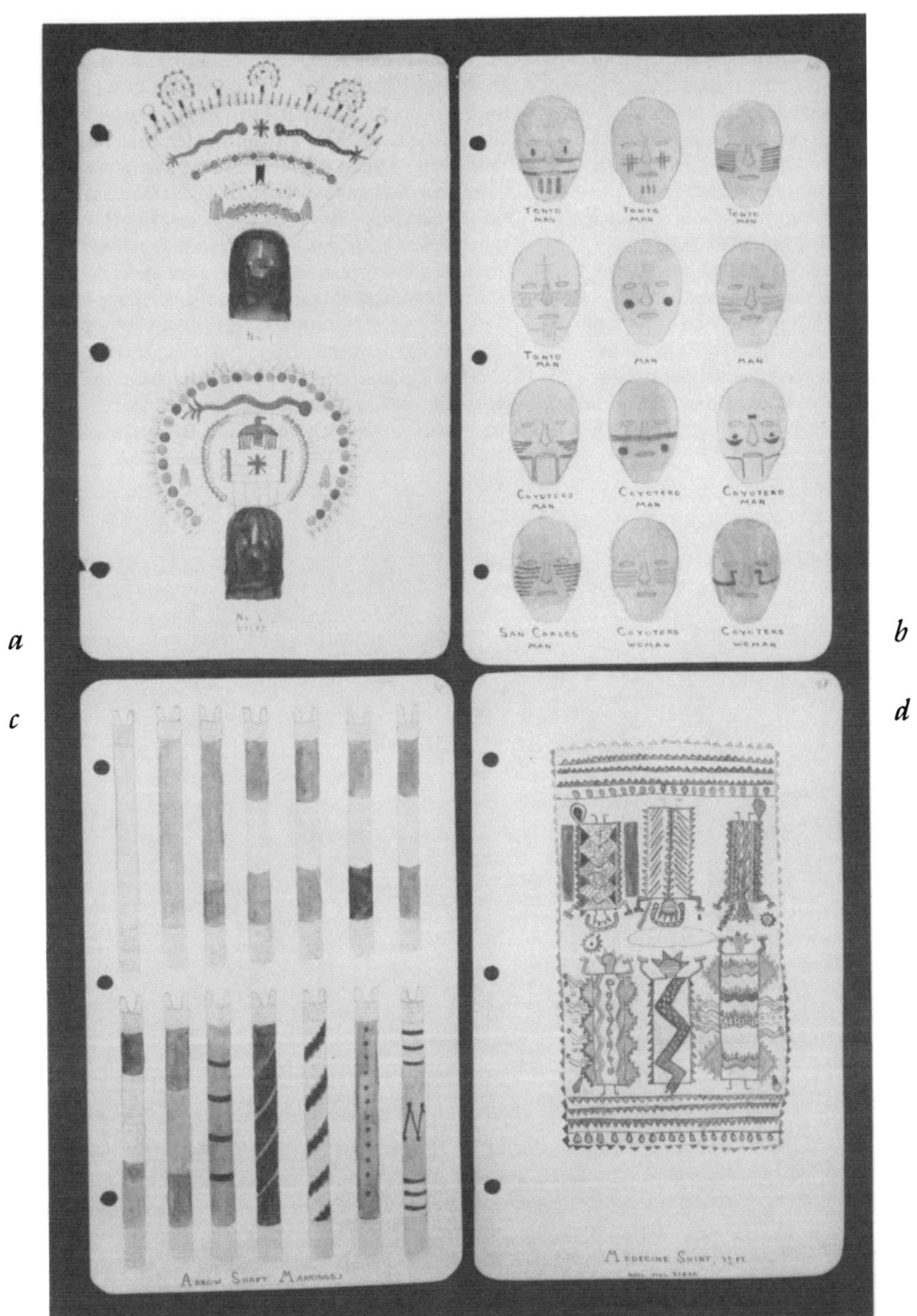

a

b

c

d

OPPOSITE: Figure 3.6. A sample of the watercolors that Grenville Goodwin painted from life and from museum specimens as records for himself and as visual aids when querying informants (see also Color Illustration 1). All were sketched first in pencil, some were then inked in and finally colored. All are done on 5 by 8 inch sheets of heavy paper and kept together in a binder (Goodwin A–77). *a, Gaan* masks: the decoration, colors, and provenience of these two masks (Bylas) suggest they were made by John Robinson, the same person from whom Goodwin purchased a complete set of similar *gaan* masks (see Fig. 7.8; compare also Fig. 7.1, showing masks that were probably also made by Robinson). *b,* Face-painting designs: face painting was done for a variety of reasons among the Western Apache (Goodwin A–66). Men and women, courting couples, and children would all paint designs for decoration. War parties might paint their faces, and one informant mentions that the absence of such paint on returning warriors was a sign that a raid had not gone well. Several types of mineral and vegetal paints were used (see Fig. 7.10 and Color Illustration 26) and could be applied with a pointed stick, a deer's lower front incisor, and one's finger or a long fingernail; parallel lines could be made by using the adjacent teeth in a lower deer jaw. A pitch-coated jar basket *(tus)* filled with water served as a mirror. Although not identified by Goodwin, this watercolor probably depicts decorative face-painting designs. *c,* Arrowshaft markings: before an arrow was fletched, that portion of the shaft just above the nock, where the feathers would go, was usually painted. A thin coat of pine pitch could be applied over the design to keep it on, and the surface of the pitch polished by turning the shaft inside a doubled-over piece of yucca leaf (Basso 1971: 230). One man told Goodwin (Basso 1971: 230), "In the old days the clans used to paint all their arrows the same way, except the *descidn* [a clan: 'horizontally red people'], who painted theirs all red." This watercolor shows a great variety in these designs, and, although not confirmed, the designs were probably copied by Goodwin from museum specimens. *d,* Painted medicine shirt: Goodwin sketched this medicine man's buckskin shirt at the Smithsonian Institution (their catalogue number 21520). The figures on the shirt are probably depictions of the *gaan*. For an indication of the accuracy and detail with which Goodwin rendered his watercolors, compare this figure (ASM Neg. 64455) with the photo of this specimen in Opler 1983, Figure 7.

more interested in them as the means by which a people carried out their purposes. It was their context and the interplay of the material and the ideological in human affairs that intrigued him. The material dimension expressed for him how well the people understood their natural surroundings and utilized their possibilities. We shall draw closer to his own conception to the extent that we think of these artifacts in use in Western Apache culture rather than as inert museum pieces.

Broadening Interests

Although Goodwin, as have so many others, began his quest by investigating the material culture of the Western Apache, this became only a first step in his research and a useful gateway to the understanding of other aspects of their life pattern. As time went on, his experience deepened, his command of the language grew, his knowledge of the literature on the Apache widened, he met other Southwestern specialists such as Edward Spicer, Harry Hoijer, Leslie Spier, and me, and he continued the formidable task to which he had set himself, namely, to provide a comprehensive picture of all aspects of Western Apache culture. He continued to make Bylas his headquarters, and he carried out intensive field researches in the Bylas area. In addition, he made trips to all parts of the Western Apache reservation with the aim of gathering comparative data concerning each of the five groups (San Carlos, White Mountain, Cibecue, Northern Tonto, and Southern Tonto; see Fig. 1.1) that together comprise the Western Apache tribe.

Goodwin made field work and the filling out of his note file his principal task for over six years, until the end of 1936. Meanwhile, beginning in 1933, he started to publish articles on Western Apache social organization, warfare practices, and religion. Since his health still remained fragile, he did not stay uninterruptedly in the field. At intervals he rested at a family home in Colorado Springs or at the home of his older brother Sage in Santa Fe.[3] Yet even at these havens his Apache work was his main concern, and he spent his time organizing his notes, writing on the basis of them, reading the comparative literature, or planning future segments of research to fill in gaps in his information. During this period, also, an important event occurred in his personal life. On November 23, 1936, Goodwin married Janice Thompson, whom he had met seven years earlier at Sage's wedding (Fig. 3.7).

As a result of his friendship with Dean Cummings, Goodwin felt a close, though informal, connection with the Department of Anthropology at the University of Arizona. In 1937, when he decided that the time had come to shift his emphasis from field work to writing, he opted to make Tucson, with its professional ties and facilities, his base. This living arrangement continued through 1938. During this period Goodwin readied a manuscript of White Mountain Apache myths and tales that was published as a Memoir of the American Folklore Society in 1939. He also revised a long manuscript dealing with the social organization of the Western Apache, which I first saw and read in 1933 and in regard to which I offered suggestions and supplied comparative data. After still further revisions, this was published posthumously in 1942 as his well-known book, *The Social Organization of the Western Apache*. In the spring of 1939, through the good offices of his long-time friend, Dr. Emil Haury, he was formally appointed a research associate in the Department of Anthropology at the University of Arizona.[4]

In the fall of 1939 Goodwin left Tucson to obtain further training in the Department of Anthropology at the University of Chicago. In this venture he was not seeking academic credits, but guidance and criticism. He hoped to benefit particularly from interaction with Harry Hoijer, the specialist in Apache linguistics, and with Fred Eggan, who was well known for his studies of the social organization of peoples of the Southwest. In October, 1939, I received a buoyant letter from him. He and his wife were enjoying the Chicago experience. He expected to stay there for one academic year. He and his wife planned to establish a permanent residence in Tucson at that time, and he looked forward to resuming his program of writing on the basis of his field materials and of continuing field research at intervals. This was the last message I received from him. Shortly afterward he was stricken by a malignant brain tumor, and by June, 1940, he was dead. His body was returned to Tucson and is buried there. He already had a number of publications to his credit and others in press. At his death he was but thirty-three years old. Yet, as a result of his industry, his cordial relations with the Indians, and his steadfastness of purpose, he left a large body of unpublished field materials of exceptional ethnographic value. Some of it has been edited and published by more recent students of the Western Apache such as Charles Kaut and Keith Basso. Still other edited works based on the Goodwin notes are promised by Basso. It is to be hoped that we shall some day have at our disposal the full results of the labors of this gifted field worker. Meanwhile, we can rejoice that so much of his legacy, such as the fine collection of Western Apache artifacts described and depicted in this catalogue, is available for our pleasure and instruction.

All those who are familiar with Grenville Goodwin's writings and field materials can attest to his industry and scholarship. In closing, I would like to say something about the man. I first met Goodwin in the winter of 1931 when I was a graduate student in the Department of Anthropology at the University of Chicago, fresh from my own initial intensive field work among the Apache and eager to begin writing my dissertation on Chiricahua Apache social organization. I was visited by this tall, fair, pleasant-looking young man of just my own age who was on his way east from Western Apache country. He was soft-spoken and modest but

OPPOSITE: Figure 3.7. Janice and Grenville Goodwin in 1937, at the home of Grenville's brother in Santa Fe, 401 Delgado Street (reproduced courtesy of Neil Goodwin).

obviously well informed. Despite his relaxed manner, one felt that he possessed drive and a determination to master the substantial research goals he had in view. He and I kept in touch through letters and occasional meetings until the end of his life, and my impression of him never varied. The same eagerness and diligence were always apparent in him. The same gentleness and thoughtfulness remained characteristic. I never heard him raise his voice in anger or speak harshly of another human being. The only annoyance I ever heard him express was with his health problem and the limitations it imposed on him. Yet even here he had learned patience and evidenced good humor. He was one of the most consistent of persons I ever knew, and to be consistently worthy is a standard too few of us can maintain.

NOTE. For other biographical sketches of Goodwin, see Cole (1941), Cole and others (1942), Spicer (1971), Opler (1973), and Brandt and others (1994).

1. Goodwin's class work at the University of Arizona included summer archaeological field work at Turkey Hill Pueblo in 1929 (see Fig. 3.5) and two semesters of classes in 1929 and 1930 in such diverse subjects as zoology, geology, botany, astronomy, military science, ethnology, and archaeology. (Note by Alan Ferg.)

2. During March of 1976, Neil Goodwin visited Tucson, Arizona, in hopes of finding someone with firsthand knowledge of the rugged and mountainous border areas of northern Chihuahua and Sonora, Mexico. This search eventually led him to contact Thomas H. Naylor and me. Neil's intent was to relocate two or three Indian camp sites that his father, Grenville Goodwin, had visited in the fall of 1931 while being guided by Bill Curtis. Grenville's field diary located these abandoned camp sites but used place names either no longer in use or unfamiliar to Naylor and Burns. However, Neil had a proof sheet of photos his father had taken that included several vistas familiar to Naylor. Using these photos and the field diary, Naylor and I surmised, in general terms, where the camp sites must have been located. We agreed to guide Neil to the general area his father had visited in 1931 and if possible actually to relocate one or more of the suspected Apache camp sites.

Shortly thereafter, a party consisting of Neil Goodwin and then University of Arizona anthropology students Thomas H. Naylor, Misse Smith, and me, left Tucson and retraced Grenville Goodwin's route, passing through Douglas, Arizona, Agua Prieta, Sonora, and Colonia Morelos, Sonora. We paralleled the Rio Bavispe to the abandoned Mormon colony of Colonia Oaxaca, Sonora, at which point we turned northeast up the narrow Pulpit Canyon. Passing through the canyon, we entered the far western edge of the historic Carretas Plains of northeastern Chihuahua. We turned south, driving up the Oso Creek drainage, and began closely examining the eastern slopes of the Sierra Azul Mountains for any of the several landmarks visible in Goodwin's photos. Our original guess that Grenville's "Cochita Hueca" [sic—Huachita Hueca] Mountains and today's Sierra Azul Mountains were one and the same soon proved correct. The distinctive pine-studded flat top of the Sierra Azul and several prominent spurs and ledges were finally matched against the set of small proof sheet photos.

After repeatedly consulting the photos and parts of Grenville's field diary, we eventually felt reasonably certain that the southernmost of the suspected Apache camp sites was nearby. After parking the vehicle, everyone spread out and began the steep ascent on foot up the eastern flank of the Sierra Azul through dense oak trees and manzanita bushes. We eventually located one portion of the hidden camp site, but only after literally walking right over it without at first recognizing it for what it was. The portion of the extended camp we found was situated on a southeasterly sloping ledge about 800 feet below the 8,097–foot summit of the Sierra Azul. Surprisingly the adobe, log, and rock structure Goodwin had sketched and photographed in 1931 had completely disappeared, leaving few, if any, clues as to its former presence. The corral noted by Goodwin had also deteriorated beyond recognition. The soggy ground mentioned by Goodwin still remained and, in fact, was the most notable feature of the site in 1976. Careful search produced a number of metal scraps and several crude stone metates, two or three of which Goodwin had actually photographed in 1931. Misse Smith found a large round piece of iron hanging from an oak tree in the ravine just north of one of the site's original house structures. This butt end of a boiler was the alarm gong found by Grenville in 1931 and provided the final proof that we, indeed, had rediscovered at least one portion of Grenville Goodwin's southern Apache camp site.

The original location of this small camp site must have been determined by the presence of the spring and seep that today is responsible for the area's soggy ground. But just as important, if not more so, is the inclined nature of the ledge on which the site is situated. Viewed from the east and even from directly below, this portion of the camp site remains out of view and completely hidden. The site really can be seen clearly only from the long and narrow flat-topped summit of the Sierra Azul. This summit is not easy of access and lies along no main trail or road.

Artifacts found at the camp site in 1931 indicated that the camp's inhabitants were in all probability Apache Indians who used traditional technologies, augmented whenever possible by objects from the Anglo or Mexican world crowding in around them. In 1976, stone metates, manos, flakes, and cores were present, along with scraps of metal and some glass fragments. Some of the pieces of metal had been hammered or filed into blades or other tools. No pottery was discovered at the site in 1976. Very few tin cans or other twentieth-century debris were noted in or near the portion of the small site we visited, nor was there any such debris below or leading up the approaches to the camp site.

While plunging through the dense underbrush heading back to our vehicle, we continued to discuss whether or not the camp site had in fact been the secret home of some band of "wild Mexican Apaches." This prompted our party to visit the Rancho Agua Blanca headquarters. The Gavilando brothers' extensive holding on the Carretas Plains includes, and included in 1931, the site we had just left. The ranch's foreman granted us a most informative and cordial interview. Neither he nor any of the ranch's longtime cowboys had ever seen any "wild Apaches" on the ranch, nor were they familiar with any stories of the ranch ever having been frequented by any such persons. Another uncle's ranch had been the scene of lots of Apache incidents, but not this Gavilando ranch. We heard a version of the story originally recorded by Grenville about a number of unsolved robberies that occurred at one of the ranch's line shacks just at the eastern base of Sierra Azul. The foreman related that sometime during the 1920s the line shack's cowboys had gone to the Las Varas ranch. Upon their return, they found the line shack ransacked and robbed of every metal utensil as well as many pieces of scrap metal. The foreman indicated that no clues were ever found as to the identity of the robbers. The ranch foreman stated that our search for any evidence of Mexico's last wild Apaches was welcomed on the ranch, but he felt it would probably be much more productive to the north toward the Sierra San Luis or to the south toward the upper reaches of Oso Creek.

Apparently the personnel of the local ranches no longer recall the discovery of the Apache camp site in 1930. We left the Gavilando ranch without disclosing that we had just visited the hidden and apparently long-forgotten camp site that lies no more than two miles from and directly above one of the ranch's line shacks. Every move made at that cow camp and along the entire length of the road leading up the Oso Creek was plainly visible from the lip of the hidden ledge. Viewed from either the road or the line shack, the Sierra Azul's contours did not even hint at the existence of any hidden camps.

The four of us left Mexico without locating any of Grenville Goodwin's other camp sites. They most certainly could be found in one of the eastern-draining canyons of the Sierra San Luis or the Sierra Espuelas. After locating the one camp site, viewing the photos Goodwin made in 1931, and reading portions of Goodwin's field diary, each of us was convinced that Grenville Goodwin had in fact visited and documented one of the last Apache sites to have been inhabited in the far northern reaches of Mexico's Sierra Madres. (Note by Barney T. Burns.)

3. Although her permanent home was in New York City on Long Island, Grenville's mother, Elizabeth Sage Goodwin (Mrs. Meredith Hare by a second marriage after divorce), kept a home in Colorado Springs, and it was probably there that Grenville convalesced from two bouts of tuberculosis in the late 1920s. While in Colorado Springs, Mrs. Hare, along with Mrs. Julie Penrose and Mrs. Alice Bemis Taylor, was instrumental in the decision to build the Colorado Springs Fine Arts Center and to make it more encompassing than most anthropology museums of the day, an all-purpose institution concerned with all the arts (see Colorado Springs Fine Arts Center 1986: 17–19, 27–29, 128, 207). Mrs. Hare was interested in the performing arts, and Mrs. Penrose in art education. The land on which the Center stands had been under the Broadmoor Art Academy, a highly regarded art school located in a former Penrose residence. The Penroses gave the land and Mrs. Taylor provided the funds to build the center, which opened on 21 April 1936. Elizabeth Sage Hare's vision and foresight played an important role in the founding of the Colorado Springs Fine Arts Center, where, appropriately, a number

of Grenville's Apache items are now housed (see Appendix C and Colorado Springs Fine Arts Center 1986: 78). She also served as the Center's first president from 1935 to 1936. Grenville's brother, Sage, was also involved with the Center's founding, having done perspective drawings for the building, as envisioned by its architect, John Gaw Meem (see Colorado Springs Fine Arts Center 1986, Figs. 16–18). Finally, Elizabeth's second husband, Meredith Hare, was one of the original members of the Indian Arts Fund in Santa Fe. Certainly Grenville was surrounded by people bent on preserving and encouraging the arts and crafts of a variety of ethnic groups in the Southwest, something clearly reflected in his careful collection of Western Apache material and nonmaterial culture and in the ultimate donation of these items by Janice and Neil Goodwin to a public museum, where they would continue to be available for use and enjoyment. (Note by Neil Goodwin, Jonathan Batkin, Curator, Taylor Museum of the Colorado Springs Fine Arts Center, and Alan Ferg.)

4. Grenville was apparently quite pleased with this affiliation. No monetary compensation accompanied the appointment, and it is clear from correspondence (in ASM Accessions File No. 2021) that Haury (on behalf of the Department) and Goodwin both looked at this association as a mutual opportunity to enrich their respective fields of knowledge and scholarship. As Goodwin noted, he was "willing and able to finance his own work," but did not wish to be thought of as "some sort of half-baked altruist," and asked that Haury enlighten anyone laboring under such a delusion. Presumably to enable Grenville to tell people that it was a paid appointment, Haury had proposed that Goodwin be reimbursed a dollar a year, something apparently deemed unnecessary by University President Atkinson. Goodwin took this loss of his entire salary with characteristic good humor, writing back to Haury: "Do not worry about the dollar a year wage. If I had it I'd probably spend it on something foolish anyway." (Note by Alan Ferg.)

Chapter Four
The Social Divisions and Economic Life of the Western Apache

Grenville Goodwin

By way of introduction it would be best to explain what peoples are included by the term Western Apache. The term is here used to designate all those Apache peoples who have lived within the present boundaries of the state of Arizona during historic times, with the exception of the Chiricahua, Warm Springs, and allied Apache, and a small band of Apaches known as the Apaches Mansos, who lived in the vicinity of Tucson. The various peoples thus classed together as the Western Apache are apparently enough like each other, and different from other Apache peoples in certain aspects of their culture, to give reason for placing them in a division by themselves.[1]

Social Divisions

At the time of the first American occupation of their territory (middle of nineteenth century) the six thousand or so people comprising the Western Apache were divided into five distinct groups,[2] each having its own territory. These groups were: (1) White Mountain Apache, (2) Cibecue Apache, (3) San Carlos Apache, (4) Southern Tonto Apache, (5) Northern Tonto Apache.[3] The five groups felt themselves to be quite distinct from one another, and hostility between certain of them was not unknown. However, among people of the same group there was a fairly close feeling of relationship in custom and speech. It was this that held them together and not any political unity.

Each one of the five groups was in turn broken up into bands or semi-bands [Fig. 4.1]. These bands were not equally distinct nor as strongly formed in all groups. The formations among the Southern Tonto cannot really be called bands in comparison

---

Reprinted from *American Anthropologist* 37(1): 55–64, 1935, by permission of the American Anthropological Association.

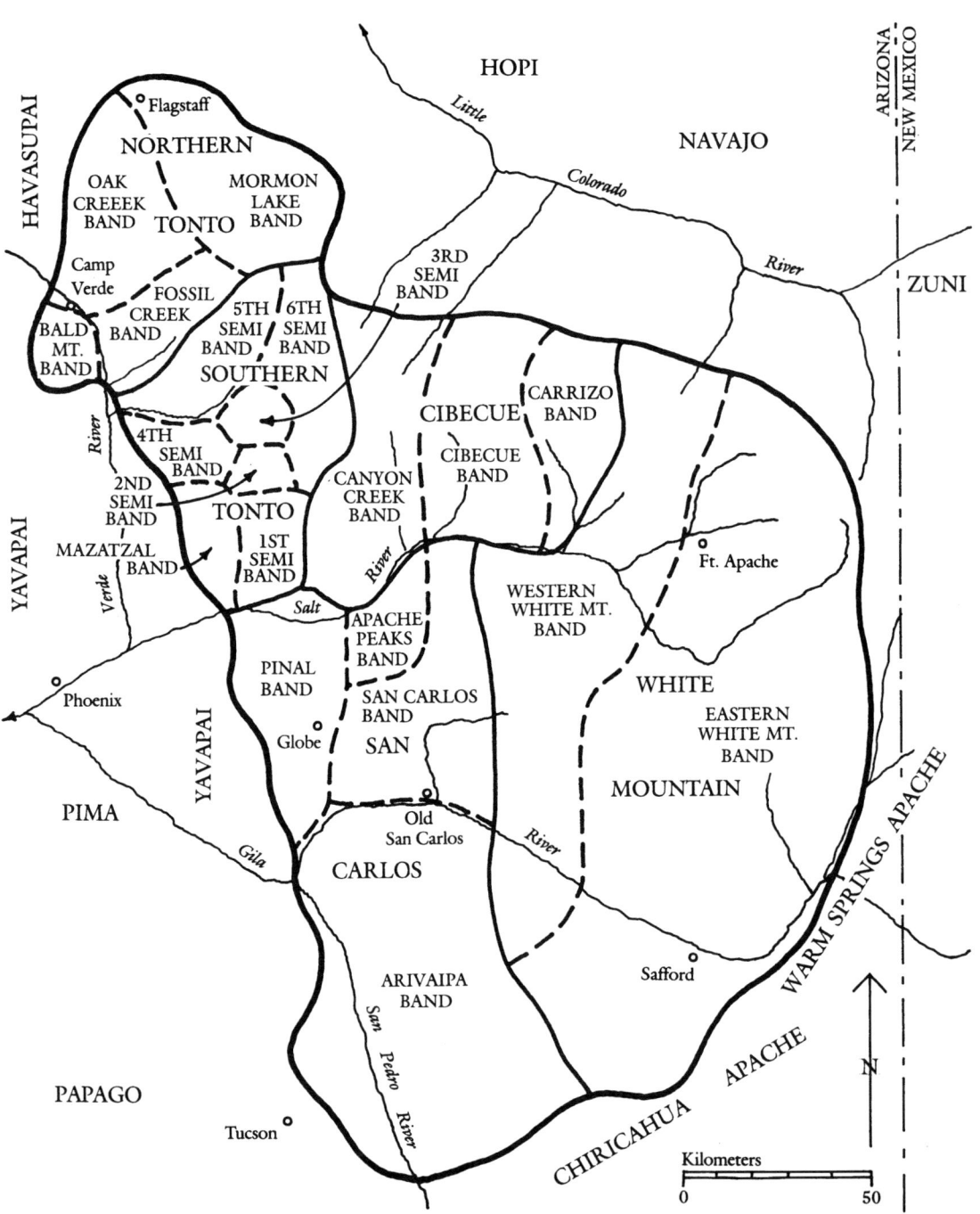

Figure 4.1. The distribution of the Western Apache groups, bands, and semi-bands in east-central Arizona. Redrafted from the original.

The Western Apache

with those of some of the other groups, and are thus termed semi-bands for convenience. Bands and semi-bands again each had their own territory and refrained from encroaching on that of their neighbors. Though the unity within a band or semi-band was naturally more intense than that within a whole group, still the people were not a political unit, and were mainly held together by common custom and clan and blood relationship.

The next unit below the band was the local group. Every band or semi-band was composed of several local groups, each having its own territory. The local group was the basic unit upon which the social organization and government of the Western Apache was built. Each local group had its own chief who led his people and directed it in matters of importance, such as war or raiding parties, food gathering expeditions, farming projects, and relations with other local groups or foreign tribes. Chiefs did not have supreme power, but instead led their people mainly by prestige and good example: attributes for which they were chosen as leaders.

Beside the chief there was another leader in the local group: the head woman or woman chief, as she was sometimes called. Her function was to counsel those about her in the ways of living and especially to organize wild-food gathering parties among the women.

In a local group there were from nine to perhaps thirty houses, and the majority of people in these generally belonged to the same clan, though some might be blood relatives of other clans, relatives by marriage, or even unrelated. This strong clan and blood relationship within the local groups was what really made them such closely knit units.

Within the local group were several family groups, say from three to six in number. These family groups were in turn made up of from three to eight households. The members of a family group were usually related within the limit of second maternal cousin, though a few relatives by marriage would be included also. Each was controlled by a head man, who directed in almost the same way as a chief, and it was from the various head men within a local group that the chief was chosen. The family group was in reality almost a miniature local group, and naturally acted even more in unison. Often it operated as a separate unit in pursuit of economic ends for short periods of time, but never permanently.

Blood relationship among these people was and is a very strong bond, involving mutual aid and responsibility. Obligations thus entailed were felt to be stronger on the maternal side than on the paternal because of matrilocal residence and the clan system. Blood relatives were considered close within the limit of second or third cousin, but beyond this strict observance of blood relationship obligations depended more on close association between the relatives concerned.

The clan system of the Western Apache is not so easy to fit into the sequence formed by the already described social divisions. Whereas each of the groups, bands and semi-bands, local groups, and family groups belonged to one area only, the clans formed cross strata of relationships which ran through the several groups, bands, etc., joining all together. Many of the clans were represented in more than one group.

Each clan had a name, usually of the place-name type, designating its legendary place of origin or first settlement. Children were born into the clan of their mother. All members of one clan were considered blood relatives and called each other by kinship terms identical with those of consanguinity. Marriage between members of the same clan was not countenanced, though marriage into the father's clan was permissible if the blood relationship was not too close. Members of the same clan were expected to aid each other in time of need, and if it was necessary the whole clan might be called together to avenge a wrong done to one of its members. However, there was no clan government or law beyond the obligations governing the actions of clan relatives to one another.

There existed a varying interrelation among the clans of all groups, and one clan might be related to another clan or several other clans. Between members of related clans the same rules of exogamy and mutual obligation held as between members of the same clan, though to a slightly less degree.

Within historic times, at least, the Western Apache clan was not primarily a territorial unit like the local group, though among certain of the bands there was a tendency to localization. The real power of the clan lay in its far flung web of interrelational obligations between its members in all the Western Apache groups.

Residence was usually matrilocal though not necessarily so. Generally neither boys nor girls married till they had proved themselves fully able to perform the tasks of men and women. In marriage proceedings between two families, the man's family first made a present to the girl's parents, and after that there might be mutual feasting and present-giving. When these evidences of friendliness and esteem were concluded, the young couple set up housekeeping for themselves. From the time of betrothal and marriage the obligations among relatives by marriage were strong, and there was a definite code for the various classes of affinal relatives with which an individual was expected to comply.

In former times a man might have more than one wife (usually not more than two or three) if he could support them, but in doing this he was expected to marry women who were of the same clan as his first wife (usually her true sisters, or daughters of her mother's sister). The same rule applied to a widower, and a widow was under obligation to marry a clan relative of her deceased husband (usually his true brother, or mother's sister's son).

When a man and woman were married, each had his share of the family work and providing. What this really amounted to was that the men did all the dangerous and very arduous or strenuous tasks (war, hunting, heavy digging or lifting, handling unruly livestock, etc.), while the women did all those things which did not require a man's strength and endurance (cooking and camp work, tanning, harvesting, etc.). Thus, though the women had the commonplace tasks, their lot kept them more steadily at work than did that of the men.

Children did not take a serious part in the culture of their people till they were about six years old. From that time on they were taught by their parents or relatives, so that they gradually became familiar with the things which they would have to know in later life. When they had reached the age of twelve or so, they took an active part in the procuring and preparation of foods, and henceforth their serious activities were increased.

The foregoing is a superficial description of the Western Apache social pattern, and it must be realized that it was merely a pattern, not a stereotyped program that the people followed regardless of all circumstances. Also it applies only to the social organization of these people within historic times, and up to the period when the United States Government first seriously started to interfere with the original balance of their culture (1871–1873), when the centralization of the Western Apache on government reservations was accomplished.

After the life on the reservations commenced, the old distinction between the groups began to break down, due to the people being thrown more closely together. At the present time group distinction plays a minor part, though the existence of a sort of rivalry between the descendents of different groups is still quite evident. The same is true of the bands and semi-bands, though with them the distinctions have lapsed even more.

The local group is no longer the close knit unit that it once was. The chiefs are gone, and their power, in great part, is now in the hands of the white agent and his employes. However, the family group still preserves a great deal of its old form. A head man directs the family affairs, and these head men still exert great influence in their communities. In the past years it has been mainly through them that the people have dealt with the agency.

The clan system also remains partially intact. Thus, though marriage between related clans is sometimes allowed, marriage between members of the same clan is not.

Marriage and family life is much the same now as formerly, except that the presents and feasting at the time of a wedding are not considered strictly necessary, a marriage license and legal marriage ceremony are required by law, and a man may not have more than one wife. Remarriage obligations are still generally in force, as well as those between relatives-in-law. However, children do not take the part in the economic life which they used to take, because they are in school during several months of the year.

At the present time the real economic unit is

the family group; the groups, bands and semi-bands, and local groups having given way to the modern, more sedentary, small farming and ranching communities, which are centralized at the seven or eight main farming locations on the San Carlos and White Mountain Reservations, and at two or three localities off these reservations.

Economic Life

To understand the economic life of the Western Apache it is necessary to know something of their natural environment. The country which comprised their historical territory can be roughly divided into two areas. The first lies in the southern and southwestern part of the territory, and is in general lower. It is a country of great open desert valleys, separated from each other by abruptly rising mountain ranges. In the valleys grow creosote bush, mesquite, yucca, chollas, sahuaro, etc., grading into oaks, junipers, and piñons on the lower slopes of the mountains. On the tops of the mountains are pines, some conifers, etc. The climate is hot in summer, mild in winter.

The second area is a more uniform upland country, averaging from five to seven thousand feet in altitude, and covered with growths of oak, juniper, and piñon. It was in this type of country that the people formerly lived during the greater part of the year. The mountains are fewer and less rugged, but higher in altitude than those in the first area. On them are thick stands of pine, conifers, etc. The climate is pleasant in summer, but from November to March and sometimes April the weather is fairly cold, with snowfalls not infrequent.

The climate is generally arid in both lower and higher areas. However, there are certain rainy seasons: in the last part of July and during August, and again during some of the winter months. The varying altitudes throughout both areas gave rise to differences in the character of the country and plant and animal life, thus affording a variety of foods.

The Western Apache had four sources from which to obtain food: wild animals and birds, wild plants, domesticated plants raised on the small farms, and livestock and agricultural products which could be taken in trade or in raids on neighboring peoples. The last source was the least important, as it was easier to obtain food at home. Its main value lay in the fact that horses, mules, burros, and cattle could be captured from the Mexican settlements in the south, and sheep and goats from the Navajo in the north to be butchered and used as food.

Of meat and plant foods, meat formed roughly about thirty-five to forty percent of the whole, plant foods about sixty to sixty-five percent. This percentage naturally fluctuated throughout the year according to the abundance of game and crops. Of edible game there used to be several kinds: bear, deer, antelope, some mountain sheep and elk as well as smaller game like rabbits, rats, squirrels, and certain birds. The larger quarry was hunted with the bow and arrow; the smaller was snared or shot with arrows, mostly by boys.

Men occupied much of their time in desultory hunting, but there were two principal seasons when hunting was given particular attention. These were late spring and fall. Late spring was a good time to hunt, coming as it did between planting and the first wild food crops of July, when the women would have time to care for hides and meat. Fall was even better, as meat and hides were prime, and a man could leave his family safely at the farms, there being nothing much to do at home. It was in the fall that the big hunting parties set out. They were not highly organized affairs, but composed only of a few men under the leadership of one of the party. Women did not usually accompany them, but instead the men butchered and skinned the carcasses, and packed the meat home to the women on horseback. This was possible because the hunting parties were only gone a few days and never ranged very far from home.

Of the sixty to sixty-five percent of plant food of the total food consumed during the year, about thirty-five to forty percent consisted of wild plant foods and the remaining twenty to twenty-five percent of domesticated plant foods. This proportion applied to those who had farms of average size. Among those who had no farms the domesticated plant foods used were only the few obtained by trade. Thus with the nonfarmers the percentage of wild plant foods used was high, often the full sixty to sixty-five percent. There were many wild food plants, and during the whole growing season (April to November) one or several plants were always available for food. Even in winter there was the mescal which could be roasted and eaten. Certain plants were staples: mescal, sahuaro fruit, acorns, mesquite beans, fruit of Spanish bayonet, sunflower seeds, fruit of prickly pear, piñon nuts, and juniper berries. Of these nine, mescal and acorns were the most important.

In the spring parties set out for the lower country and prepare mescal. In July the sahuaro fruit was ripe there and also certain of the prickly pears. Late July and August was the season for gathering acorns, summer that for mesquite beans. Later, in early September the Spanish bayonet fruit was ripe. When October and November came, the last crops, piñon nuts and juniper berries, were harvested.

As the food was gathered it was either eaten or stored for winter. Storage was usually in caves in sealed olla-shaped baskets, or in the dwellings of the families themselves.

Since most of the principal plant foods grew at different altitudes, it was necessary to keep moving from place to place to harvest them. These journeys lasted from ten days to a month, and as many women and girls were needed to help, the whole family usually went along. However, the men spent the time hunting, as it was not their task to help gather and prepare any of the wild plants except mescal.

Among the Western Apache every family did not have a farm. The farming opportunities of the area varied and even some families who could have did not wish to farm. In the northwestern part of the area many of the people did not farm because of their exposed position to enemy tribes and the resulting danger of living on farming sites. The varying degrees in the amount of agricultural activity between the several groups stands out best when a comparison is made. Among both bands of the White Mountain group and all three bands of the Cibecue group most of the local groups farmed. Among the four bands of the San Carlos group, and the second, third, fifth, and sixth semi-bands of the Southern Tonto group the majority of local groups had farms. In the Mazatzal band and the first and fourth semi-bands of the Southern Tonto group only about half the local groups farmed. Of two bands of the Northern Tonto group the majority of local groups did not farm, and in the other two there was no farming at all.

Farming, as can be seen, was not necessarily carried on by all families in one group, band or semi-band, or clan, but it is true that if some of the families in a local group farmed then the majority of families of that local group did, usually all at the same site. This does not mean that the farm was a local group institution. It pertained essentially to the family.

Among these people agriculture was not a complex affair. Fields were small: about half an acre or so, often less. On them were raised corn, some beans, squash, and later wheat, but corn was the main crop and formed a staple food. Clearing and tilling fields was done with the digging stick, and in seeding, the planting stick was used. Farming sites located in country high enough to get sufficient rainfall were not irrigated, but those in low country were and the neighbors helped each other in the construction of dams and ditches. Preparing the fields and planting took about a month. All the members of the family group were expected to help if needed. When the corn was about three feet tall, most of the people moved away for the summer to harvest the various wild plant foods. In September they returned to harvest and store the crops, this again taking about one month's time. Much of the corn was stored in large ground caches for future use.

After harvest part of the population remained at the farms, and part moved down to lower country to escape cold weather and to be within close raiding distance of enemy settlements. Though away from the farms for much of the year, yet these were the places that the people considered their real homes.

The old way of life of the Western Apache shows that these people had a mixture of three modes of living. They hunted large game, but did not depend on meat to such a degree that they ever exhausted or drove the game from their territory and had to go long distances for it. They farmed to some extent, but by no means enough so that they could depend on crops for sustenance throughout the year and so remain in one place. They made use of wild plant foods and small game, but this was not sufficient for them to forego the hunting of big game, though it did allow a minority of them to do without agriculture. Thus their existence kept them moving about within a limited territory in which they were able to practice all three ways of living and follow out their seasonal schedule.

One point of importance was the method of travel. In spite of accessibility to the Mexican ranches of Sonora, the horse never became indispensable in travel, and travel by foot still remained general. The horse was used very often as a pack animal. When families had to move on foot they packed their belongings on their backs in burden baskets. The Western Apache, it must be understood, were never a stock-raising people.

Though much of the population had semi-permanent homes at their farms, they moved too much from one place to another to develop any of the arts that a more sedentary people might have. Their dome-shaped, brush-covered dwellings were easily reconstructed and set up in a new place when necessary. On account of frequent travel their belongings had to be conveniently transportable and thus, though they made some pottery, the art was never carried far. They did no textile weaving in cotton or wool, but made their clothing and blankets from skins. However, there was one real art which they did develop and which fitted perfectly to their mode of life. This was basketry; an art carried to perfection among them.

The old type of subsistence has not been given up altogether: even today [1935] a good many of the more common of the wild plant foods are used, mescal and acorns still being staple foods. However, due to lack of game, beef is now the principal meat food. In spite of the many changes of recent years the most popular type of dwelling is still the old style house.

Unfortunately the reliable material already published on the Western Apache is not abundant. What little there is deals mainly with separated aspects of their culture so that it is impossible to get a clear perspective of the people as a whole. Therefore it is interesting to look forward to the time when a thorough understanding of the Western Apache and their position in the Southwest can be made possible not only in relation to the other Apache peoples and the Navajo, but to the whole area.

SANTA FÉ
NEW MEXICO

---

1. The material upon which this paper is based has been collected during the years 1930–1933 under the auspices of the University of Arizona, in a project which entails the study of the culture of the Western Apache now living on the San Carlos and White Mountain Indian Reservations, and at various settlements off the reservations in the state of Arizona, near Camp Verde, Payson, etc.

2. The terms "tribe" or "tribal group" may possibly be more suitable than "group," but the latter is here used until some one term becomes established for designation of these Western Apache units.

3. The reasons for the naming of these five groups in the above manner, as well as for naming the bands as they are on the map, is not here explained. The whole subject is fully discussed in a manuscript now completed on the social organization of the Western Apache, which will be published shortly [Goodwin 1942]. The three western-most bands of the Northern Tonto Apache intermingled with Yavapai people who shared the region with them.

Chapter Five
Subsistence

Alan Ferg and William B. Kessel

OVERLEAF: **Preparing mescal.** Figure 5.1. Mrs. Jewett Wright patting out cooked, mashed mescal onto a forming tray (see Figs. 5.10, 5.11) at Bylas on June 1 of either 1931 or 1936. Cooked mescal was a Western Apache staple that was dried and stored or traded to the Navajo, Hopi, and Zuni (Goodwin 1942: 73, 74, 81; photo by Grenville Goodwin, ASM Neg. 18193).

Quivers, bows, and arrows. Figure 5.2. Quivers were made from a variety of animal skins including horse, steer, peccary, deer, wolf, coyote, gray fox, bobcat, and mountain lion, the last being the most valued (Basso 1971: 234; Goodwin 1939: 20, fn. 2). A bearskin quiver is also mentioned in White Mountain myth (Goodwin 1939: 172). If the skins had nice tails, they were left on for decoration. The quiver at bottom, 75 cm long, is made from a single piece of coyote hide from the body, neck, and head, folded over and sewn shut with buckskin thongs around a long stick, with a rawhide disc base. The stick and base keep the quiver rigid and maintain its flattened cylindrical shape. The lip is finished with a piece of yellow ochre-dyed buckskin, a wide yellow band of buckskin girdles the quiver, and the holes near the base where the ears were cut off are also patched with yellow buckskin. A piece of an old commercial leather belt was attached as a shoulder strap. This quiver and the arrows in both quivers (all 21359) came from San Carlos.

The quiver at top (E–9240) lacks specific provenience information and may not be Western Apache. It is made of a single piece of buckskin folded over and stitched shut with sinew around a long stick at the back. The base is a rawhide disc. Around the top and bottom are strips of red flannel with black and white beadwork trim. The bow case is a similarly constructed sleeve of buckskin but without a stick or a base and is attached only at the two points where the shoulder strap is sewn on with buckskin thongs. According to one of Goodwin's informants, plain quivers were the earlier style, and attached bow cases were copied from the Chiricahua (Basso 1971: 234).

The bow (21356) in the bow case is made of mulberry, roughly shaped but not finished, as it would have been traded to the Navajo. It was made by Palmer Valor in 1932. The bow at top (EEG 45; 120 cm long) has no specific provenience but may have come from East Fork or Whiteriver in the 1920s. It is semicircular in cross-section and carefully shaped and smoothed. Both of these are single arc bows. Double arc bows were known but not preferred. Basso (1971: 223–226) provides more information on bows and a photo of a double arc bow. Bows apparently had definite tops and bottoms: "When you are shooting a bow, you always keep the side with the buckskin down to the ground and the other end up" (Goodwin A–67). This statement makes sense when one examines the decorated bow (E–9243, not illustrated) that made a set with the plain quiver and arrows (21359): it has a buckskin thong tied to the bowstring just above where the string is tied to one end of the bow. This single strand hangs down 21 cm, has one knot tied in it, and presumably indicates the "bottom" end of this bow.

Types of arrow points. Figure 5.3. This selection of arrows collected by Goodwin shows the various point types used by the Western Apache. At left are two arrows tipped with points cut or filed from sheet metal (21359–d, –k). The next four arrows (26535–x–6, x–11, x–9, x–4) are part of a group of 14 (with 21358–b), probably made by Sherman Curley in 1932. The consistent workmanship of these white stone and brown bottle glass points (and two more white stone points not illustrated), coupled with the knowledge that the Western Apache preferred white flint when making their own points (Basso 1971: 231; Gifford 1940: 120) and that they are known to have made glass points (Bourke 1891: 18), indicate that the points probably were made by Curley. As such they are good examples of what points *made* by Western Apache look like stylistically, a matter that has been largely open to question because points of various ages and cultural affinities commonly were scavenged from prehistoric sites for use as charms and, presumably, sometimes to tip arrows. The arrow seventh from left (21359–b) is tipped with what appears to be a prehistoric point. The next arrow (21370) has four small wooden crosspieces tied about midway up the foreshaft with sinew, a type

Subsistence

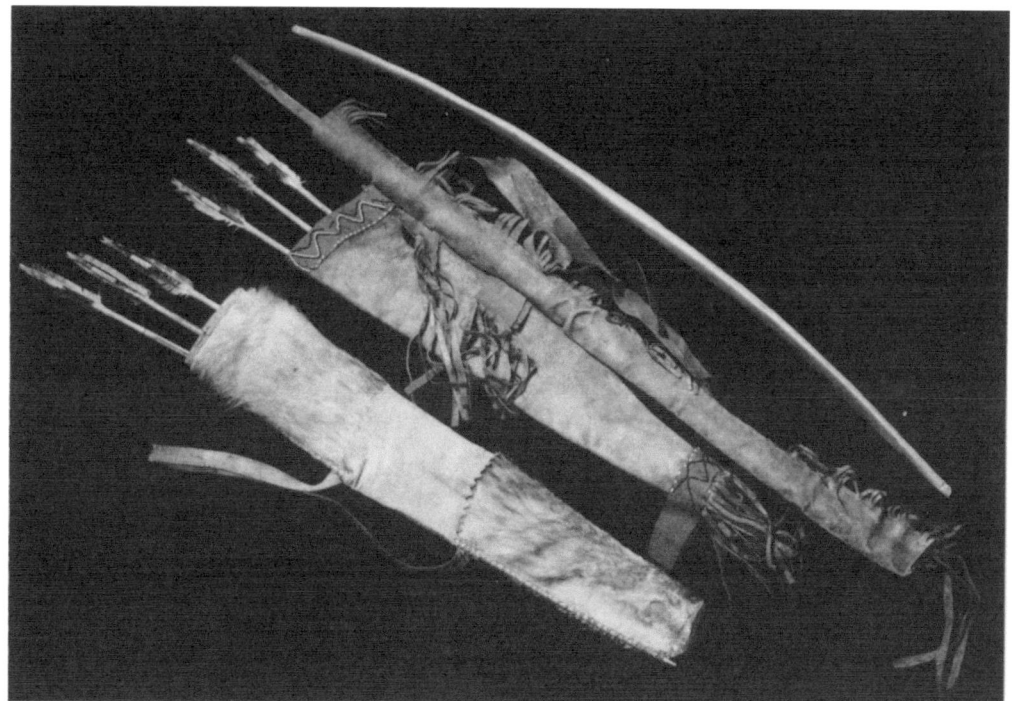

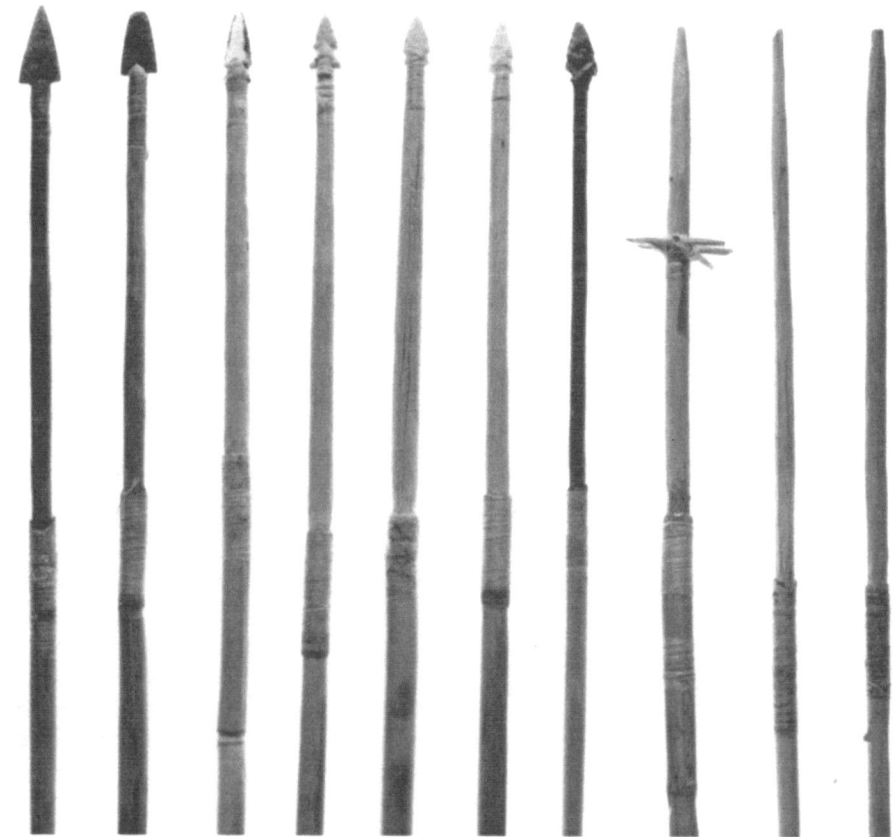

Top: Figure 5.2. Quivers, bows, and arrows (ASM Neg. 56710).

Bottom: Figure 5.3. Types of arrow points (ASM Neg. 64303).

used to hunt small birds and occasionally small mammals. The crosspieces were designed to hit the small target, even if the shaft missed (Basso 1971: 231). Second from the right is an arrow (21437–b) with a plain foreshaft. All of these are composite arrows, with a wood foreshaft inserted into the end of a cane (usually *Phragmites*) shaft. The all-wood arrow (*right*, 21437–c), however, was carved to look like a composite arrow and wrapped with sinew just as were the others illustrated. Making all-wooden arrows reputedly was learned from the Navajo (Basso 1971: 230); such arrows appear to have been considered inferior (by older Navajo as well; see Kluckhohn, Hill, and Kluckhohn 1971: 35), and it is probably not a coincidence that the one shown here was identified as a boy's arrow. The points are bound into notches in the foreshafts with sinew, and the binding of 21359–b is also secured with pitch. The foreshaft of the plain arrow and that of the bird arrow are set into their cane shafts with pitch. The foreshafts of 21359–b and –d are painted black, and that of –k is red. For more information on arrows and fletching, see Basso (1971: 227–231) and Figure 3.6.

Archery paraphernalia. Figure 5.4. Wrist guards were rags simply wrapped around the wrist or were fancy, made of leather, and notched around the edges (*upper left*, 21438; Goodwin A–67). This guard was made by Jewett Wright in 1935, has a buckskin tie, and was cut from the heel of a man's commercial work shoe; its orange stitching identifies it as not of military issue. At top right is a rock (21395) with the kind of lichen used to make one of several types of arrow poison for war or deer hunting (Goodwin A–67). The lichen probably did not make any chemical or catalytic contributions to the poison, but because they grow on rocks lichens are "heavy," and "whatever is shot with it will get heavy like it" (Goodwin A–67), causing the man or deer to slow down or drop. The arrowshaft smoother and straightener (*bottom*, 21443; 11.2 cm long) is a rounded rectanguloid of basalt originally found in a cave near Rice (the arrow on top is 21359–f). Apparently the Western Apache made no distinction between straighteners and smoothers (Basso 1971: 229) as have other groups (Cosner 1951); such tools were both made by the Apache and scavenged off prehistoric sites, and traded to the Zuni (Goodwin 1942: 81, 82; see also Fig. 7.16 herein and Opler 1983, Fig. 3).

Turkey tail decoy. Figure 5.5. This decoy consists of the whole tail of a turkey with the three feathers in front stuck in backwards (21442; about 46 cm high). The worn condition of the feathers is indicative of summer plumage; Jewett Wright probably took the bird just before he made the decoy, in July of 1935. The base is buckskin with buckskin stitching and headstrap. This decoy could be either worn as a hat by the hunter or used in the manner described by John Rope (Goodwin A–70): "The tail was cut all off at the base with the flesh. The flesh was cleaned out and the bases of the feathers were tied together all with buckskin. . . . One buckskin loop was put about the thumb, the other about the little finger . . . so that when . . . the hunter . . . spread his fingers it opened and spread. . . . A man would practice opening and shutting the tail with his hand till he was good enough and then he would go out hunting. But he made no noise like turkey at all; he just used the tail."

Deadfall trap sticks. Figure 5.6. Goodwin himself apparently made this set of deadfall sticks (21367) as instructed by Harvey Nashkine. The trap stick (45 cm long), upright, and trigger stick are made of arrow weed with the bark left on, the ends cut with a metal knife, and the trap stick notched at one end to seat the string. Although Goodwin did not record how the sticks were set up, the drawing shows a likely arrangement common to many groups, both north and south of the Western Apache (Kluckhohn, Hill, and Kluckhohn 1971, Fig. 8.8; Fontana 1979, Fig. 26). Among the Western Apache this type of deadfall was used for catching packrats and other small rodents.

Bird cage. Figure 5.7. This interesting yucca basket (21317), unfortunately, was not listed in Goodwin's personal catalogue, but presumably it was made sometime in the 1930s by one of his informants, perhaps Anna Price. It is about 35 cm tall with a door about 9 cm square (middle left of basket). The ASM card simply says "bird

Subsistence

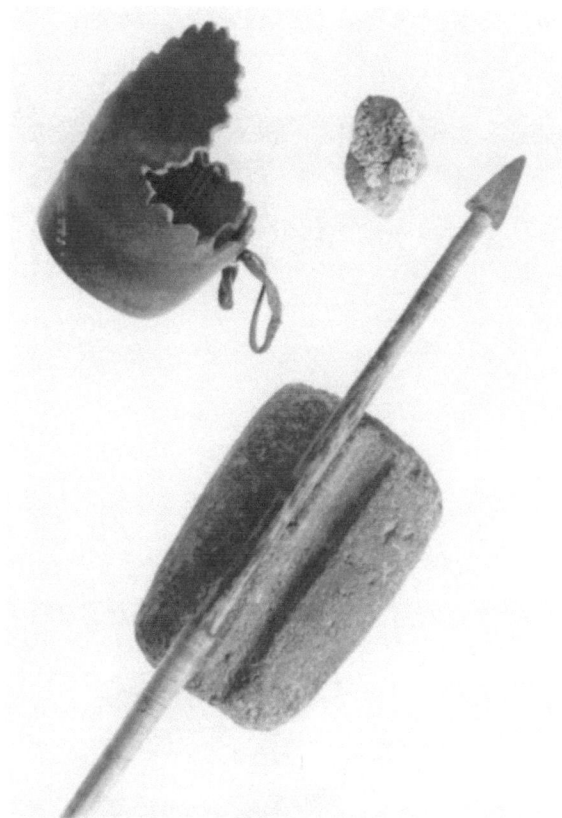

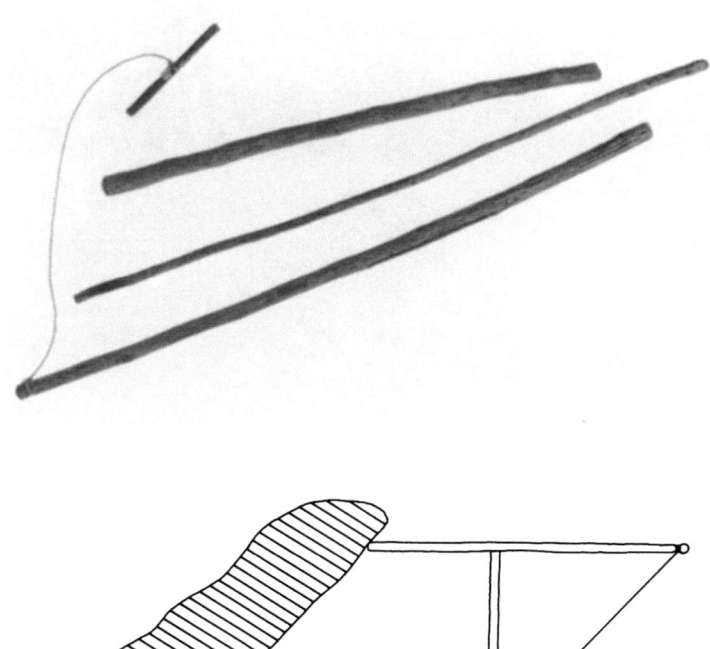

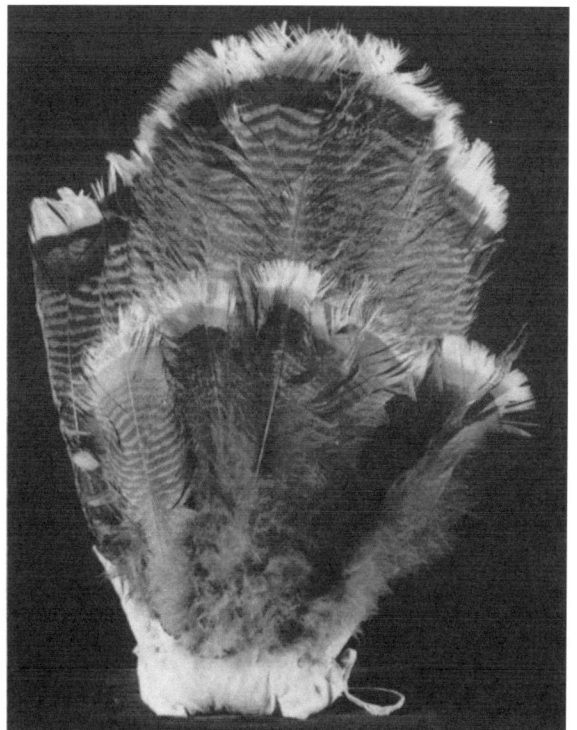

TOP LEFT: Figure 5.4. Archery paraphernalia (ASM Neg. 56708).

LEFT: Figure 5.5. Turkey tail decoy (ASM Neg. 32079).

TOP RIGHT: Figure 5.6. Deadfall trap sticks (ASM Neg. 32100).

LEFT: Figure 5.7. Bird cage (ASM Neg. 56663).

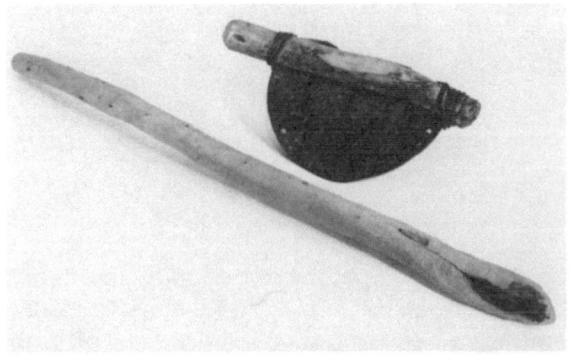

RIGHT: Figure 5.8. Digging stick and mescal knife (ASM Neg. 32094).

BOTTOM: Figure 5.9. Mescal roasting camp at Bylas (ASM Neg. 18219).

OPPOSITE: Figure 5.10. Mescal drying rack (ASM Neg. 18208).

Subsistence

cage—used for captive wild birds, [such] as quail, mockingbirds, etc." John Rope stated (Goodwin A–70): "In the old days we never used to keep wild birds for pets, like people keep quail. . . . We were on the move too much to pack them about. But nowadays we have no enemies and can stay in one place, so we have them." His observation suggests that cages for pet birds were a reservation period innovation. Anna Price (Goodwin A–70), however, noted keeping a variety of animals, including "quail, doves, bandtailed pigeon, mockingbird, antelope [presumably she is referring here to an antelope squirrel, *Citellus harrisi* or *C. leucurus,* and not a pronghorn], chipmunks, king birds, rock squirrels, etc., in woven basketry cages" and Goodwin's notes (A–70) indicate that at least the birds were kept in fact as pets and not, for example, as food. That pet bird cages were a pre-Reservation trait, contrary to John Rope's statement, is strongly suggested by the fact that virtually all the things Anna Price discussed with Goodwin, or made for him, were as they had been in the old days. (See also Fig. 5.49.)

Digging stick and mescal knife. Figure 5.8. The digging stick (*bottom,* 21373; 80 cm long), constructed of catclaw with the broad digging end bevelled, was made by Anna Price. This type of tool was used in farming or, with a rock, was pounded in around the base of a mescal plant to uproot it. The knife (*top,* 22273; 36 cm across), used for trimming the leaves off the mescal head, has an iron blade (an old shovel blade?) set between the halves of a split mesquite handle held in place with a wire wrapping at each end. It was made in 1933 by Mrs. Francis Drake, and purchased from her in 1936.

Mescal roasting camp at Bylas. Figure 5.9. Mrs. Jewett Wright, two of her sons, Neil Buck, and others under a mesquite tree and ocotillo shade at left rear on June 1 of 1931 or 1936. A brush drying rack with a forming tray frame on it is at right rear and, in front, is the pit in which the mescal was roasted. The cottonwood leaves that were used to cover the cooking mescal are scattered about the heaps of earth and burned stones surrounding the pit.

Mescal drying rack. Figure 5.10. Mrs. Wright took the finished sheet of cooked mescal that she was making in Figure 5.1 and turned the forming tray over onto the brush drying rack, leaving the sheet of mescal to dry *(left)* and the forming tray *(right)* free to be used again. The drying rack is built tilted slightly toward the south so as to take full advantage of the sun.

Mescal forming tray. Figure 5.11. On this tray (21385; 40 cm wide, 75 cm long) cooked, mashed mescal was patted out into a rectangular sheet, 3 to 5 cm thick; it was then flipped off the tray onto the drying rack. The frame is of split sotol stalks tied together with yucca *(left)*, with bear grass lashed to the top *(right)* with more yucca strips. This tray was made for Goodwin by Mrs. Jewett Wright, although she actually used larger ones, about 75 cm wide and 120 cm long, during the gathering trip that Goodwin photographed (Figs. 5.1, 5.9, 5.10; Goodwin A–68).

Mescal head, ready to roast. Figure 5.12. Although now somewhat desiccated, this mescal head (21421; 20 cm in diameter) is trimmed of its leaves, prepared for the roasting pit. It was cut by Anna Price in September of 1931 and given to Goodwin. The two leaves left partially intact and tied in a knot may have served as a strap to carry the head from where it was dug up to the pit. Two of Goodwin's informants also noted tied leaves as one of several ways for a woman to distinguish her mescal heads from those of others roasted in the same pit at the same time (Goodwin A–68).

Cactus fruit pickers. Figure 5.13. At top is the end of a long pole (21895) used to hook or knock off ripe fruit from the tops of saguaros. The single sotol stalk is 11 feet (3.44 m) long with a mesquite(?) hook lashed on with yucca strips. At right is a pair of tongs (21362; 27 cm long) used to pick prickly pear fruit, constructed by doubling over a half-round mesquite(?) stick made to hold its form by heating or steaming the wood. At bottom is a round plaque (bottom side up to show construction, 43 cm long) and brush (both 21383) used to gather prickly pear fruit and brush off the spines. The tray has a mesquite stick, peeled and shaved flat, for a hoop frame that is strung with yucca, with a bed of vine-mesquite grass tied down with more yucca. The brush has vine-mesquite grass on the outside, a core of burro brush, and a handle of tied yucca. All four items were made by Mrs. Jewett Wright. The cactus fruits are not ethnographic.

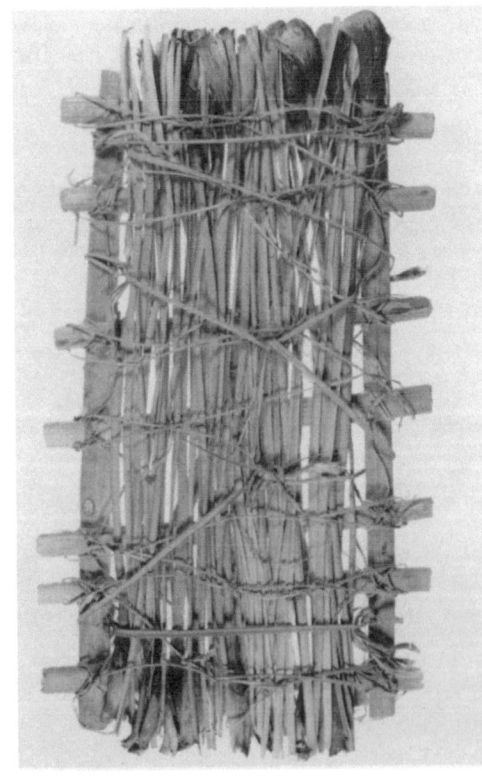

Figure 5.11. Mescal forming tray (*left*, ASM Neg. 32058; *right*, 32057).

Subsistence

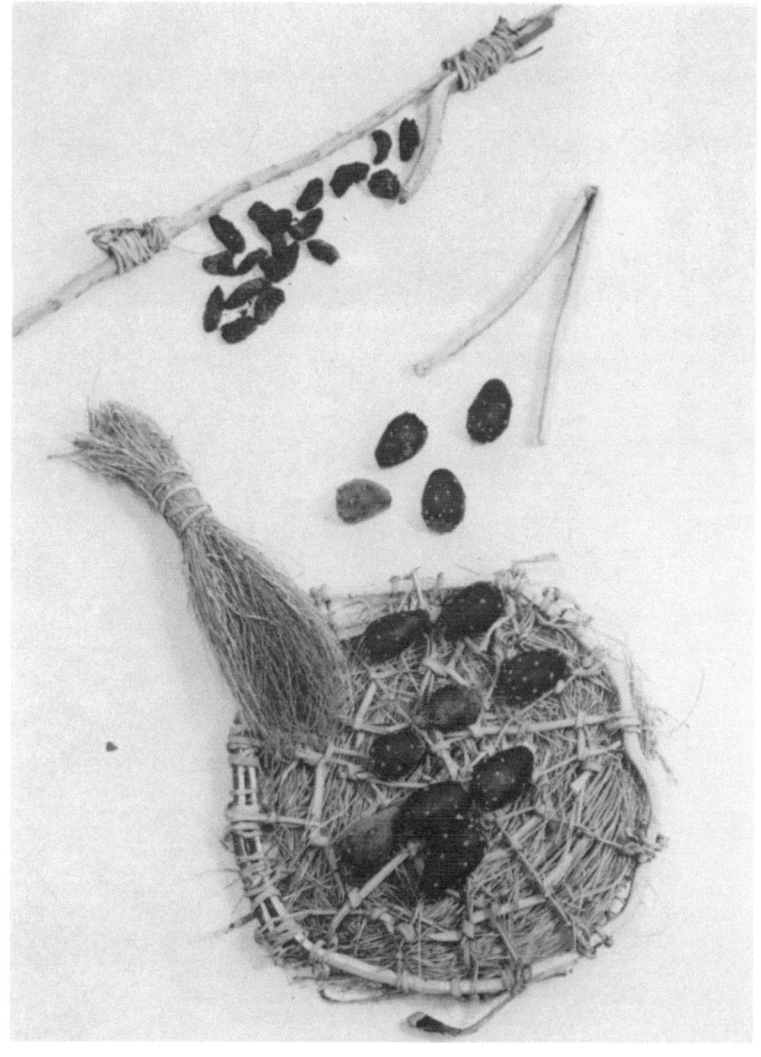

Top: Figure 5.12. Mescal head, ready to roast (ASM Neg. 56720).

Right: Figure 5.13. Cactus fruit pickers (ASM Neg. 56667).

LEFT: Figure 5.14. Seed beaters and baskets (ASM Neg. 56668).

BOTTOM: Figure 5.15. Salt-drying tray and salt cake (*a*, ASM Neg. 32090; *b*, 32116).

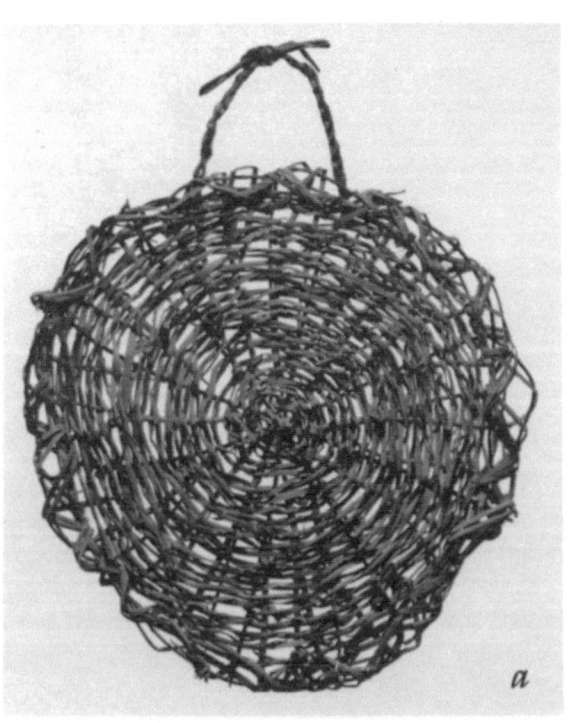
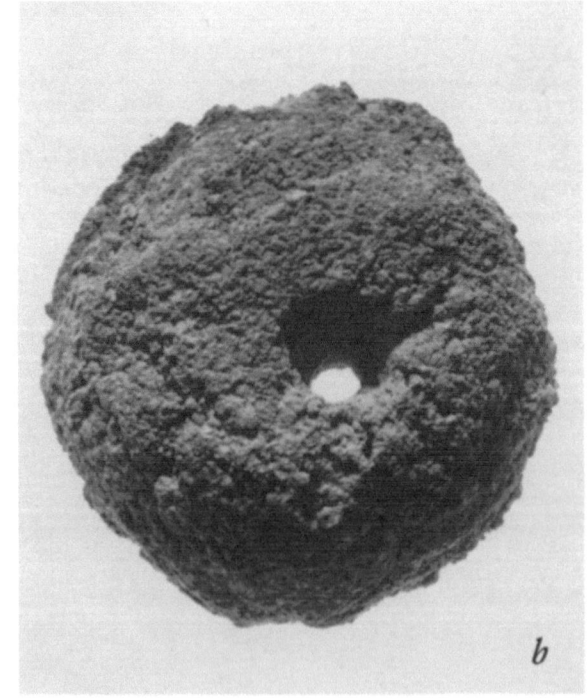

Subsistence

Seed beaters and baskets. Figure 5.14. Plaited seed beaters were used to sweep small seeds into bowl baskets or possibly burden baskets (Fig. 5.35; Goodwin A–68). The beater at right (21377; 43 cm long) was made by Anna Price of split tamarix twigs with yucca strips securing the ends and forming a handle. The beater at left (21318) is made of cottonwood shoots, also with a yucca-wrapped handle. The stick (21444; 64 cm long) is a section of sotol stalk. It was laid across the mouth of a burden basket, a bundle of sunflower heads was laid atop it, and the seeds were beaten loose with a second stick just like it. It was purchased from Mrs. Jewett Wright in 1936. The sunflower seeds in the bottom basket (EEG 68) are not ethnographic. The Emory oak acorns (21427) in the top basket (EEG 84) were given to Goodwin at Bylas. The tansy-mustard seeds (21399) in the basket at right (EEG 69) were collected by George Wright's children, possibly using seed beaters, in April of 1932, probably near Bylas. These kinds of seeds were ground, boiled, and eaten as a mush. The three baskets were obtained by the Guenthers at East Fork between 1911 and 1919. Goodwin (1939: 123, fn. 2) also noted that in pre-Reservation days, seed gathering often was made a social event by groups of courting boys and girls.

Salt-drying tray and salt cake. Figure 5.15. To obtain salt the Western Apache traveled to Zuni Salt Lake in New Mexico, about 45 miles south of Zuni Pueblo. Circular trays about four or five feet in diameter with a four inch high rim were taken on which to spread the salt. A model (*a*, 21316; 43 cm in diameter) of such a drying tray was made for Goodwin by Mrs. Jewett Wright. It is plain twined, up to the right with yucca and unpeeled willow warps, and yucca wefts. Neither the warps or wefts are split. Both the fag and moving ends are joined by knotting on both faces. At the edge, the warps are turned to the left and finished with a loose rim-wrapping of yucca. This model lacks a raised rim. A braided yucca loop handle is attached to the top. Although the ritual observances for salt gathering by the Western Apache (as recorded by Goodwin A–68) are simpler than those of the Navajo (Hill 1940), their shared traits are another clear reflection of the relative closeness of ceremonial practices between these two Southern Athapaskan groups (see also Goodwin 1945).

In their own territory the Western Apache gathered the much less pure salts that precipitated out along the banks of some streams and rivers. It was dried, ground, and then moistened and formed into a cake. A hole was made through the middle with a stick and the cake was hung on yucca string to dry between two fires. The cake of salt (*b*, 21420) made by Anna Price at Bylas in 1932 is 15.7 cm in diameter and weighs 1252 g. Formed in the traditional manner described, it appears to be almost as much dirt as salt, an unavoidable result of the way in which it had to be collected.

Grinding tools and corn. Figure 5.16. Western Apaches made their own metates and manos but also scavenged them off prehistoric sites. In years past discarded ground stone artifacts from archaeological field schools on the reservations have also been a rich source of these items. Flat (slab) metates seemed to be preferred. Goodwin's informants were also familiar with trough metates and metates with either two small legs or a ridge on the bottom at one end, designed to keep the metates steady and correctly angled during grinding (Goodwin A–71). The center metate (EEG 235a; 39 cm long) was collected around 1980 from a prehistoric site near Forestdale. When found, it was slightly trough or basin shaped; however, Emma Cosay of Whiteriver wanted a flat surface and she pecked down the offending edges. She planned to use it to grind corn and juniper berries and as a weight to keep green cradleboard frames flat while they dried. Mrs. Andrew Stanley told Goodwin (A–71): "We had two kinds of manos, one was sort of round so that you could roll it over in grinding, and [the] other was sort of flat so that you just keep the one side of it to the metate. You did the same with the other also, but you rolled it just a little. Both were called by the same name." The manos illustrated include flat, two-handed manos (21899 *on metate*, EEG 236b at *front center*), a flat handstone (E–6815–x–4, *front left*), and a rounded type (EEG 235b *in the mortar*).

Mortars and pestles were also made or

Figure 5.16. Grinding tools and corn (ASM Neg. 56712).

Subsistence

Figure 5.17. Gathering corn (photo by Paul Mayerhoff).

scavenged, or sometimes prehistoric bedrock mortar holes were used. The mortar shown here (EEG 236a, *upper left*) was found by Yale, Emma's husband, just east of Whiskey Flat near Whiteriver. Mortars were used to grind mesquite beans and walnuts, and Emma planned to pound up acorns with this one. She also thought the bottom was fairly flat and might be worth pecking down into a metate. When this mortar and metate were purchased, she asked more for the mortar as such tools were harder to find. All of the ground stone shown is basalt except for the handstone, which is quartzite.

The corn at bottom (21416) is 14–rowed Pueblo Flour collected from Laban James' farm on North Fork, and that at top (21422) is 12–rowed (the red and variegated ears) and 14–rowed (yellow and two white ears) Pueblo Flour corn given to Goodwin by Anna Price at Bylas. The top ears have their husks pulled up and tied with yucca strips for hanging over a pole or for easy packing on a horse (Fig. 5.17).

Gathering corn. Figure 5.17. Corn was packed out of the fields on horseback, both in bags and tied in bundles as shown in Figure 5.16. This photo probably was taken near East Fork between 1896 and 1903.

Making fry-bread. Figure 5.18. Bart Tonay *(right)* making fry-bread at Sadie Stone's puberty ceremony at East Fork in 1912. Two fry-bread holders with bread on them are at rear and at right, and balls of dough are in the girl's hands and in the white enamel bowl at lower right.

Fry-bread holder. Figure 5.19. This fry-bread holder (EEG 118; 73 cm long, 36 cm in diameter) belonged to Shima and was obtained by the Guenthers between 1911 and 1945. Although such holders were usually made of heavy wire, this specimen is more substantial than most with a carefully shaped frame of quarter-inch reinforcing rod. The head is strung with wire.

Corn beer strainer. Figure 5.20. This strainer (79–95–1; 15.2 cm high, 42.4 cm long) was fabricated from a one-pound Hills Brothers coffee can lashed to a forked stick handle with a single piece of wire. The stick was peeled and shaved flat on the inside of both arms to facilitate their bending and to seat them more snugly against the can. The holes probably were punched with a commercial wire nail, and they

Subsistence

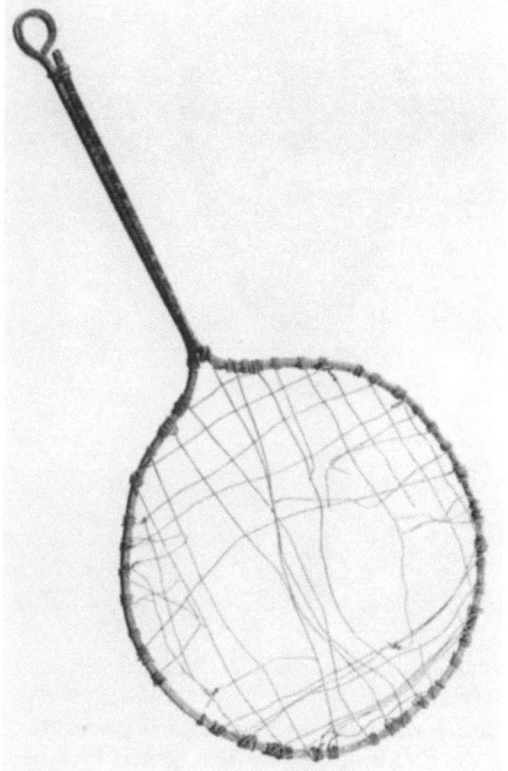

OPPOSITE: Figure 5.18. Making fry-bread (photo by E. E. Guenther).

LEFT: Figure 5.19. Fry-bread holder (ASM Neg. 56715).

TOP: Figure 5.20. Corn beer strainer (ASM Neg. 56714).

cover the whole surface and bottom of the can. Some strainers of this type have their holes punched in a decorative pattern. This specimen was obtained at Carrizo in the early 1960s by Arthur Guenther, and strainers like this have been in use for as long as cans or lard pails have been available to the Western Apache. Corn beer formerly played an important role in Western Apache subsistence and history. According to an informant (Goodwin A–68) it was "first introduced to the White Mountain Apaches by the Chiricahuas, who in turn got it from the Mexicans." The "Mexicans" may have been Spanish or more probably Indian groups such as the Opata (Hinton 1983: 325) or the Tarahumara. Corn beer is a long established and integral part of Tarahumara culture and social organization (Kennedy 1963; Pennington 1963: 149–153). A sequence of photos showing the preparation of corn beer among the Tarahumara, which is much the same as that practiced by the Western Apache, is in Figure 2 of Merrill 1983.

The terms *tiswin* and *tulpai* often are used, interchangeably and confusingly, for the alcoholic beverages made from maguey and from fermented ground sprouted corn. The consumption of corn beer commonly was cited as the cause of everything from Geronimo's fleeing the reservation in 1884 (Thrapp 1967: 312) to fighting, discontentment, immorality, indolence, ill health, and a general lowered resistance to disease (Reagan 1930: 298; Hrdlička 1908: 31). The nutritious qualities of corn beer rarely were mentioned, even though recognized to some extent by Apaches and Anglos alike (Opler 1941: 368–370; Kessel 1976: 144; Hrdlička 1908: 26). An attempt by the U.S. Army and the Bureau of Indian Affairs to stamp out the use of corn beer may be cited as a continuing point of conflict and major source of stress in Apache and Anglo relations, from the founding of the reservations on into the twentieth century (Bullis 1888: 7; Johnson 1892: 220; Clum 1875: 216; Pierce 1886: 40).

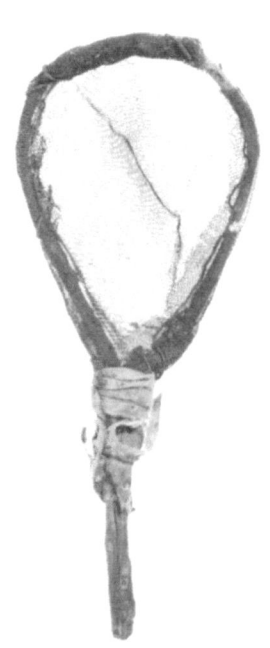

Top: Figure 5.21. Food strainers (*left*, ASM Neg. 32092; *right*, 56713).

Bottom: Figure 5.22. Food preparation tray (ASM Neg. 32056).

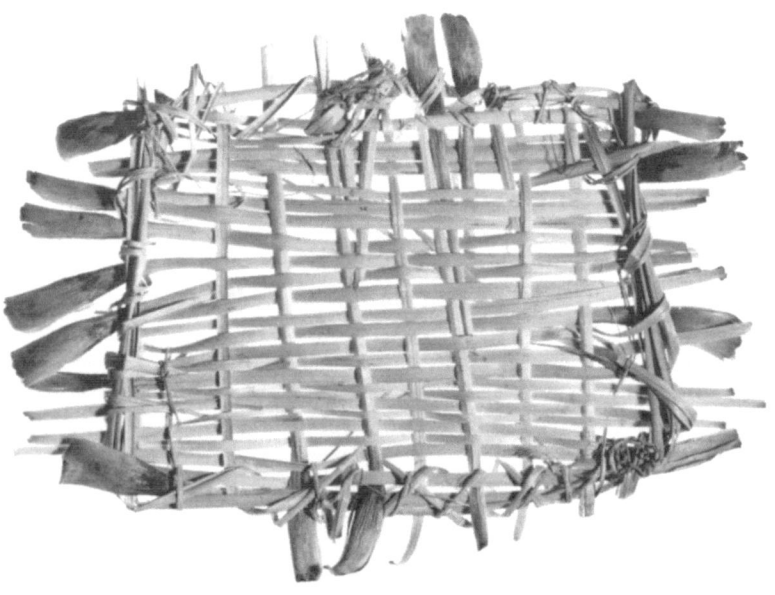

Food strainers. Figure 5.21. The strainer on the left (21382) was made in the old style, probably specifically for Goodwin, by Mrs. Jewett Wright in 1932. It is plaited of bear grass, is 37 cm long and 20 cm wide, with the handle thickened and secured by wrapping with more bear grass. The strainer at right (21867; 33 cm long, 14 cm wide) was collected by Goodwin from a camp at Kinishba in 1936. It is a more modern version of the bear grass strainer, made of a single thickness of window screen lashed to a forked stick frame with a single piece of wire. The stick was peeled and the arms were bent into a loop and tied with yucca. The screen, wire, and a wrapping of strips of commercial cloth were all cemented to the crotch of the stick with pine pitch. Goodwin indicates that these were "used in cooking," but he does not identify them any more specifically; conceivably these, too, could be corn beer strainers (Fig. 5.20).

Food preparation tray. Figure 5.22. Goodwin identified this plaited bear grass item (21384) as a tray "used to spread puddings [including a corn 'pudding'] and other soft foods on during preparation." It was made by Mrs. Jewett Wright in 1932 and is 62 cm long and 46 cm wide; some of the edges are strengthened with yucca ties.

Subsistence

Figure 5.23. Chipped stone tools (ASM Neg. 64307).

Chipped stone tools. Figure 5.23. At left is a flake (21324; 7.9 cm long) identified by Goodwin as a type of knife used by the Apache. In the early days when metal was scarce, mescal knives were made from a type of rock that split into tabular pieces, sometimes with the thin edge sharpened by flaking (GP 49410–x–1, second from left) and sometimes with a handle shaped by grinding (Goodwin A–71). At right are two hard-hammer-flaked choppers (21325, 21897) of the type used in pre-Reservation times for chopping meat, gristle, and bone. All of these stone tools could have been prehistoric items, prehistoric but reused by Apaches, or made by Western Apaches. Although their actual association with Apache sites is tenuous, they do serve as examples of the type of chipped stone tools the Western Apache made or scavenged.

Stew spoon. Figure 5.24. This old style spoon (21380; 10 cm long) for eating stew consists of the bases of two yucca leaves; yucca strips bind them together and form a handle. It was made by Anna Price in 1932. This spoon originally may have had a third leaf, and similar spoons were made of a single leaf base (21379, not illustrated), bear grass leaf bases, or turkey breastbones (Goodwin A–71). In pre-Reservation times, supposedly only men used such eating utensils and women used their hands (Goodwin A–68).

Sherd ladle. Figure 5.25. This ladle (21397; 25 cm long, 18 cm wide) was picked up by Goodwin at an old Apache camp at Dewey Flat. It was made from a prehistoric plain, polished brown ware jar sherd, and undoubtedly it was fashioned by Apaches as indicated by grooves from a metal file on all the worked edges.

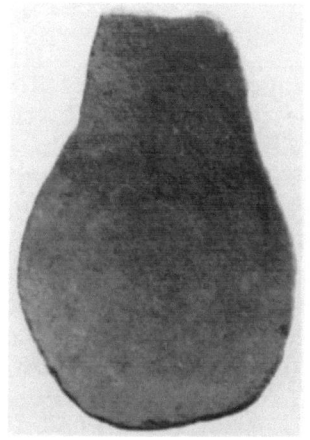

TOP: Figure 5.24. Stew spoon (ASM Neg. 32095).

RIGHT: Figure 5.25. Sherd ladle (ASM Neg. 56675).

LEFT: Figure 5.26. Pottery (ASM Neg. 56674).

BOTTOM: Figure 5.27. Stirring sticks (ASM Neg. 32107).

Pottery. Figure 5.26. Because of their seminomadic life style, the Western Apache never achieved the high level of sophistication in pottery making that they did in basketry; where ceramic utensils were used by puebloan groups, forms of basketry were substituted by the Western Apache. Some plain ware jars were made, occasionally decorated with incised lines, fingernail indentations, or tooled rims. Jars were used primarily for boiling meat, corn, or corn beer, but also were used to store shelled corn food caches, seed corn, and tobacco, to melt pitch for coating basketry water bottles, and as drums (Goodwin A–66, A–68, A–70, A–71). Pottery making began to decline in the 1880s and virtually had disappeared by the turn of the century. The large globular jar (*back,* EEG 129; 35 cm high) is from the Carrizo area and was found by Frieda Knoop, probably between 1919 and 1923. The pointed-bottom jar (*right,* 21430; 27 cm high) was found near Tonto National Monument and purchased by Goodwin from

Subsistence

Mrs. Frances J. McCormack of Globe (additional San Carlos Apache materials from the McCormack Collection now belong to the National Park Service, Western Archeological Center, Tucson). In June of 1932 Anna Price made two pots (presumably jars) for Goodwin and started the base of another (*center right,* 21419) by molding the clay over her knee. The pots were built by coiling and thinned with a gourd scraper (*front left,* 21376). None were fired, and unfortunately the two completed pots were not housed at the Museum and their present whereabouts are unknown. The polishing stone (*front right,* 21877) was found on what Goodwin thought was an old Apache camp near Kinishba. Stone polishing is rare on Western Apache pottery, however, and even when present is minimal. (The raw clay shown is not Western Apache.)

Stirring sticks. Figure 5.27. Although Goodwin's informants provided scant information on stirring sticks (Goodwin A–68), this implement is briefly described in Western Apache myth (Goodwin 1939: 56), and Mrs. Jewett Wright probably made this example (21363) specifically for Goodwin. All three sticks (each about 35 cm long) are made from the scrubby variety of tamarix and are tied together at one end with sinew. A metal knife appears to have been used to cut the sticks, shave off the bark, and notch the ends for the sinew tie. Stirring sticks were used to stir liquids being cooked in a pot. The Navajo made this same type of stirrer, with a variable number of sticks (Kluckhohn, Hill, and Kluckhohn 1971: 124–126).

Firedrills and torch. Figure 5.28. The firedrill and hearth shown in use (19584) are both made of bear grass stalk (64 cm and 46 cm long, respectively); the hearth has four holes, two used. The second set (21366) has a bear grass stalk drill (51 cm long) and a sotol stalk hearth (20 cm long) with two used holes and notches for three more. Tinder was usually dry cottonwood bark. Firedrill sets were carried in quivers. When a hearth had six used holes, it was considered old and no good for making fires. It was then stuck into the interior wall of the wickiup and told: "I have kept you a long time for fire, so you sit in here now" (Goodwin A–71).

The torch (21425; 65 cm long) is composed of strips of juniper bark bound with yucca. Such

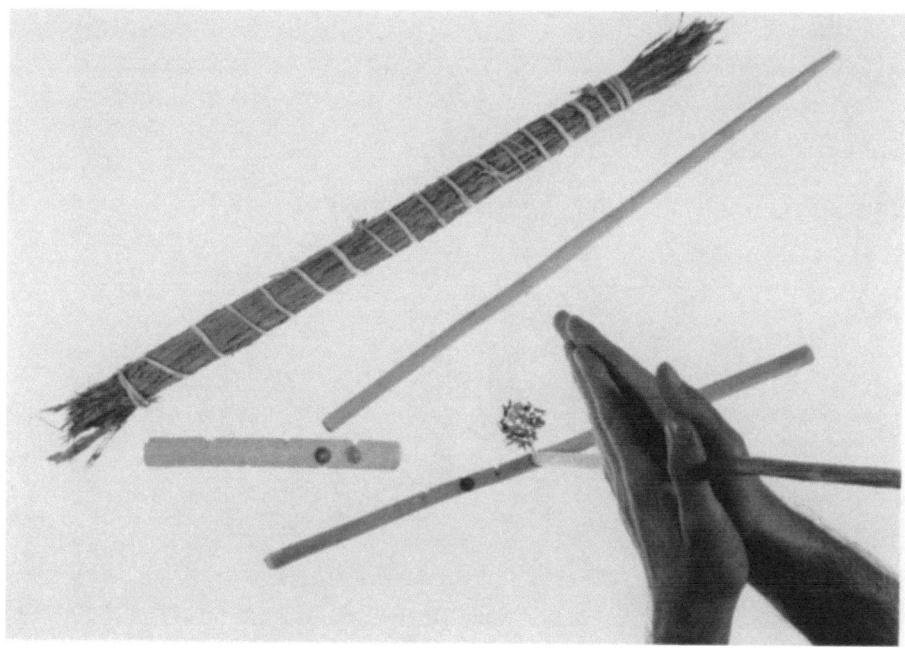

Figure 5.28. Firedrills and torch (ASM Neg. 56717).

torches were used to carry fire from camp to camp (Goodwin A–71), and in the fall and winter boys and girls hunted quail at night by torch light (Goodwin A–68).

Carrying water in a *tus*. Figure 5.29. Two Apache girls carrying water in a *tus*, probably near East Fork between 1896 and 1903. Leaves were stuffed in the mouth of the *tus* as a plug, and note the metal pan and the manner in which the tump rope is positioned. According to Anna Price (Goodwin A–71), women always positioned tump lines in this manner (see also Figs. 5.36 and 5.37), and men always positioned them across the shoulders. Of interest also are the calico dresses, moccasins with "noses" (Fig. 6.10), and necklaces and bracelets of beads and mirrors.

LEFT: Figure 5.29. Carrying water in a *tus* (photo by Paul Mayerhoff).

OPPOSITE: Figure 5.30. Containers (ASM Neg. 56673).

Subsistence

Containers. Figure 5.30. At far left is a shallow saguaro callus or "boot" (21389) that Anna Price was using as a cup in 1932. Cups were also made from oak boles and cow horns (Goodwin A–66). Saguaro boots, if of a suitable size and shape, were used also as water bottles and to pack saguaro fruit or juice back to camp (Goodwin A–66, A–68). Archaeological data suggest they may have been used also for storage (Gifford 1980: 132–133, Fig. 66a). At top center is a water bottle (21435; 34 cm high) made from the base of an agave stalk by Mrs. John Roberson in 1935. It was constructed by hollowing out the stalk and patching the bottom with a piece of canvas and pine pitch. Gourds also were made into water bottles and ladles (Goodwin A–68). At top right is a container made from a large cushaw squash (21863) with a burlap and flour sack cover and carrying strap; its specific use was not recorded. The sack was from the "Arizona Flour Mills/Phoenix, Mesa, Tucson, Safford, Ariz." A pottery jar with a notched rim (*bottom right*, 21861; 31 cm high) was found about fifteen miles north of Rice; it could have been used in a variety of ways (see Fig. 5.26). At bottom center is a *tus* with three wooden handles (EEG 197; 20 cm high) made by Mary Keyes of East Fork between 1911 and 1922; these pitched basketry jars usually were used to carry water or store food (Goodwin A–68). The commercial white enamel metal cup (*bottom left*, EEG 233) from Canyon Day is of a type that was readily available to the Apache in the early reservation days.

Subsistence

OPPOSITE: Figure 5.31. Pitched basket *(tus)* manufacture (ASM Neg. 56672).

RIGHT: Figure 5.32. *Tus* handle attachment (ASM Neg. 56669).

Pitched basket (*tus*) manufacture. Figure 5.31. A *tus* was twined, usually of squawberry or sumac. The bundle of unpeeled sumac twigs (E–52; about 60 cm long) was collected by Goodwin as a sample of basketry material. The coils of prepared fine (21865) and coarse (21866) basketry splints (tentatively identified as arrow weed) were collected by Goodwin at a camp near Kinishba in 1936; both are tied with yucca. Of the three finished but not yet pitched baskets, one has no handles *(front left,* EEG 209), one has two twig handles (EEG 208), and one has two splint handles and a woven-in black design of devil's claw (EEG 226). The first two were obtained at East Fork between 1911 and 1922. The third is of unknown age but, with its coarser weave and elaborate decoration, looks more recent and may have been spawned by the craft market. With a woven-in design it resembles coiled jar baskets but, being twined, takes less time to weave. *Tus* baskets were caulked with a paste of ground juniper leaves and then sealed with pine pitch melted in a pot and applied with a brush; pitch on the interior was evened out by rolling hot stones around inside the basket (Goodwin A–66). The brush (21378; 21 cm long) was made from a single split yucca leaf, the ends frayed, and the halves tied back together; it has traces of pitch on it. On some baskets black clan symbols were painted around the shoulder prior to pitching (see Tanner 1982, Fig. 2.8), and if a reddish *tus* was desired, powdered hematite was mixed with the juniper paste; the finished *tus* here (EEG 204; 40 cm high) exhibits both these features.

***Tus* handle attachment.** Figure 5.32. This *tus* (E–9257) was made by the daughter-in-law of Laban James and purchased from her by Goodwin in 1931. The closeup shows how the angled twig handles were carefully notched to better seat the splints that hold them to the basket body and were shaved to a pleasing point; usually the handles were simply lashed on with no such extra effort. The notching may well be superfluous, but is an interesting stylistic variation. Handles also were made from horsehair, recycled commercial leather belts or harnesses, and twisted bark with copper wire (Roberts 1929: 152). Handles are usually two or sometimes three in number, but one or none are not unknown.

Top: Figure 5.33. Pitched basket *(tus)* shapes (ASM Neg. 56671).

Opposite: Figure 5.34. *Tus* designs used by Clan I.

Pitched basket (*tus*) shapes. Figure 5.33. The full range of *tus* forms known are illustrated here except for what may be an early pointed-bottom form (see Tanner 1982, Fig. 4.4). The enormous *tus* (*left rear*, EEG 201; 70 cm high) was made by Ruthena Dale Henry of Cibecue, probably in the late 1960s or early 1970s. Although its large size may have been designed to attract a buyer, in fact *tuses* of this size were described to Goodwin (A–66) as used to bury food caches. At right rear and front are two *tuses* (EEG 203 and 202) of normal size for water carrying or storage. Two apparently nontraditional forms are the cylindrical *tus* (*center*, EEG 117) and the bowl (*left front*, EEG 116). The bowl form came from Whiteriver in the early 1960s, and the cylinder was purchased in Whiteriver but made by Lassie Wright of Cibecue in the late 1960s or 1970s; the purpose of both these shapes is unknown, but may be simply experimentation in hopes of discovering a new, saleable form. The bilobed form (*left*, E–9) commonly was used as a water canteen; a carrying rope was tied around the middle (eliminating the need for handles) and the mouth plugged with grass or juniper bark. This one probably was made by Mrs. Jewett Wright in 1932, and it has an unusual decoration of spiral lines. Clan I shoulder designs are on EEG 201–203 (see Fig. 5.34). Worn out *tuses* often were stuck on a stick and used as torches when hunting quail at night (Goodwin A–68), the burning pitch creating quite a light (see also Fig. 5.28).

***Tus* designs used by clan I.** Figure 5.34. Goodwin (1942: 117) stated that "A privilege enjoyed only by clan I was the right to paint a decoration about the shoulder of their basketry water bottles.... If individuals of another clan dared to decorate their bottles likewise, people of clan I might destroy the vessels." Goodwin (1942: 119) also noted that at the time he was writing, the 1930s, such restrictions were not strictly observed. The first, second, and fourth of the designs (from Goodwin 1942, Fig. 1) may be seen on baskets in Figures 5.31 and 5.33, but the clan affiliations of their makers are unknown.

Burden baskets. Figure 5.35. Goodwin's informants distinguished two types of burden baskets:

> ... [one] has crossed sticks on the bottom, and ... [the second] has no crossed sticks on the bottom and ... is not ornamented with buckskin as is the first. The first kind we used to pack our belongings in, on our backs, when we moved camp.... The second kind we used more for gathering foods in. We used to gather mescal heads in this kind. The juice of roasted mescal we used to smear on the inside of the basket, so that when we gathered small seeds they wouldn't leak out (Goodwin A–66).

The baskets at lower left (EEG 220) and center (EEG 219) are reinforced with two U–shaped crossed sticks woven into them; both were collected at East Fork between 1911 and 1922. The basket at lower right (EEG 217) is of the food gathering type, collected at Carrizo between 1919 and 1923. All three of these baskets have woven-in black elements of devil's claw and red painted designs. An atypical small basket (*upper right*, EEG 222), without crossed sticks but with buckskin, has a completely painted yellow exterior with red and blue designs; it reputedly was made by and belonged to Shima. The modern basket (*upper left*, EEG 216; 33 cm high) was made by Mrs. Taylor of Whiteriver around 1975. The lack of crossed sticks and the presence of buckskin ornamentation may be explained for this basket as a logical result of commercialization: heavy reinforcements are unnecessary, and buckskin fringes (and metal tinklers on others) are attractive to prospective purchasers. This one is typical of most modern burden baskets, as is an increasing tendency toward conical shapes.

Figure 5.35. Burden baskets (ASM Neg. 56666).

Subsistence

Top: Figure 5.36. Packed to go to the fields (photo by Paul Mayerhoff).

Right: Figure 5.37. Woman gathering corn in burden basket (photo by Paul Mayerhoff).

Packed to go to the fields. Figure 5.36. Tom Friday's wife packed to go to the fields, probably near East Fork, between 1896 and 1903. She is using the type of burden basket with crossed sticks and buckskin ornamentation, with the tumpline worn across the forehead in appropriate female fashion (see Fig. 5.29). The little girl at right carries another child in a cradleboard. Of interest are the calico dresses, buckskin moccasins with "noses," and the dog.

Woman gathering corn in burden basket. Figure 5.37. The woman is throwing corn into her burden basket, probably at East Fork, between 1896 and 1903. The tumpline is worn across the forehead, and the basket is of the type described for gathering food (Fig. 5.35), that is, lacking heavy reinforcing crossed sticks and buckskin trim.

Figure 5.38. Coiled basketry (ASM Neg. 56670).

Subsistence

Coiled basketry. Figure 5.38. Early coiled basketry was made primarily of mulberry, valued for its strength and durability, but by the 1930s it was being supplanted by willow and cottonwood; devil's claw continued to be used consistently for the black portion of designs (Roberts 1929: 137). Bowl baskets predominate among coiled forms; it is possible that jar forms, oval trays, and almost certainly flat plaques were relatively late innovations, started perhaps in the second half of the 1880s in response to Anglo purchases and demands (Mason 1904: 284–285; Roberts 1929: 142, 167; Tanner 1982: 31). For further discussion of technology and decoration of Western Apache coiled baskets see Roberts (1929) and Tanner (1982).

This selection of baskets from the Guenther collection illustrates the variety of forms and decoration in coiled basketry. An unfinished basket collected by Goodwin from Mrs. Jewett Wright in 1932 is shown bottom side up (21400, partly covering the plaque) to indicate what the splints looked like before being trimmed. The oval tray (*left*, EEG 91) and smaller jar basket (*top*, EEG 93) came from either Carrizo or East Fork between 1919 and 1924. The larger jar basket (EEG 98) was purchased at Florence Junction in the 1930s. The small flat plaque (EEG 92) and the bowl basket at upper left (EEG 89) were obtained at East Fork between 1911 and 1919; the latter has red-dyed splints highlighting the black designs. The two small bowl baskets in front (EEG 71, 76) came from Whiteriver sometime after 1919. The bowl basket at left with lizard designs (EEG 66) came from Cibecue at an unknown date. The bowl basket in the center (EEG 30) was used to dispense pollen at Sadie Stone's puberty dance at East Fork in 1912 and was given to the Guenthers afterward by Sadie's grandfather, Y–1 (see Fig. 7.6). The bowl basket at right (EEG 73) was purchased by Rev. Guenther from the maker at Cedar Creek in 1922. The date "January 7, 1922" was taken unprompted from a calendar that Guenther had given the woman, but the inspiration for the five dollar symbol is unknown. Perhaps it was the price she hoped to get for the basket. Tanner (1982, Figs. 4.28–4.32) describes additional baskets from the Guenther collection that are not in the Arizona State Museum (as she so indicated then for Fig. 4.28). Most of those baskets probably date from the first thirty years of this century and come from the Fort Apache Indian Reservation, but Mrs. Guenther could not recall any specific dates or places for them. (Figs. 2.4, 5.14, 5.49, 7.3, 7.36, and 7.37 herein show additional examples of coiled basketry.)

Preparing hide. Figure 5.39. Woman scraping a hide near Bylas, sometime in the 1920s. Goodwin's informants differed on what type of wood should be used for the pole on which the hide was scraped; one claimed that a food-bearing tree had to be used such as pinyon, oak, or walnut, while another said it simply had to be

Figure 5.39. Preparing hide (ASM Neg. Pix 783–x–4).

smooth wood such as mesquite or cottonwood (Goodwin A–66). These poles were saved and reused. Hide scrapers were made by beveling the end of a deer metacarpal to a chisellike edge, sharpening the edge of cow or horse ribs and using them like a drawknife, or making a composite elbow scraper (Fig. 5.40) with an angled wood handle and a metal blade (Goodwin A–69). All were women's tools and were made and kept by their owners. In this photograph the woman is using an actual drawknife that is missing one handle. The enamel basin holds water to keep the hide wet. This photo may have been taken by Gracie S. Taylor, a Bureau of Indian Affairs nurse stationed at Bylas and later at San Carlos.

Rope twister and tanning tools. Figure 5.40. The rope twister at top (21364) was made by Jewett Wright in 1932. This type of twister was used to make horsehair rope; the handle is 36 cm long, and all shaping of both sticks apparently was done with a metal knife. Heavier versions of this same tool were used to make rawhide rope. At left is a hide scraper made by Mrs. Jewett Wright in 1936, and a gneiss whetstone with which to sharpen it (both 21319). This elbow scraper has a heavy mesquite handle shaped with an ax or knife and a thin sheet metal blade lashed to the underside with buckskin. Some of the buckskin is dyed yellow, and this wrapping extends well down onto the handle; total tool length is 28 cm. The piece of shaped vesicular lava (*bottom right*, 21426) was used to smooth a hide after it had been tanned. Hide grainers such as this were easily pecked to shape with a hammerstone and were often made in quantity by old people and used in trade at Zuni (Goodwin A–66; 1942: 82).

Temporary cradleboard. Figure 5.41. If no permanent cradleboard was ready the day after a baby's birth, a hastily constructed temporary one was made. The specimen shown here (E–10; 75 cm long) appears to have been constructed "like an old time one" by Mrs. Jewett Wright in 1932 (Goodwin A–1087), but may have been made by Anna Price (Goodwin 1942: 429). Temporary cradleboards formerly were made of native woods; this one uses unpeeled tamarix for the two arcs of the oval frame and for the four transverse ribs that support the 33 long tamarix twigs making up the bed of the cradleboard (*left*, back view). All the frame members are lashed together with cloth strips that largely cover the transverse ribs. At the foot of the cradle the twigs of the bed are bent up and out, with the ends brought up along the frame edges and the bent-over end projecting slightly beyond the end of the frame. The hood frame is a wickerwork band of bear grass (*right*, front view) with the sharp ends and lower edge covered with cloth. The top of the hood was not put on, but would have been buckskin. Buckskin side flaps are stitched to the frame with buckskin thongs, and a buckskin carrying strap is tied to the back of the frame. Opposing slits in the flaps are laced with a buckskin thong to secure the child. A pad of jungle-rice grass and shredded inner cottonwood bark placed on the bed completes this cradle.

Figure 5.40. Rope twister and tanning tools (ASM Neg. 56716).

Subsistence

Figure 5.41. Temporary cradleboard (*left*, ASM Neg. 64292; *right*, 64293).

Permanent cradleboards. Figure 5.42 and Color Illustration 2. Normally a newborn was placed in a temporary cradleboard (Fig. 5.41) unless an expectant mother had prepared a permanent one ahead of time or had saved the cradle of a previous child (if its infancy had been a healthy one). Usually a baby had only one permanent cradle, made about three months after birth, but occasionally a second, larger one was made. After outgrowing the cradle and beginning to crawl, a child was often transported in a carrying-jacket (Fig. 6.7).

The cradleboard at top (EEG 248) was made by Melvina Bourke of Whiteriver in 1981, a person well-known for her cradleboards. This exceptionally large one (97 cm long) is symmetric and carefully finished, with a hood of vertical yucca slats. At right is a smaller cradle (EEG 138; 68 cm long) made around 1970 by June Beatty of San Carlos. It has a hood of horizontal twigs and rick-rack trim. Although various explanations of the significance of using vertical versus horizontal slats in the cradle hood have been given (White Mountain versus San Carlos style, North Fork versus East Fork style, cradles for boys versus girls), there is little concensus; Goodwin (1942: 431–432) noted but did not discuss the differences. "In former times permanent carriers were made identical with those used now, except buckskin was used in place of cloth . . . frequently painted with a yellow ocher, as was the exposed wooden portions of the hood" (Goodwin 1942: 432). Both of these cradles have the wood painted or stained yellow, and the predominance of yellow cloth on modern cradleboards is doubtless related to the former use of yellow buckskin. This tendency appears to have been strengthened by tourists having seen yellow cradles and then specifically seeking yellow cradles, to the extent that little else may be seen now—a rare example of tradition reinforced, rather than altered, by commercial demands. The plain cradle (*lower left*, EEG 128) was made for Mrs. Guenther by Mrs.

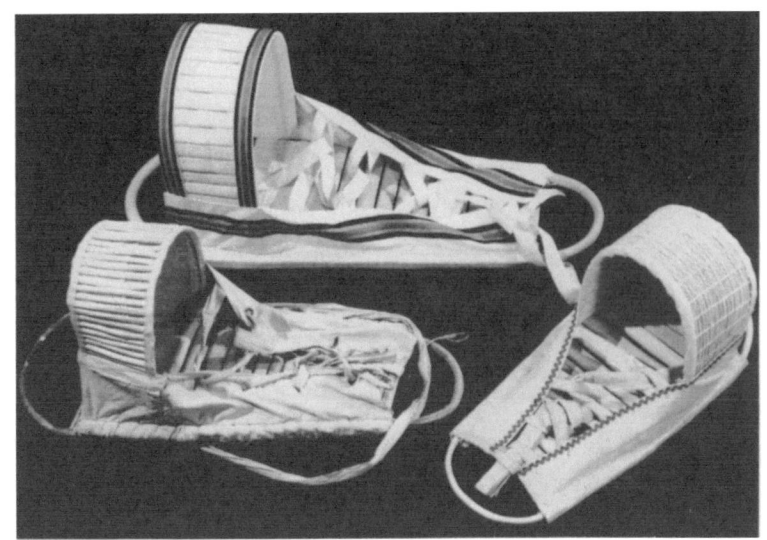

RIGHT: Figure 5.42. Permanent cradleboards; see also Color Illustration 2 (ASM Neg. 56684).

BOTTOM: Figure 5.43. Permanent cradle, doll, and diaper: *top,* closed (ASM Neg. 56683); *bottom,* open (56682).

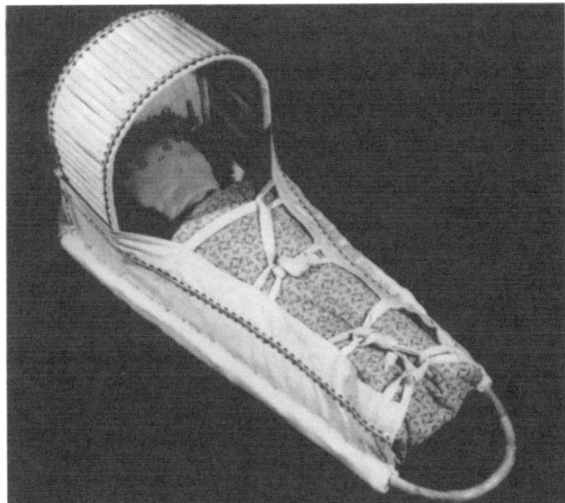

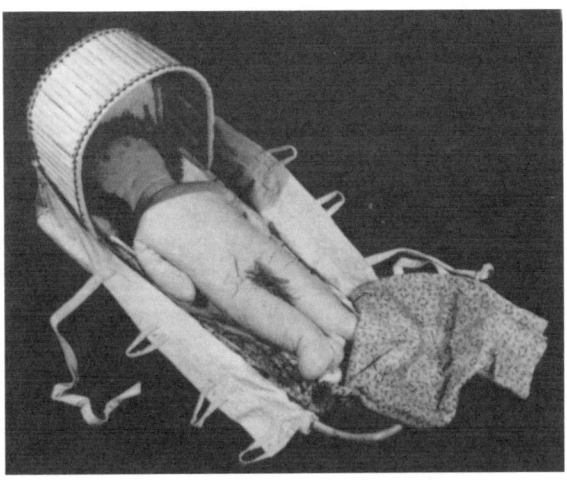

Jack Keyes in February of 1912, right after Wenonah was born. Wenonah was carried in it (Fig. 2.3), as were Mrs. Guenther's other eight children. Unlike most modern cradles made for sale, this one has the requisite carrying strap. Rev. Guenther rigged a spring with a hook to the top edge of the windshield on the passenger's side of their Model-T Ford so that Mrs. Guenther could hook up the top of the cradle and let the bottom rest in her lap, allowing the baby to see her and at the same time leave Minnie's hands free to do other things; an interesting forerunner of today's rear-facing safety carseats for infants (Tai 1980). Eventually the top of the cradle frame wore thin and broke, necessitating the metal tube and wire repair visible at the far left. Goodwin (1942: 429–440) provides additional information on cradleboards.

Permanent cradle, doll, and diaper. Figure 5.43. A full-size permanent cradleboard (EEG 127; 80 cm long) was obtained by the Guenthers at East Fork between 1911 and 1919. The hood and side-flaps were made of a heavy orange cloth ornamented with cord and rick-rack trim. To occupy the child, five buckskin thongs (three missing) strung with graduated green glass beads hung from the front of the hood. The stuffed cloth doll has yarn hair and sewn-in facial features. This set shows how a child actually was

Subsistence

bundled up, with the cover blanket passing under the child. A softer cloth pad with absorbent shredded juniper bark was placed where the child would wet, with extra bark at the side. Goodwin's informants (1942: 433–434) described this same sort of diaper, the bark or rabbit skin pads, and pillows of beaver or Abert's squirrel skin.

Old-style saddle. Figure 5.44. Top and bottom views of an early type of horse saddle (21407) made by Anna Price, for Goodwin, in 1932. The two rolls of untanned cowhide are filled with bundles of Johnson grass tied with yucca, with the rolls tied shut and to each other with buckskin thongs. The larger roll is about 45 cm long. The whole was held in place on the horse with a rawhide cinch strap, 170 cm long (not illustrated). This style of saddle among the Western Apache might be an adaptation of even earlier dog pack-saddles (Clark 1963: 241) or may have been inspired by similar Mexican horse pack-saddles of the 1700s (Treutlein 1949: 95).

Rawhide horseshoes. Figure 5.45. This pair of horseshoes (21406) was made in the old style by Jewett Wright, for Goodwin, in 1932. They are made of cowhide with the hair left on, with a drawstring of the same material that was probably brought forward from a back corner, around the front of the hoof, laced through the opposite front corner and tied in front as shown in Baldwin (1965: 87). Each shoe is about 15 cm across, and this pair is identified as for the front feet; whether Goodwin meant this particular pair actually had been made for a horse's front feet or was implying that shoes for the rear feet were somehow different is unknown.

Some horseshoes also had holes cut in the bottom to let out gravel. Horseshoes were used on raids and long trips, or after such journeys (Goodwin A–71; 1942: 89; Basso 1971: 32), and were made of oxhide, cowhide, or horsehide. They were used by the Apache as early as the 1750s (Treutlein 1949: 147) and by the Spanish and other Southwestern Indians as well (Clark 1963: 246). Shoes of this type, but smaller, also were made for burros (21441, not illustrated), and buckskin boots were made for dogs (Goodwin A–70).

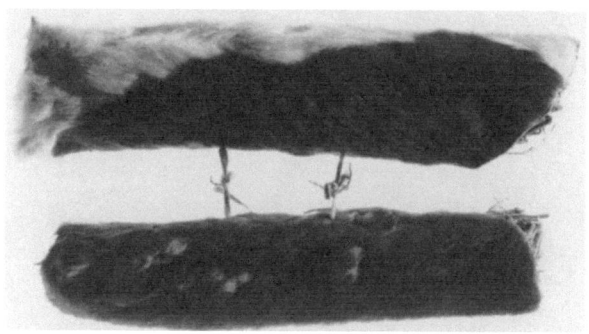

TOP: Figure 5.44. Old-style saddle (*top*, ASM Neg. 32125; *bottom*, 32102).

BOTTOM: Figure 5.45. Rawhide horseshoes (ASM Neg. 32074).

Figure 5.46. Quirts (*top*, ASM Neg. 56718).

Quirts. Figure 5.46. An old-style riding whip for horses (top, *left*, 21374; 75 cm long) was made for Goodwin by Anna Price in 1932. The handle is carved from a sotol stalk and it has a buckskin wrist loop and rawhide whip. Holes for the wrist loop and whip are carved, not burned through, and the whip is made from a single strand of cowhide ingeniously "knotted" in place (bottom).

The braided horsehair quirt (top, *right*, EEG 57) was made by Silas John Edwards, probably between 1912 and 1916 at East Fork, and was purchased from him by the Guenthers (see also Figs. 6.16 and 6.21). The foundation is apparently two (or more) strips of tanned leather, the ends of which extend past the horsehair and form the whips. The wrist loop has a slide so it can be cinched up tightly. The whole quirt from butt to tip of whips is 85 cm and it is made with black and white horsehair.

How traditional or widespread the use of horsehair was among the Western Apache and from whom they learned the craft are unclear. Utilitarian use of horsehair such as for ropes (Goodwin 1942: 471) may extend back in time. However, the Western Apache may have learned to make elaborately braided craft items from the Navajo, who were making similar horsehair quirts for sale at least as early as 1910 (Franciscan Fathers 1910: 314). This knowledge by both groups may ultimately derive from Mexicans. (See also Figs. 6.16, 6.21; Kluckhohn, Hill, and Kluckhohn 1971: 96.)

Packed for a trip on horseback. Figure 5.47. This woman was photographed between 1896 and 1903, probably near East Fork. She is holding a cradleboard and sitting astride some sort of large folded tarp(?) atop the saddle. Behind her leg (note her buckskin moccasins with "noses") is a bulging set of rawhide saddlebags, a *tus*, and a buckskin-decorated burden basket with crossed sticks, the type used for moving (see Fig. 5.35). Certainly this woman appears to be moving her camp or perhaps heading out on some sort of food gathering trip.

Bag and saddlebags. Figure 5.48 and Color Illustration 3. At left is a cloth bag (21440; 41 cm wide) for carrying or storing things, made by

Subsistence

Figure 5.47. Packed for a trip on horseback (photo by Paul Mayerhoff).

Mrs. Jewett Wright, but whether for her own use or for Goodwin, is unknown. It was closed and carried by a drawstring and was constructed of white cloth with decorative bands of yellow, black, and red cloth with a fringe of untwisted rope; virtually all stitching was done on a sewing machine. In pre-Reservation times such bags may have been made of rawhide and used primarily for gathering and storing acorns and seeds (Goodwin A–68, A–71; see also Fig. 3.4). The saddlebags at center (EEG 115) were obtained by the Guenthers from Chief Alchesay's household between 1918 and 1928. These are full-size saddlebags for a horse, measuring 130 cm high when folded in half as shown and made of rawhide and decorated with rawhide cut-outs

Figure 5.48. Bag and saddlebags; see also Color Illustration 3 (ASM Neg. 56687).

and red cloth. Smaller saddlebags of this type were made for burros (EEG 114, not illustrated) and miniatures were made as children's toys (Fig. 8.11). Saddlebags were made from cow, deer, or elk rawhide or buckskin (Goodwin A–71). The saddlebags at right (EEG 229) are made of decorative red, blue, black, and green cloth strips on white cloth, with a cloth fringe; length is 110 cm when folded in half. All stitching was done on a sewing machine. This pair, of the type now made for sale to tourists, was acquired by Mrs. Guenther probably before 1961, but similar saddlebags may have been used by the Apache at one time (Fig. 7.22).

Subsistence

Figure 5.49. Trade goods; see also Color Illustration 4 (ASM Neg. 56665).

Trade goods. Figure 5.49 and Color Illustration 4. In pre-Reservation times various Western Apache groups and bands maintained trade relationships with the Hopi, Zuni, and various segments of the Navajo and Yavapai (Goodwin 1942: 72–91). Items traded included bowl baskets, burden baskets, *tuses,* unfinished bows, stone arrowpoints, arrowshaft smoother-straighteners, prepared arrow feathers, turkey feathers, live turkeys, horses, buckskins, hide grainers, cooked mescal, sunflower seeds, and saguaro fruit. Materials obtained by the Western Apache included guns, powder, lead, iron hoes, cloth, blankets, sashes, sheep skins, buffalo skins, turquoise, white shell beads, abalone shell discs, brass tacks, corn, and, specifically from the Yavapai, saguaro fruit and mescal knives made of old shovel blades.

The rough, handspun wool blanket used as a backdrop here (21900) was purchased by Goodwin from Charlie Sego at Bylas in 1931. According to Charlie, it had been obtained by his mother "long ago" in a trade with some Navajos who were visiting Fort Apache. Curiously, Goodwin identified it as Navajo in one place and Zuni in another. This blanket has 4½ warps per inch and 17 wefts per inch and measures 190 by 123 cm. Warps are natural white handspun wool. Wefts are natural white, brown-gray, and dark gray handspun wool, and a black that may be analine dyed. End selvages are twined with two strands of light brown 2–ply wool. The side selvages and corner tassels were extensively repaired with a 4–ply commercial yarn at some unknown time. Long lazy lines occur in the white areas. Though apparently obtained from Navajos, it is possible that this natural-colored striped pattern blanket was woven at Zuni. Both Navajo and Zuni weavers have produced striped blankets and used lazy line patterns. The missing selvages preclude using these features to assign the piece to one group or the other. Technology, design, and particularly the quality of the wool suggest this blanket was made probably sometime in the late 1800s to early 1900s.

The two bowl baskets (*left*, EEG 90; *right*, EEG 67) came from East Fork between 1911 and 1919 and are of the type that was traded, particularly to the Zuni (see also Tanner 1982: 104–113 for illustrations of early Western Apache bowl baskets collected at Zuni). In earlier times prepared abalone shell discs were obtained at Zuni (to be used for a girl's forehead pendant at her puberty dance or on buckskin caps), although in recent years the Apache have had access to whole shells (EEG 232) from several sources. Turkey tails and wing feathers similar to these (EEG 234) were traded "as-is" or split and trimmed for fletching arrows.

The unusual wickerwork basket at top (21871; 44 cm long) has large unpeeled willow twigs for the warps and small twigs for the wefts. It was found by an Apache on an old Apache camp site and sold to Osborne's store in Bylas (or Rice?), where Goodwin bought it in 1932. Goodwin's notes identify it as: "turkey basket to carry young turkey pets—very rare." Pet turkeys are mentioned in White Mountain myth (Goodwin 1939: 63) and apparently young turkeys actually were kept as pets. Probably children cared for them until they had gotten adult plumage and were suitable for trading to the Zuni (Goodwin 1942: 81). Anna Price recalled: "We used to make little baskets of open work to carry our pet young turkeys in long ago. We called these *taji bi tats a*. I made them for my turkeys when I was young" (Goodwin A–66). "When I was a little girl I had four pet turkeys. They were caught when they were little. That's the way some of our people used to do—catch young turkeys and raise them. One Mexican woman, a captive, used to raise quite a few. We used to take these turkeys over to the Zuni and trade them for striped blankets" (Goodwin A–70).

Although it is clear from the foregoing that turkeys were kept and transported in special baskets, the one shown here is technologically and stylistically indistinguishable from the rib-type baskets made throughout rural America by Anglos. Such baskets were copied by eastern American Indian tribes (Lamb 1972: 142–143) using a form that was of European derivation (see Teleki 1975: 25–27, Fig. 5, Plates 14, 16, 53, and especially 61). Even the "under-rim openings" for handles are the same. Although it may have been found on an Apache camp by an Apache, probably this basket originally was made by and obtained from an Anglo, and Goodwin's equation of it with Anna Price's little openwork turkey baskets is a case of mistaken identity. Turkey baskets most likely were simply larger versions of the type of bird cage shown in Figure 5.7, which is much more suitable for containing a bird than the open-top basket shown here.

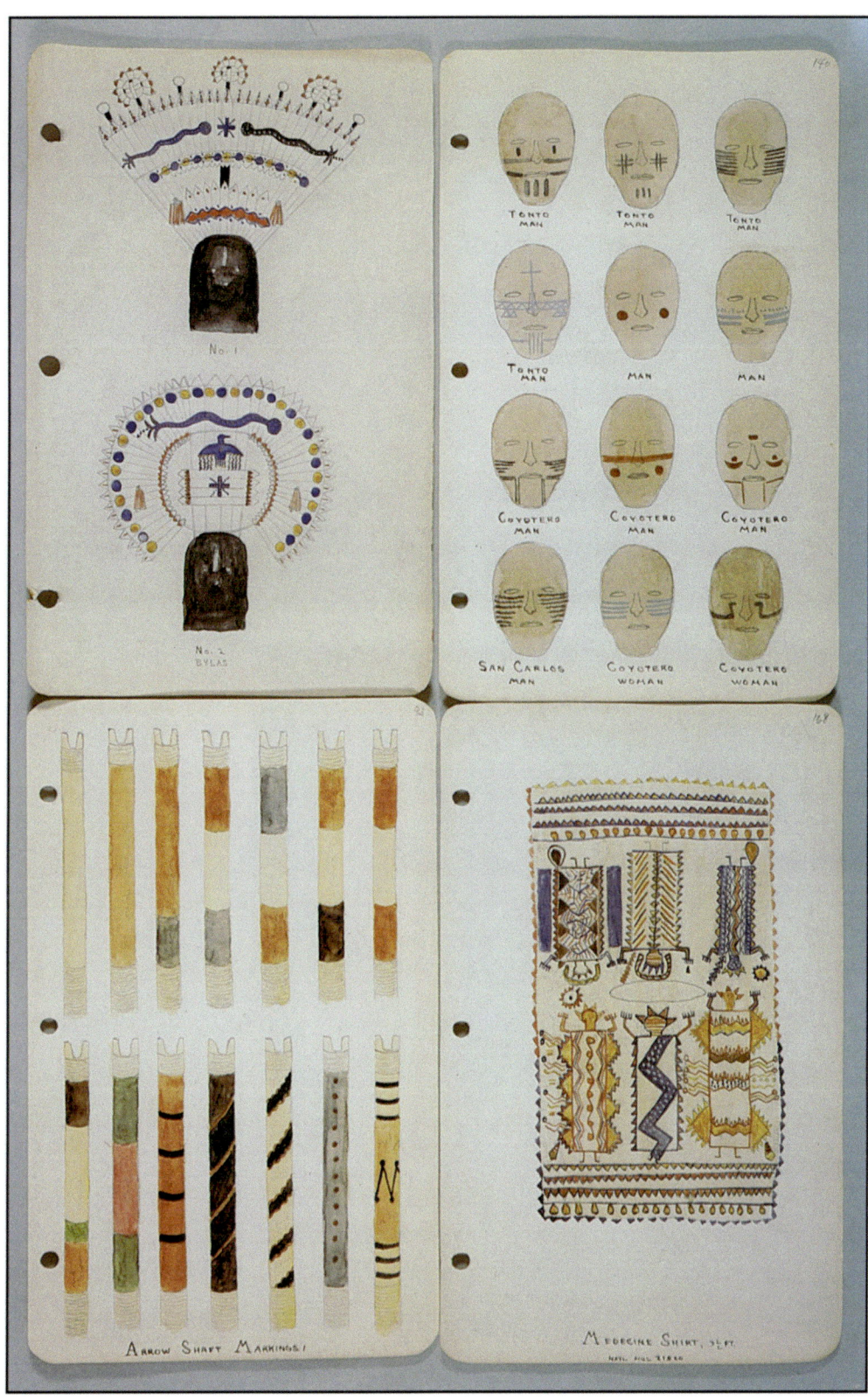

Color Illustration 1. A sample of watercolors painted by Grenville Goodwin. (Fig. 3.6. ASM Neg. C–20499.)

Top:
Color Illustration 2.
Permanent cradleboards.
(Fig. 5.42. ASM Neg. C–15119.)

Bottom:
Color Illustration 3.
Bag and saddlebags.
(Fig. 5.48. ASM Neg. C–15121.)

Opposite:
Color Illustration 4.
Trade goods.
(Fig. 5.49. ASM Neg. C–15112.)

OPPOSITE:
Color Illustration 5.
Dolls with 1880s clothing, back view.
(Fig. 6.2. ASM Neg. C–15115.)

TOP:
Color Illustration 6.
Man's buckskin shirt of the mid–1800s.
(Fig. 6.4. ASM Neg. C–15100.)

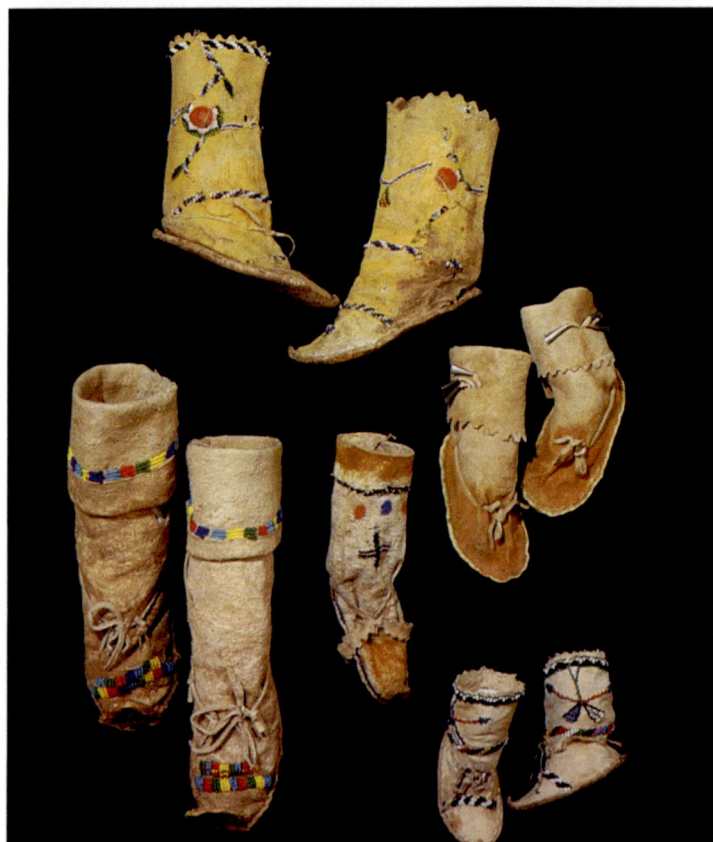

Top:
Color Illustration 7.
Child's carrying-jacket.
(Fig. 6.7. ASM Neg. C–15098.)

Bottom:
Color Illustration 8.
Children's moccasins.
(Fig. 6.9. ASM Neg. C–20435.)

Top:
Color Illustration 9.
Beaded awl or knife cases.
(Fig. 6.11. ASM Neg. C–15081.)

Bottom:
Color Illustration 10.
Girls' hair ornaments.
(Fig. 6.13. ASM Neg. C–20436.)

Color Illustration 11. Rectangular buckskin pouches. (Fig. 6.14. ASM Neg. C–15123.)

Color Illustration 12. Round buckskin pouches. (Fig. 6.15. ASM Neg. C–15122.)

Color Illustration 13. Watch fobs. (Fig. 6.16. ASM Neg. C–15080.)

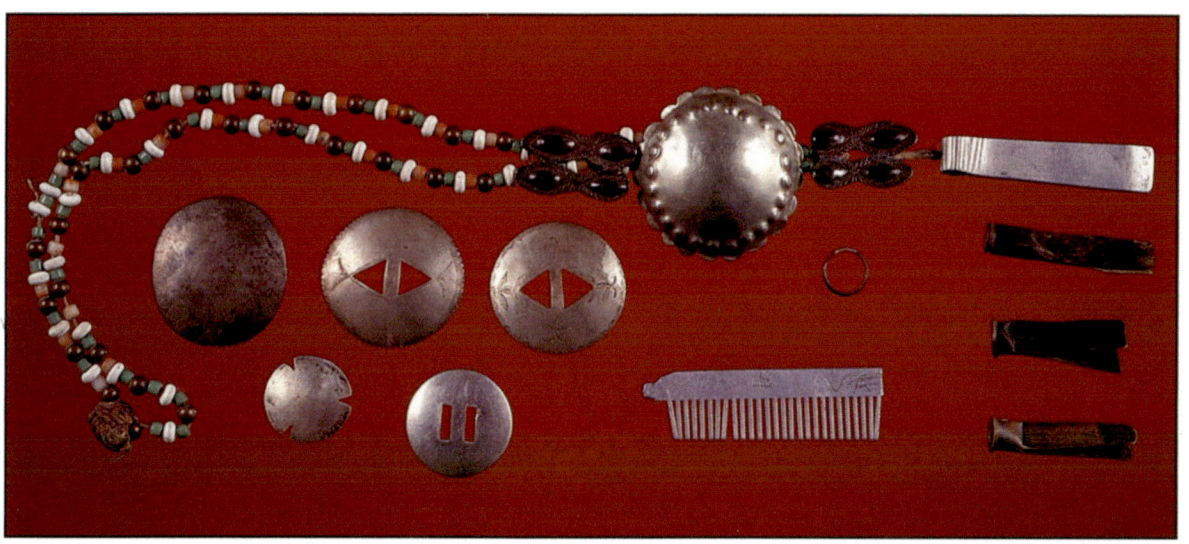

Top: Color Illustration 14. Metal jewelry. (Fig. 6.17. ASM Neg. C–20437.)

Bottom: Color Illustration 15. Beaded purses, 1911 to 1914. (Fig. 6.18. ASM Neg. C–15124.)

Color Illustration 16. T–necklaces, 1911 to 1944. (Fig. 6.25. ASM Neg. C–15083.)

Color Illustration 17. T–necklaces, 1911 to 1970. (Fig. 6.26. ASM Neg. C–15084.)

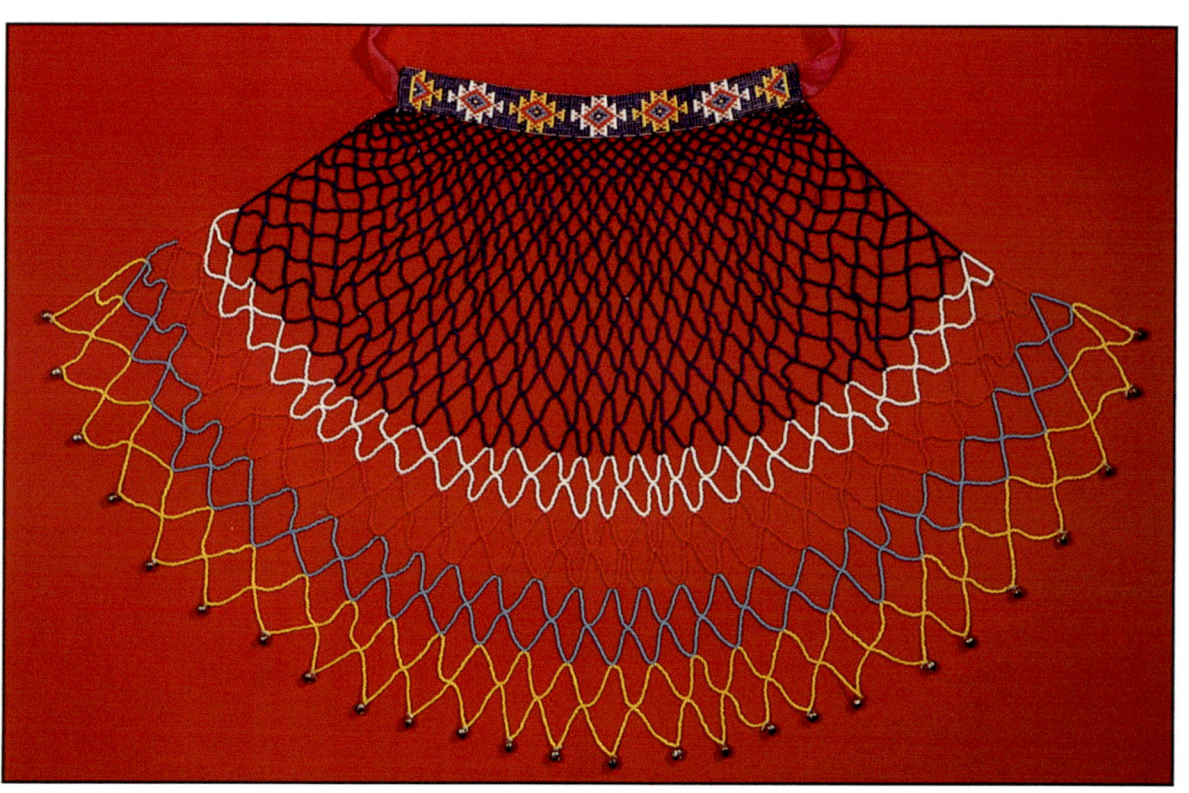
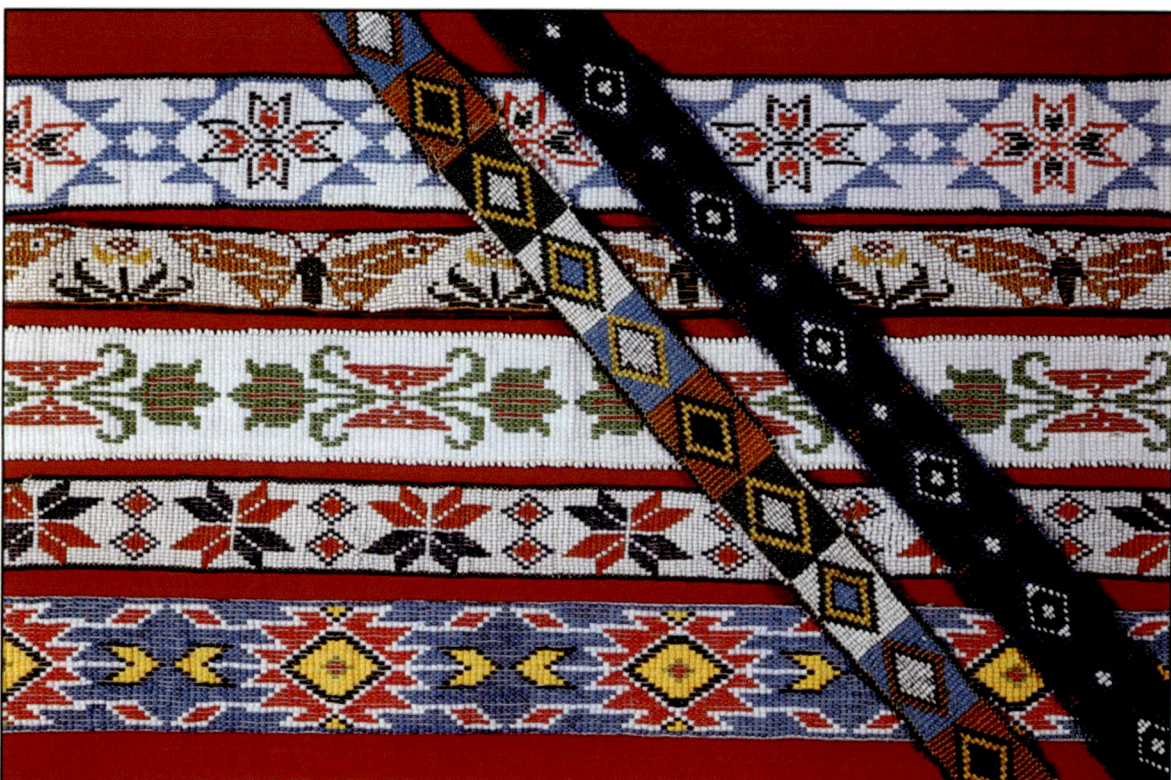

OPPOSITE, TOP: Color Illustration 18. Shawl necklace. (Fig. 6.28. ASM Neg. C–15092.)

OPPOSITE, BOTTOM: Color Illustration 19. Beaded and beadwork belts. (Fig. 6.29. ASM Neg. C–20498.)

RIGHT: Color Illustration 20. Commercial craft items. (Fig. 6.31. ASM Neg. C–15079.)

OPPOSITE:
Color Illustration 21.
Girl's puberty ceremony buckskin dress.
(Fig. 7.2. ASM Neg. C–15103.)

TOP:
Color Illustration 22.
Girl's puberty ceremony paraphernalia.
(Fig. 7.3. ASM Neg. C–15135.)

BOTTOM:
Color Illustration 23.
Girl's puberty T–necklace, made before 1912.
(Fig. 7.5. ASM Neg. C–20497.)

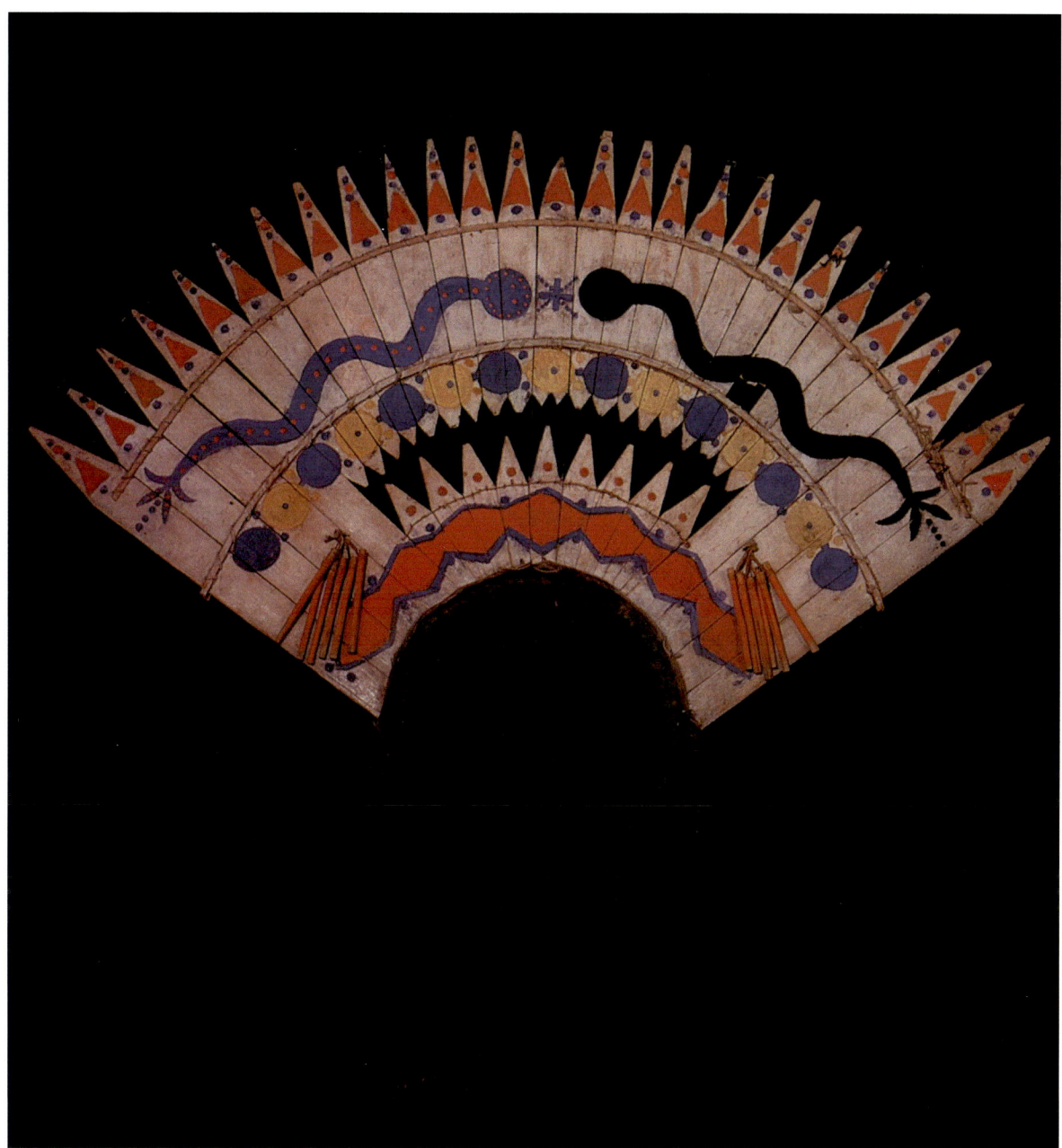

OPPOSITE:
Color Illustration 24.
Gaan mask made by John Robinson in 1901.
(Fig. 7.8*a*. ASM Neg. C–20426 DUP.)

TOP:
Color Illustration 25.
Gaan mask made by John Robinson in 1901.
(Fig. 7.8*b*. ASM Neg. C–20429 DUP.)

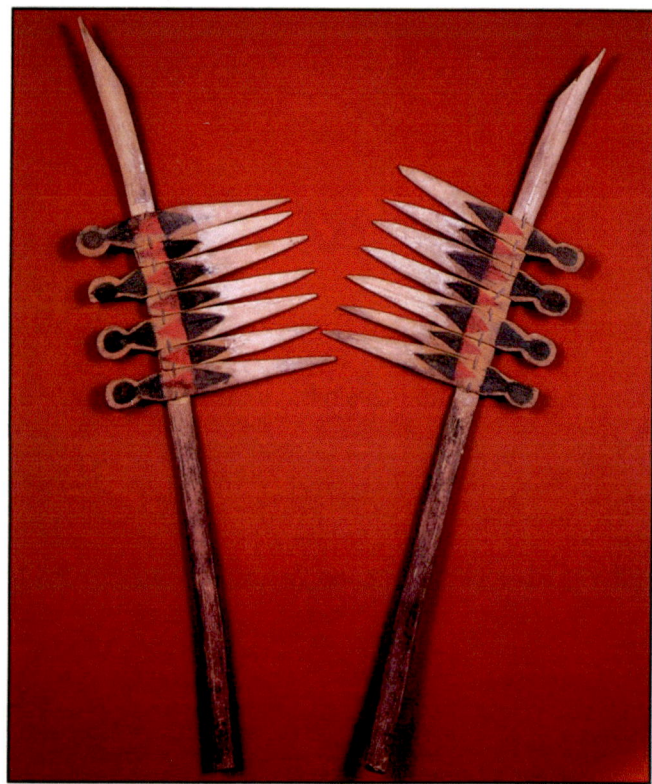

Top:
Color Illustration 26.
Mineral paints.
(Fig. 7.10. ASM Neg. C–15138.)

Bottom:
Color Illustration 27.
Pair of *gaan* dancer's wands.
(Fig. 7.11. ASM Neg. C–20432.)

Opposite:
Color Illustration 28.
Medicine charms.
(Fig. 7.14. ASM Neg. C–15089.)

Top:
Color Illustration 29.
Men's buckskin war caps.
(Fig. 7.20. ASM Neg. C–15107.)

Bottom:
Color Illustration 30.
Turkey feather *(right)* and owl feather *(left)* buckskin caps.
(Fig. 7.23. ASM Neg. C–15108.)

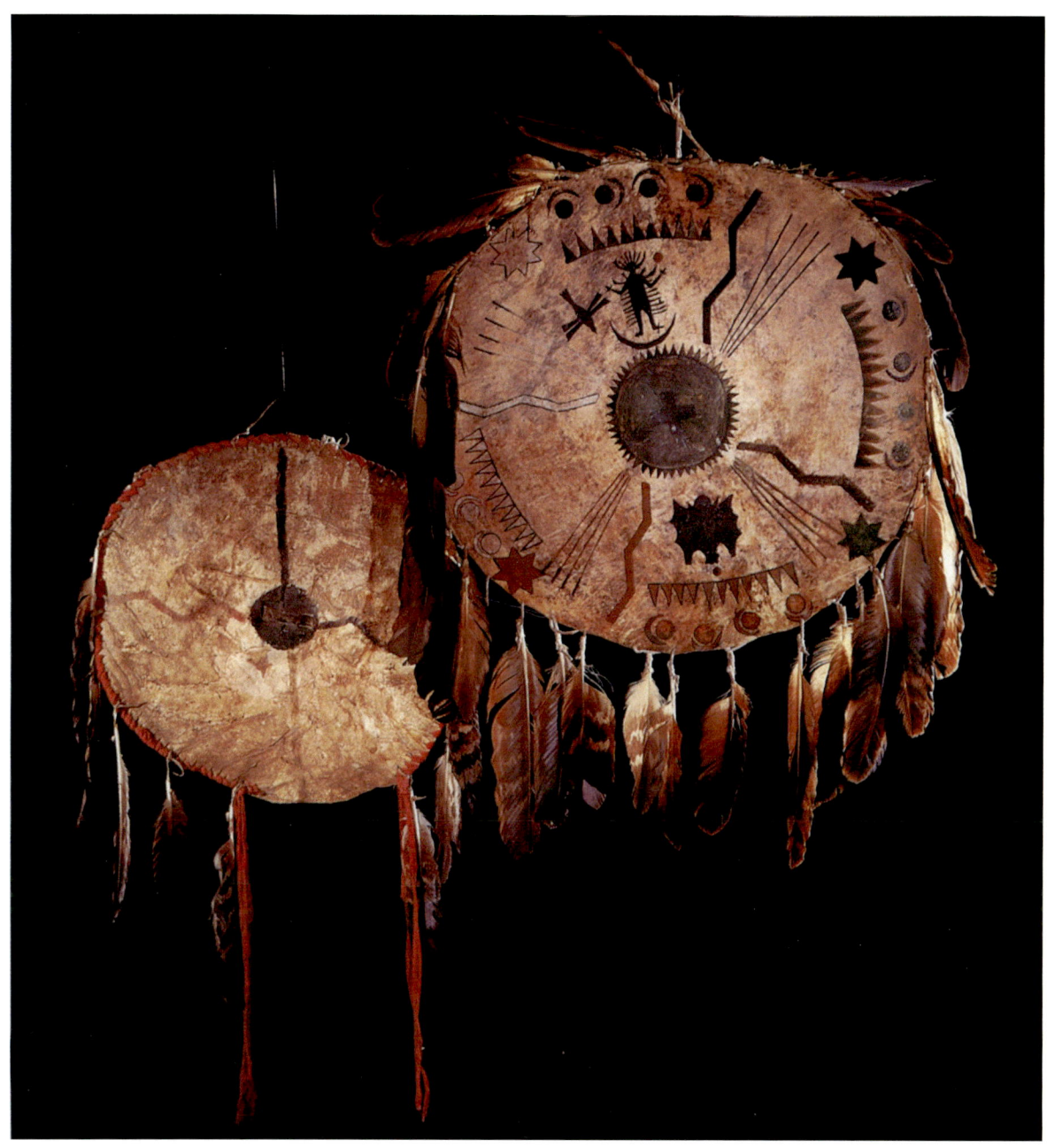

Color Illustration 31.
Rawhide war shields.
(Fig. 7.27. ASM Neg. C–15131.)

Color Illustration 32. Musical instruments. (Fig. 8.13. ASM Neg. C–15136.)

Chapter Six
Clothing

Alan Ferg and William B. Kessel

OVERLEAF: **Baha and Eskiaga.** Figure 6.1. Rev. Paul Mayerhoff took this photo between 1896 and 1903, probably in the East Fork area. It was labeled "Baha and Eskiaga," and it is conceivable that the youngster on the left is young Baha, son of Chief Alchesay, and Alchesay's successor. Both wear buckskin moccasins with "noses" and headbands. The man wears a cloth breechclout, choker-type bead necklace, and what appear to be three silver ornaments with notched bottom edges on his vest (see Fig. 6.17).

Dolls with 1880s clothing. Figure 6.2 and Color Illustration 5. The front *(left)* and back *(right)* views of dolls made by Mrs. Jewett Wright in 1932 and 1935 show the 1880s style of dress for a Western Apache man and unmarried woman. The female doll (21408; 54 cm high) wears buckskin moccasins, a white and red cloth skirt with black trim, a fringed buckskin poncho, and a girl's hair ornament. Her moccasins are the type worn on dress occasions, partially painted with yellow ochre, with high tops, "noses" (see Fig. 6.10), and fancy-cut cuffs and laces. The poncho is a single piece of buckskin with a hole cut for the head. It is trimmed with beads, brass studs, and black cloth on the shoulders, the lower half (front and back) is dyed with yellow ochre, metal tinklers hang in front and back, and strips of squirrel(?) skin are tied to all four corners. Underneath the poncho is a red cloth blouse with black and white cuffs. The doll's hair ornament is the standard hourglass-shaped piece of rawhide with brass studs, beadwork and tinkler fringe, and a black cloth tie. The doll also wears beadwork bracelets, a choker-type necklace, and long earrings in what would have been pierced ears (Goodwin A–66). The hair may be horsehair (it is not human), and the facial features are simply blue ink(?) dots on the cloth head. The torso foundation is a piece of board with two additional small sticks nailed(?) on for the legs; the arms are stuffed with cloth(?). The doll also wears a petticoat and camisole of calico.

Figure 6.2. Dolls with 1880s clothing; see also Color Illustration 5 *(left,* ASM Neg. 56680; *right,* 56679).

Clothing

The male doll (21436; 52 cm high) has a wood foundation similar to the female doll. He wears white cloth breeches, shirt, and breechclout. His buckskin moccasins are much the same as those of the female doll, with the addition of red cloth ties at their tops and an unidentified feather tied into the laces of the right foot. He wears beadwork bracelets, a choker necklace, earrings in pierced ears, and a leather belt ornamented with brass and silver studs. His hair (not human, possibly horsehair) is held in place by a red cloth headband with white, orange, and black trim and scalloped ends hanging down in back (see Fig. 6.3). A silver stud, a Red-shafted Flicker feather, and two pieces of eagle down are affixed to the back of the headband as well. Facial features are sketched on the cloth head in ink. Around the doll's waist in back, rolled up and with its ends tucked into the belt, is an unidentified cloth object. Attached to the belt is a rectangular beaded buckskin pouch. Over his right shoulder is a medicine cord with (visible in front) a steatite disc bead, a quartz crystal, another Red-shafted Flicker feather, an obsidian point, and (visible in back) a semicircular beaded buckskin pouch containing a piece of glass (perhaps to represent a signal mirror), another steatite disc bead, and a chalcedony point base. Attached to his bead necklace in front is a pair of metal tweezers and an unidentified bundle of twigs. Attached to a strand of beads that loops under his right arm is a pouch of buckskin painted red, probably to hold pollen or tobacco.

Although doubtless functioning as a charm, the specific significance of the Red-shafted Flicker feathers is not clear. An informant (Goodwin A–66) noted that "long ago, when they went to war, men used to stick a tail feather of red flicker in their head band or hat" but did not know specifically why. Perhaps, like the flicker feather on the child's carrying-jacket (Figure 6.7), it serves "to keep away all sickness and misfortune" (Goodwin 1942: 440–441). As on the child's jacket, the prehistoric arrow points on the war charm on this doll may serve to ward off lightning. The rolled cloth may represent a poncho. The bundle of sticks may represent a torch, but attached as it is to his necklace and tweezers, it more likely portrays a hairbrush or a charm. On their first two raids, young men wore a drinking tube and scratching stick analogous to those worn by a girl at her puberty ceremony, but this bundle of sticks does not particularly resemble either.

Three Apache men. Figure 6.3. These men were probably Western Apaches, with buckskin moccasins, cloth breechclout, and beaded choker necklaces. The man at right wears a fancy headband and Navajo(?) blanket; the headband is the same type as that on the male doll in Figure 6.2.

Figure 6.3. Three Apache men (photo courtesy Arizona Historical Society, Neg. 41151).

Man's buckskin shirt. Figure 6.4 and Color Illustration 6. Sometime between 1919 and 1923, Arnold Knoop obtained this shirt (EEG 126) at his store in Carrizo. An Apache widow, M–2, came in, said that her father had worn it when she was a girl, noted the holes in the back of the collar and shoulders (which she had recently caused?), and traded the shirt for food. The Apache name of M–2 was Dodzondiski, and in 1900 she was fifty-six years old and already a widow (U.S. Army Census 1900). When the Knoops met her she would have been seventy-five to seventy-nine years old, implying that the shirt dates to the 1860s or earlier. In her notes Frieda Knoop gave a date of 1844 for this shirt, but the reason for this assignment is not stated.

The shirt is about 60 cm long from the collarless neck to the bottom of the waist fringe. The outside appears to have been colored all over with yellow ochre (usually mixed with yucca juice; Goodwin A–66). The buckskin fringe across the chest and upper shoulders and the upper fringe at the waist are sewn on; the other fringes are cut from the edges of the body or sleeve pieces. Under the armpits, where the sleeves join the body, holes were left open for ventilation (Goodwin A–66). Nearly all of the beadwork is sewn on in a lazy stitch with sinew. Most of the stitching on the whole shirt is sinew, but there is some commercial thread as well. Frieda Knoop carefully stitched up the numerous tears in the upper back and patched the holes with uncolored buckskin. This shirt buttoned up the front with 12 buttons (1 missing), had 2 more buttons at the throat, 3 buttons at each cuff (the right ones are gone), and 51 buttons around the shoulders as added decoration. These brass buttons appear to be stamped out, with a brass eye with a foot soldered to the back; they are 0.50 inch (1.28 cm) in diameter. Although difficult to date precisely (none bear any design or marks), commercial buttons of this type date in the first half of the 1800s and could have been used anytime after that (Olsen 1963, Fig. 1*h*; South 1964, Type 18 buttons).

Shirts of this style were fairly standardized in design and ornamentation (Goodwin collected a similar one, 23020, not illustrated; see also Mails 1974: 38) and, according to Goodwin (A–66), probably were first made in the mid-1800s, stimulated by the shirts and coats of Mexicans and Anglos. Usually only wealthy men owned this type of shirt. Earlier styles included sleeveless shirts or a garment consisting of sleeves connected by a yoke (Figs. 6.5, 6.6).

Clothing

OPPOSITE: Figure 6.4. Man's buckskin shirt of the mid–1800s; see also Color Illustration 6 (*left*, ASM Neg. 56650; *right*, 56651).

Man's sleeveless buckskin shirt. Figure 6.5. A sleeveless shirt was worn by men who did not have enough buckskins to make up the kind of elaborate shirt shown in Figure 6.4. It is probably a more traditional style, uninfluenced by the cut of Anglo or Mexican clothing. These shirts were made of a single buckskin folded over, with a head opening cut in the fold and the sides laced together under the arms. Harvey Nashkine said: "They used to make these to wear on the warpath in Mexico so as not to get cut up by the brush in traveling" (Goodwin A–66). This sketch is taken from Goodwin's record of remarks by John Rope about shirts (Goodwin A–66).

Man's buckskin shirt, sleeves only. Figure 6.6. Another type of shirt, described by John Rope (Goodwin A–66), consisted of sleeves and yoke. No details of its manufacture are given, but it apparently has buckskin fringes down the insides of the arms and around the shoulders (at seams?) and is laced together down the front of the yoke.

Child's carrying-jacket. Figure 6.7 and Color Illustration 7. This buckskin jacket (21327; 32 cm from collar to waist) was made by Mrs. Jewett Wright in 1936. Tied to the front (not shown) are two pine twigs, one quartz crystal, one *Olivella dama* whole-shell bead, and one white arrow point. On the back of the jacket (shown) are a quail's head, one black stone bifacial tool, one commercial green glass bead, and two flicker feathers. Goodwin (1942: 440–441) described these jackets in detail.

A special type of little buckskin shirt was worn by infants after they outgrew their carriers [cradleboards]. This had a . . . belt . . . by which the child could be lifted and

BOTTOM LEFT: Figure 6.5. Man's sleeveless buckskin shirt.

BOTTOM RIGHT: Figure 6.6. Man's buckskin shirt, sleeves only.

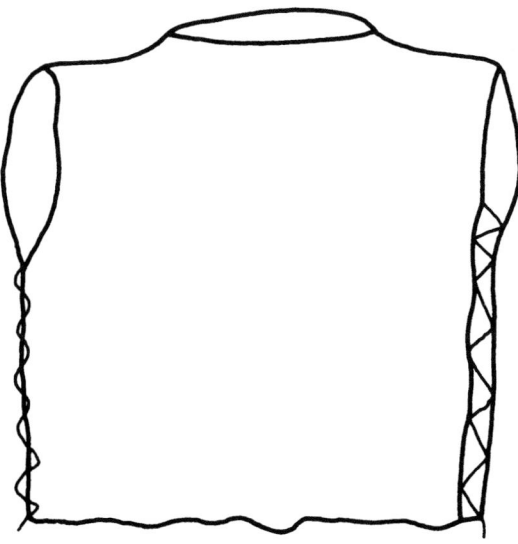

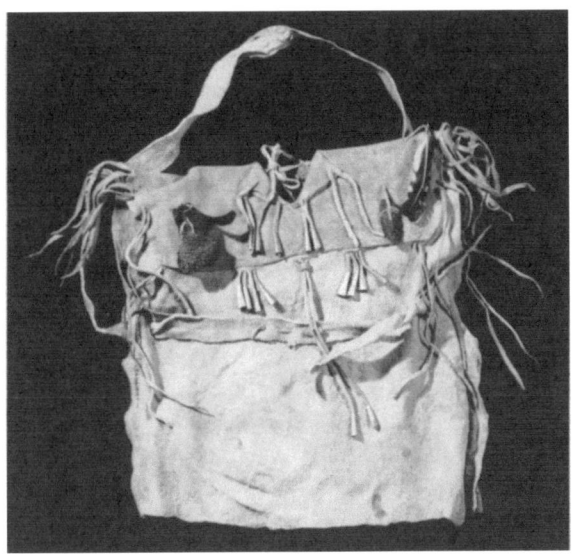

Top: Figure 6.7. Child's carrying-jacket; see also Color Illustration 7 (ASM Neg. 56648).

Bottom: Figure 6.8. Babies' moccasins (ASM Neg. 32120).

slung over the shoulder of the mother or from the horn of a saddle. It is said the infants did not mind this. . . . Charms which had been attached to the hood of the baby-carrier were often removed and tied to the shoulders or back of this little jacket. . . . It [ASM 21327] is made of two pieces of buckskin attached . . . over each shoulder and sewn together down the sides, leaving holes for the arms . . . [and] for the head at the top . . . and the turned-over edges at the collar are worn in back. The jacket is decorated with buckskin tassels and short flaps . . . painted with native yellow ocher. . . . Several charms are attached: quartz crystal to protect during darkness, two pine twigs with the bark eaten off and thrown down from the top of a yellow-pine tree by the Abert squirrel, which spends his life in high trees and never falls, to protect the child from being hurt by falling; the head of the male Gambel's quail to keep away sickness, because quail is never sick; a red-shafted flicker feather, also to keep away all sickness and misfortune; a black stone knife blade, known as "thunder knife," to protect from lightning . . . and a white chert arrow-point with white-shell bead attached, also to keep away sickness and evil. . . . These shirts could be used for another child when outgrown or might be put away and kept by the mother, some day to be shown with pride and sentiment to her grown child.

Babies' moccasins. Figure 6.8. These moccasins (21411) are essentially small bags constructed of two pieces of buckskin with a seam along the sole of the foot (Goodwin A–66), with buckskin drawstrings at the ankles. They were made by Mrs. Jewett Wright in 1932 and are 17.5 cm long from toe to cuff. "This type of boot was sometimes worn by babies still in the carrier [cradleboard] and were sometimes used until the child was four or five years old. However, these little boots were not always worn and many small children went barefoot. Sometimes these little boots were taken apart to form the uppers of a child's first pair of real moccasins [see Fig. 6.9], the soles being of rawhide and made exactly like the adults'" (Goodwin A–66).

Clothing

Figure 6.9. Children's moccasins; see also Color Illustration 8 (ASM Neg. 64290).

Children's moccasins. Figure 6.9 and Color Illustration 8. A pair of tiny beaded buckskin moccasins (*lower right,* EEG 182; 10 cm high, 11 cm from toe to heel) was made by Shima for the Guenthers' first child, Wenonah, in 1912 or 1913. Born in 1912, Wenonah was an early, energetic walker (Fig. 2.4). Shima made Wenonah a second pair (*top,* EEG 175) around 1919 or 1920, decorated with a red paint dot surrounded by beadwork. Another pair (*lower left,* EEG 176) was made by Shima at about this same time for the Guenthers' second child, Edgar. The single right moccasin (*center,* EEG 177) was found at East Fork between 1911 and 1920. It is quite fancy, with beadwork, scalloped laces, the top of the cuff and top of the foot painted yellow, two red and one blue dot below the cuff, a blue line around the top of the sole, and, as a final touch, the inside of the "nose" is painted red. At right is a pair of moccasins (21328) purchased by Goodwin from Palmer Valor's daughter-in-law in 1932. They had belonged to her son and had scalloped cuffs and four metal tinklers on each boot.

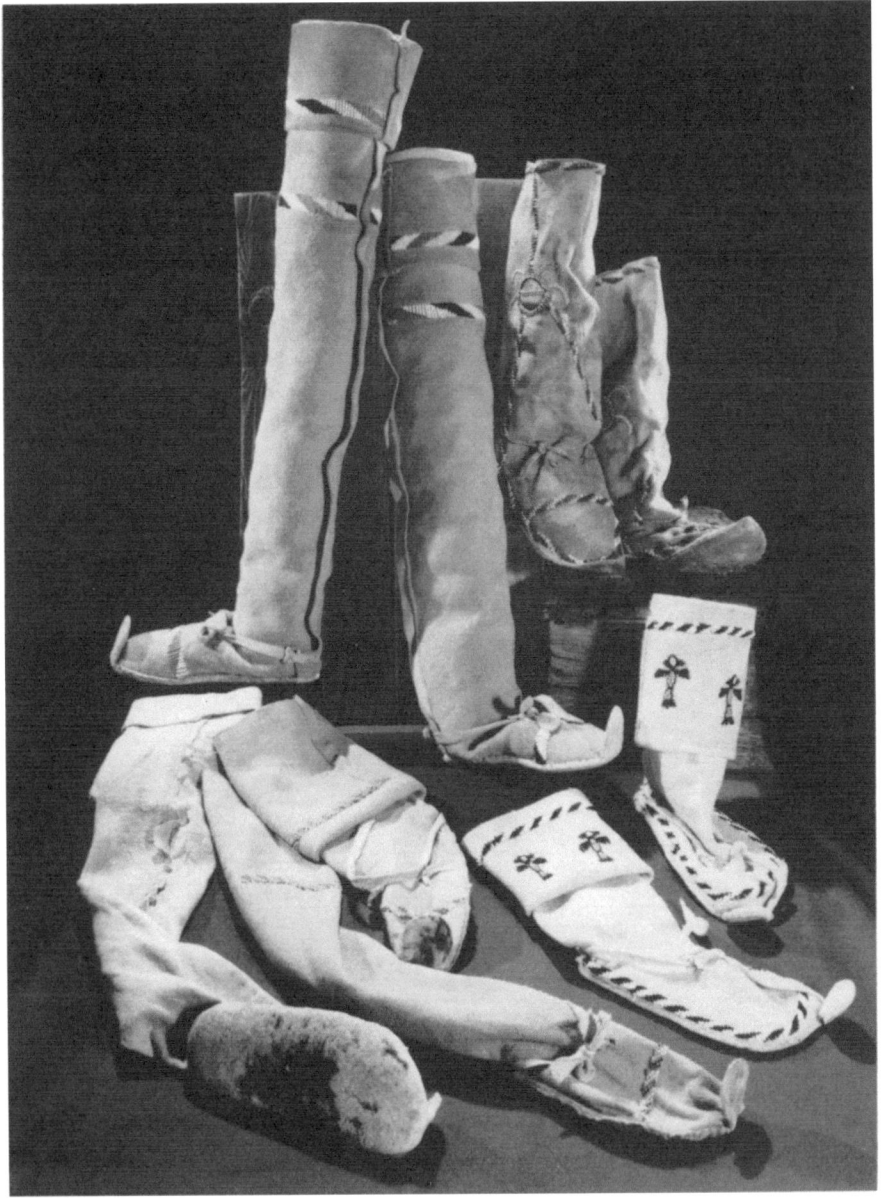

Figure 6.10. Adults' moccasins (ASM Neg. 56644).

Adults' moccasins. Figure 6.10. According to informants (Goodwin A–66), in pre-Reservation times there were three lengths of men's moccasins: to the knee, half way up the calf, and to the ankle. The two shorter types may have been the result of cutting away the upper worn parts of the cuff, although some may have been made these lengths initially. Women apparently always wore the high tops. Several informants agreed that moccasin "noses" (toe tabs or "protectors") were an innovation derived late in time from the Chiricahua during joint raids into Mexico. The "noses" were purely decorative, to be put on dress moccasins, and had nothing to do with protecting the toes, as is popularly repeated (Tanner 1968, Fig. 7.7; Dutton 1980: 211–212). They were specifically noted as something that might cause the wearer to stumble.

Clothing

Dutton (1980) provides a well-illustrated description of how a similar pair of moccasins was made.

The pair of calf-high beaded moccasins (*upper right,* E–9248) is probably Western Apache. The pair at bottom center (EEG 179), the pair with beaded birds at bottom right (EEG 178), and a right moccasin (of a plain pair) at bottom left (EEG 180) were purchased by the Guenthers at East Fork between 1911 and 1922. The pair at upper left (EEG 174) was obtained in Whiteriver in the 1960s; these tall moccasins stand 70 cm high from heel to top of cuff. "Noses" are on all of the Guenther moccasins, and an alternating diagonal "rope" design in beadwork is on all the decorated pairs. The plain right moccasin is painted with yellow ochre on the top of the foot. All the soles appear to be cowhide with the hair left on intentionally.

Beaded awl or knife cases. Figure 6.11 and Color Illustration 9. At right are three beaded buckskin cases (*left to right:* EEG 1, EEG 3, EEG 2) obtained by the Guenthers in the early 1920s at East Fork; EEG 2 and 3 are beaded on their backs as well, EEG 1 is plain. Another case (*left,* EEG 4) from the same time period (plain back) has the tag band number B–33 at the top. It was probably made by Nagaahoun, the wife of Bezho; Bezho's tag number was B–33 (U.S. Army Census 1900). Second and fourth from the left are an awl case (beaded front and back) and a 14–cm long wooden awl (both 21402) made in the old style by Anna Price in 1932. Commonly used in hide working, basketry, and even shelling corn, awls in pre-Reservation times also were made of deer ulnae and antler tines (Goodwin A–66, A–71). The Guenthers obtained the knife (EEG 183; 27 cm long) at East Fork between 1911 and 1922. The home-made wood handle is attached to the steel blade with three nails(?); the blade appears to be commercial but might have been crafted by an Apache from some other item. In early times metal knives were stolen on raids or fashioned from such things as barrel hoops traded from the Navajo (Goodwin A–71).

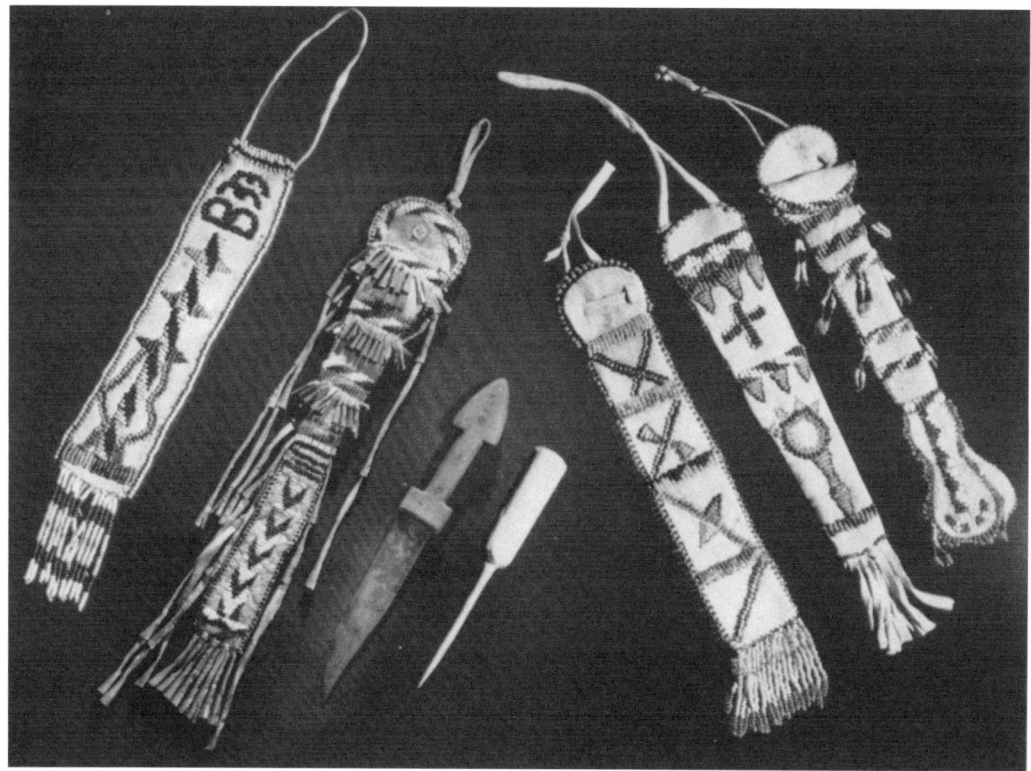

Figure 6.11. Beaded awl or knife cases; see also Color Illustration 9 (ASM Neg. 56629).

Apache girl wearing hair ornament. Figure 6.12. From the time a girl started to menstruate, around age fourteen or fifteen, until after she was married and pregnant, her hair was rolled up at the back (sometimes around an hourglass-shaped piece of antelope hide) and secured with a cloth or buckskin tie attached to a hair ornament. After her first child was born, she wore her hair loose around her shoulders (Goodwin A–66). Hair ornaments were usually made of beadwork or brass tacks on a cloth-covered piece of rawhide, often with a beadwork fringe as in this picture. In pre-Reservation times, the brass tacks were obtained in trade from the Zuni, one exchange value cited as one large Apache bowl basket for enough tacks for one hair ornament (Goodwin 1942: 81). This photo probably was taken at East Fork between 1896 and 1903.

RIGHT: Figure 6.12. Apache girl wearing hair ornament (photo by Paul Mayerhoff).

BELOW: Figure 6.13. Girls' hair ornaments; see also Color Illustration 10 (ASM Neg. 64296).

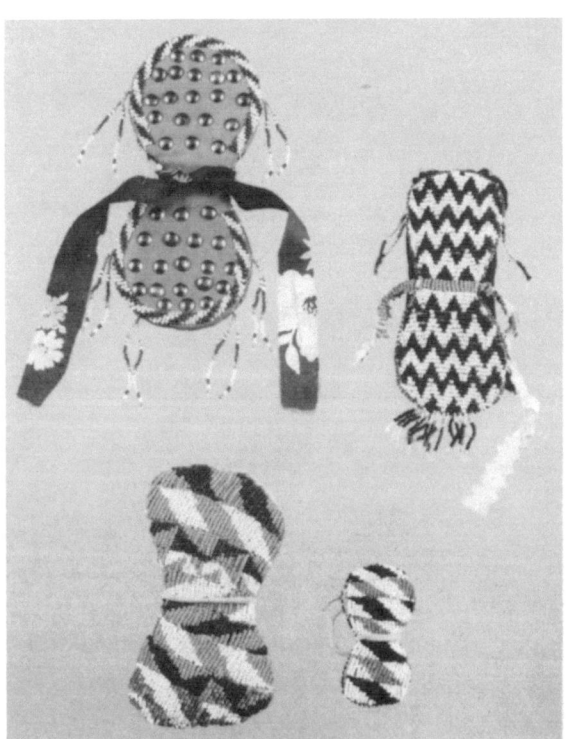

Girls' hair ornaments. Figure 6.13 and Color Illustration 10. The upper left ornament (21323; 18.8 cm high) was made by Harvey Nashkine's daughter in 1932 and purchased by Goodwin; whether Goodwin commissioned this piece is unknown. Tacks are pushed through what feels like a rawhide foundation and bent over on the back. These look like thumbtacks or upholstery tacks rather than the earlier buttonlike discs shown in Figure 6.12. The upper right ornament (EEG 21) has the beadwork stitched directly onto a buckskin backing, has a long black cloth tie, and was made in 1912 or 1913 by Kitty Savage of East Fork. The two at bottom (large, EEG 19; small, EEG 20) are both beadwork on a cloth-covered rawhide(?) foundation. Both were probably made by the same person (the backings are of the same cloth) and were purchased in the late 1910s or early 1920s at either East Fork or Whiteriver by Mrs. Guenther. The small size of one and lack of ties or fringes on both raise the possibility they were unfinished, or perhaps made specifically to sell and left this way intentionally.

Clothing

Rectangular buckskin pouches. Figure 6.14 and Color Illustration 11. The pouch at upper left (23021) has a flap closed with a commercial metal button. The center pouch (21401) has the flap closed by buckskin thongs, and was made by Mrs. George Gray at Bylas in 1932. The other three pouches were collected in the early 1920s by the Guenthers, probably at East Fork or possibly at Whiteriver, with a silver (coin?) button-closed flap (*upper right,* EEG 7), a commercial bone button (*lower right,* EEG 5), and a buttonless flap (*lower left,* EEG 6; 29 cm long from pouch top to fringe bottom). All the pouches have plain backs.

The center pouch may have been made specifically to sell to Goodwin and, if so, leaving the metal cones off might have been viewed as an acceptable omission. This idea presumes that the other four pouches were made for Apache use and is of interest because some of Keith H. Basso's Cibecue informants in the 1960s and early 1970s indicated that only women's pouches had cones and that men's never did, presumably to avoid noise while hunting or on a raid. The presence of cones on these four rectangular pouches and their absence on all of the round pouches (Fig. 6.15) suggest that there may have been preferred or prescribed shapes for each sex as well.

Round buckskin pouches. Figure 6.15 and Color Illustration 12. The two pouches at top are painted front and back. The pouch at upper left (21403, front shown) had a flap closed with a metal button (now missing), and was purchased by Goodwin in 1932 in "Osborne's store" in Bylas. The pouch at upper right (EEG 10, back shown) has a flap closed with a mother-of-pearl button; it and the four beaded pouches are believed to have been obtained by Frieda Knoop at Carrizo between 1919 and 1923. The center pouch (EEG 12) has an open mouth and a less elaborate beaded back; the right center pouch (EEG 13) has an open mouth with a drawstring. The pouch at lower left (EEG 9; 36 cm long from pouch top to fringe bottom) has a metal button-closed flap (button missing), a metal button as part of the front ornamentation, and a plain back.

TOP: Figure 6.14. Rectangular buckskin pouches; see also Color Illustration 11 (ASM Neg. 56689).

BOTTOM: Figure 6.15. Round buckskin pouches; see also Color Illustration 12 (ASM Neg. 56688).

LEFT: Figure 6.16. Watch fobs; see also Color Illustration 13 (ASM Neg. 56628).

BOTTOM: Figure 6.17. Metal jewelry; see also Color Illustration 14 (ASM Neg. 64298).

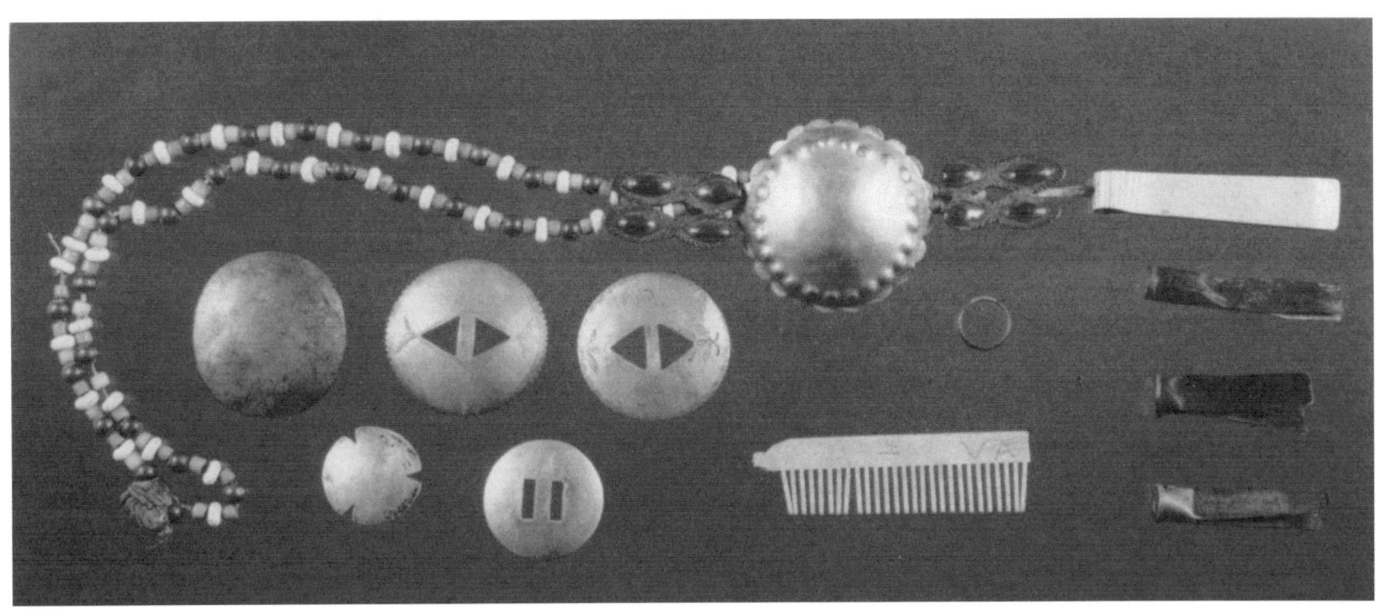

Clothing

Watch fobs. Figure 6.16 and Color Illustration 13. At upper left (EEG 23) and lower right (EEG 22) are two beadwork fobs collected at East Fork by the Guenthers between 1911 and 1919 (see also Fig. 7.7). From the top of the beadwork to the bottom of the fringe, EEG 22 is 15 cm long.

One fob of beadwork on buckskin (*upper right,* EEG 24) incorporates the claws from both feet of an eagle (probably Golden Eagle); it was made by Bertha Alchesay sometime in the 1920s and belonged either to her father, Chief Alchesay, or more probably her brother, Chief Baha. The use of eagle claws by Baha was probably not fortuitous, because he was a member of what Goodwin called clan I whose "relatives" included all eagles and hawks. Although eagles were relatives to other clans as well, as a prominent member of one of the largest White Mountain clans, Baha's use of eagle claws was wholly appropriate, in the same way that members of clans related to bears wore bear claws or paws (Goodwin 1942: 114–116, 578, 600). Apparently Rev. Guenther admired Baha's watch fob, for he commissioned Bertha to make a similar fob for him (*lower left,* EEG 25), which, however, appears to have had little or no use. An X-ray photograph of both these fobs reveals that Baha's has the eagle claws intact, with the bones in place and unmodified, and Rev. Guenther's has the chitin sheaths pulled off the bones and used "hollow."

The braided black and white horsehair fob (*bottom center,* EEG 54) made by Silas John Edwards, probably between 1912 and 1916 at East Fork, was purchased by the Guenthers. Silas John apparently learned how to make horsehair items and rattlesnake belts from his father, Yoohn, who may have learned to make such items in prison (Kessel 1976: 113, 153–154, 156). Silas' father was known to Anglos at Fort Apache as Johnnie Yuma, which could be construed as support for the belief that he learned these skills in prison. Braiding horsehair curios was one of a variety of crafts practiced by the prisoners at the Yuma Territorial Prison to sell to get pocket money. Silas, like his father, supported himself for a time by selling horsehair and rattlesnake items to the soldiers at Fort Apache. (See also Figs. 5.46, 6.21, and 7.41.)

Metal jewelry. Figure 6.17 and Color Illustration 14. The necklace (E–11) has glass beads strung on a buckskin thong with two Navajo(?) silver ornaments attached, a large silver(?) concho, and aluminum tweezers. On the part of the necklace hidden behind the concho are four small blue beads; whether their number and location have any ritual significance is unclear. This necklace, 57 cm long, belonged to Chrysotile Charlie of San Carlos and was acquired by Goodwin in 1938. Some tweezers like these, of silver and brass, were undoubtedly acquired from Navajo silversmiths (Frank and Holbrook 1978: 91; Rosnek and Stacey 1976: 62), although others may well have been made by the Apaches themselves and were used to pluck facial hair (see Mails 1974: 116, 224 for additional photos). More common were Apache-made tweezers fashioned by splitting and hammering flat brass rifle cartridges. Below the necklace (*right,* from top to bottom) are tweezers (21876) constructed from a Springfield 30–06 cartridge that was manufactured in March of 1909, tweezers (EEG 109) from a 45–70 cartridge (manufactured February 1887), and tweezers (EEG 110) from a 30–40 Krag (manufactured May 1895). All are military issue ammunition manufactured at the Frankfort Arsenal.

Although the more elaborate Western Apache bracelets, rings, and buttons were probably acquired in trade with the Navajo (Frank and Holbrook 1978: 58–59; Rosnek and Stacey 1976: 15), simpler ornaments and buttons undoubtedly were made by the Apaches themselves (Bourke 1891: 477), particularly those used as religious charms (Goodwin and Kaut 1954: 391–392, 396, 398; Frank and Holbrook 1978: 61; see also Figs. 7.33, 7.35). The last two tweezers above and the following items were apparently collected by the Knoops, presumably at Carrizo or East Fork, between 1919 and 1924. Left of the tweezers is a finger ring (EEG 62) hammered out of a U.S. twenty-five-cent piece (the flattened words "QUARTER DOLLAR" are still legible on the interior). A section of a commercial aluminum comb (EEG 231; 9.5 cm long) has "A–19" stamped into one face, perhaps the owner's tag number. The five buttons shown probably represent several different sources. That at top left (EEG 64–x–5) is probably Apache-made, apparently hammered out of a coin, with a Horstmann button-back soldered to it and five small notches filed along what is presumed to be the lower edge (see Fig. 6.1). The button at lower left (x–4) also may well be Apache-made. Two Plains-style conchos (*top center*, x–1; *top right*, x–2) probably were obtained in trade, but from what group is unknown. The design on the first is scratched on, the second is rocker–engraved; x–1 is a hammered-out fifty-centavo piece. The button at lower right (x–3) is commercially stamped out steel(?), probably originally a saddle ornament.

Beaded purses. Figure 6.18 and Color Illustration 15. Shown front *(top)* and back *(bottom)*, these beaded bags are believed to have been made by the same person, a daughter of Chief A–100, between 1911 and 1914. Mrs. Guenther used the buckskin bag at left (EEG 14, made in 1911 or 1912) as a purse for many years. During a visit she made to Watertown, South Dakota, Mrs. Guenther's mother-in-law (Mrs. Emma Guenther) and aunt (Emma's sister, Mrs. Augusta Rau) saw this bag and commissioned similar articles, each providing a commercial hinged clasp and chain. Mrs. Guenther believed she placed this order with the same woman that

Figure 6.18. Beaded purses, 1911 to 1914; see also Color Illustration 15 (*top*, ASM Neg. 56690; *bottom*, 56691).

Clothing

had made her bag, and the result was Emma's purse with a metal clasp (*center,* EEG 15) and Augusta's purse with a false tortoise-shell clasp (*right,* EEG 16), both made in 1914. Not including carrying straps, these bags (*left to right*) are 30 cm, 37 cm, and 39 cm long.

Dolls with modern clothing. Figure 6.19. Both dolls (EEG 169) were made by Mrs. Joe Crocker, probably in the 1950s, and were purchased by Mrs. Guenther. They have pliable cloth bodies with stiff reinforcing in the shoe soles and the man's hat. Sewing appears to be a mixture of handwork and sewing machine. The male doll (34 cm tall) has sequins and beads on his belt and bandanna and pencilled-on facial features. The female doll (30 cm tall) has a beadwork necklace, sewn-on facial features, and panties of the same material as her dress. Women in the 1930s usually wore "two blouses . . . at a time and almost always two or more skirts, the older ones underneath. This style of clothing was probably borrowed from the white womens' of the eighteen sixties, seventies and eighties. Heavy underskirts are often worn and the younger generation wear modern panties" (Goodwin A–66).

Figure 6.19. Dolls with modern clothing (ASM Neg. 56678).

Figure 6.20. Four Apache women at East Fork around 1912 to 1916 (photo by E. E. Guenther).

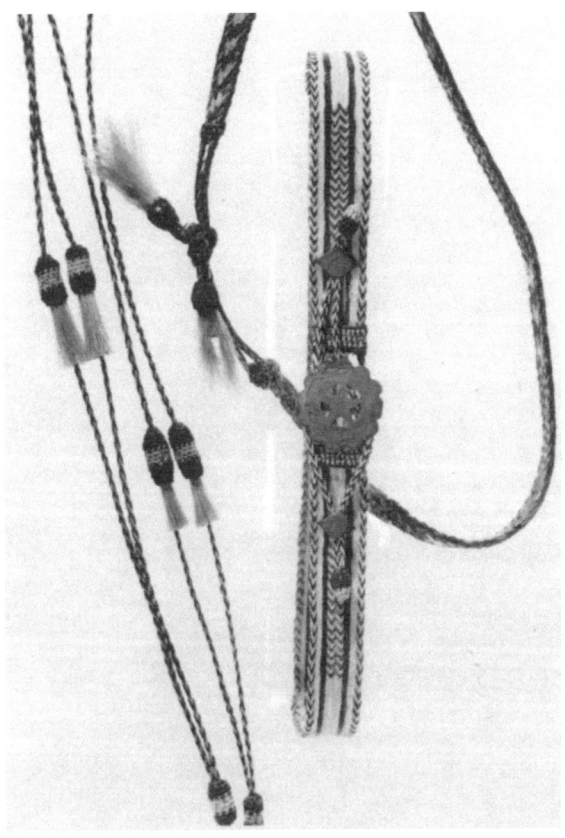

Figure 6.21. Horsehair hatbands and watch chains (ASM Neg. 56642).

Four Apache women at East Fork around 1912 to 1916. Figure 6.20. These women wear two-piece skirt and blouse "camp dresses," three have buckskin moccasins with "noses," and all but the youngest have shawls. They wear bead necklaces and bracelets and metal finger rings and bracelets.

Horsehair hatbands and watch chains. Figure 6.21. These items were made by Silas John Edwards, probably between 1912 and 1916 at East Fork, and were purchased by the Guenthers (see Figs. 5.46, 6.16). At left are two women's loop watch chains (EEG 55, 56; each about 59 cm long), black and white horsehair, to be worn around the neck, each equipped with a slide (at bottom) to cinch them up as far as the two decorative tassels, with a small loop at the bottom to attach the watch. At right are two hatbands, the lower (EEG 53) of black and white horsehair with tassels knotted in front, and the upper (EEG 52) of black and white horsehair with brown hair used to create the nested "Ws" in the middle of the band. Both are adjustable, the lower with a horsehair slide, the upper with a more elaborate arrangement of a central, circular rocker-engraved silver slide flanked by plain diamond-shaped silver slides. Whether the silverwork was done by Silas John or acquired from Navajos is unknown. (See also Fig. 6.22).

Clothing

Apache men wearing Anglo clothing. Figure 6.22. B–18 (Santa Cruz) and Carl Gass, probably at East Fork between 1911 and 1919, wearing all-Anglo clothing; the man at left has a horsehair hatband. In the 1930s Goodwin (A–66) noted: "Nowadays the men dress like white ranchers in store-bought shoes or cowboy boots, blue jeans or khaki pants with the typical jacket and broad-brimmed hat. All use underwear under which some of the older men still wear the gee-string. . . . Very few men have long hair anymore—only an old-timer here and there—and they have it cut like the Whites."

RIGHT: Figure 6.22. Apache men wearing Anglo clothing (photo by E. E. Guenther).

BOTTOM: Figure 6.23. Anna Price (photo by Grenville Goodwin, ASM Neg. 18265).

Anna Price. Figure 6.23. Anna Price and an unidentified companion in the 1930s wear skirts, blouses, and shawls. Anna has buckskin moccasins, and her friend wears shoes and carries a staff. Goodwin (1942: 513) noted that: "When old people began to have difficulty in walking, they used a straight, undecorated staff. . . . This they made for themselves or had made for them by a son or some other younger member of the family. The material was either the stalk of a yucca, bear grass, or sotol, or some heavier wood like willow or sycamore. Four feet, or slightly more in length, the staff often became shortened in time, because the old person frequently used it as a fire-poker." Anna Price probably witnessed the changeover from predominantly buckskin clothing to cloth garments. According to Goodwin (A–66) cloth was probably rare before about 1830, well-known and fairly common by 1850, but buckskin remained the most common material as late as the 1860s.

LEFT: Figure 6.24. Woman's dress and cane (ASM Neg. 56655).

OPPOSITE LEFT: Figure 6.25. T–necklaces, 1911 to 1944; see also Color Illustration 16 (ASM Neg. 56631).

OPPOSITE RIGHT: Figure 6.26. T–necklaces, 1911 to 1970; see also Color Illustration 17 (ASM Neg. 56632).

Woman's dress and cane. Figure 6.24. Frieda Knoop acquired this blue paisley print cotton dress and plaid shawl (EEG 214) at East Fork in 1923 or 1924. Both the skirt and separate blouse are decorated with red, yellow, and white trim and have string ties. Most of the stitching was done on a sewing machine, and Goodwin (A–66) noted that in the 1930s nearly every camp had a sewing machine, purchased from traveling salesmen or on the installment plan, and that "the sewing machine man is a familiar figure seen going from one dwelling to another trying to collect payments."

The cane (EEG 47; 94 cm tall, 3 cm in diameter) was acquired at an unknown date from an old Apache woman. Mrs. Guenther wondered if it was store-bought because of the tight curve on this relatively heavy piece of wood, but said she had seen several canes of this type whose owners all claimed to have made them themselves.

Clothing

T–necklaces. Figure 6.25 and Color Illustration 16. The origin of this type of woman's beaded necklace, which appears to be unique to the Western Apache, is unknown at present. The earliest documented example dates some years prior to 1912 (Fig. 7.5). In recent years T–necklaces are usually worn by the girls at a girl's puberty ceremony, and now commonly are made specifically to sell. These five relatively early examples undoubtedly were made to be worn. At bottom left (EEG 150) is the necklace of Mary Keyes (daughter of Jack Keyes, Edgar Guenther's first interpreter), worn at her puberty dance at East Fork in 1911; it has a large Plains-like, rocker-engraved silver concho. The necklace at bottom center (EEG 155) was obtained around 1914, and those at bottom right (EEG 154) and top right (EEG 153) date between 1911 and 1922; all are from East Fork. At top left is the necklace worn by Mrs. Nora Vlasquez Tortice at her dance on 14 July 1944 (EEG 28); it is 40 cm high, including fringe.

T–necklaces. Figure 6.26 and Color Illustration 17. Both old, personal necklaces and new, made-for-sale examples are in this selection. The necklace at bottom right (EEG 149) came from East Fork between 1911 and 1918, and that at upper left (EEG 152) between 1911 and 1922. The large necklace (*bottom left*, EEG 156) was probably made in the 1960s or 1970s in the Whiteriver area; the main body is 39 cm tall, including the fringe. The necklace with American flags and eagles (EEG 157) was obtained in Whiteriver around 1970. The necklace with a *gaan* dancer (EEG 159) was made by Sylvania (Alchesay) Lee of Whiteriver. Sylvania is thought to be the first person to use *gaan* motifs on T–necklaces, beginning around 1968. It is unknown how many of this style she made; however, the one shown here was the fourth that Mrs. Guenther acquired (two of which are still owned by her children), purchased about a week before Sylvania was killed in a car accident in 1974. Since then other necklace makers have started using *gaan* motifs on T–necklaces. Through time, at least as represented by the Guenther collection, the average width of T–necklaces from the East Fork and Whiteriver area has steadily increased, the most recent being over twice as wide as the earliest. All the earlier necklaces appear to be woven with a net-like "peyote stitch" construction (Pardue 1982), but more recent pieces are all loom made.

Shawl necklace. Figure 6.27. Beaded collars or shawl-type necklaces appear to have been most common and the most developed among Colorado River groups, including the Yuma (Quechan), Mohave, and Cocopa (Forde 1931: 231; Stewart 1983, Fig. 12; Williams 1983, Figs. 5, 6). The Western Apache may have learned this netted type of beading, or obtained examples to copy, from their closer neighbors to the west, the Yavapai, or possibly learned directly from the Yuma when some of the latter were placed briefly on the San Carlos Reservation in the last quarter of the 1800s (Goodwin 1942: 88). This example (EEG 160) was made sometime in the 1920s and obtained by the Guenthers at either Whiteriver or East Fork. Its inside diameter is about 18 cm, maximum dimension is about 50 cm.

Shawl necklace. Figure 6.28 and Color Illustration 18. This beadwork shawl or collar (EEG 162) lacks provenience data. It appears to be recent (1960s or 1970s?) and was probably purchased in Whiteriver by Mrs. Guenther. It has cloth ties at top and small commercial bells at the end of each loop of the necklace's edge. The whole necklace measures approximately 90 cm across and, when worn, completely covers the shoulders but does not meet in back. In recent years a shawl necklace has been commonly worn under a T–necklace by a girl at her puberty dance or at special public functions where she wanted to be as dressed-up as possible (see the covers of *Arizona Highways,* July 1962 and July 1977).

Beaded and beadwork belts. Figure 6.29 and Color Illustration 19. These belts, ranging in length from 70 to 90 cm, are from the Guenther collection but lack specific provenience information. The belts at top (EEG 188; 5 cm wide), center (EEG 189), and bottom (EEG 190) are all carefully made, are cloth-backed, have hook-and-eye fasteners, and are completely clean and undamaged, suggesting they are relatively new; they were purchased by Mrs. Guenther no later than 1961. The belt second from the top with butterfly and plant designs (EEG 193) is cloth-backed and sewn onto a commercial, size 32 "HICKOK" brand leather belt with a brass buckle with the letter "K" on it; this belt may well have belonged to Arnold Knoop, Frieda's husband, and could have been

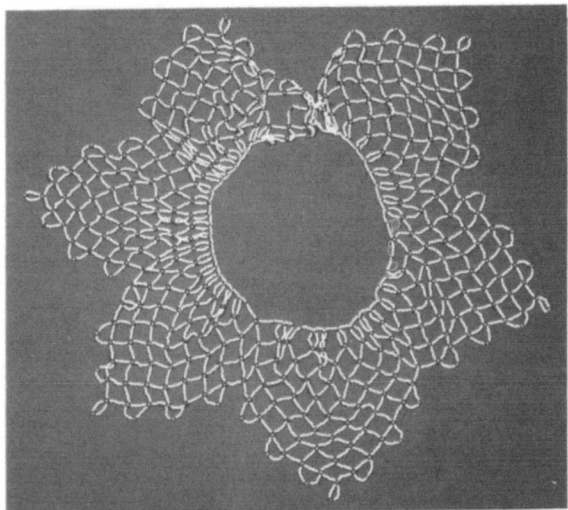

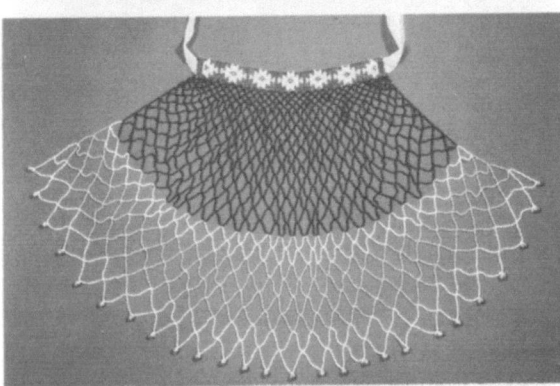

TOP: Figure 6.27. Shawl necklace (ASM Neg. 56640).

MIDDLE: Figure 6.28. Shawl necklace; see also Color Illustration 18 (ASM Neg. 56641).

BOTTOM: Figure 6.29. Beaded and beadwork belts; see also Color Illustration 19 (ASM Neg. 64454).

Clothing

made between 1919 and 1924 at Carrizo or East Fork. The remaining three belts all show wear or damage, but their ages are unknown. The top diagonal belt (EEG 191) and the second belt from the bottom (EEG 192) are both cloth-backed with hook-and-eye fasteners. The lower diagonal belt (EEG 194) has cloth ties, no backing, is rather short (52 cm), and conceivably could have been a headband.

Commercial jewelry and accessories. Figure 6.30. At top is a beaded barrette or hair clip (E–9885) made by Gloria Elgo at San Carlos in 1971. The beaded buckskin wallet(?) at left (EEG 27; 11.5 cm long) probably was made in the early 1960s, reportedly by Mrs. Nora Vlasquez Tortice of Whiteriver. Surrounding it is a juniper berry seed necklace (EEG 210) of unknown age from the Whiteriver area; each tassel is tipped with three gold-colored glass beads. At bottom left and center are two pairs of earrings for pierced ears, purchased from Harry Tortice (Nora's son) in the late 1960s or 1970s. The two miniature burden baskets (the left pair, EEG 124) are woven of agave(?) with buckskin trim and metal tinklers. To their right is a pair of miniature beaded buckskin moccasins (EEG 132). The beaded buckskin keyring (*far right*, 74–68–1) was made in 1974 in the Fort Apache area. The "rope" necklace (*right*, EEG 186), from either Whiteriver or East Fork, consists of a hollow beaded tube with tassels; its age is uncertain, but Gloria Guenther noted that when she arrived in Whiteriver in 1947, there were no necklaces of this style. However, Curtis (1907–1930, Plate 61) shows a Mohave woman wearing a necklace of this style, suggesting the possibility that it, along with shawl-type necklaces, was inspired among the Western Apache by the beadwork of their more westerly neighbors. Also, the American Museum of Natural History possesses a White Mountain Apache example of this type of necklace that was collected in 1910 (AMNH Cat. 50/9126). The rope necklace surrounds a rounded buckskin-backed beaded earring with a commercial metal screw (EEG 184), which is also from either Whiteriver or East Fork. Above this earring is a miniature cradleboard (EEG 133); it was designed as a pendant for a woman's dress, to be pinned through the back of the

Figure 6.30. Commercial jewelry and accessories (ASM Neg. 56634).

beaded buckskin rectangle. Made in the late 1960s, this pendant probably was inspired by the two pendants at center. Both are in the shape of a miniature *tus* of beads, the upper (EEG 147) with a beaded buckskin rectangle with a safety pin sewn into it, and the lower (EEG 148) with a suspension loop of beads. According to Mrs. Guenther, both were made by B–6's daughter at East Fork, the first apparently on her own, the second at Mrs. Guenther's request, around 1918 and 1919, respectively, when the girl was about seventeen and a student at the East Fork school.

Figure 6.31. Commercial craft items; see also Color Illustration 20 (ASM Neg. 56627).

Commercial craft items. Figure 6.31 and Color Illustration 20. The three pairs of miniature buckskin moccasins (*upper right,* EEG 119, 121, 123) were obtained from Harry Tortice, probably in the late 1960s; the smallest pair is 2 cm high excluding the suspension thong. At bottom right (EEG 170) is the first attempt at basketry by an unidentified Whiteriver girl. The large beaded pouch (*center,* EEG 26; 26 cm tall, excluding thong and fringe) with an abalone bangle covering the button probably was made by Mrs. Nora Vlasquez Tortice in the early 1960s. The use of a *gaan* motif on secular items is a relatively recent development, perhaps related to increasing commercialization of various crafts. For this pouch, in particular, the fact that the beadwork forms the front face of the pouch, with no buckskin backing, further illustrates its strictly commercial intent. Below it are two miniature cradleboards (EEG 134, 135) made in the late 1960s, each complete with a miniature cloth doll. At upper left is a "medicine bean"; this one (EEG 185) is a bead-encased coral bean of unknown age from the Whiteriver or East Fork area. Previously used as protective amulets, these beans are now largely a curio item (Fig. 7.17). Below it is a beaded doll (EEG 187) with a cloth core and beadwork suspension loop, age unknown, from the Whiteriver or East Fork areas. Below it is a miniature beadwork burden basket (EEG 171) with a white plastic bottle cap(?) as a foundation; it was made in early 1980 by an unidentified Whiteriver girl. At bottom left are two of an original set of eleven beadwork napkin rings (EEG 17, 18), possibly made as early as the 1920s, commissioned by the Guenthers of an unknown person in the Whiteriver or East Fork area. Rev. and Mrs. Guenther and each of their children had one. (See Tanner 1968, Fig. 7.13 *right,* for more napkin rings and "medicine beans.")

Chapter Seven
Ritual

Alan Ferg and William B. Kessel

OVERLEAF: **Masked dancers.** Figure 7.1. A group of masked dancers impersonating the supernatural spirits, or *gaan*. These dancers perform at various curing ceremonies and at a girl's puberty ceremony. They have been variously referred to as Crown Dancers and, incorrectly, as Devil Dancers or as actually being the Mountain Spirits or *gaan* that they are representing. This group of dancers posed for Forman G. Hanna in the Red Knolls Amphitheater, a natural amphitheater near Eden in Graham County, on 6 December 1925. The masks these dancers are wearing may well have been made by the same man that made those pictured in Figure 7.8, judging by the construction and decoration of both sets. McCoy (1985) provides a general discussion of *gaan* masks and dancers. (Photo courtesy of the Arizona Historical Society, Neg. 65199.)

Girl's puberty ceremony buckskin dress. Figure 7.2 and Color Illustration 21. The girl's puberty ceremony (*na ih es*), also known as a coming-out dance or sunrise dance, is a complex ceremony held for a pubescent girl, after which

Figure 7.2. Girl's puberty ceremony buckskin dress; see also Color Illustration 21 (ASM Neg. 56653).

Ritual

she has "come of age" and is considered an adult. The ceremony promotes longevity, physical strength, a good temperament, and prosperity for the girl. For the community it is a time to reaffirm kinship ties, participate in social dancing, and benefit from the supernatural power with which the girl is imbued for the four days following the ceremony. During these days she can cure sickness, and bring rain by sprinkling water on the cane given to her for her ceremony. *Gaan* dancers also commonly perform at puberty ceremonies, and it is the combined images of *gaan* dancers and the pubescent girl in her elaborate buckskin dress at *na ih es* that most non-Apaches first visualize when thinking of Western Apache ritual. Basso (1966) has published a full discussion of this ceremony.

For the ceremony, the pubescent girl is provided with a number of items, the most conspicuous of which is her buckskin dress, consisting of a poncho and skirt. The example shown here (21329) was made by David Longstreet for his daughter as a replacement for the dress she had actually worn at her puberty ceremony (which he had also made). She had sold her *na ih es* dress, apparently later regretted it, and asked her father to make her another one to keep (Goodwin A–66). Whether this dress was ever given to her is unknown, but Goodwin purchased it from David Longstreet in 1935. Longstreet had learned to make puberty dresses from his mother, and both of them were acknowledged as very skillful. They made several, both for relatives and when commissioned by others (see the *na ih es* poncho on the structure behind Longstreet in Basso 1971: 186). In the mid-1800s a person commissioning a dress paid with a horse or cow or buckskin (when these items were very valuable) and had to provide the buckskins for the dress itself. A relative could borrow such a dress for free, but a nonrelative was expected to pay something substantial for this privilege such as a horse or buckskin (Goodwin A–66). Girls wore the dress at *na ih es* and anytime thereafter until their marriage and first pregnancy. At that time the dress might be given to a younger sister or close maternal relative.

This dress required six buckskins. For the poncho, one buckskin made up the body of the garment, and two more were needed for the fringes. Three more buckskins were used for the skirt, one each for the front, the back, and the fringes. In addition to the extensive fringes, ornamentation included cutting circular tabs around the bottom of the poncho and adding bands of beadwork, yellow paint, and innumerable tin cones on the poncho and skirt. The use of decorative metal cones on puberty dresses may go back into the 1700s and conceivably into the 1600s, although in early times metal was much scarcer and the number of cones proportionately less. Palmer Valor (Goodwin A–66) said that "long ago" dresses had only plain fringes. David Longstreet (Goodwin A–66) stated: "I don't remember a time when we had no metal dangles like this, though I have heard that long ago there were none. In the old days when our people went raiding in Mexico, they would capture tin from the Mexicans and bring it home to make these dangles. A girl who had no relatives to go on raids must do without metal dangles on her dress." Raiding into Mexico goes back to the late 1600s (Goodwin 1942: 94), but the use of metal cones probably did not become common until tin cans became readily available in the 1800s. During the years of hostilities with the U.S. Army, use of cones was probably kept to a minimum because they might make noise at inopportune times (see Fig. 6.14). With the establishment of the reservations, the numerous sources of cans and sheet metal that accompanied them, and a growing tourist market for crafts, the use of decorative cones assumed at least the levels of popularity that they enjoy today. It is possible that prior to the use of metal, or while metal was scarce, the Western Apache might have used perforated deer hoofs as decorative dangles as did their neighbors, the Southeastern Yavapai (Gifford 1932: 227), although no Western Apache examples are familiar to the authors. Frank and Holbrook (1978: 54) illustrate a Navajo awl or needle case from the 1870s that uses *both* deer hoofs and brass cones as bangles.

The skins from the deer's legs were sewn to the front and back corners of the poncho; these were ornamental, but it was apparently important to Longstreet "to show that the garment is truly made from the skin of a black-tailed deer" (Goodwin A–66).

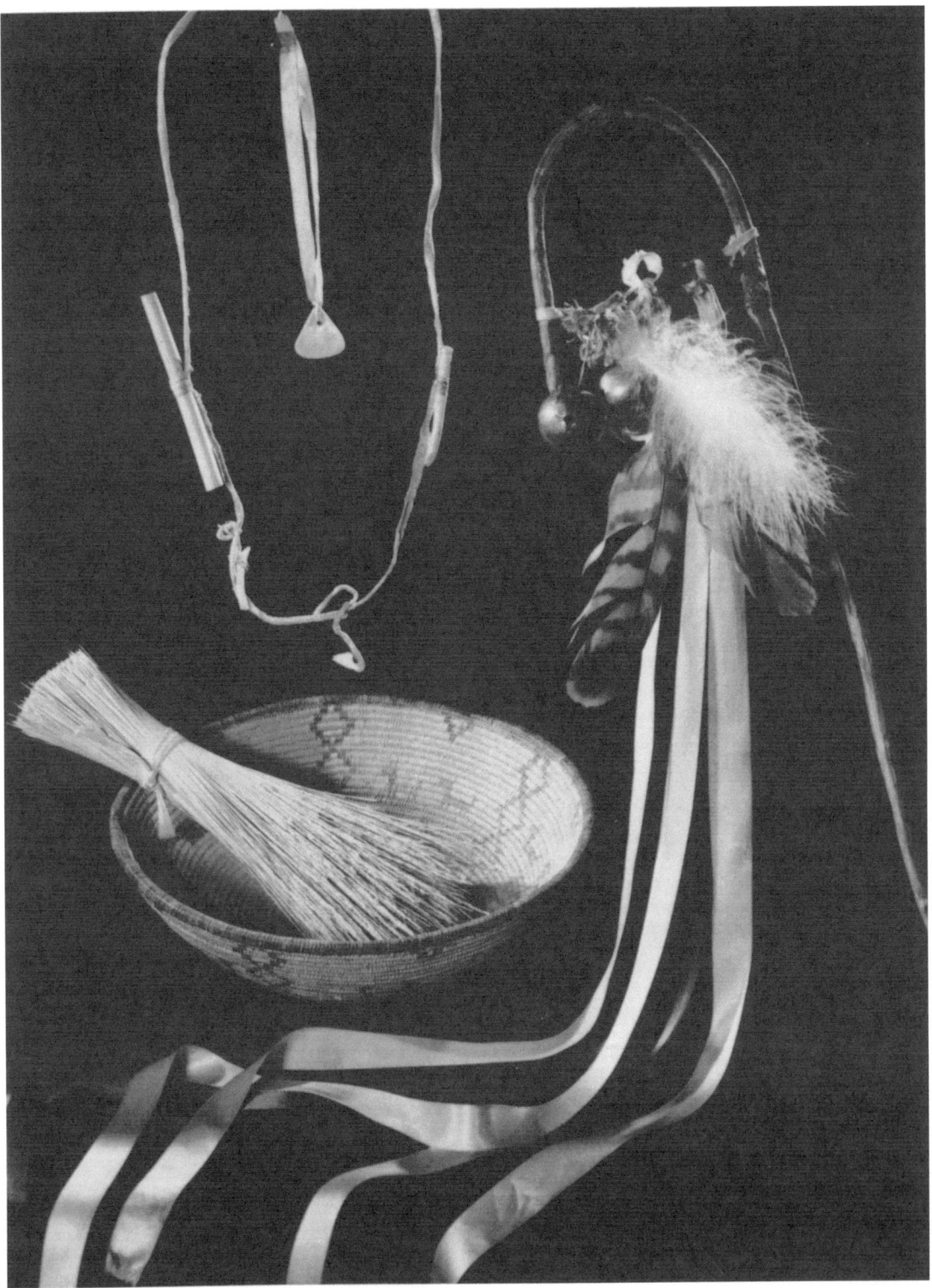

Figure 7.3. Girl's puberty ceremony paraphernalia; see also Color Illustration 22 (ASM Neg. 56702).

Ritual

Girl's puberty ceremony paraphernalia. Figure 7.3 and Color Illustration 22. The girl's cane (*right*, EEG 48) was obtained by the Knoops at either Carrizo or East Fork between 1919 and 1924. This cane is an integral part of several phases of *na ih es*, and in later years may be used as a walking staff. It is made from a peeled stick bent into a crook at one end and held in place with a buckskin thong, and this one is just over a meter long. To the buckskin are tied an eagle down feather, an owl wing feather, three large commercial metal bells, and four ribbons (black, green, yellow, tan) representing the cardinal directions, all knotted at their midpoints around the buckskin thong to create eight streamers. Basso (1966: 143–145) notes other particulars of manufacture, including the usual presence of a turquoise bead and oriole feathers, the latter because orioles are happy and have a good disposition and will cause the girl to be the same way.

At top is a drinking tube and a scratching stick tied to a buckskin thong loop about 30 cm in diameter (21869) that was worn by the pubescent girl. Both the cane tube and the carved scratching stick each have a zigzag line lightly incised down their length, and they and the buckskin loop are liberally coated with yellow ochre. Oriole feathers might also be attached to the drinking tube, as they may be on the cane. Another such necklace collected by Goodwin (21398, not illustrated) does have oriole feathers tied to *two* drinking tubes that are tied to each other at right angles, forming a cross. On the necklace illustrated here, a band fragment from a prehistoric *Glycymeris* shell bracelet is tied below the drinking tube with a piece of string. Although this shell charm is not coated with ochre and appears to be a later addition, it is not inappropriate in its attachment to the necklace inasmuch as shell is symbolic of Changing Woman (also known as White-Shell-Woman). Throughout her ceremony, and particularly for the four days thereafter when she has "power" and is holy, the pubescent girl is to drink only through the tube (if water touches her lips she would develop facial hair, which was considered unsightly on both women and men) and scratch only with the stick (else sores appear where she touched herself; Basso 1966: 145, 160). On a boy's first two raids he was subject to a number of proscriptions and various types of training. Along with a special buckskin cap he was given a necklace with a drinking tube and scratcher identical to a girl's puberty example, for much the same reasons (Basso 1971: 288–298). The girl's necklace shown here was made by David Longstreet at Bylas, probably in 1932.

Suspended within the necklace is an abalone pendant (EGG 172; about 3 cm high) of the type worn in the pubescent girl's hair, the pendant resting on her forehead. It is ground to shape from a piece of Black Abalone *(Haliotis cracherodii)*, with a drilled suspension hole, and strung on a yellow ribbon. Being made of shell, this pendant symbolizes the girl's personification of Changing Woman. Like the scratching stick and drinking tube, it is worn for the four days following the ceremony (Basso 1966: 160), although David Longstreet said it was worn for two months and that the girl "takes it off going into . . . water as it comes from water and she might get sickness from that" (Goodwin A–72).

At lower left is a bowl basket (EEG 103; 32 cm in diameter) and a hair brush of Spike Muhly grass stalks tied with a yellow ribbon (EEG 104). These are reportedly the basket and brush used to dispense pollen at a large dance held in 1943 for five girls at Whiteriver and featured in Reg Manning's regular newspaper cartoon, "Big Parade," in *The Arizona Republic* (Phoenix) for 10 September 1943. The uneven end of the hair brush was used to spread pollen, but it is the even end that is used to brush hair.

Girl's buckskin puberty poncho. Figure 7.4. The Guenthers obtained this poncho (EEG 31) probably around 1950 in Whiteriver. When this piece was originally made is unknown, but in the course of being repeatedly loaned out by the Guenthers to Apache friends to use at puberty ceremonies, it underwent numerous minor modifications. For example, in a photo of a girl's puberty ceremony published in Baldwin (1965: 114), the pubescent girl's sponsor is wearing this poncho, which on that occasion had some sort of bead or sequin decoration sewn onto the front, just below the head-opening; this decoration is no longer present. This same poncho is in another photo (of the same ceremony?) on the preceding page (Baldin 1965: 113). The body is

Figure 7.4. Girl's buckskin puberty poncho (ASM Neg. 56649).

Ritual

made from a single buckskin, with the fringes probably made from another one or two skins. The head-opening was made by cutting an "X" in the center of the buckskin and folding back the four triangular flaps so created. This makes four "lapels" (two front, two back), whose corners are secured here by four commercial faceted plastic "jewels" (red, green, blue, and yellow for the cardinal directions) and whose edges are outlined in a continuous band of beadwork. Other decoration includes the traditional yellow ochre around the shoulders, beadwork, several kinds of commercial metal bells and buttons, red cloth with sequins around the bottom, many large cone tinklers cut from cans (reading the inside of the cones reveals many to be from coffee and baking powder cans), and a fine fringe of buckskin thongs, each thong sewn once through the poncho edge to make two fringes. The fringes are up to 65 cm long, and total height of the poncho, fringe included, is 115 cm.

Girl's puberty T–necklace. Figure 7.5 and Color Illustration 23. This necklace (EEG 158) was given to the Guenthers by John Riley sometime between December 1912, when he married his sixth wife, and his death in 1916. Although Mary Keyes' T–necklace (Fig. 6.25) was collected in 1911, this necklace was reputedly worn by each of Riley's wives at her wedding, presumably making it considerably older than 1912. Although this particular necklace was apparently worn in weddings, it is of the type commonly worn by a girl at her puberty ceremony and is illustrated here as the earliest known example of a T–necklace. Now an apparently standard part of the pubescent girl's attire (Figs. 6.25, 6.26), T–necklaces seem only to have been in existence since about the turn of the century, and early photographs of puberty ceremonies often do not show them (Fig. 7.6).

The vertical panel is 4.2 cm wide and total height of the necklace is 36 cm. It is woven with a peyote stitch. The incorporation of a cross-and-crescent motif into the design at the top and bottom of the vertical panel is unusal. Whether its use is purely decorative, religious, or somehow related to the 1903 to 1906 religious movement among the Western Apache (see Figs. 7.32–7.39) is unknown.

Figure 7.5. Girl's puberty T–necklace, made before 1912; see also Color Illustration 23 (ASM Neg. 64453).

Sadie Stone's puberty ceremony. Figure 7.6. The first girl's puberty ceremony that the Guenthers attended after arriving in Arizona was that of Sadie Stone, in the summer of 1912 near East Fork. Shown here is Sadie Stone in a buckskin poncho and cloth skirt, holding her cane, with her grandfather, Chief Y–1, on her right (wearing gloves and breechclout). Sadie's father, Lambert Stone, is supposedly also in the photo, but has not been identified. At far left, hiding his face behind his blanket, is Johnson O'Hell. Y–1 was also known as Y–1 #1, Skilskoy, and William White (U.S. Army Census 1906). On the ground in front of Sadie are the numerous blankets on which she will be dancing, kneeling, and lying during various phases of the ceremony. Y–1 later gave the Guenthers the bowl basket used to dispense pollen at this ceremony (see Fig. 5.38).

Lambert Stone and several hundred other Apaches (mostly White Mountain) were featured in the 1950 movie "Broken Arrow," a story of the 1872 peace negotiations between the Chiricahua Apache and the U.S. Army conducted by Cochise (played by Jeff Chandler) and Tom Jeffords (James Stewart). Utley (1977) reports fully on the actual events. It was at this time that Geronimo broke with Cochise, choosing not to accept the offer of a reservation. When being cast for the picture, Lambert Stone reportedly said: "It was a bad thing when I went with Geronimo. I will play a part [in the movie], but this time I must do the right thing and stay with Cochise. He was the true leader" (*The Arizona Daily Star*

Figure 7.6. Sadie Stone's puberty ceremony (photo by E. E. Guenther).

Ritual

1950). "Broken Arrow" contains what are probably the most accurate portrayals of Apache material culture in a movie to date.

Girl's puberty ceremony near Fort Apache. Figure 7.7. Taken between 1912 and probably 1919 by E. E. Guenther, this photo shows an unidentified girl at her puberty ceremony, wearing a cloth dress with eagle feathers apparently attached across the shoulders. She is also wearing a beadwork T–necklace, partly obscured by the eagle feathers. Her cane is by her side. The man to her right holds a buckskin-headed drum and curved drumstick (see Fig. 8.13). Also the fourth man from the left in the front row is wearing a beadwork watch fob similar to those collected by the Guenthers (see Fig. 6.16).

Set of *gaan* dancers' masks. Figure 7.8 and Color Illustrations 24 and 25. Early in his field work among the Apache, Goodwin apparently served as an intermediary for the Arizona State Museum in the purchase of this set of masks (19839 through 19843), accessioned in August 1932 and acquired in Bylas, "Purchased from John Robison [sic], thru Grenville Goodwin." The catalogue card for one of the masks bears the cryptic remark: "One of a set of Devil Dancer masks said to be *the first made at Bylas in 1901*" (emphasis ours). Whether this implies that this was the first set *ever* made at Bylas (which seems unlikely), or that it is simply the first set *of 1901*, is unclear. Regardless, this set of masks serves nicely to document the shapes and designs in use in the Bylas area at the turn of the century. Soon

Figure 7.7. Girl's puberty ceremony near Fort Apache (photo by E. E. Guenther).

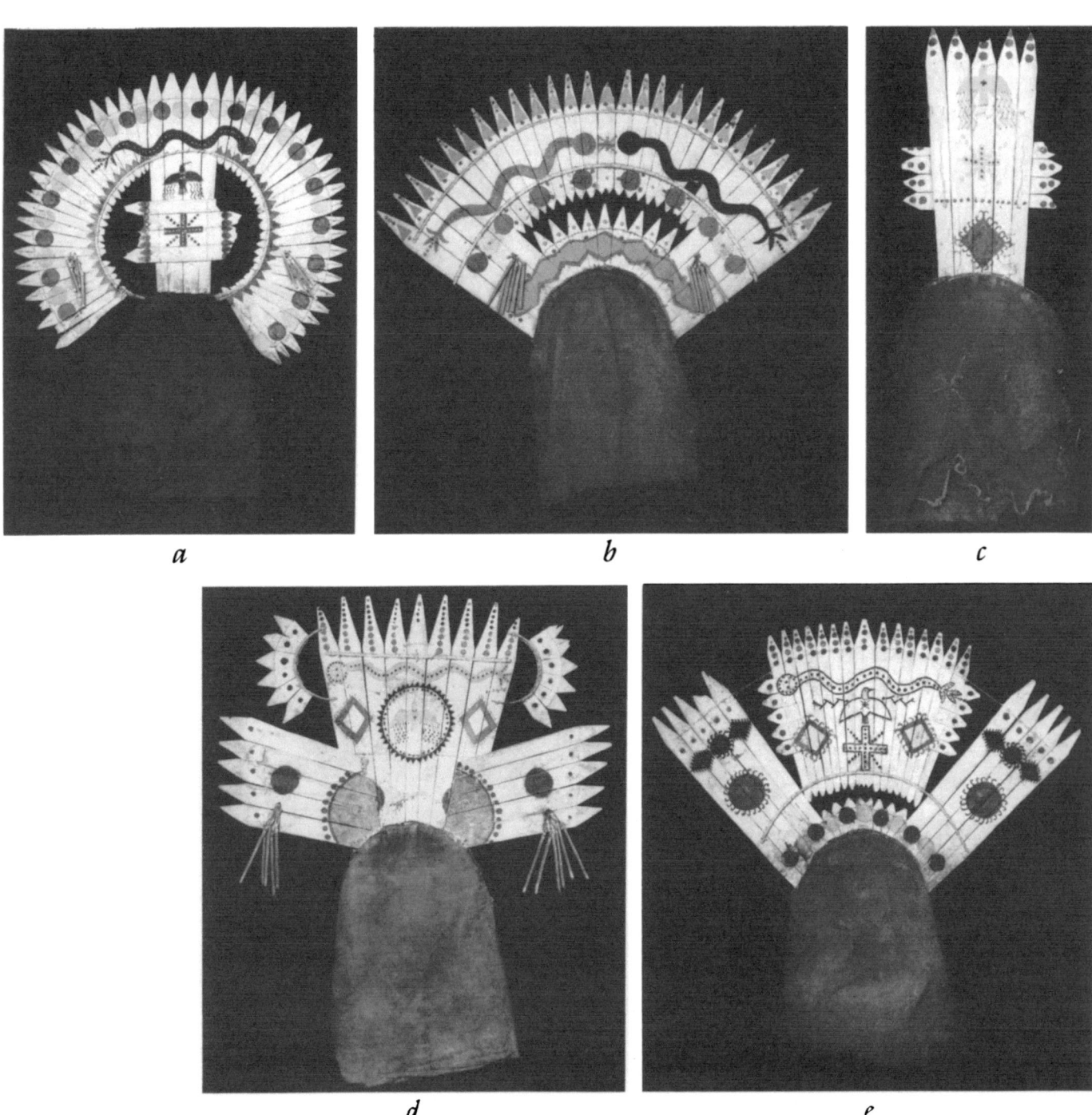

Figure 7.8a–e. Front of *gaan* masks made by John Robinson in 1901; see also Color Illustrations 24 and 25 (ASM Neg. numbers in text).

Ritual

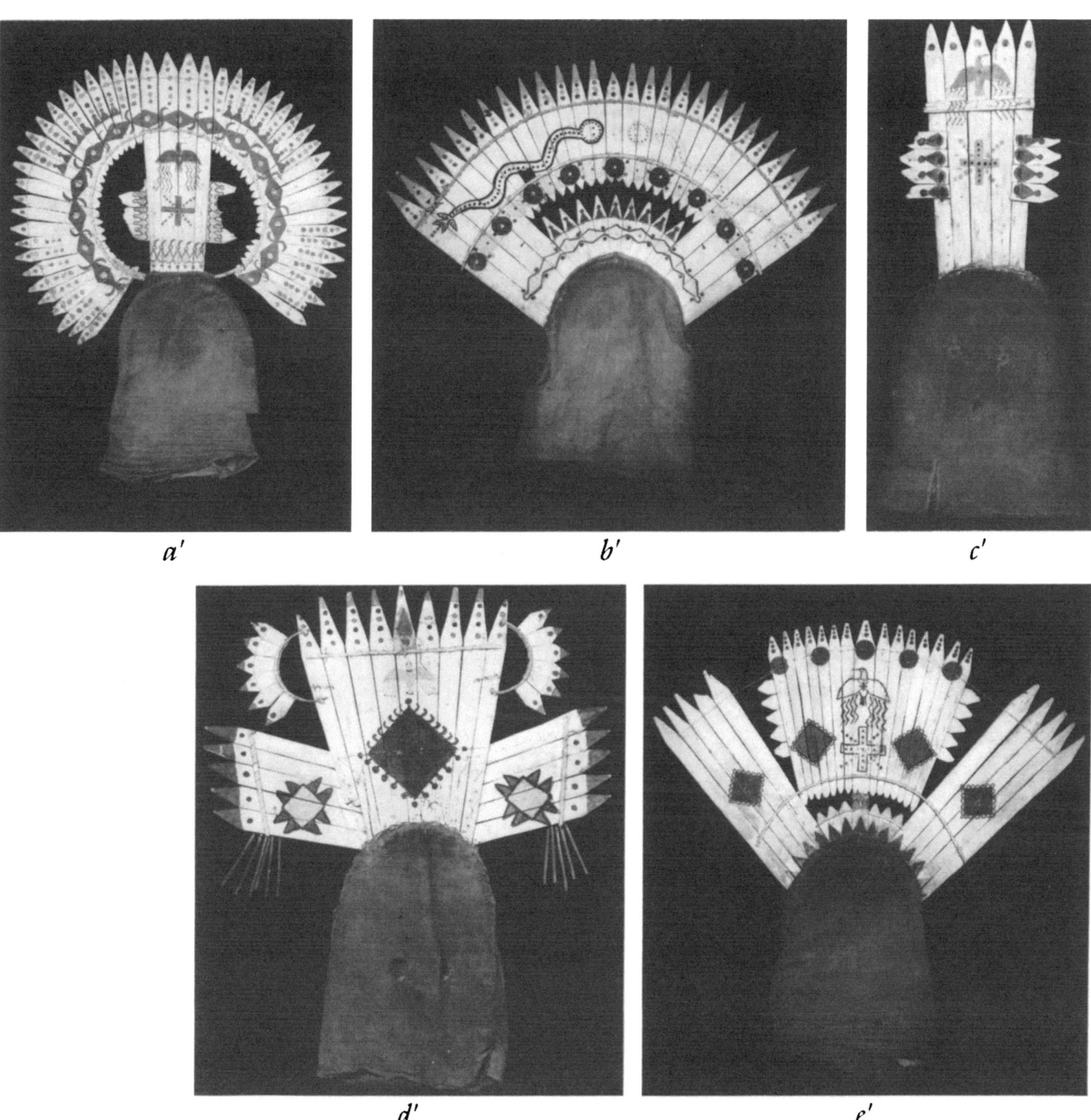

Figure 7.8a′–e′. Back of *gaan* masks made by John Robinson in 1901 (ASM Neg. numbers in text).

after their purchase, additional documentation on these masks was obtained by Dorothy Francis Gay, a University of Arizona student working on her Master's thesis in anthropology (Gay 1933). She interviewed "John Robinson, a Devil Dance Priest at Bylas" as to the meanings of the designs on this set of masks, which he made "many years ago" (Gay 1933: 26, 30, 32). After examining the masks' construction, the designs on them are discussed.

All *gaan* masks have the same basic construction. The laths are all of split yucca or sotol stalks, shaved to a half centimeter or less in thickness, and secured to each other and to supporting framework pieces with twine, buckskin thongs, sinew, small nails, or, in more recent specimens, glue. This fan-shaped assembly is set into the top of a semicircular (or more precisely, an upside down "U") stick, which has been partially split to receive it. This U–shaped headpiece slides down on either side of the head and cloth strips tied to each of its ends are tied together under the chin to keep the mask on. A cloth hood (formerly buckskin) is sewn over the headpiece, usually black in color, but sometimes gray, white, or painted, especially the clown's. When the mask is put on, holes are cut for the eyes and mouth, and a red strip of cloth passes around the back of the neck and across the chin, helping to keep the mask on tightly; eagle feathers often hang down from this red strip. Short sticks are tied in a bunch on either side of a mask's front and clack when the dancer shakes his head.

The masks shown here have a combination of buckskin and twine ties and at one time had eagle down feathers attached to the tips of some of the laths (see Fig. 7.1). The hoods are of dyed cloth bags; on several the company names are legible. Figure 7.8*a* and *a'* (19839; *a*, ASM Neg. 64283; *a'*, 64274) is 66 cm wide and has multiple eye and mouth holes on the front. Figure 7.8*b* and *b'* (19840; *b*, ASM Neg. 64278; *b'*, 64277) is 81 cm wide, has eye and mouth holes on the front and a hood made from an "El Toro Western Portland Cement" bag. The clown mask, Figure 7.8*c* and *c'* (19843; *c*, ASM Neg. 64285; *c'*, 64289), is 25 cm wide, has eye and mouth holes front and back and a hood of another Western Portland cement bag. Figure 7.8*d* and *d'* (19841; *d*, ASM Neg. 64276; *d'*, 64275) is 63 cm wide, has eye and mouth holes front and back, and a hood of a "STAR Semi-Hard Wheat Valley Milling Safford, Arizona" bag. Figure 7.8*e* and *e'* (19842; *e*, ASM Neg. 64279; *e'*, 64280) is 76 cm wide, has eye and mouth holes on the front and a hood made from a "Gila Valley Mills" bag. The skins of walnuts were often used to make black dye for cloth.

Gay (1933: 5) was commendably cautious in "interpreting" the designs used on these masks. Also, because she was working through an interpreter (Gay 1933: 31), we have no way of knowing how much simplification or subtle alteration of meaning John Robinson's remarks may have undergone. Nevertheless, any early record of such explanations is of interest, especially because John Robinson was apparently a medicine man and had painted, or had presumably supervised the painting, of these masks himself. Gay (1933: 30–33, Plates 20–22) has three pages of designs drawn by John Robinson and his explanations of them. Based on these, Gay identifies the designs on the front of masks 7.8*a*, *b*, and *d*. The snakelike figures are:

> . . . the voice of the lightning, or the reverberations that are heard after the clap of thunder. John Robinson was most emphatic in stating that this was not a snake, nor was it intended to represent one. He gave an ingenious explanation for the forked tail: 'The forks of the tail work in the same way that the antennae of a radio do. The sound is caught by them and is amplified, and thus we are able to hear it.'

The birds are hummingbirds, the creature that lead the Apache into upper worlds and that presently serves as a messenger between the Apaches and the supernaturals (Figs. 7.21, 7.27; Goddard 1918: 27–28). A cross with dots between its arms appears on all of the masks except 7.8*d* and *d'* and is part of a representation of the sun (or possibly Sun, the supernatural?); the serrated circle around the hummingbird on 7.8*d* is likewise identified as a partial sun symbol. The complete sun symbol has the cross within the circle, although in this instance, with its beak straight up, the hummingbird presents a cruciform outline and might be considered the equivalent, or a variety, of a cross.

Although these "explanations" leave us without any real understanding of the specific purpose of such designs on the masks or of the possible significance of their various groupings and color combinations, they do illustrate the conservative nature of religious motifs among the Western Apache. John Robinson supposedly learned "the way these things are to be drawn" from his father, and modern (1980) *gaan* dancers' masks from the San Carlos area continue to have "lightning"-snake, "sun," hummingbird, and cross designs.

Three final points are considered: (1) the age of these particular masks, (2) the relationship between lightning and snakes, and (3) the time-depth of lightning-snake designs. These masks were ostensibly made in 1901 but were not acquired from Robinson until 1932. Where had they been for thirty years? Supposedly such masks would have been used in 1901 and then permanently cached, as was expected of this type of ritual item. These masks also *strongly* resemble masks in use in 1925 that, based on similarities of construction, decoration, time, and place, also may have been made by John Robinson (compare Figs. 7.1 and 7.8). Conceivably the masks in Figure 7.8 could date to the 1920s with the 1901 date being a miscommunication; additional research on John Robinson, the Western Portland Cement Company, the Gila Valley Mills or Valley Milling in Safford might resolve the matter. For now, however, these masks are considered as having been made in 1901.

John Robinson's "emphatic" statement that the designs on his masks represented lightning and definitely not snakes is somewhat curious. Although they can be distinct entities, lightning and snakes do seem to be closely associated with one another and with precipitation or water, and it appears they can be used interchangeably, in some situations, as symbols or designs. Goodwin (1938b: 25) states:

> Certain species of snakes, some from earth and some imaginary ones, with porcupine, lizard, and skunk, fly about in space just beneath the sky. From certain of these animals comes the dangerous lightning. A great snake in the underworld communicates with a lightning being above concerning certain happenings on the earth. The connection between snakes and lightning is an important one.

Unfortunately, Goodwin does not elaborate. Although Bourke (1892) may not have recorded the whole story, he does describe a ceremony in 1884 supposedly intended to bring rain, which employed a cross with a snake design on it (p. 479); a Chiricahua *gaan* mask with snakes and snake heads, the latter representative of hail (pp. 582–583); and a "serpent lightning" design on a painted wooden charm (p. 587). Opler (1941: 196) notes two versions of a Chiricahua myth in which lightning and water are juxtaposed:

> Through the mythology an association is established between water and lightning. In most versions of the birth of the culture hero, his mother is impregnated by Water, but in one variant Lightning strikes at the divine woman four times and thus causes her to conceive Child of the Water. Another version, after describing the impregnation by Water, relates that Lightning tests the hero, discovers him to be his son, and later helps him conquer a giant.

Flood waters may be brought by mythological snakes (Kessel 1976: 123), and lightning, flood waters, and supernatural snakes all figured in a medicine man's vision that Kessel (1976: 162–163) recounts. Finally, "lightning power" and "snake power," of all the kinds of power available to man (see Basso 1969: 30–31), are the most powerful and rarely obtained; medicine men who possess either of these powers are especially respected and influential (Goodwin 1938b: 29, 31–32; Kessel 1976: 196). Although undoubtedly distinguished when appropriate, snakes, lightning, and water are all interrelated, and it is not surprising that their depictions grade into one another.

In 1985 a San Carlos Apache indicated that the carved serpentine figures at the top of a modern *gaan* mask were snakes (Fig. 7.9*f*), and that their use on *gaan* masks dated from the Silas John religious movement that began around 1920 (discussed below, see Figs. 7.40, 7.41). The use of live rattlesnakes in curing ceremonies and snake depictions on religious paraphernalia were both conspicuous features of Silas John's religion, and Silas is thought to have had "snake" or "lightning power" or both (Kessel 1976: 142–185). Although Silas John's emphasis on the use of snakes was extreme by traditional standards (Kessel 1976: 166, fn. 3), snakes had been employed by medicine men earlier. Bourke (1892: 479, 504–505, 582–583), speaking of the Western Apache and Chiricahua in the 1880s, mentions "snake dances" and snake depictions. Corbusier (1886: 336–337) speaks of Yavapais being treated by Tonto medicine men using rattlesnakes. Reagan (1930: 320) notes a curing ceremony on Carrizo Creek in 1901 that employed a nonpoisonous snake. Goodwin (1938b: 34) also notes the former use of live snakes in ceremonies. So, although Silas John may have popularized the use of snakes and snake designs, they do appear to have been a limited but consistent component of traditional Western Apache ritual and iconography. Carved snakes virtually identical to those on the modern *gaan* mask mentioned above can be seen in photographs taken in the 1920s or 1930s at San Carlos (ASM Pix–783–x–19) of a girl's puberty ceremony. John Robinson's painted designs for *gaan* masks (Fig. 7.9*d, e*; Gay 1933, Plates 20*b*, 21*b*) may date as early as 1901. Gay (1933: 31) indicates that the four dots at the tail of Figure 7.9*d* (and presumably *e* as well), "are representative of the fireballs sometimes observed at the end of forked lightning." Rock art sites in Western Apache and Chiricahua territories show what are presumably mythological snake or lightning or water depictions (Schaafsma 1980: 333–341) that almost certainly date even earlier, although how much earlier is unknown (Fig. 7.9*a–c*). The common use of dots on these designs as well as split tails (forked lightning?) shows a continuity in their depiction. Of the snake with a head at either end (Fig. 7.9*b*), Schaafsma (1980: 339) cites Newcomb and Reichard's (1937: 53) similar description of Big Snake, a mythological being often shown in Navajo sandpaintings, and Bourke (1892: 583), speaking of a *gaan* dance held at Fort Marion, Florida by captive Chiricahua in 1887, notes three of the dancers had snakes painted on their arms, one depicting a snake with a "head at each extremity."

Snake or snakelike designs. Figure 7.9. These designs are: *a*, a pictograph from Chiricahua territory (after Schaafsma 1980, Fig. 282); *b, c*, pictographs from Western Apache territory (after Schaafsma 1980, Fig. 283); *d, e*, designs drawn by John Robinson (after Gay 1933, Plate 21 and ASM Cat. 19840); and *f*, a carved and painted figure from atop a *gaan* mask (ASM Cat. 85–40–1) made on the San Carlos Reservation in 1980.

Figure 7.9. Snake or snakelike designs.

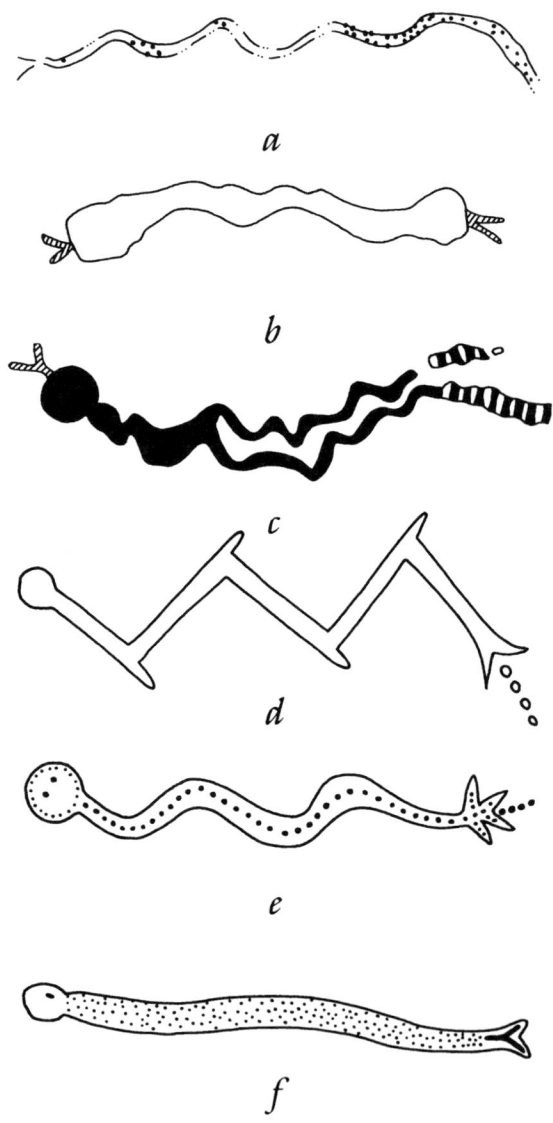

Ritual

Figure 7.10. Mineral paints; see also Color Illustration 26 (ASM Neg. 56719).

Mineral paints. Figure 7.10 and Color Illustration 26. Many of the paints used aboriginally by the Western Apache were powdered minerals of various colors. Goodwin either collected samples of raw materials himself or obtained them from his Apache friends, along with an identification of their source whenever possible. Clockwise from the right is a lump of red scoria with minute feldspar crystals (21892) from Rose Peak; it is sitting on an unmodified tabular river cobble (21396; 14.5 cm long) found at an old Apache camp at Dewey Flat and catalogued by Goodwin as a paint palette. The green paint stone (21894) is a malachite coating on calcite, unidentified as to source. The white paint stone is an especially gritty caliche from Canyon Day, composed of calcium carbonate, clay, and some limonite (21893). At lower left is a concretion of clay, limonite, and some sand (21896) that, broken open, serves for yellow paint; the source of this specimen is unknown. The three stones at upper left (21429) are specular hematite used for a silvery sheen, hematite for red, and an unidentified manganese oxide-iron mineral for black, all from Bylas or the Blue River.

An informant (Goodwin A–66) stated that the juice of the Spanish bayonet (yucca) was used as a binder for the powdered mineral paints. Prepared cakes of paint were made by adding water to the powdered mineral and letting it dry; John Rope noted that "Sometimes with . . . red paint they ground up plants or their flowers that smelled good so that the paint would smell good." This scented paint was first worn by young men when they were courting (presumably as face paint), and it could then be worn throughout adulthood.

At top is part of a *gaan* mask dating around 1920, showing the use of what appear to be commercial water colors, colored pencils, and possibly some vegetal paints. Various items were also decorated with charcoal, commercial enamel paints and stains, crayons, and inks. This clown mask (EEG 163) was obtained at Carrizo by Frieda Knoop.

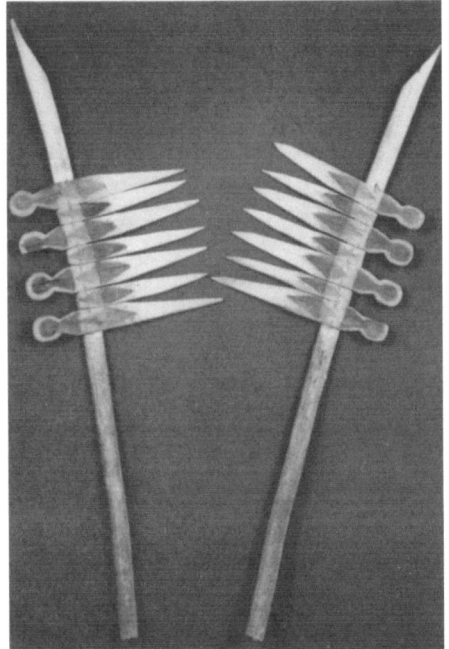

LEFT: Figure 7.11. Pair of *gaan* dancer's wands; see also Color Illustration 27 (ASM Neg. 64282).

RIGHT: Figure 7.12. Oil painting of a *gaan* dancer by Curry Clawson (ASM Neg. 56661).

Ritual

Pair of *gaan* dancer's wands. Figure 7.11 and Color Illustration 27. In ceremonies, each *gaan* dancer carries a matching pair of wands except the clown, who generally carries a wand in one hand and whirls a bullroarer intermittently with the other.

Goodwin purchased the rather ornate pair of San Carlos wands shown here (21372; each 84 cm high) at Manuelito, New Mexico, in 1930. Both the handles and crosspieces are made of yucca or sotol laths and assembled with buckskin ties. The handle tops and crosspiece tips (front and back) are coated with a chalky white paint. On the backs of both wands, opposite the crosspieces, the handle is painted black, and the crosspieces themselves lack the green paint found in the design on their fronts.

Other forms of wands also occur, including wands that lack crosspieces altogether or that have a single semicircular stick attached near the top of the wand, with the open side of the stick pointed upward. Usually wands have three or four crosspieces that are carved the same on both ends (as opposed to those shown here with one end round and the other end pointed).

Oil painting of a *gaan* dancer by Curry Clawson. Figure 7.12. This untitled painting (EEG 247) of a *gaan* dancer at night in front of a fire is 12 inches by 18 inches, oil paint on masonite. It is signed 'C.CLAWSON "79"' and was painted in 1979 at his home in Cedar Creek; it was sold to Mrs. Guenther in Whiteriver in the summer of that year. *Gaan* dancers have been a natural subject matter for Apache artists for years (Tanner 1973: 407–424), but, like many of his fellow Apache artists, Clawson paints non-Apachean subjects also and particularly enjoys landscapes. Neither this painting nor the carved wooden figures in Figure 7.13 are ritual items, but both utilize *gaan* motifs, which are becoming more and more popular as subject matter for secular craft items (see Figs. 6.26, 6.31).

***Gaan* dancers carved by Ray Thompson.** Figure 7.13. This set of wooden *gaan* dancers (EEG 245) was carved in the spring of 1981 by Ray Thompson at his home in Canyon Day. The figures stand between 17 cm and 19 cm high and were carved from pieces of commercially cut 2-by-4 boards. The figures are painted with watercolors and have red cloth kilts and neckbands, adhesive tape belts, and chicken feathers on their masks. They are carved from a single piece of wood except for the wands, the clown's bullroarer, and the mask slats. The slats usually are carved from yucca or sotol stalks and affixed with white glue.

A number of carvers in recent years have gained notoriety for their *gaan* figures, including Ray Thompson, Cain Hastings, Philip Titla, B. Beaty, Bill Stevens from Mescalero, Rodney Banashley who is Apache-Zuni (see Hess 1980: 285, 287; Nicholson 1984), and Vincent Dowahongva, a Hopi married to an Apache and living at Fort Apache (some of his carvings are illustrated unidentified in Guy 1977: 18).

Figure 7.13. *Gaan* dancers carved by Ray Thompson (ASM Neg. 56662).

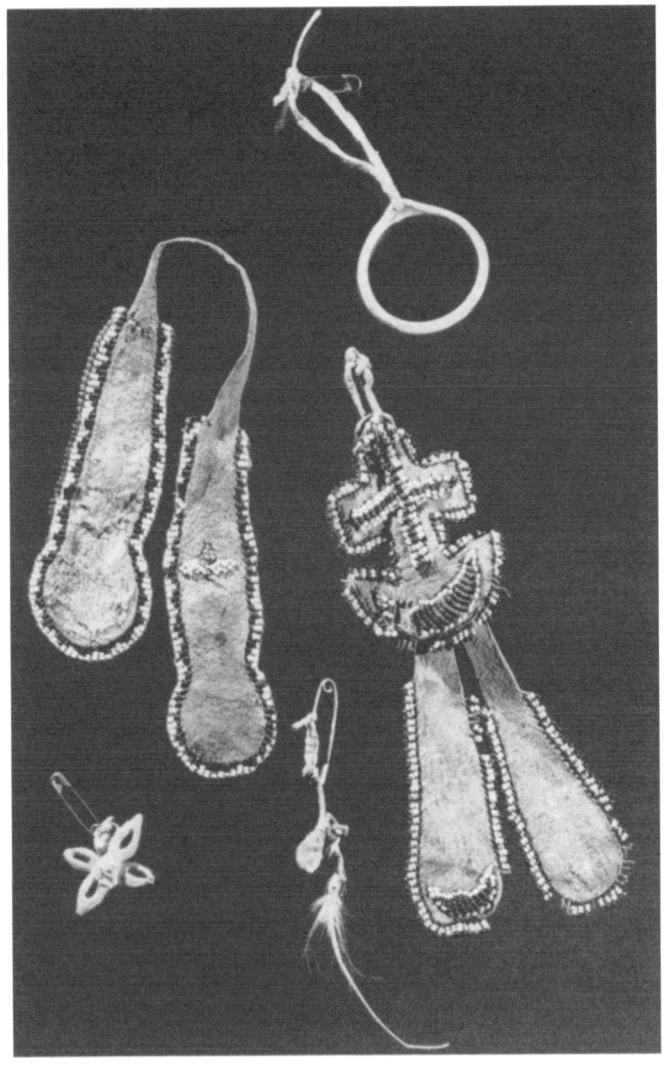

Figure 7.14. Medicine charms; see also Color Illustration 28 (ASM Neg. 56637).

Medicine charms. Figure 7.14 and Color Illustration 28. Objects such as quartz crystals and pendants of turquoise, abalone, or silver were often attached to medicine caps; however, all of the charms shown here were either pinned to a person's shirt or blouse during a curing ceremony or were tied around medicine-pollen bags. The charm at left center (EEG 43) is a single piece of buckskin, with a cross or 4–pointed star done in beadwork on each tab. It was obtained with Coyote's medicine cap in 1914, but could date much earlier (see Fig. 7.20). In 1910 Pliny Earle Goddard collected a virtually identical White Mountain charm tied around a buckskin pollen bag for the American Museum of Natural History (AMNH Cat. 50/9083). The charm at right center was obtained with Loco Jim's medicine cap (both EEG 36, cap not illustrated) in either 1920 or 1922, but possibly dating earlier. This charm (22 cm high) has a cross-and-crescent-shaped pouch of two pieces of buckskin sewn together and beaded. At the top (top arm of the cross) a buckskin thong passes through both faces of the pouch and through a turquoise pendant in front; this suspension loop does not seal the pouch, but does make it difficult to open, and the small mouth would not admit anything larger than a few millimeters in size. Neverthe-

Ritual

less, something was felt in the bottom of the pouch that gave the crescent a padded, lumpy appearance. An X-ray photograph revealed grains of a radio-opaque material, and a sample shaken out through a hypodermic had the appearance of ground galena. A spectroscopic analysis confirmed this identification, indicating this ore was primarily lead with a small component of silver. Although ground galena could be used for a sparkling paint, as is specular hematite (Fig. 7.10), the small amount in this difficult-to-open pouch-charm suggests that it may have had some more esoteric use or properties for Loco Jim. Attached to the middle of the pouch's back by another thong is a piece of buckskin with two tabs, much like EEG 43 but with a beadwork crescent at the bottom of one tab and a cross on the other (not visible). The buckskin pouch and the front of the attached buckskin strip-tabs are painted with yellow ochre. The cross-and-crescent designs on these charms and Goddard's collection of a similar specimen along with other objects apparently associated with the *daagodighá* movement both suggest that these two Guenther charms do date to the *daagodighá* religious movement of 1903 to 1907 (Figs. 7.32–7.39).

At top is a prehistoric plain *Glycymeris* shell bracelet with a buckskin thong passed through the suspension hole in the umbo (EEG 61); a safety pin on the thong served to pin it to clothing. This and the pendant at bottom center (EEG 60) were obtained by the Knoops at either Carrizo or East Fork between 1919 and 1924. EEG 60 consists of the shaft of an unidentified feather, an obsidian flake, a turquoise pendant, a piece of quartz, a rectangular orange bead, and three disc beads, one each of white shell, red argillite, and black steatite, all tied to or strung on a thin buckskin thong, itself tied around a safety pin. The combination of beads on this charm is not accidental; the four "sacred jewels" and their associated colors and directions (Goodwin 1939: 2, 19) are: black jet or steatite or shale (Black, East), turquoise (Green or Blue, South), "red stone" or argillite (Red or Yellow, West), and white shell (White, North).

At bottom left is a cross (EEG 59) made of two pieces of carved cholla skeleton tied together at right angles with commercial string, and the string tied through a safety pin. It was made by Silas John Edwards for a curing ceremony (see also Figs. 7.40, 7.41), but there is no other specific provenience information.

Baby's charm necklace. Figure 7.15. At times, necklaces of charms were made to protect babies and were worn about the child's neck. This buckskin thong loop (21870; about 10 cm in diameter) was made (probably specifically for Goodwin) by Mrs. Jewett Wright in 1936. Tied to it with sinew are four quartz crystals to protect the child at night; the fifth and largest crystal has a buckskin fringe painted red and is "chief" for the other four. Two segments of peeled cholla stem painted red are strung on the thong and held in place with knots. Fourteen yellow corn kernels are strung on heavy commercial string and tied to the thong. Both the cholla and corn keep off disease and bad luck. The red paint on the cholla and chief crystal fringe promote health. (See also Goodwin 1942: 441 and, for another child's charm necklace with different attachments, Hildburgh 1919: 82, Plate F–Fig. 3.)

Figure 7.15. Baby's charm necklace (ASM Neg. 32108).

Figure 7.16. Prehistoric items used ceremonially (ASM Neg. 64295).

Prehistoric items used ceremonially. Figure 7.16. At right is a large (11.0 cm long), bifacially flaked, white chalcedony knife (21390) of prehistoric manufacture. These types of objects were said to be the points with which lightning strikes, and medicine men searched for them at the base of lightning-riven trees. They were used in curing ceremonies or as charms. This one was found by Jewett Wright some distance north of the Gila River, north of Bylas, and was sold to Goodwin in 1932. At top center is a large flake of clear quartz (21874) found by Goodwin on an old Apache camp site near Kinishba in 1936; this crystal may have been found by Apaches in the Kinishba ruins. Quartz crystals were used as protective charms and could be looked into to foretell events and to find lost objects. At left are a tubular pipe and arrowshaft straightener (both EEG 107), both made of blue-black steatite, both found in a prehistoric site near Carrizo by V–50. Frieda Knoop recorded that he carried these items in his pocket for a long time, but late in 1922 came into the Carrizo trading post and traded them for food. These two items are included here because of their origin and because the pipe could have been used for smoking, which, at that date, might still have had predominantly ritual associations (see Fig. 7.19). The straightener could have been used to trade in earlier days (Goodwin 1942: 82), but, depending on the circumstances under which it was found, V–50 might have felt it had some power. Frieda noted that V–50 had "made the marks on the arrow straightener [and] also put his brand on it." Six incised vertical parallel lines are on one side, but nothing resembling a cattle brand, if that is what Frieda meant, is apparent. This marking is of interest in that a straightener (apparently prehistoric) obtained by Goodwin from an Apache at Camp Verde (not illustrated) also has incised marks that appear to be recent, presumably Apache, additions. Such marks may have served to identify personal property or, conceivably, to identify it in the owner's mind as Apache and as his own, thus no longer belonging to the prehistoric people.

Ritual

Witchcraft charms or "medicine beans."
Figure 7.17. At bottom center are a coral bean *(Erythrina flabelliformis)* seed pod and loose seeds, and at upper left are mescal bean *(Sophora secundiflora)* pods and loose seeds. Coral beans are native to far southeastern Arizona, southwestern New Mexico, and onward south into Mexico; mescal beans are found in extreme southeastern New Mexico, much of southern Texas, and on south into Mexico (Merrill 1977, Figs. 3, 4). In pre-Reservation times and the early decades of this century, the Western Apache could have obtained coral beans when raiding into Mexico, possibly from Chiricahua friends, or on other trips. These beans were sewn into fringed buckskin cases like the one at lower left (21404) made by Charlie Sego in 1932, and "worn on inside of shirt as a protection against bad medicine [witchcraft] which some other person might try to make on you." This charm is made from two strips of buckskin, tied at the top, cut into fringes at the bottom, and sewn shut around the two beans with commercial thread. Each bean is visible through holes cut out of the buckskin, one big hole on either face for the top bean, five small holes on either face for the bottom. In recent years beadwork has replaced buckskin, and "medicine beans" are a popular tourist item. At lower right is a beaded specimen made in the early 1970s in the Whiteriver area (74–61–1; see also Fig. 6.31 and Tanner 1975, Fig. 7.13 "necklaces"). In 1980 Mrs. Guenther received a single specimen done in the old style (*upper right,* EEG 242) in buckskin with cut-outs, made by Loretta Dazen of Whiteriver, who was around age fifty at the time. Beadworkers who sold things to Mrs. Guenther identify these items as "medicine beans" that promote the general good health of the owner or, more importantly, the bean is supposed to crack with a loud noise if someone is telling a lie about the owner or if a witch is nearby. At top are fourteen coral beans with suspension holes burned through them transversely strung on heavy commercial thread (EEG 230). Some whitish substance is spattered on several of the beans; it is not pollen, but cannot be further identified. Unfortunately there is no provenience on this specimen other than that it is presumed to be Western Apache in origin.

All early examples of such charms would be expected to contain coral beans (as do all of the charms shown here). However, at least as early as the late 1960s, Anglos in Tucson were supplying mescal beans through the Guenthers to Apaches in the Whiteriver area, and researchers should not be surprised to find mescal beans and coral beans used interchangeably in recent craft items. Nonnative mescal shrubs are used occasionally in landscaping in Tucson. To fill a growing craft demand, Western Apaches have utilized the easily gathered mescal beans and made trips on their own to southeastern Arizona to gather native coral beans themselves. (See Merrill 1977 for a full discussion of coral beans and mescal beans and their aboriginal uses in North America.)

Figure 7.17. Witchcraft charms or "medicine beans" (ASM Neg. 56635).

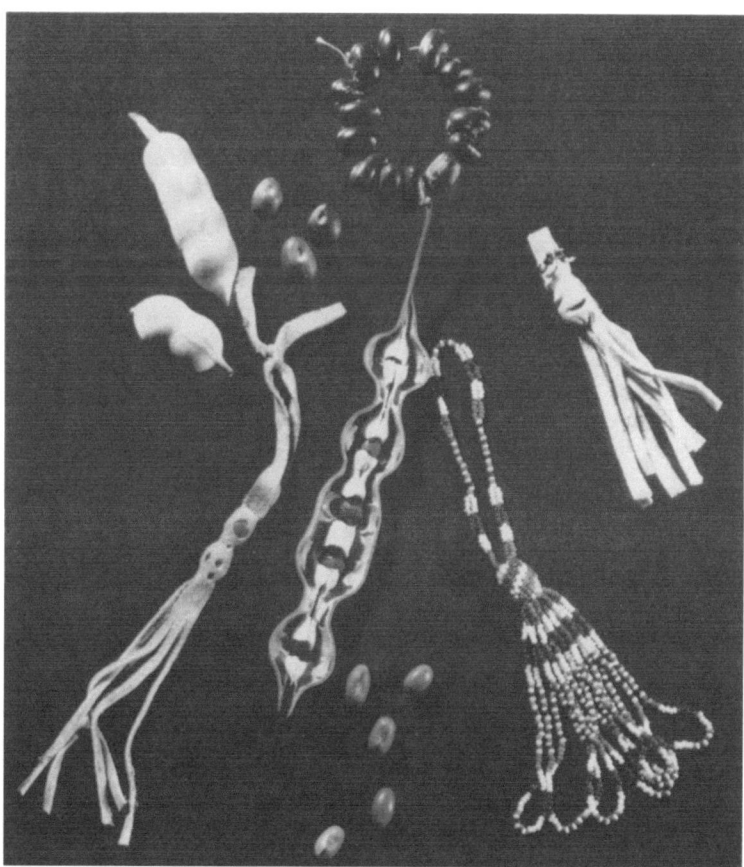

War charm necklace. Figure 7.18. Necklaces such as this were worn by men over the right shoulder and under the left arm, primarily to protect themselves in raiding or warfare but also as a good luck charm at home or when traveling. They are most often mentioned as warding off blows and missles, especially bullets, for a man wearing one and for the men under a leader wearing one into battle. Additional discussions and illustrations of war charms are in Basso 1971 (pp. 243–245), Bourke 1892 (pp. 550–554), and Hildburgh 1919.

This necklace (21326; about 40 cm in diameter) was made by George Gray at Bylas in 1935 and sold to Goodwin. It is made of two buckskin thongs, themselves twisted and then braided together in a Z–twist. There are numerous objects tied on with sinew, including twenty-two small translucent white chalcedony nodules, twenty-five flakes and small tool fragments of obsidian, and ten other flakes and unmodified pebbles. Suspended at top and bottom (as oriented in this photo) are two charms for protection against witchcraft, consisting of three coral beans sewn inside two buckskin "jackets" with fringes and holes through which the beans are visible (see Fig. 7.17). Suspended at lower left and right are eagle (cf. *Aquila chrysaetos*) wing

Figure 7.18. War charm necklace (ASM Neg. 22943).

Ritual

feathers; around the base of each is tied a piece of eagle down and some yellow Hooded Oriole feathers. In addition to the stone items already noted are two obsidian and four chert points or point bases; one obsidian and one chert have eagle down attached, and a second chert point has Hooded Oriole feathers. All of the points appear to be prehistoric, and the chert points in particular may be late Archaic in age; all presumably were attached because of their generally protective properties, possibly specifically with regard to lightning. At upper left is a yellow and black Hooded Oriole's head (with the cranium removed). The significance of this and the feathers is uncertain, but pieces of Bullock's Oriole nests were sometimes attached to cradle-board hoods for luck (Goodwin 1942: 434), and whole skins occasionally were attached to medicine caps.

Tobacco smoking paraphernalia. Figure 7.19. Statements made by informants (Goodwin A–71) indicate that in pre-Reservation times smoking was an activity for men and was restricted to a certain degree to older men. Tobacco was a highly valued, often scarce commodity. Men carefully planted small plots of tobacco hidden in the hills. The ground was

Figure 7.19. Tobacco smoking paraphernalia (ASM Neg. 32111).

usually prepared by burning off the brush first. When harvested, the dried leaves were crushed and carefully stored in bags made specifically for that purpose, fashioned from the skin of a whole fox or young deer, or of two Abert's squirrel hides sewn together; less often tobacco was stored in a pottery jar cached in a rock shelter. The dried seed pods were beaten with a stick and the seeds husbanded for the next year's planting.

Not everyone had tobacco; it was given away sparingly, even to close friends or relatives ("not more than it would take to cover a coyote track"), and commanded valuable goods when it was traded. One fistful was worth a large black-tailed deer buckskin; two fistfuls, a horse. Other items mentioned as traded for tobacco were blankets and canes for arrows. Four cigarettes rolled with corn husks were worth a buckskin or four or five arrows. As tobacco became more readily available from Anglos, smoking became a more secular activity, practiced by younger men and boys, and chewing-tobacco and commercial cigarettes also were used. In early days, smoking had strong associations with prayers and health and luck and particularly success in hunting deer—"that is what tobacco is made for." Older men joked with a youngster asking for tobacco: "'Well, did you catch badger yet?' 'No.' 'Well, nothing doing, no smoke for you yet.'" If the boy believed the old men, it might be sometime before he asked again, as catching a badger was a difficult and dangerous undertaking.

Tobacco was rolled into cigarettes using corn husks saved for that purpose, such as the bundle shown at top (21381) tied up by Anna Price in 1932. Modeled tubular clay pipes were made also, sometimes fired like the one at bottom left (21393) or just dried like the one at bottom center (21392). The fired pipe had a pattern of diamonds incised into the wet clay surface, and it has a buckskin thong tied around the middle; Goodwin purchased it at a trader's store in Whiteriver in 1930. The unfired pipe (5.7 cm long) was made by Palmer Valor in 1932 and given to Goodwin, who noted that Valor never fired his pipes. Stone pipes (presumably found on prehistoric sites, see Fig. 7.16) also were used. If a clay pipe was unavailable, a strip from a yucca leaf was wound up into a pipe shape and filled with tobacco, like the one at bottom right (21391) made by Charlie Sego in April of 1932 and given to Goodwin. After a yucca pipe was smoked, "we always undid that thing before we threw it away."

Buckskin caps. Five types of men's buckskin caps were described for Goodwin (A–66), all related to ceremonialism or warfare. A sixth type, made of beaver skin (with the fur on?), appears to have been a secular article of cold-weather clothing, possibly made by only some of the Western Apache (Goodwin A–66).

Although the five types of caps have various physical attributes that distinguish them, their functions related to curing, warfare, and protection often subtly overlapped. The first type (Figs. 7.20, 7.21 *upper right*) may have no feathers at all, but commonly has from one to several eagle flight feathers attached to the top. This type is consistently identified as being worn to war, but may have been used also by medicine men in other ritual contexts.

The second type of cap (Fig. 21, *left*) has only a few eagle down feathers on top, along with charms of turquoise, silver, shell, and other materials that the owner might attach, depending on the "powers" he possessed and the purposes for which the cap was intended. One informant said that Wood Ibis feathers also had been used on such caps, as they had "the same power" as eagle down. This type of cap was made and used only by medicine men.

A third type had "two buckskin horns sticking up, one on each side, stuffed with something so they stood up stiff." These apparently were worn only by the leader of a war party and had to be made for him by a medicine man. Opler (1941, Plate XI, *top*) illustrates a heavily beaded Chiricahua example of this design.

The fourth type of cap was covered with bundles of iridescent turkey breast or body feathers, and the buckskin was cut so that there were tabs or scalloped fringes hanging down in back. This type might have only turkey feathers (see Opler 1983, Fig. 9), but usually had two big eagle flight feathers standing up on top (Fig. 7.23, *right*). The usual identification of this type as war caps or medicine men's caps may be misleading, as one of Goodwin's informants stated that this type was "only to dress up in and wear at dances," while another agreed but added: "They used to wear them on the warpath also, but this was just because they liked to wear them. There used to be lots of this kind. When the wind blew the eagle feathers, it made them turn this way and that." The manner in which the eagle feathers were made to stand up but be free-turning is described below.

The fifth type of buckskin cap is covered with split owl flight feathers, and two painted triangular or trapezoidal tabs in the back appear to be standard as well. References as to who wore owl caps and why are varied and not specific. A Western White Mountain band member said only San Carlos bands wore this type. One informant said any class of men (as opposed to medicine men) could wear owl caps, and another said only old men wore them. Finally, one old man, when asked why he always wore an owl cap, replied: "Well, when you walk alone at night and wear it, nothing bothers you. You can't hear any owls at all" (Basso 1971: 282). Basso (1971: 318) also notes that hearing an owl meant that the ghost of a deceased relative was near and might cause the hearer to become ill. Young men wore such caps too, however, including Apache Scouts in the U.S. Army (Fig. 7.24; Opler 1983, Fig. 10; Basso 1977: 38). Taken altogether, it may be that any man could wear such a cap, and that it served to protect the wearer from harm in general and perhaps owls and ghosts in particular.

Basic construction of all five types of caps was quite similar. The skullcap was made concave and fitted to the wearer by sewing together curved pieces of buckskin, by cutting out darts and sewing the remaining edges together, or both. The edge of the resulting approximately hemispherical cap was left unmodified, was turned out and back on itself, had a separate strip sewn to the outside, or had a separate strip folded in half lengthwise and sewn to the bottom. These edges and trim could be scalloped and were usually ornamented or held in place with beadwork, metal tacks, shell buttons, and strips of red or black cloth.

Individual feathers usually were lashed with sinew to a buckskin thong that went through the crown of the cap and was knotted on the inside. Large feathers might have the end of the quill cut off, and the thong passed up through the shaft, out a hole made in the side, and was knotted. The bundles of turkey and owl feathers on the fourth and fifth type of caps described above were made by doubling over the ends of several feather shafts, binding them with sinew, and passing a buckskin thong through the resulting loop.

Chin straps were usually a thin buckskin thong, sometimes a wider strip, or even string. They attached on either side of the cap, next to the intersection of the main seam or dart with the cap's edge, and tied under the chin.

Other construction variations doubtless exist, but these methods are the most common and are found on one or more of the caps in the Goodwin and Guenther collections.

One other type of cap should be mentioned, similar to the first type above for men, the one made for a boy to wear on his first two raids: "The war cap of a boy novice is different from that of a man. There is no power in the former's, but it has four different feathers in it, quail, eagle down, oriole down, and two wing pinfeathers of hummingbird for speed" (Basso 1971: 290–291).

Men's buckskin war caps. Figure 7.20 and Color Illustration 29. These three caps are of the first type described by Goodwin's informants and were used primarily in raiding or warfare. All three have beadwork cross-and-crescent emblems on them, conceivably related to the 1903 to 1907 *daagodighá* religious movement (see Figs. 7.32–7.39). Although both the cross and the crescent appear to have been in common use long before 1903, generally they were not used in combination with one another, suggesting that these caps may indeed have been used during the movement. The sheer number of caps with cross-and-crescent decorations make it hard to believe that all were made or modified for *daagodighá*; it is possible, however, because many of the caps in collections were obtained in the early part of this century, when *daagodighá* paraphernalia was relatively common. Also, considering the Apache fear of the dead and that this movement had come to a close with the deaths of three prominent medicine men, participants in this movement may have been relatively willing to

Top: Figure 7.20. Men's buckskin war caps; see also Color Illustration 29 (ASM Neg. 56657).

Bottom: Figure 7.21. Men's buckskin caps (ASM Neg. 56656).

Ritual

part with such caps. The full significance and time-depth of cross-and-crescent designs has not been fully explored, and good provenience information for objects with these designs is essential to any attempt to link them to *daagodighá*.

The three caps shown here cannot be clearly associated with *daagodighá*. That at lower left (23029) is an unprovenienced specimen collected by Goodwin. It had at least ten and possibly twelve feathers at its crown. It has four sets of beadwork crosses and crescents, one set each in yellow, blue, white, and black, the colors relating to the cardinal directions. Although these elements are now side by side, thread holes in the buckskin show that they formerly were arranged with the crosses above the crescents, as on the other two caps shown.

The cap at top (EEG 39) has a confused history; it belonged to a medicine man, possibly with an "M" tag-band number, and was collected in the 1920s from either Carrizo or Cibecue. This cap presently has remnants of ten eagle flight feathers at the crown, and may have had as many as fifteen. On one thong between the cap and feather is a dark stone(?) disc bead. At one time there were eight large round buttons (presumably silver) evenly spaced around the lower edge, with two more near the crown, as shown by less soiled circular outlines with single or paired shank-suspension holes at their centers. At least one crown and two of the edge buttons (and the other seven, too?) were removed before a beadwork cross-and-crescent insignia was stitched on the front and back. Both crosses are a combination of black and white beads; the crescent visible is black with orange tips, and the back crescent is white with blue tips.

The cap at right (EEG 40) belonged to Coyote (Fig. 7.22). When baptized into the Lutheran church at East Fork in 1914, he came with this cap and gave it to Rev. Guenther. A single eagle secondary feather is attached to the crown, and four silver buttons are strung on a thong along one side. All the buttons appear hammered from coins, and the interiors of the two end buttons still have legible inscriptions that identify them as U.S. coins. There are two cross-and-crescent symbols done in black and white beads, one on the front, one in back. The blue, yellow, and green painting was a late modification applied after the beadwork had already begun to fall off; blue, yellow, and green paint is smeared on beads in each color zone, and particularly around the cap's lower edge. The green was clearly applied around the segments of what was formerly a continuous band of black and white beads. The green band appears to have had triangles projecting point upward from it into the yellow band above.

Men's buckskin caps. Figure 7.21. At upper right is another example of the first type of cap described (21410), worn primarily during raiding or warfare. Purchased by Goodwin at a trader's store in Bylas in 1930, this cap has ten eagle flight feathers (probably all Golden Eagle) attached at the crown, and on either side above where the chin strap attaches is a plain silver button. A double row of various size hemispherical metal tacks extend around the edge. Each tack has two prongs protruding from a drop of solder on its back and was attached by pushing the prongs through the buckskin and bending them over. Lines of such paired prong holes remain where tacks previously formed a cross on one side and a crescent on the other. These symbols might have been taken off to remove the cap's "power" if the owner no longer wished to use the cap, or perhaps if he wanted to sell it. If this cap was used during the *daagodighá* religious movement, which had the cross-and-crescent as its insignia, the cap's owner may have wished to retain the cap but not its associations with the movement and so removed the cross and crescent.

Goodwin's catalogue entry for the other cap (*lower left*, 21409) says: "made for C.G.10 by a medicine man, about 1898. It has lost its power now. The humming birds on it were supposed to act as go be-tweens from this earth to the skye, and holy things. Purchased from C.G.10 at Bylas, July 1932." Five Golden Eagle body down feathers are attached to the top. Strung on the buckskin thong between one of these feathers and the cap is a well-polished, heart-shaped turquoise pendant. Now much weathered, the painted designs on the cap are nearly obliterated, but one hummingbird on the body of the cap and circles around the lower edge can still be discerned.

Coyote and his family. Figure 7.22. This photo probably was taken near East Fork between about 1915 and 1920. Whether or not all of the young women and girls are Coyote's daughters is unclear, but everyone appears older than the girls in another family photo taken by E. E. Guenther around 1913 (see Herbert and Herbert 1962: 41), and Coyote died in 1922. Coyote wears a buckskin cap decorated with silver buttons, a silver cross and a crescent, and topped with what appear to be down feathers, which would correspond to a medicine man's cap as described by Goodwin's informants. Coyote's son wears a similar cap but probably just for this photo, as children did not wear buckskin caps. The boy also wears a medicine cord of some sort, possibly his own (see Fig. 7.15) but more probably also something that belonged to his father.

Other interesting items in this photo are the cross-shaped (beaded buckskin?) charms worn by several of the girls; Coyote's necklace with tweezers, silver crescent, and possibly a cross-and-crescent emblem; the bridle, saddle, and rope next to Coyote; the cloth saddlebags hanging in the juniper at left (see also Fig. 5.48); and the blankets on the wickiup at right.

Figure 7.22. Coyote and his family (photo by E. E. Guenther).

Ritual

Turkey feather and owl feather buckskin caps. Figure 7.23 and Color Illustration 30. At upper right is an example of the fourth type of cap described by Goodwin's informants, made primarily to be worn to social dances and only occasionally when raiding. Mrs. Guenther saw this cap worn at a war dance held in 1916 between Fort Apache and Whiteriver. It was staged the night before the Apache Scouts were to set out with the U.S. Army cavalry to go to Old Mexico in pursuit of Pancho Villa. Supposedly Loco Jim wore this cap at the dance, and Mrs. Guenther obtained it (from Jim?) the next day. Covered with tight bundles of iridescent turkey body feathers, it also has two eagle flight feathers rigged to stand up on the crown (see Fig. 7.25). These two eagle feathers are not the originals. In 1961 the Guenthers loaned this cap to then Fort Apache Reservation Tribal Chairman Lester Oliver to wear in President John F. Kennedy's inaugural parade down Pennsylvania Avenue in Washington on January 20. Prior to going, Oliver replaced the worn original feathers with new ones. The new feathers have had their edges cut. This type of cap is the most appropriate Western Apache headgear that could have been worn by Oliver, made as they were for dress-up social occasions. The buckskin at the back of the cap was cut into an elaborate fringe, and the front edge was decorated with a strip of black cloth placed behind the upturned toothed edge of the buckskin, both held in place and ornamented with hemispherical silver-colored metal tacks.

An example of the fifth type of cap described to Goodwin (*lower left*, 21432) is covered with bundles of split Great Horned Owl flight feathers. This cap was originally from San Carlos, but was purchased from Mrs. Frances J. McCormack of Globe. The exterior of the whole cap was painted or rubbed with yellow ochre, and then the tips of the toothed buckskin strip on the front and the two trapezoidal tabs in the back were decorated with glittering purple specular hematite paint. The toothed front strip is also decorated with two rows of mother-of-pearl two-hole buttons. In addition to the split flight feathers are three bundles of downy owl feathers at the back of the cap and three eagle flight feathers (see also Fig. 7.24).

Figure 7.23. Turkey feather and owl feather buckskin caps; see also Color Illustration 30 (ASM Neg. 56658).

Man wearing an owl feather cap. Figure 7.24. This man is wearing the fifth type of cap described by Goodwin's informants, covered with bundles of split owl flight feathers and with buttons around the lower edge, similar to the Goodwin specimen in Figure 7.23. Iverson (1982: 48) identifies this individual as a Yavapai, while the Arizona Historical Society's print (reproduced here) says "Ya-Va-Ki-Shi Apache Scout photo by G. H. Rothrock in Phoenix." The name, in fact, does sound Yavapai. However, no references can be found to the Yavapai making owl feather caps, and hence regardless of the tribal affiliation of this man, the cap is almost certainly of Western Apache manufacture, as may be the tweezers he is wearing.

Turkey feather cap mechanism. Figure 7.25. This drawing shows the rather elaborate mechanism used on the Guenther turkey feather cap (EEG 42, Fig. 7.23) to keep the two eagle feathers standing upright, but leaving them free to swivel in the breeze. It is a view of the back left side of the cap; the turkey feather bundles, front trim, and back fringe are not shown. A carefully shaped piece of wood, bent into a tight curve at the upper end and a gentle arc at the base, is tied down the back of the cap with buckskin laces. A hollow crosspiece of a cut section of bird bone is secured at the upper end of this stick (bindings not shown here). Each eagle feather has the tip of its quill cut off and a hole cut in its side about 5 cm above the tip. The dotted line shows how a thin buckskin thong passes through the feathers and crosspiece and is knotted on the inside of the cap. Each of these feathers can rotate about 180 degrees, and the whole mechanism can flop a little side-to-side, all of which must have given a very animated appearance to the cap and its wearer. Some variation on this type of mechanism apparently was used on all caps of this type with upright eagle feathers.

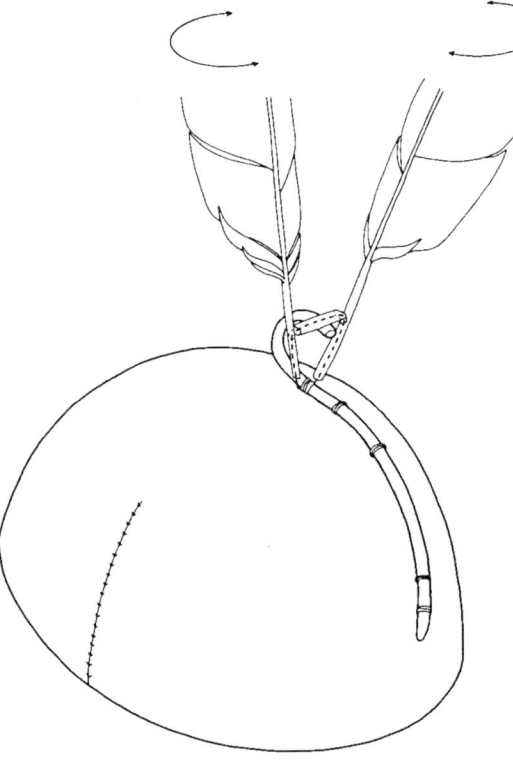

TOP: Figure 7.24. Man wearing an owl feather cap (photo courtesy Arizona Historical Society, Neg. 20802).

BOTTOM: Figure 7.25. Turkey feather cap mechanism. (View of the back left side of the cap; turkey feather bundles, front trim, and back fringe not shown.)

Figure 7.26. Lance, with closeup of blade (lance, ASM Neg. 22946; blade, 22945).

Lance, with closeup of blade. Figure 7.26. This lance (21355) was made by Anna Price to be used at a celebration held at Ft. Huachuca, probably in 1931 or 1932, presumably related to Apache Scouts in the U.S. Army. It is made of a sotol stalk, slotted at the bigger end to receive a 42-cm-long iron blade. A sleeve of rawhide (probably a section of cow's tail) was slid down over the blade and, as it dried, it held the blade snugly in place, aided by the notches filed into either edge of the blade's base (see closeup). The blade itself was made from an unidentified piece of iron, with the sides and tip filed to sharp edges. An ironic source of lance blades in the 1700s was captured Spanish short sword and sabre blades (Treutlein 1949: 146), and the U.S. Cavalry involuntarily supplied similar material in the 1800s (Bourke 1891: 40; Woodward 1943: 38; Basso 1971: 234). Anna Price's lance is constructed just as several of Goodwin's informants recalled earlier lance manufacture (see Basso 1971: 234–237) and is 174 cm (over six feet) long.

The blade on Anna Price's lance has a sheen to it as if it had been slightly varnished or lacquered. Since it was made for a public function at Ft. Huachuca, it is conceivable that it was varnished to make it look nice. In this connection, however, Palmer Valor spoke of lance blades made of mountain-mahogany, which, when finished, had the juice of a small cactus (probably *Echinocereus* sp. or possibly *Mammilaria* sp.) painted on them, and "when this dried, it made it [the lance blade] shine. Now it was ready to use" (Goodwin A–67).

Rawhide war shields. Figure 7.27 and Color Illustration 31. Shields were imbued with great protective and concealing powers and could only be made safely by men with knowledge of the appropriate "power." To make a shield without such knowledge was to risk grave, supernaturally induced illness. This being the case, a man who could make shields was well paid for his work, and not everyone could afford a shield (Goodwin A–67; Basso 1971: 239–243). "Only a man who knew about making these shields and 'enemies-against power' could make one. . . . The other men would go to him and get him to make them one. Only rich men who know about war medicine used these shields. They had to pay the equivalent of about thirty or forty dollars to the maker" (Basso 1971: 239, 240). Shields were not destroyed upon the death of the owner, but were passed on to a relative rather than permanently cached as were medicine caps, *gaan* masks, and other such items.

Shields were made of one or two thicknesses of cow, bull, or horse rawhide taken from the neck, shoulder, or hips where the hide was thickest. The front was painted with "medicine figures" and on the back, where only the owner could see it, was faintly painted a "medicine-sign" that helped the owner be successful in war (Goodwin A–67; Basso 1971: 242). Around the edge of the shield were hung eagle or hawk feathers, and when red cloth became available, a strip was attached to the upper edge under the feathers. John Rope noted that a crow feather was hung on each side of a shield where the eagle feathers stopped, "like a prayer to the crow for some reason" (Basso 1971: 242). Shields were stored in covers of buckskin or cloth, but no mention was made by Goodwin's informants of these covers having been painted, as were the covers of many Pueblo and Plains Indian shields (Wright 1976; McCoy 1984).

The smaller shield at lower left (21415; 58 cm in diameter) was made by Jewett Wright at Bylas in July of 1932 "as a model," probably at Goodwin's request. It is made of a single thickness of cowhide with a rawhide strap handle that passes through two slits in the shield center and is knotted in back. It is trimmed with strips of red cloth laced through slits in the shield's edge; the cloth does not extend all the way to the bottom. Twelve eagle flight feathers are nearly evenly spaced around the edge. The front is painted with a black central dot with a straight black line going up, a straight yellow line going down, and a blue and a red zigzag line going to either edge of the shield. The four colors and the quartered layout of the design are related to the four cardinal directions.

The larger shield (EEG 125; 70 cm in diameter) was obtained by Frieda Knoop in the summer of 1920 at the Knoop's trading post in Carrizo. An Apache known to the Knoops by his tag-band number, V–18, came in wearing only a breechclout and moccasins, with the shield on his arm, and wished to trade the shield for coffee, sugar, salt, and bacon, which Frieda did. As recorded in the U.S. Army Census (1900), V–18's Apache name was "Tinilzay," and he was fifty years of age in 1920. No other provenience information is known. Obviously no precise assignment of age can be made for this shield, but it presumably dates back into the 1800s, possibly well back.

This shield is flat, made from a single thickness of rawhide. The painted front is actually the inside of the hide, and analysis of hair remnants from the back of the shield (the hide exterior) identifies it as brown cowhide. The handle is now broken but was a piece of three-quarter-inch-wide leather harness(?), held by two copper rivets punched through the hide, 42 cm apart. One rivet is visible at the left shoulder of the anthropomorphic figure near the top, the other is below the bat figure near the bottom. Although it presently has thirty-nine eagle flight feathers around the edge, a multitude of old holes along the edge and recent repairs to the lower feathers make it clear that the trim on this shield has undergone several refurbishings.

The painting is done in black, blue, a dark green, a brown that may originally have been more yellow, and white. When examined closely, the black paint sparkles from many tiny points and may have some finely ground galena or specular hematite mixed up in it. The center of the shield is a large green dot with a toothed edge, outlined in black; barely visible at its center is a blue equal-arm cross. The zigzag lines, sets of four lines radiating from the center, sets of four circles and crescents, lines of triangles, and stars

Ritual

are all repeated four times with the designs in each quadrant executed in one main color and outlined in another, again related to the four cardinal directions. White is outlined by black, yellow (now brown) is outlined by green, and green is outlined by yellow. The black quadrant's triangles are actually dark green outlined in black, and the four radiating lines have their outer ends outlined in yellow. The yellow, green, and black stars are seven-pointed; the white star is eight-pointed. The green quadrant's line of triangles has thirteen elements, and the others each have eleven. Finally, the green quadrant's "moons" have green circles but blue crescents.

At the top of the shield above a crescent is a single black anthropomorph, possibly depicting a *gaan* but more probably representing Slayer of Monsters, a culture hero and son of Sun. "The most important power for war is 'enemies-against power'. It is the real war power. This power comes from Slayer of Monsters, for in the beginning he was the one who went all over the earth doing things and killing monsters, and he was the first one to use his power in doing this, so it all comes from him" (Basso 1971: 270, phraseology slightly modified). Next to him on the shield is a bird depicted in blue, with four wings, probably representing a hummingbird

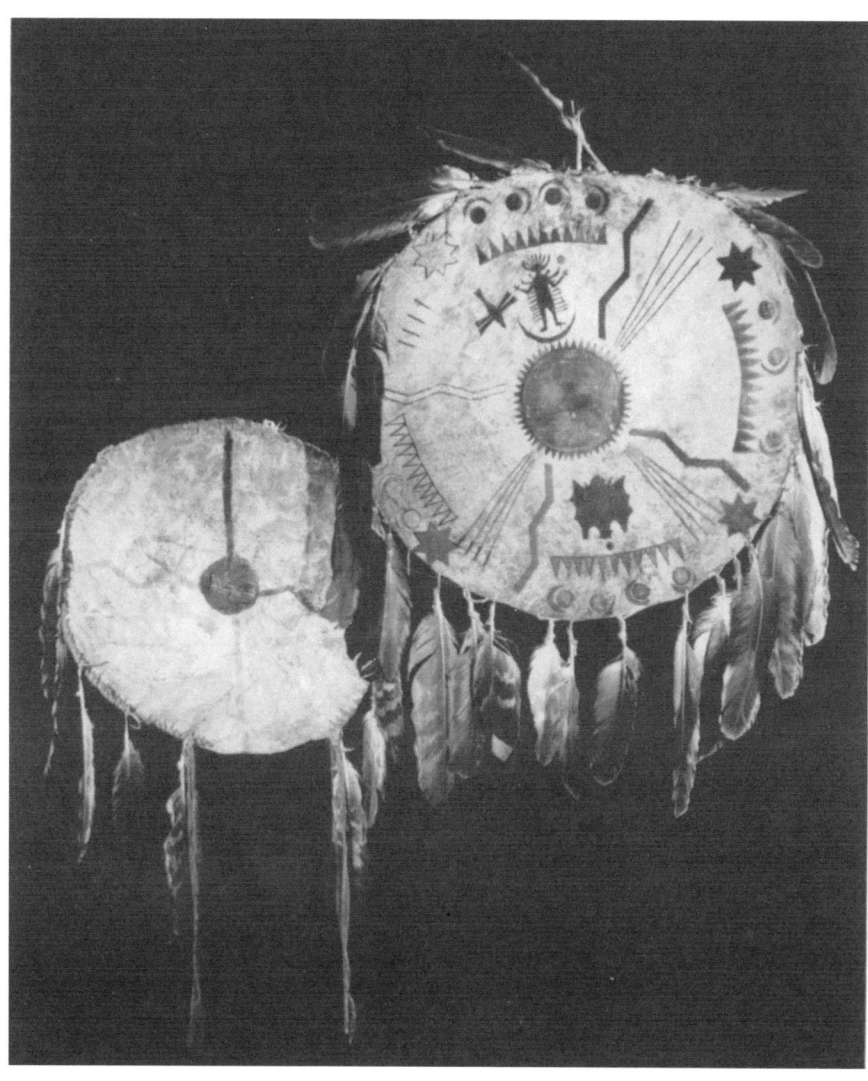

Figure 7.27. Rawhide war shields; see also Color Illustration 31 (ASM Neg. 56696).

TOP: Figure 7.28. Detail of shield design (ASM Neg. 64458).

BOTTOM: Figure 7.29. Detail of shield design (ASM Neg. 64457).

who acts as a messenger between the earth and supernatural powers (see Fig. 7.8 and Goddard 1918: 27–28). The hummingbird may also help a warrior run fast and be hard to see, like hummingbirds, which go so fast no one can see them (Basso 1971: 290).

At the bottom of the shield is a black bat, undoubtedly because: "Warriors are made like bats by a medicine man . . . so they can't be hit. 'Bat power' makes them elusive" (Basso 1971: 273). Clearly bats would be efficacious medicine figures for a shield.

Mrs. Guenther recalled being told that the bird was indeed a hummingbird and was given explanations virtually identical with those proposed above for it and for the bat. The wide zigzag lines supposedly represented thunder; the sets of straight lines, lightning, and the triangles, rain; and the fourfold repetition of these elements was related to the four directions or possibly the four seasons. The central green dot was the sun. Mrs. Guenther was uncertain as to the identity of the black anthropomorph. Kessel had been told, however, that the green "sun" actually represented "Giver of Life" (also known as "In Charge of Life" or "Rules over Life," a being sometimes, but not always, synonymous with Sun; Goodwin 1938b: 26), and that the blue cross within the green disc represented the hero twins, Slayer of Monsters and Born from Water. Kessel feels that if this is correct, then the black anthropomorph is most likely a *gaan*. (However, see also the identification as a sun symbol of a disc with a cross in it used on *gaan* masks by John Robinson, Fig. 7.8.)

Detail of shield design. Figure 7.28. This detail of shield EEG 125 (Fig. 7.27) shows probably Slayer of Monsters (11.5 cm high) and a hummingbird (7.4 cm long, beak to tail). The copper rivet head above the anthropomorph's left shoulder holds the upper end of the leather carrying strap on the back of the shield.

Detail of shield design. Figure 7.29. This detail of shield EEG 125 (Fig. 7.27) depicts a bat (9.6 cm high), probably to make the shield and its owner difficult to hit, as bats are. The copper rivet head directly below the bat holds the lower end of the shield's carrying strap.

Ritual

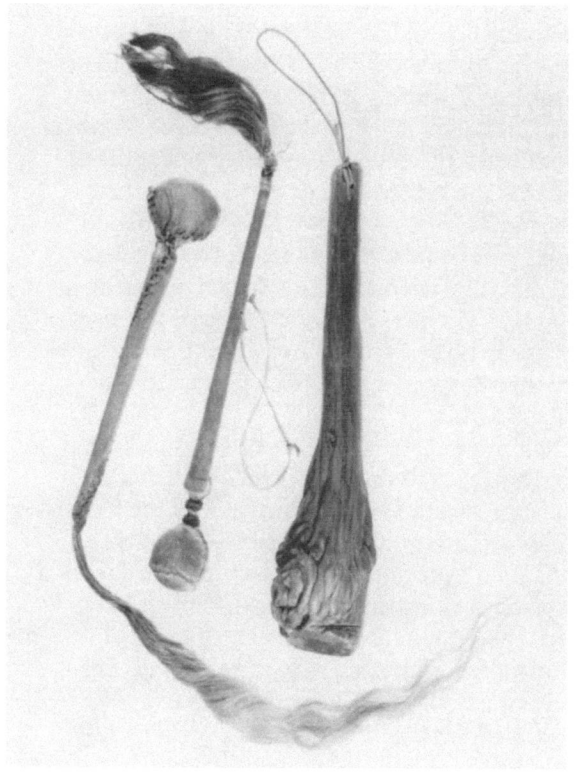

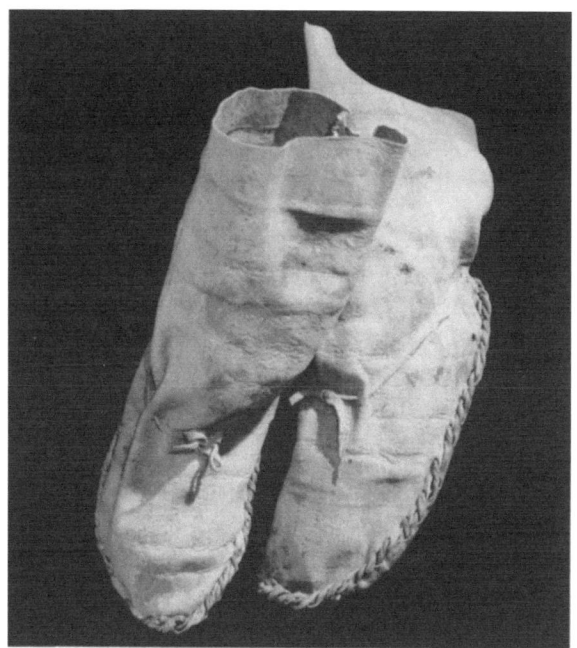

Left: Figure 7.30. Warclubs (ASM Neg. 56700).

Right: Figure 7.31. Makeshift moccasins (ASM Neg. 56643).

Warclubs. Figure 7.30. At left and center are traditional Western Apache warclubs, the one on the left (21452) purchased by Goodwin from Osborne's Store in 1931, the center one (EEG 38) obtained by the Knoops between 1919 and 1924 at either Carrizo or East Fork. John Rope described their construction: "They took a peeled cow's tail and shoved a hardwood stick down inside it. At the end they sewed a round rock inside the rawhide. Sometimes they sewed the tail up along the stick also. They put a thong in the handle so that you could slip your wrist through it. I have never seen or heard of one of these being painted" (Basso 1971: 239). Goodwin's club is stitched with rawhide thongs and measures 97 cm long, including the tail. The Guenthers' is stitched with heavy commercial string, and the rawhide covering the stone is a separate piece from that covering the handle. The whole club is 64 cm long, with several non-Apache string and buckskin repairs at each end of the handle.

The solid wood club (*right*, EEG 37) was cut with a saw from a gnarled juniper branch, 48 cm long, with the bark stripped off it. The handle was drilled for a leather wrist-loop. It was made by Loco Jim and sold to Rev. Guenther sometime between 1919 and 1928. Jim, a medicine man in his eighties at the time (M. Guenther 1928), knew of the traditional style clubs but said that this, too, was an Apache warclub. Most likely it was made specifically to be sold to the Guenthers; it appears to be unique and completely nontraditional.

Makeshift moccasins. Figure 7.31. This pair of moccasins (21412) was made by Jewett Wright in 1932, apparently as an example for Goodwin of the type made when men were raiding or at war, and pressed for time. The buckskin uppers and rawhide soles are of the usual type, but they are assembled with rawhide thongs sewn in big stitches on the exterior, rather than the careful, fine sewing with sinew hidden on the interior as in regular moccasins.

Religious cult movements. Four religious cult movements have occurred among the Western Apache since 1880. The Goodwin and Guenther collections include several items related to the second and fourth of these movements. The brief descriptions below are drawn or quoted directly from Kessel's (1976) history of these movements.

In late 1880 a medicine man from Cibecue, Noch-ay-del-klinne (also known as Bobbydoklinny), began the religious movement known as *na'ilde'* (a reference to a return from the dead). He proclaimed that he would raise the dead, Whites would somehow be gone from Apache country by the time the corn was ripe, and Apaches would take possession of the U.S. Army horses and belongings and defeat all of the Apaches' traditional enemies. In the summer of 1881 he claimed he would raise two popular chiefs from the dead (Eskiole and Diablo) to help in the process. Not surprisingly, the U.S. Army was perturbed by such announcements, and as a result of the arrest of Noch-ay-del-klinne by the Army, a fight broke out on 30 August 1881 between Noch-ay-del-klinne's followers, aided by Apache Scouts, and the Army detail. Known as the "Cibecue Massacre," eight Anglos and an estimated eighteen Apaches were killed, including Noch-ay-del-klinne. A medicine man reportedly sang over the body, and "On the morning of the fourth day, a large boulder was heard to rumble down the side of a nearby butte. This was a sign from Knoch-e-da-klinne that he would not return" (Meader 1967: 22–23). With this, *na'ilde'* came to an end.

From 1903 until about 1907 both the San Carlos and Fort Apache reservations experienced a second movement, *daagodighá,* the name meaning "rising upward" or "they will be raised up." The movement was again started by a Cibecue medicine man, Daslahdn, who proclaimed a prophecy. Followers of the movement would be raised up into the sky in a cloud. After this a great flood or earthquake would purge the earth of its evil, and the followers would then be set back on the rejuvenated earth where they would live in peace and plenty (Goodwin 1938b: 35; Goodwin and Kaut 1954). After several years of dancing for this end, many followers became discontented; much time had been spent in preparation for the new earth, but there was no sign of its impending arrival. To reestablish his influence, in 1906 Daslahdn had his followers cut his head off as a means of proving he could return from the dead. His failure to return to life in three days as he promised, the deep-seated Apache fear of the dead, and the subsequent deaths of two other *daagodighá* medicine men in 1907 and 1908 brought the movement to a close. No one had been raised up in spite of faithful participation in the dances. A cross-and-crescent motif was used extensively by this group, and a number of items from this movement have been preserved (see Figs. 7.34 through 7.39).

The third religious movement was short-lived, from June of 1916 until late 1917. A medicine man from Turkey Creek known as P–1 started *'aaghode'* ("it is going to happen"). P–1 also proclaimed a prophecy, that at a prescribed time and place the long deceased mother of an old Apache Scout would return to earth riding a white horse and dressed in white clothing. She would carry back all worthy Apaches to a new world. People were instructed to dress in white, carry a bag of cattail and corn pollen purchased from P–1, and await an appointed day. When this day passed without incident, the followers returned home. In 1917, P–1 and a number of other influential medicine men held numerous dances intended to hasten the removal to the new world. After several months of such intensified activity with no results and growing uncertainties about their leaders, participants abandoned the *'aaghode'* movement and returned to their normal routine.

The fourth religious movement was started in 1920 by a medicine man named Silas John Edwards and is sometimes referred to as *sailis jan bi'at'eehi* ("Silas John his sayings"). The movement introduced completely new ceremonial dances and a unique writing system for recording prayers (Basso and Anderson 1973), had a strong emphasis on healing with rattlesnakes and on cross symbols employed at "holy ground" dance areas, and conferred protective blessings on all who believed. Silas' possession of "snake" or "lightning power," his familiarity with handling snakes, and his knowledge of Christian symbolism related to crosses and snakes gained while working as E. E. Guenther's interpreter

Ritual

undoubtedly all contributed to his unconventional utilization of snakes in dances and healing. By the end of the 1920s his movement had followers throughout the Fort Apache and San Carlos reservations and had spread to the Fort McDowell and Mescalero reservations as well. In 1933 Silas was falsely convicted of the murder of his wife and sent to the United States Penitentiary at McNeil Island, Washington. Paroled in 1955, Silas resumed his ceremonies for about ten years, but failing health forced him to stop, and he was eventually placed in an American Indian rest home in Laveen, where he died in 1977. Only within the last ten years has his movement shown signs of diminishing. A number of objects made by Silas prior to starting his movement and two items used during his teaching were saved by the Guenthers (see Figs. 7.14, 7.40).

Daagodighá(?) **wickiup.** Figure 7.32. Prominent among the *daagodighá* prophets was a medicine man from Bylas named Big John, who was responsible for a number of innovations. At one point he instructed that various objects be made specifically for use at his dances, in particular white buckskin clothing, and that silver ornaments in the form of a cross-and-crescent be worn on the clothing and medicine caps (Goodwin and Kaut 1954: 391–392, 396, 398). Buckskin pollen sacks were to be decorated in black and white beads, and horses, a *tus,* a burden basket, and a bowl basket were to be brought to the dances because they would be needed in the new world; some women put cross-and-crescent designs in their baskets "because they wanted to." In 1906 Big John also directed that a special camp be built near Ash

Figure 7.32. *Daagodighá*(?) wickiup (photo courtesy American Museum of Natural History, Neg. 14468).

Flat, with all the wickiups "in four rows, the lines running north and south. Each one had two doorways: one to the east and one to the west; so that by looking through the door of one wickiup you could see right through the two doors of the next one and so on. We made them of good stout juniper poles, and they were all made well. Some of the poles are still standing there [1936] . . . we . . . cut big pine for poles and dragged them in by horses . . . made them extra strong as a heavy snow might fall sometime" (Goodwin and Kaut 1954: 394, 397). Apparently this camp was to be a gathering point for when the good people were to be raised up. Similar camps were reportedly built near Cedar Creek. This photo is probably of a wickiup at one of these camps. Basso (1983, Fig. 15) identifies this same structure and a cross-and-crescent emblem collected by Goodwin (Fig. 7.34) as coming from the Silas John movement, but this is unlikely. This structure was photographed in March of 1910 by Pliny Earle Goddard and identified as "House of a White Mountain Apache, showing crescent cross of new religious movement." Goddard is known to have been familiar with the *daagodighá* movement (Goodwin and Kaut 1954: 387, fn. 7), and as strong as these wickiups were built in 1906, there is no reason that they should not have been in reasonable repair four years later. Conversely, Silas John did not even start to preach his doctrines until at least 1916 and more probably 1920 (Kessel 1976: 157, fn. 2), and no such building of special wickiups or camps has been recorded for the Silas John movement other than the designation of "holy grounds" dance areas, around which were usually placed staffs or crosses (Opler 1969, photo on p. 90; Kessel 1976: 164, 182–183). Finally, although the cross-and-crescent emblem saw use before *daagodighá* in ritual contexts, primarily on medicine caps, and is still used in this way, this emblem seems clearly to have been most closely associated with and popularized by *daagodighá*. The preeminent symbols associated with Silas John were the cross and the snake, often in association with one another (Kessel 1976: 155, 172–173, 175, 176, 182–183).

Neil Buck stated that: ". . . [Big John] never told us what the cross and crescent signified. I never heard the cross was for the sun and the crescent for the moon" (Goodwin and Kaut 1954: 398). This sounds like a response to a remark or question probably posed by Goodwin, and suggests that at least some Apaches *did* interpret the symbol this way. Farrer and Second (1981) discuss Mescalero cosmology, which could be viewed as supporting the idea that the cross may represent Sun and the crescent a crescent moon and Changing Woman.

Drawing of *daagodighá* emblem. Figure 7.33. This drawing (from Goodwin and Kaut 1954, Fig. 1) is a rendering of the type of silver ornament-charm that Big John ordered worn on men's shirts or medicine caps and on women's blouses during *daagodighá* ceremonies. One could wear a single such charm or two, one on the left and right side. This drawing is taken from Neil Buck's description of this charm as "a cross made of silver with a crescent moon over it and from the bottom of the cross hung four or five conchos, made of dimes hammered out and strung on a piece of buckskin by little wire loops soldered to them" (Goodwin and Kaut 1954: 391–392).

***Daagodighá*(?) emblem of iron.** Figure 7.34. This rusted iron emblem (21453; 5.2 cm high) was cut from sheet metal, with a blob of solder on the back at the intersection of the arms of the cross. It was found (by Goodwin?) at Ash Flat in 1931. Ash Flat was the location of the special camp that Big John ordered built in anticipation of the time when all would be "raised up" (Fig. 7.32). Pliny Goddard collected a similar cut sheet metal charm in 1910 for the American Museum of Natural History (AMNH Cat. 50/9142), along with other probable *daagodighá* paraphernalia (see Fig. 7.14).

***Daagodighá* pollen sacks.** Figure 7.35. These three pollen sacks are tied together with a buckskin thong. Goodwin's catalogue entry for this item (21433) reads:

> Three small pollen bags of buckskin made by Mrs. Andrew Stanley of Bylas, and purchased from her, July 1933. The one with the large metal cross [*right*] was her's; the one with the smaller metal cross [*left*] she made for her daughter; and the one with the metal crescent [*center*] she made

Ritual

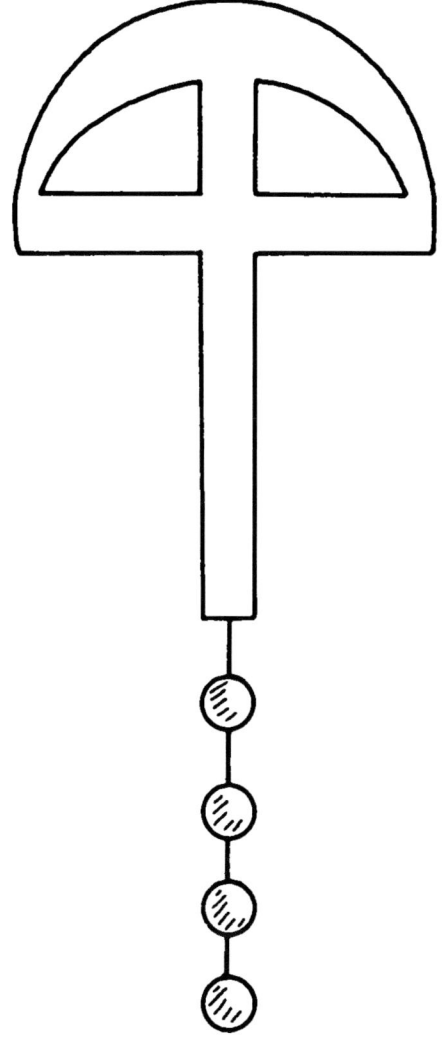

LEFT: Figure 7.33. Drawing of *daagodighá* emblem.

RIGHT: Figure 7.34. *Daagodighá*(?) emblem of iron (ASM Neg. 32097).

BOTTOM: Figure 7.35. *Daagodighá* pollen sacks (ASM Neg. 32076).

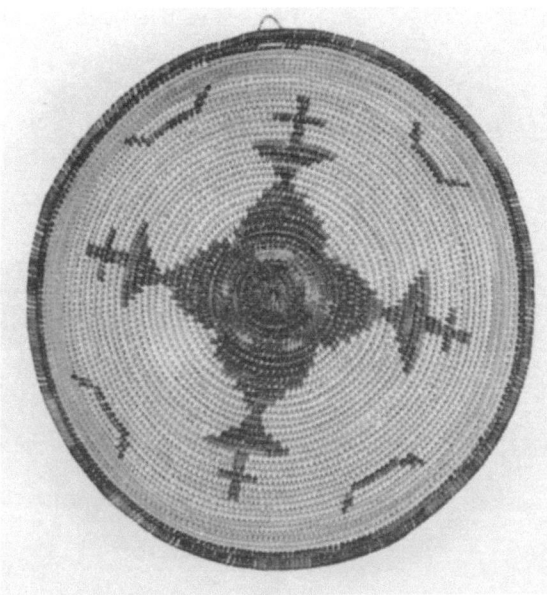

TOP: Figure 7.36. *Daagodighá*(?) bowl basket (ASM Neg. 56664).

BOTTOM: Figure 7.37. *Daagodighá*(?) bowl basket (ASM Neg. 56960).

for her husband. These were made at the time of the *da-xo-di-yá* in 1906.

The longest arm of the larger cross is 4.5 cm across. Each sack has the rim around its mouth and a cross and a crescent done in black and white beads. The center pouch has a small pierced crescent tied to its back. The cross at left is apparently of nickel, blue-black in color, and strung through a square patch of commercial gold cloth atop a blue cloth ribbon. Both crosses have copper wires soldered to the center of their backs. The specific use of black and white beads on pollen sacks, and the use of both nickel and silver for ornaments, are all recorded in Neil Buck's account of the *daagodighá* movement (Goodwin and Kaut 1954: 392, 396, 398).

***Daagodighá*(?) bowl basket.** Figure 7.36. Goodwin purchased this basket (E–1; 29 cm in diameter, 8 cm deep) in 1938 from a collection made on the Fort Apache Reservation around 1906. He noted that the rawhide loop was used to hang the basket up inside a wickiup, and he felt that this basket had been used in *daagodighá*, based on the crosses and crescents woven into it and the time and place of its collection.

***Daagodighá*(?) bowl basket.** Figure 7.37. This unprovenienced specimen from the Guenther collection (EEG 80; 25 cm in diameter, 7 cm deep) is not among the pieces donated to the Arizona State Museum. The cross-and-crescent designs suggest this basket may have been used in *daagodighá*, especially because of their arrangement one above the other (see Figs. 7.32 to 7.34). Roberts (1929: 130, 205) attributes the introduction of cross-and-crescent motifs into basketry as stemming directly from their use in *daagodighá*. She illustrates a bowl basket similar to Figure 7.36 above, with the crosses and crescents separated and placed up near the rim (Roberts 1929: 202, Fig. 14*d*).

***Daagodighá*(?) burden basket.** Figure 7.38. Collected at Globe in 1916 by former Arizona Governor George W. P. Hunt, this burden basket (1611) is illustrated because of its cross-and-crescent motifs, of which there are four evenly spaced around the basket and interspersed with single crosses. Although trimmed with buckskin, this basket (28 cm high and 28 cm in

Ritual

Figure 7.38. *Daagodighá*(?) burden basket (ASM Neg. 64294).

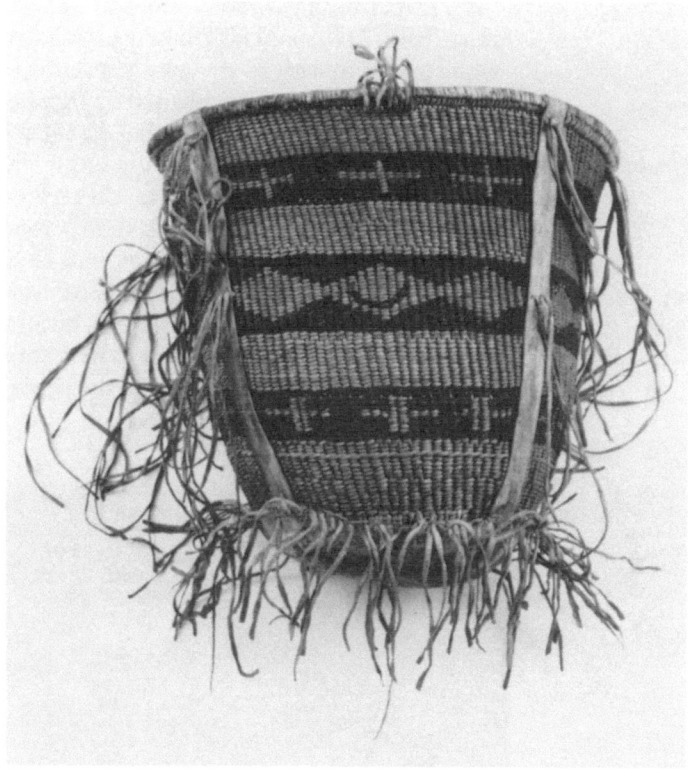

Figure 7.39. *Daagodighá*(?) burden basket (ASM Neg. 64287).

diameter) does not have reinforcing cross-sticks as might be expected (see Fig. 5.35).

***Daagodighá*(?) burden basket.** Figure 7.39. This is an unprovenienced specimen (E–8466) with buckskin trim and reinforcing cross-sticks, 35 cm high and 40 cm in diameter. It was collected in Arizona by James W. Manson. As originally woven, it had upper and lower bands with negative crosses and a middle band of negative, connected diamonds. Subsequently a black crescent was stitched in devil's claw into the central negative diamond on each of the basket's four sides. Interestingly, Roberts (1929: 205) found two baskets with crosses and crescents in which the crescents were later additions, embroidered atop the basket's weave; she does not indicate whether these were bowl, jar, or burden baskets. These were the only examples of embroidery of any kind on Apache baskets that she was aware of, and led her to remark on the possible role of "religious zeal" as a stimulus for technological innovations. The important inference to be drawn here, however, is that these three baskets with embroidered crescents were probably not originally made for *daagodighá* (as those baskets with both the cross and crescent woven in may have been), but were almost certainly converted for such use between 1903 and 1906.

Silas John's medicine shirt. Figure 7.40. This shirt (EEG 211; about 65 cm long) is made of white buckskin with an irregularly serrated bottom. The body of the shirt is a single piece of buckskin, sewn up the sides with a slit cut for the head-opening. Fringes encircle the shoulder seams except for the armpit areas; they were made by threading fine buckskin thongs through the seam once, so that each thong creates two strings of the fringe. Similar fringes extend from elbow to mid-forearm on each sleeve, but these are sewn through the sleeve *next* to its seam (and the seam runs down the outside of the sleeve).

Identical triangular flaps are attached front and back at the head-opening, each ornamented with a fringe and a seven-bead-wide band of lazy-stitch beadwork in white, red, yellow, light blue, and dark blue beads. Identical beadwork bands follow the shoulder-seam fringes. There is no other ornamentation. The flaps are darkened by grime, not by paint or ochre.

This shirt is clearly not of Western Apache manufacture (see Fig. 6.4) and may be Mescalero Apache in origin or, less likely, Jicarilla Apache, based on its attributes (although see Appendix C, fn. 2). Because of Silas John's close relationships

Ritual

with the Mescalero and no known contact with the Jicarilla, a Mescalero origin for this shirt is probable. Mescaleros came to his dances on the San Carlos Reservation as early as 1921, by no later than 1928 he had set up "holy grounds" at Mescalero, and by 1929 his visits and influence there were sufficiently disturbing to the Bureau of Indian Affairs that he was forbidden to enter the Mescalero Reservation (Kessel 1976: 172, 177). Silas, then, may have obtained this shirt himself at Mescalero, or it could have been brought or sent to him in Arizona. Even after being banned at Mescalero, Silas continued to carry on religious business by mail (Kessel 1976: 177). Hence he could have acquired it probably anytime between about 1921 and his incarceration at McNeil Island in Washington in 1933.

In 1971 Mrs. Guenther indicated to Wesley Jernigan that the shirt was sold, presumably by Silas, "when he was jailed." This could refer to any of several incidents from 1920 on (Kessel 1976: 157–158), but would most likely refer to his Washington imprisonment in 1933.

Silas John and his father. Figure 7.41. E. E. Guenther took this photo of Silas John Edwards

OPPOSITE: Figure 7.40. Silas John's medicine shirt (ASM Neg. 56652).

RIGHT: Figure 7.41. Silas John and his father (photo by E. E. Guenther).

and his father, Yoohn, probably at East Fork around 1912. Yoohn was also known to Anglos as John, Johnnie, and Johnnie Yuma. Yoohn spent four years with the Apache Scouts, was reputed to have spent some time in prison, and eventually worked a farm near East Fork (Kessel 1976: 153–154). Apparently while in prison, Yoohn learned to make horsehair items and to skin rattlesnakes to make belts, skills passed along to Silas John (see Figs. 5.46, 6.16, 6.21). Yoohn was also an influential medicine man, possessing "snake," "lightning," or "deer power," or possibly all three (Kessel 1976: 154), which doubtless influenced Silas John's own development as a medicine man and the innovative use of live rattlesnakes in his ceremonies.

Chapter Eight
Recreation

Alan Ferg and William B. Kessel

OVERLEAF: **Men playing hoop-and-pole.** Figure 8.1. In this photograph taken by Paul Mayerhoff, probably near East Fork between 1896 and 1903, men are playing the hoop-and-pole game. The hoop has just been thrown and can be seen between the ends of the two poles. The clothing is predominantly Anglo in style, but long hair, cloth headbands, and buckskin moccasins are worn by some of those present.

Hoop-and-pole paraphernalia. Figure 8.2. Goodwin (1936: 53, fn. 29) briefly described the hoop-and-pole game as follows:

> Hoop and pole was one of the most important games. . . . Only the men played it, and women were not allowed where a game was going on, as they were said to start trouble with their prattle [this is probably the Reservation-period reason; in pre-Reservation times, it was thought that women might be harmed by the hoop-and-pole power "loosed upon each other" by the competing men (Goodwin A–69)]. Only two men played at a time. Each had a pole, and each took a turn at throwing the hoop. . . . The hoop was thrown just hard enough so that by the time it got to the furrows [see Fig. 8.3*b*] it fell sideways on the ground and lay there . . . both men threw their poles so as to have them slide along the ground . . . and the hoop . . . land on or under the butt of the poles. . . . The scoring system was a complicated one, and the game required a great deal of skill. It is not played at the present time.

The poles apparently were made and kept as sets, one (usually with the butt painted red) referred to as female, one (usually with the butt painted blue) as male (Goodwin A–69). The set (21360) shown here, including the hoop, was made by Charlie Sego in 1931. The poles are both well-smoothed, straight Gambel oak, 234 cm (over seven feet) long, each made up of three overlapping pieces ranging from 90 cm to 129 cm long. Where the poles overlap, each is flattened to seat against the other and usually secured with sinew (string in this set). The butt is rounded and on the first 23 cm are various divisions and grooves demarcating nine counting areas (Culin 1907, Fig. 593); this counting section is painted orange (female) on one pole and is unpainted (male) on the other. The tip of each pole is tapered to a dull point. The hoop is also of Gambel oak, 22 cm in diameter, shaved flat on the inside to facilitate bending, and flat on the outside probably to help it roll; the ends are secured with buckskin. The thong stretched across the hoop is buckskin, wound with a buckskin thread making fifty-one "beads," each worth one point, on each side of a large central "bead" that counted as one point either direction, for a total of 104 possible points (Goodwin A–69). Culin (1907: 454–455) describes a hoop with fifty beads on either side of a central, one-point bead, totaling 101 possible points. Supposedly actual beads were used in the early days. On either side of the hoop's circumference are cut nine notches, with the two attachment points for the thong making a total of eleven scoring points on the hoop. Score is computed based on the overlap of the butt of the pole by beads on the thong and points on the hoop circumference. Culin (1907: 449–457)

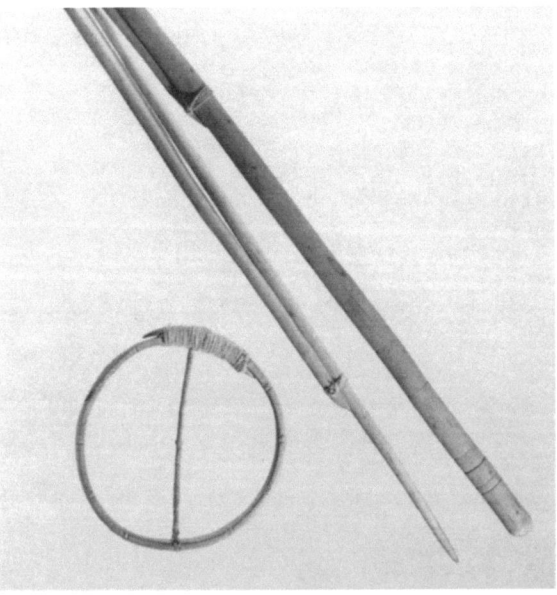

Figure 8.2. Hoop-and-pole paraphernalia (ASM Neg. 56705).

Recreation

a

b

Figure 8.3. Playing hoop-and-pole (photos by Paul Mayerhoff).

provides a more detailed discussion of the intricacies of scoring and reports the length of the playing ground as 36 yards (32.9 m). Straw, grass, or pine needles were spread to help the poles slide (Goodwin A–69).

Playing hoop-and-pole. Figure 8.3. These photographs of the hoop-and-pole game, probably taken near East Fork between 1896 and 1903, show men throwing the poles as the hoop is rolling *(a)* and scoring the throw *(b)*.

Stick game staves. Figure 8.4. Three types of stick games predominated among the Western Apache: the basket-game, played with anywhere from four to fourteen short wood staves (Culin 1907: 91; Goodwin A–69), the 3–stick game; and the 4–stick game. On top is a set of half-round 3–stick staves (21368), one of Gambel oak (with bark left on the round side) and two of juniper, each 29 cm long. All three have a diagonal, black-painted cut on their flat face. In this game, also known as "throw-sticks," the staves were thrown down on end and bounced off a flat rock, with the score kept on forty stones arranged in a circle around it (see Fig. 8.5). In 4–stick or "drop-sticks," the staves were simply dropped on the ground. The set on the bottom (21369) has half-round, shaved batamote staves, each 61 cm long, with the flat side painted black on one and orange on three. Both sets of staves were made by Charlie Sego in 1931; they apparently were carved with a knife and have battered and flattened ends from use.

Many slight variations on the rules for all three games existed, usually concerned with scoring or who and how many could play (Culin 1907: 86–91). Instances of men, women, or mixed groups playing both 3–stick and 4–stick are known; however, 3–stick seems to have been played most often by women (see Fig. 8.6). Although both men and women could make the staves used in each game, apparently men usually did so. All of Goodwin's informants agreed that there was no ritual involved in the manufacture of the staves, nor was there any power or lucky words that could help a player win (Goodwin A–69). Harvey Nashkine noted that 4–stick staves "were carried in a small buckskin case, stuck in the belt in back," and Anna Price remarked that the Western Apache had learned 4–stick from the Chiricahua (Goodwin A–69).

Figure 8.4. Stick game staves (ASM Neg. 32093).

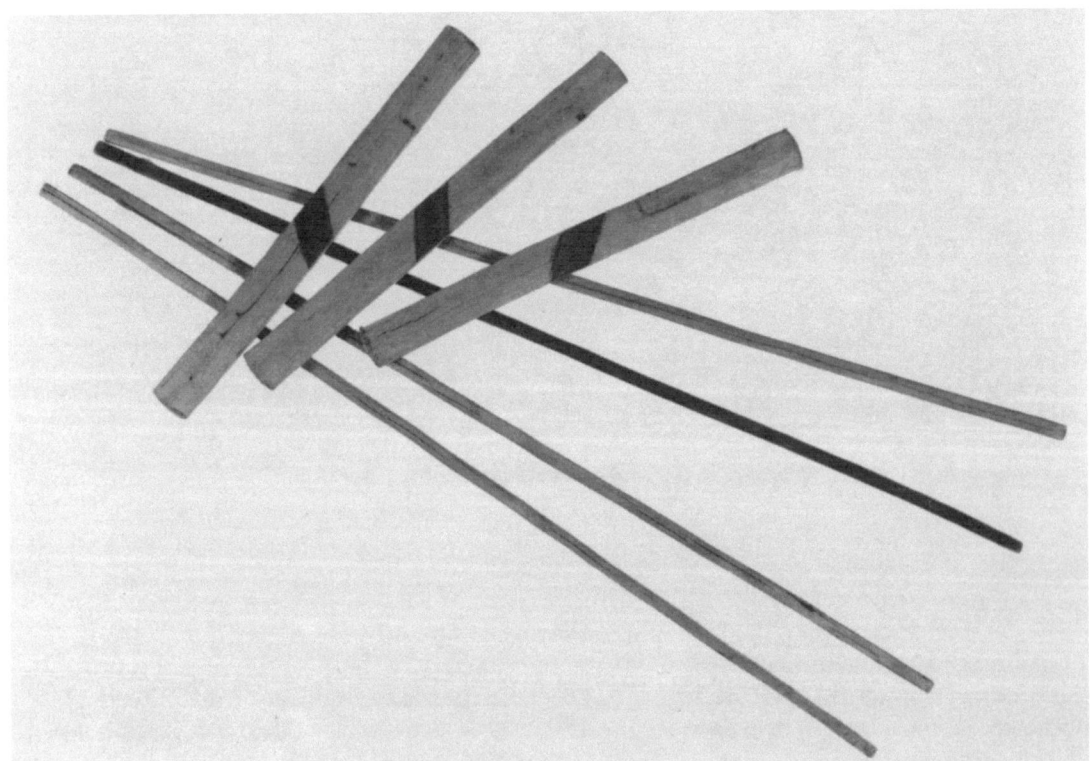

Recreation

RIGHT: Figure 8.5. Arrangement of stones and players in the 3-stick game.

BOTTOM: Figure 8.6. Women playing the 3-stick game (photo by Paul Mayerhoff).

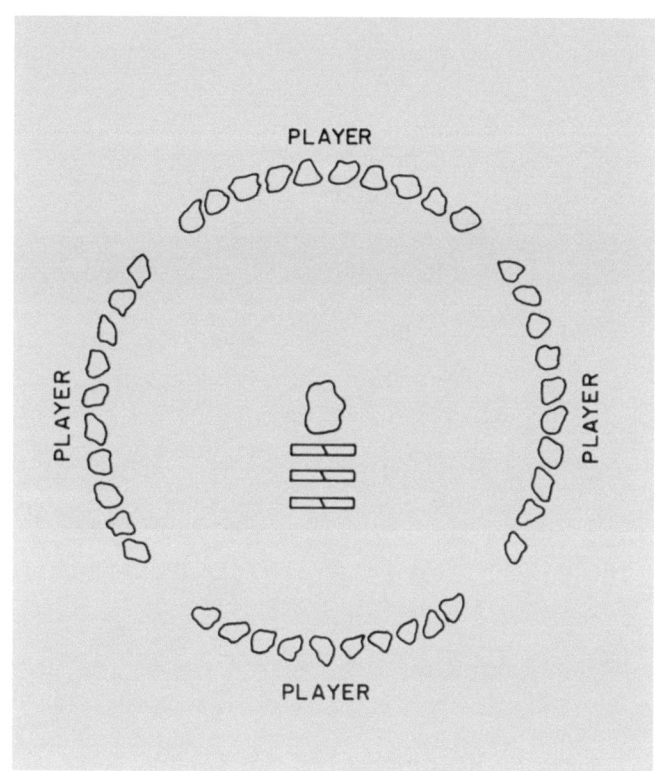

Arrangement of stones and players in the 3–stick game. Figure 8.5. This arrangement was used among the White Mountain Apache (after Reagan in Culin 1907, Fig. 86).

Women playing the 3–stick game. Figure 8.6. This photo of women playing the 3–stick game was taken sometime between 1896 and 1903, probably near East Fork. Descriptions of both the game rules and sets of the staves sent by Rev. Paul Mayerhoff to the Field Columbian Museum in Chicago are in Culin (1907: 87–88).

Figure 8.7. Shinney ball (ASM Neg. 32096).

Figure 8.8. "Dirt Hill Night Ball" game paraphernalia (ASM Neg. 64297).

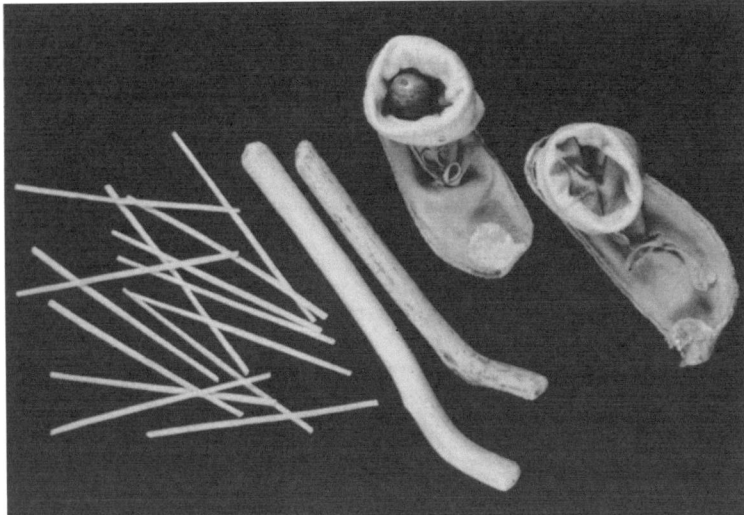

Shinney ball. Figure 8.7. This buckskin ball (21405; 5.5 cm to 7.5 cm across) was filled with a light, resilient material (agave fiber?) and sewn shut with a buckskin thong. It was made by Charlie Sego in 1932. Shinney is played something like hockey without ice. According to informants (Goodwin A–69), the game was played by young men and women, in two teams of from two to ten members each. Two bushes about 150 yards (137 m) apart at each end of an open, level piece of ground served as goals. The number of goals needed to win was decided on before the game started and was usually three or four. Kinds of balls reported included the type shown here, with agave fiber stuffing, rounded bone joints (probably like that in Fig. 8.8), and "coyote pumpkin" (*Cucurbita palmata*) gourds and "finger-leaf" gourds (*C. digitata*), although it is hard to imagine the gourds standing up to any hard play. Shinney sticks were made of mesquite or mountain-mahogany, crooked on the end, well-smoothed, and about a meter long (Navajo sticks are illustrated in Culin 1907: 623 and Kluckhohn, Hill, and Kluckhohn 1971: 381, 383). The game was started at mid-field by two opposing players, "one with the ball in his hand which he would pretend to drop several times and then quickly drop it . . . and then both players would hit at it with their sticks." The object was to hit the ball downfield and hit the goal bush. "When the ball was near a goal, then everyone would be trying to get it. Lots of times they would miss the ball and crack you on the shins."

"Dirt Hill Night Ball" game paraphernalia. Figure 8.8. "Dirt Hill Night Ball," or the hidden-ball game, was played by two teams, one side hiding a ball and the other trying to find it (Goodwin A–69). Teams could number more than twenty members on a side. In pre-Reservation times women played among themselves, or with old men, but in Reservation times the game seems to have been most commonly played by men only; it was inappropriate for a married woman to mingle with so many men, and women usually watched and bet but did not play. This game was played in the winter; it started several hours after sundown and was supposed to stop before dawn. If the game was still in

Recreation

progress and sunrise was imminent, the players put streaks of charcoal under their eyes to lessen the glare. The same was done at night if there was glare from snow on the ground.

Hidden-ball had two major variants. Among the San Carlos Apache the ball was actually buried under piles of dirt arranged in a variety of standardized patterns in a pit, and a team had to win two fourteen-point games (in a row?, two of three games?) in order to win the competition. Each team had its own pit, with the pits placed on opposite sides of the fire. Among the White Mountain Apache, four moccasins were buried on each side of the fire with about three inches of cuff showing, the ball was hidden in one, and the opposing team used a stick to thump moccasins which they wanted eliminated or in which they thought the ball was hidden. The moccasins used could be either old or those of someone at the game, men's or women's, with toe tabs or without. Only one game was played, consisting of 106 or 160 points. Apparently the White Mountain "moccasin game" fell into disuse first, and by the 1930s only the San Carlos variant was still being played.

This paraphernalia includes a pair of worn moccasins (EEG 173), a ball made from the proximal head of a domestic cow's left femur (21322), and two tapping sticks with the requisite crook, one of mesquite (21320; 44 cm long) and one of tamarix (21321; 36 cm long); these were used in the White Mountain variant. Jewett Wright made the sticks and ball for Goodwin in 1936. The fourteen yucca counters (21434) are each about 25 cm long, with both ends cut off rounded and are of the type used in the San Carlos variant. This set was collected by Goodwin after a game at Calva in February of 1935.

Balls also were carved out of yucca. One could cheat in the San Carlos variant by burying two balls at the same time, at different depths or in different areas of the pit, and acknowledging the one that scored the fewest points for the opposing team; to preclude this, the ball used normally had marks cut or burned into it in everyone's presence at the start of the game. Balls, sticks, and counters were discarded without ceremony or were cached where the game had been played, to be used some other time.

Figure 8.9. Cloth dolls, old and new (ASM Neg. 56681).

Cloth dolls, old and new. Figure 8.9. At left (EEG 167) and right (EEG 168) are two modern dolls of the type made to sell to tourists; both were made in the late 1960s, possibly by the same person, and were purchased by Mrs. Guenther. The larger is about 75 cm tall, with two beaded pouches on her belt. The smaller is about 50 cm tall, carrying a shawl, pitched water bottle, and a pair of moccasins. Both have cloth bodies, yarn hair, sewn facial features, beadwork jewelry, moccasins, slips or petticoats, and panties, with the clothing sewn on a sewing machine. At left center (EEG 165) is an entirely hand-sewn doll made by Shima for Mrs. Guenther's first daughter, Wenonah, in 1913 or 1914 (see Figs.

2.4, 2.5). About 40 cm tall, it has a cloth body, thread hair, sewn facial features, and a beadwork T–necklace. At right center is a third modern doll (EEG 166), not in the ASM collections, with no provenience information.

Toy cradleboards. Figure 8.10. These six miniature cradleboards (EEG 141 through 146) were given to Mrs. Guenther by Apache school girls at East Fork, between 1911 and 1922. Whether all were made by the girls themselves, or by their mothers, is unknown. The largest (EEG 141; 49.3 cm long) has black, blue-and-white-striped, and red-and-white-striped seed bead trim, and the cradleboard cloth is made from a La Junta, Colorado, "Blue Bell," 24–pound, bleached hard wheat flour sack.

Figure 8.10. Toy cradleboards (ASM Neg. 56685).

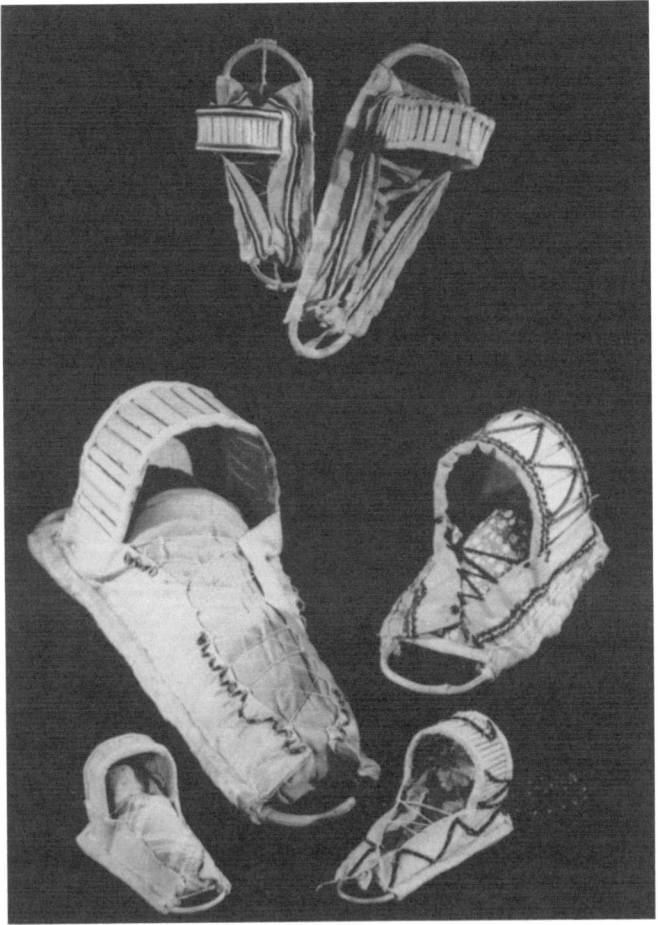

Children's toys made by adults. Figure 8.11. The doll at left (EEG 223; about 55 cm tall) was made on a two-stick foundation, one forked stick forming the legs, torso, and head, with a straight stick attached transversely to form the shoulders. The sticks were padded with a green and white print commercial cloth and covered with under-clothing of the same material. The doll was then dressed in a beaded buckskin poncho, skirt, and boots. The eyes are sewn-on black beads and the black thread hair is tied at the back with a beaded hair ornament (Figs. 6.12, 6.13). The T–necklace appears to be a later addition. Twelve colors of beads were used. This doll was obtained by Frieda Knoop from an unknown source but was noted by her as having been made in 1877. (See Figs. 6.2 and 6.19 for other dolls.)

At center is a bow and two arrows (EEG 44) made for one of the Guenther children. The bow is juniper with a buckskin string, and the arrows, each about 67 cm long, have cane shafts and juniper foreshafts. Each arrow is fletched with three turkey feathers, two wing and one tail. One arrow has the nock area painted green, the other blue, and the painting on both was placed over the sinew bindings. (Additional painted nocks and hafting styles are shown in Figs. 3.6 and 5.3.)

At right is a pair of miniature saddlebags (EEG 112) made between 1918 and 1928 for the Guenther children by someone in Chief Alchesay's family. It is ornamented like the full-size bags (see Fig. 5.48), with red cloth, fancy-cut leather trim, large blue glass beads, smaller black and white beads, metal tinklers, and black and red paint. Folded in half, it is about 53 cm tall.

At lower left are two bumpy, chocolate-colored mudstone concretions (21868). Goodwin obtained these at Bylas in 1936 and refers to them as "marbles, kind used by Apache boys in early reservation days."

At bottom left is a miniature beaded buckskin pouch (EEG 8) made for one of the Guenther children. The zigzag beadwork design is done in red, white, and blue beads, with a metal tinkler fringe at the bottom. The back is plain. The rectangular shape and presence of tinklers suggest it may have been made for a boy (see Fig. 6.14).

Recreation

Figure 8.11. Children's toys made by adults (ASM Neg. 56686).

At bottom right are five walnuts (21388) that Goodwin purchased from Mrs. Jewett Wright in 1932. They, or five round stones of about the same size, were used in the "Five Stone Game," sometimes referred to as a girl's juggling game; it was played by girls or young women of any age up until they were married. From two to four played, taking turns trying to complete fourteen different plays, each being some combination of holding some stones and catching others thrown into the air, analogous to, but more complex than Anglo "jacks" (Goodwin A–69).

At bottom center is an unfired clay doll (21386; 15 cm tall) of the style that may have preceded both the buckskin and cloth (Fig. 8.9) types. It was made by Anna Price and given to Goodwin in December 1932. This doll has a hair ornament attached by agave(?) fiber embedded in the clay, a "necklace" of punctate dots, and a "buckskin dress" with a "fringe" depicted by incised lines at the base. Arms, feet, and facial features are not depicted.

Musical instruments. Figures 8.12, 8.13, and Color Illustration 32. Drums were used in both ceremonial and social contexts. Originally they were made with a piece of buckskin tied over the mouth of a pottery jar that had a little water inside to keep the buckskin damp (Goodwin A–71). The small pot-drum shown (*right*, E–56)

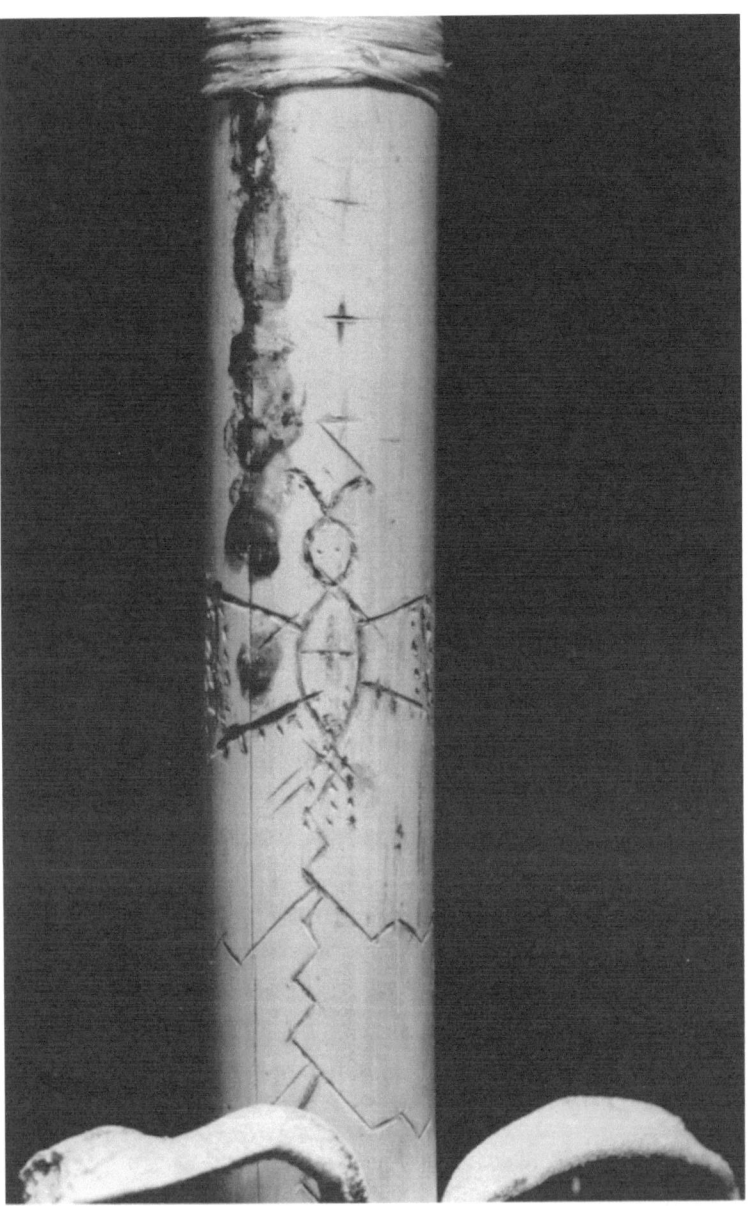

Figure 8.12. Closeup of cane flageolet (ASM Neg. 56704).

is actually Navajo, but is analogous to the Western Apache type; the drum stick with it (EEG 35) is Western Apache, 32 cm long, shaved flat on the inside where it is bent into a circle, and secured with sinew. As pottery making declined, iron kettles or large cans were substituted (Bourke 1892: 462, 583; Baldwin 1965: 111; see also Fig. 7.7). Pueblo-style drums constructed from sections of cottonwood logs have also been made recently. The large log-drum and drumstick (*left*, EEG 140) were made by Ted Bourke of Whiteriver in 1961 or 1962. The end visible has a geometric design, and the opposite rawhide head has a *gaan* mask, wands, and the words "WHITE MOUNTAIN APACHE" painted on it. The drumstick is completely wrapped in buckskin.

Flutes were made primarily by young men to be used in courting, although men apparently also played them occasionally for their own amusement (Goodwin A–71). The cane from which flutes were made (presumably *Arundo donax*, giant reed) was usually collected on raids into Mexico. This flute (*bottom center*, 21361; 45.5 cm long) was made by Ambrose Swift at Bylas in 1932. It is tied with sinew in three places and has three finger holes. The sound hole was created by cutting a hole through the outer wall of the cane and partially through the septum in the cane joint, then partially covering this over with a piece of buckskin; technically this instrument is a flageolet. Pitch was used apparently to keep air from leaking out a crack in the upper body. Geometric decorations and a butterfly are cut and burned into the cane (Fig. 8.12). Goodwin's catalogue notes that the "butterfly on it is to attract women or girls when it is played," and the association of flutes, butterflies, and courtship is well described in Apache myth (Goodwin 1939: 27–28).

Fiddles were used to play a variety of ceremonial songs, social dance songs, love songs, and corn-beer drinking songs, but usually were played by men for their own entertainment or for a small group of friends, and not at dances or ceremonies. Fiddles, made from century-plant flower-stalks (*Agave* sp.), exhibit a variety of manufacturing techniques, and have from one to three horsehair strings (Bourke 1886, illustration opposite p. 49; Dittemore 1978). At bottom

Recreation

Figure 8.13. Musical instruments; see also Color Illustration 32 (ASM Neg. 56703).

right is a one-string fiddle (21431; 26 cm long), with red designs and burned-in holes, both decorative and for the tuning peg. It was collected by Goodwin in Whiteriver in 1933. The large two-string fiddle and its bow (*upper left,* 5871) were collected by Goodwin in 1931. Although additional provenience information is lacking, this elaborately decorated fiddle undoubtedly was made by Amos Gustina of Bylas (Ferg 1981). At upper right are two one-string fiddles and bows, each 45 cm long (*right,* EEG 33; *left,* EEG 34), obtained by Frieda Knoop at either Carrizo or East Fork, between 1919 and 1924.

Appendix A
The Southern Athapascans

Grenville Goodwin

The Navajo and Apache collectively are termed Southern Athapascans, because they speak Athapascan languages and are the most southerly representatives of this important North American linguistic stock. Athapascan speaking peoples are geographically divided into three groups: Northern Athapascan in Alaska and Northwest Canada, Pacific Coast Athapascan located intermittently from British Columbia south to Northern California, and Southern Athapascan already mentioned [Fig. AA.1]. The Northern group number roughly from 15,000 to 17,000, the number of the Pacific Coast group is far smaller, and the Southern group today number approximately 57,000. Thus, though the linguistic stock has been named for a Canadian region inhabited by the Northern divison, the number of people in the Southern group today is vastly larger, and even several hundred years ago was probably at least as large as the Northern group. Between the territories occupied in the Southwest by the Southern Athapascans and those held by the other groups were vast intervening regions belonging to alien tribes. Because Northwest Canada and Alaska are in the main peopled by Athapascans, it is suggested that this stock was probably one of the most recent arrivals from Asia, and consequently that the Southern group must have split off from the Northern group and pushed south. The date of this southward push, if we can accept this theory, is uncertain. However, we know that Spanish explorers encountered peoples in the Southwest as early as 1540 who were very probably Athapascan speaking, and it is by no means impossible that the forbears of the Navajo and Apache entered the Southwest some time in the 13th and 14th centuries.

Within historic times the Southern Athapascans have been composed of seven distinct divisions, based on territorial limits, culture, and language: Navajo, Western Apache, Chiricahua, Mescalero, Lipan, Jicarilla, and Kiowa-Apache. In 1870 the approximate populations of these divisons were respectively 15,000, 3,600, 1,000, 830, 300, 769, and 320. Due to Navajo numerical superiority and certain striking cultural peculiarities, as blanket weaving, silver work, dwelling type, Pueblo dress, sheep raising, and wealth of spectacular ritual, it has been the custom to consider them a distant entity, as opposed to the remainder of these people who are collectively termed Apache and who, it has been supposed, are far more closely interrelated in langauge and culture than any of them are thus related to the Navajo.

Reprinted from *The Kiva* 4 (2): 5–10, 1938, with permission of the Arizona Archaeological and Historical Society. (Accompanying figures selected by Alan Ferg.)

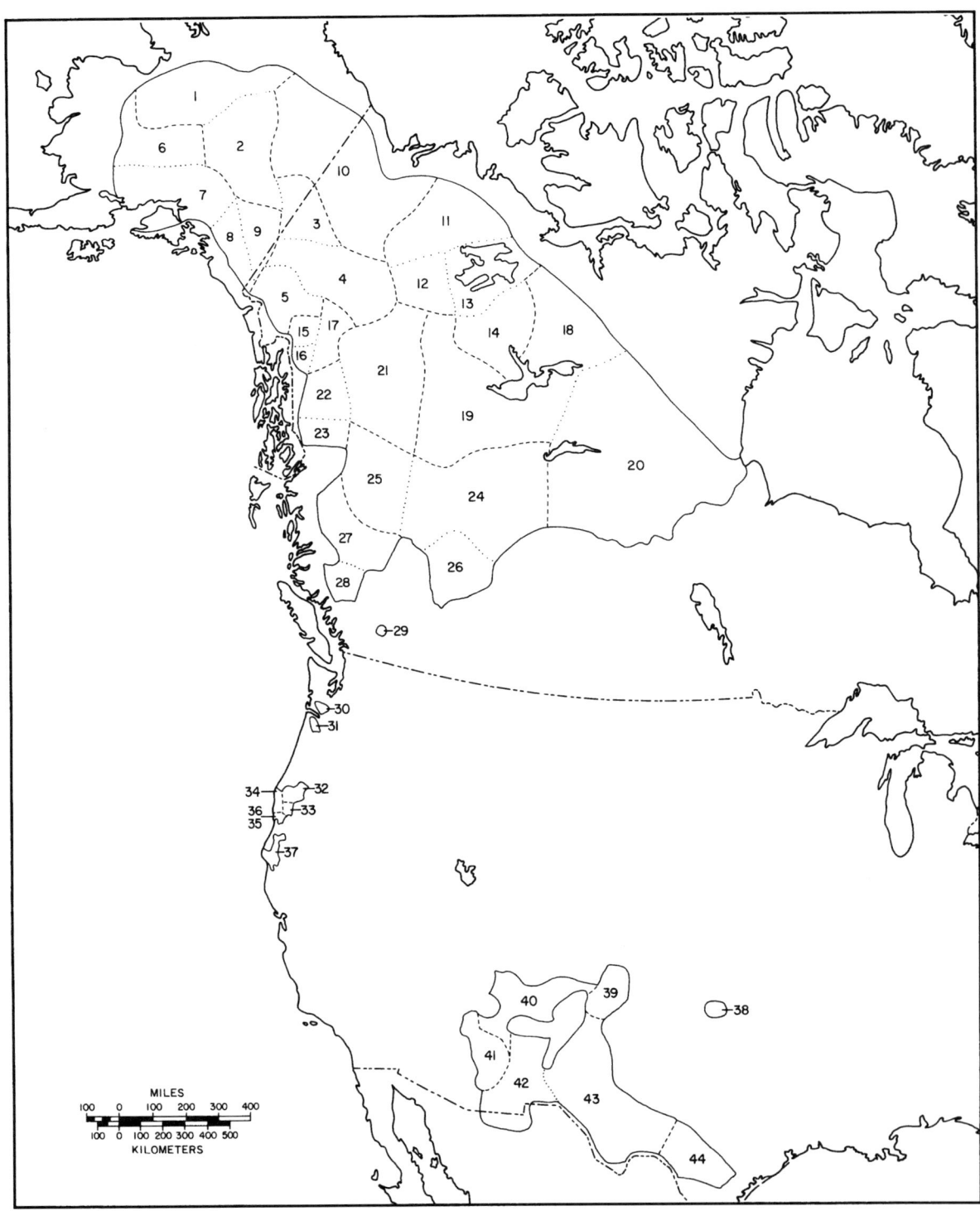

Figure AA.1. Distribution of Athapascan tribes in North America. The boundaries and relationships shown and the names and spellings used follow Driver and others (1953) except in their inclusion of Toboso. The Toboso may have been Uto-Aztecan speakers, but are perhaps best left unclassified (Griffen 1983).

The Southern Athapascans

NORTHERN ATHAPASCANS

1. Koyukon
2. Tanana
3. Han
4. Tutchone
5. Southern Tutchone
6. Ingalik
7. Tanaina
8. Ahtena
9. Nabesna
10. Kutchin
11. Hare (Kawchodinne)
12. Mountain
13. Bear Lake (Satudene)
14. Dogrib (Thlingchadine)
15. Tagish
16. Atlin
17. Teslin
18. Yellowknife (Tatsanottine)
19. Slave
20. Chipewyan
21. Kaska
22. Tahltan
23. Tsetsaut
24. Beaver (Tsattine)
25. Sekani
26. Sarsi
27. Carrier
28. Chilcotin (Tsilkotin)
29. Nicola

PACIFIC COAST ATHAPASCANS

30. Kwalhiokwa
31. Clatskanie
32. Upper Umpqua
33. Middle Rogue River
34. Lower Rogue River
35. Chetco
36. Tolowa
37. California Athapascans

SOUTHERN ATHAPASCANS

38. Kiowa-Apache
39. Jicarilla
40. Navajo
41. Western Apache
42. Chiricahua
43. Mescalero
44. Lipan

That the Navajo do not merit such a segregation has become evident through a fuller knowledge of the Apache cultures and languages. Such differences as the Navajo show are not caused by something inherent within themselves, but are due to acculturation from an alien people, mainly the Pueblo. They are an extreme, but not the only acculturation extreme among Southern Athapascans. On the east we have the Kiowa-Apache who have apparently taken over Plains traits wholesale. Acculturation is to be found to varying lesser extent among the other divisions. It is because Navajo assimilation has been from one of the most intense and colorful cultures in North America, that it has been given undeserved prominence. Actually Kiowa-Apache warrant just as much distinction of this kind. If we are to think in terms of true linguistic and cultural variation between the seven Southern Athapascan divisions, we must consider them as one people, and not as a dual division, Navajo-Apache.

The Navajo were originally located in Northwestern New Mexico and extreme Northeastern Arizona. Their extension further west into Arizona came in the 19th century. The Western Apache, composed of the five groups, White Mountain, Cibecue, San Carlos, Southern Tonto and Northern Tonto, occupied an area in Eastern Arizona bounded roughly on the north by Flagstaff and on the south by Tucson. The Chiricahua held extreme Southeast Arizona and Southwestern New Mexico west of the Rio Grande. The Mescalero ranged through South Central New Mexico and down into the Big Bend region of Texas, Chihuahua and Northern Coahuila. Early in the 18th century the Lipan inhabited the Southern Panhandle region of Texas, but under the impact of the Comanche they were gradually forced to Southern Texas, between Corpus Christi and Del Rio, and the adjacent part of Coahuila. The Jicarilla held Northeastern New Mexico and an adjacent area in Colorado bounded on the north by the Arkansas river. The Kiowa-Apache were located in Southeastern Kansas, Western Oklahoma, and the Northern part of the Texas panhandle. Recent research indicates that the Southern Athapascan languages may be divided into two groups, Eastern and Western. In the Eastern group belong Lipan, Jicarilla and Kiowa-Apache, with the latter people showing some distinctions from the first two. In the Western group are placed the Navajo, Western Apache, Chiricahua, and Mescalero, the Navajo being distinct from the other three, and Chiricahua and Mescalero closely similar.

Economic Life

Hunting was important to all divisions, for to a great extent they depended on the use of meat and hides. Deer, antelope, and small animals were the most common game. Buffalo were important as a food source to Mescalero, Lipan, Jicarilla, and Kiowa-Apache, particularly the latter for whom they were almost the staff of life. These last people held policed communal buffalo hunts of the Plains type. Though occasionally Navajo made journeys to the plains to hunt buffalo, such activities were economically unimportant. The Western Apache were too far removed from buffalo range to hunt them, and the same is true of the Chiricahua with the possible exception of the Eastern Chiricahua. The fact that Navajo territory was somewhat inferior as a game country may have influenced the early acceptance of sheep raising and agriculture by these people.

Piñon nuts, juniper berries, prickly pear fruit, and yucca fruit were extensively eaten by Navajo, Western Apache, Chiricahua, Mescalero and Jicarilla. Mescal and mesquite beans were important to Western Apache, Chiricahua, Mescalero and

BOTTOM: Figure AA.2. Navajo earth-covered forked-stick hogan at "Cave Springs" in the Chinle Valley, northeastern Arizona; photograph taken by A. V. Kidder around 1912. Note the buckboard in the background (ASM Neg. Pix 1470–x–6).

OPPOSITE, TOP: Figure AA.3. Western Apache wickiup on the San Carlos Reservation; photograph taken by Grenville Goodwin in the 1930s (ASM Neg. 18077).

OPPOSITE, BOTTOM: Figure AA.4. Jicarilla camp of Tofilo Venuio, showing canvas(?) tipis and a brush shade; photograph taken by Pliny Earle Goddard in September of 1909 (photo courtesy American Museum of Natural History, Neg. 14317).

The Southern Athapascans

probably Lipan, and the acorns of Emory's oak were much used by the Western Apache. Sahuaro fruit, though available to the latter people, was not as important as it was among the Papago and Pima. Wild plant foods were of utmost importance to Chiricahua and Mescalero, as these people were nominally without agriculture. Information from the Kiowa-Apache and Lipan is incomplete, but we know that both utilized wild plant foods. The Western Apache, Jicarilla and Navajo with their agriculture were less dependent on them than the others, especially the latter.

The Kiowa-Apache lacked agriculture and among the Lipan it was not of importance; Chiricahua and Mescalero farming was negligible. Only a few families planted and very little care was expended in raising the crop. Among Navajo, Western Apache, and Jicarilla, agriculture reached considerable development. Dry farming and irrigation were practiced, and corn, beans, squash, and gourds were raised. Though Navajo agriculture slightly exceeded that among the Western Apache, it was by no means comparable to Pueblo or Pima farming.

Stock raising did not occur till after the Spanish colonization of Northern Mexico. Though the Western Apache, Chiricahua and Mescalero continually raided Mexican settlements for horses and cattle, they did not seriously attempt to raise stock of their own. It seems probable that among the Lipan, Jicarilla, and especially Kiowa-Apache with their Plains orientation, horse raising was of some importance, though raiding other tribes and Mexican ranches for horses was continually indulged in. The Navajo raised horses to some extent and took over sheep and goat raising from the Pueblo and Spanish speaking peoples in the upper Rio Grande Valley. This last became an important industry among them.

Material Culture

Methods of travel and conveyance varied. Before acquisition of the horse, the Jicarilla and probably the Lipan and Kiowa-Apache used dogs for transportation, though it is not certain whether the dogs carried small packs or were made to pull a travois. All but the Kiowa-Apache, and possibly the Lipan, made use of the carrying basket. With the introduction of horses, riding and packing of them became important, especially among Jicarilla, Lipan and Kiowa-Apache. The Jicarilla and Kiowa-Apache as well as the Mescalero and probably the Lipan, used the travois with the horse, but it was absent for the remainder of the Southern Athapascans, except among the easternmost of the Chiricahua. All employed baby carriers of varying design.

Three dwelling types occurred [Figs. AA.2–AA.4]. The Navajo used the earth covered hogan, the Western Apache, Chiricahua, Mescalero, and Jicarilla the wickiup covered with brush or grass, and the Mescalero, Lipan, Jicarilla and Kiowa-Apache the buffalo hide tipi of the Plains. Among Jicarilla and Mescalero we find both tipi and wickiup, but apparently in former times the wickiup was the more favored of the two.

Southern Athaspascan pottery is unique in the area. Raised or incised decoration, markedly conical bottom, and flaring rim are its main characteristics. It has no parallel in the Southwest except among the Ute, Southern Paiute, and Taos and Picuris Pueblos. It was made fairly commonly by the Navajo, slightly less so by Jicarilla, decidedly less frequently by Western Apache, and to a slight extent by Chiricahua and Mescalero. So far as is known the Lipan and Kiowa-Apache made no pottery. The Navajo were the only ones who made decorated ware similar to the Pueblo. This they did to a limited extent. It should be noted that among them, where pottery making was more prevalent, basketry did not attain the finesse or importance it did among other divisions using it.

The Kiowa-Apache made no basketry and data are lacking on Lipan basketry, but it was common among all the other divisions. Coiled, twilled, and twined weaves were used. The most popular forms were coiled trays or bowls, pitched water bottles of coiled or twilled weave, and burden baskets of twined or twilled weave. Twilled weave was frequent for Western Apache, Chiricahua and Mescalero, but was apparently absent or at least extremely uncommon among Navajo and Jicarilla. The basketry of each division is clearly distinguishable. Weaving of blankets, garments, or cloth of any kind was confined entirely to the Navajo, who wove in wool on upright looms.

Clothing varied from division to division [Figs. AA.5–AA.7]. Mescalero, Lipan, Jicarilla, and Kiowa-Apache men wore the hair in two braids and dressed in buckskin shirt, leggings and moccasins of Plains type. Western Apache and Chiricahua men wore the hair loose and held in place by a head-band. Though they used buckskin shirts and leggings to some extent, these differed slightly from the Plains type, as did also their boot-like moccasins. Jicarilla and Kiowa-Apache women's dress was of buckskin, reaching from the

The Southern Athapascans

TOP LEFT: Figure AA.5. Dolls showing pre-Reservation dress for a Jicarilla man (*left*, E–22) and woman (*right*, E–23); both acquired in the 1930s by Goodwin on the Jicarilla Reservation in New Mexico. The male doll is 41 cm tall, with the hair worn in braids, and has low-top moccasins, leggings, and breechclout. The female also has the hair in braids and wears the typical wide leather belt (ASM Neg. 64299).

TOP RIGHT: Figure AA.6. Dolls showing pre-Reservation dress for a Mescalero man (*left*, E–27) and woman (*right*, E–28); both acquired in the 1930s by Goodwin on the Mescalero Reservation in New Mexico. The male doll is 42 cm tall, with the hair worn in braids, and has low-top moccasins, leggings, and breechclout. The female has the hair in a queue (ASM Neg. 64301).

LEFT: Figure AA.7. Dolls showing pre-Reservation dress for a Lipan man (*left*, E–29) and woman (*right*, E–30); both acquired in the 1930s by Goodwin on the Mescalero Reservation in New Mexico. The male doll is 30 cm tall, with the hair worn in braids, and has low-top moccasins, leggings, and cloth breechclout. The female has the hair in a queue. Goodwin noted that both dolls were virtually identical to the Mescalero dolls, and might show Mescalero influence rather than a true depiction of Lipan clothing (ASM Neg. 64302).

shoulders to below the knees and with an extra buckskin cape or poncho over the head and shoulders. Women of both peoples wore the hair in braids and Jicarilla women at times wore it in two queues at the back of the head. Lipan, Mescalero, Chiricahua, and Western Apache women wore a buckskin skirt and a buckskin poncho-like upper garment. All wore boot-like moccasins and among all the hair style was either a queue at the back of the head, braids among the Lipan and Mescalero, or loose hair among Chiricahua and Western Apache. Though apparently the Navajo used buckskin garments of a native design, within the last century, at least, they completely adopted the Pueblo type of dress: loose drawers, woven shirt, and ankle high red moccasins for men, the two blanket dress with moccasin puttees for women. Both sexes wore the hair in a queue at the back of the head. Among the Mescalero, Jicarilla, Kiowa-Apache and probably Lipan, the Plains war bonnet occurred. The Navajo, Western Apache, and Chiricahua used a peculiar type of buckskin cap, and the Mescalero also may have used a slightly similar one.

Weapons consisted of shield, lance, war club, bow and arrow. The main variations occur in type of bow and arrow. The self bow was Western Apache and Chiricahua, the sinew backed bow Navajo, Jicarilla, and probably Mescalero, Lipan, and Kiowa-Apache. The wooden arrow, closely resembling a Plains type, was the most common among Navajo, Mescalero, Jicarilla, Kiowa-Apache, and probably Lipan. The cane arrow with foreshaft was the favorite among Western Apache and Chiricahua, and is also said to have been once used by the Navajo.

Social Organization

Kinship terminologies are apparently of two types. In the first are classed those of Western Apache, Chiricahua, and Mescalero, in the second those of Jicarilla, Lipan, and Kiowa-Apache. The predominant Navajo system belongs in the second group, but also has alternative terms in several positions which closely link it with the first group. Matrilineal descent and closest association of the individual with the mother's blood relatives, seems to be common to all divisions except the Kiowa-Apache, where though it may exist, it is said not to be as vital as elsewhere. Only the Navajo and Western Apache have clans. These are matrilineal and closely resemble those of Hopi and Zuñi.

Marriage was usually arranged by the boy's parents who made a gift to the girl's family which might or might not be reciprocated. Marriage ritual was apparently absent except for the Navajo. The couple most commonly lived near the wife's family and the husband had a definite obligation to work for and help his parents-in-law. He had also to show them certain respects which they were obliged to return. Mother-in-law avoidance for men was present except for Lipan. Likewise polygamy was practiced by all except these people and the sororate (various rights and privileges of a man over his wife's younger sisters), and levirate, (wife inheritance by a deceased man's brother), were common in every division.

Joking relationships (privileged familiarity between individuals of specified relationships), occurred in certain of the divisions, but were entirely absent from Chiricahua and Mescalero. The most marked of these were between cross-cousins, and between siblings-in-law of the opposite sex. (Siblings are children of the same parents.)

The principal social and economic unit was the extended family, under the leadership of one man, the family head. Several of these extended families tended to inhabit one locality and together formed what may be called a local group. The most influential head man in the local group acted as its chief. Authority of chiefs depended mainly on their personal influence and no absolute rights were vested in them except on very limited occasions. When several local groups inhabited a given range, they might form a band, though not necessarily so, for among Navajo, Kiowa-Apache, and some Western Apache, band formation was practically non-existent. As a chief's authority did not go beyond his own local group, no chief controlled a whole band.

The Southern Athapascans have been famous for their raids and war parties against Europeans and outside Indian tribes. Even hostilities between certain of the division were by no means infrequent. To some extent raiding for stock and other booty was of economic importance. Though data are lacking on Lipan and Kiowa-Apache, the war dance was probably common to all, and the same may be said of the victory dance on the return of a successful war party. Scalping, though practiced by all, was not important among Navajo, Western Apache, and Chiricahua. Formal boasting of war prowess, a Plains trait, occurred among Mescalero, Jicarilla, Kiowa-Apache, and possibly Lipan, but was absent elsewhere.

Religion and Ritual

Certain elements in mythology are common to almost all Southern Athapascans. Chief among these are the doings of the culture heroes, "Slayer of Monsters," and "Born from Water." Emergence from an underworld, a Pueblo theme, is present in Navajo, Jicarilla, and Western Apache mythology, but absent from that of the Chiricahua and Mescalero. No mythological material is yet available from Lipan and Kiowa-Apache, and data on religious concepts of these two divisions are also lacking. The other peoples consistently show a strong tendency to personify animals, plants, and elements, and to view these personifications as both destructive and constructive supernatural agencies in their religions.

There are two main types of ceremonies: those derived through direct contact of the shaman with the supernatural sources of his power, and those which are traditional rites passed down from generation to generation. The Navajo have only the latter, but the Jicarilla and Western Apache have both traditional and personal rites with stress on those of traditional type. The Chiricahua, Mescalero, and Lipan ceremonies are almost entirely non-traditional. The one ceremony which is traditional wherever it occurs, is the important girl's puberty rite, found in all divisions but the Kiowa-Apache and possibly the Lipan. Though data are lacking for the Kiowa-Apache we know that all the others had rites in which masked dancers comparable to and probably originating from the Pueblo kachina, appeared. Curing rites were common to all and the Navajo, Western Apache, and Jicarilla had agricultural and rain making ceremonies. Hunting rites and rites used in divination are recorded for all but Lipan, Jicarilla, and Kiowa-Apache, but very probably existed among them as well. The Kiowa-Apache participated in an annual sun-dance, and had four dancing societies of the Plains type with ceremonial bundles. Such striking Plains characteristics as these were apparently non-existent among other Southern Athapascans, though no negative data have yet been published for the Lipan. Lipan, Mescalero, and Kiowa-Apache had a peyote rite.

Navajo ritual is conspicuous by its extreme complexity of terminology and minute ceremonial classification. It also employs ritual complications and paraphernalia far beyond those in use by other divisions. Thus, though the Jicarilla and Western Apache both make intricate ceremonial sand paintings, the number used by them is negligible compared to that among the Navajo. But only in its Pueblo veneer, its strong traditional character, and its peculiar use of a complex category for ceremonies, is Navajo ritual markedly differentiated. Basically it is very close to Western Apache and probably to Jicarilla. There is hardly a major Navajo ceremony which does not have a simplified counterpart among the Western Apache.

Lipan material concerning death and death customs is wanting. That from the other divisions shows a consistent and striking similarity. All share a fear and horror of death, all believe in a land of the dead where life goes on as it does on earth, and all bury the dead in the ground or in a rock crevice. To mention the names of the dead is taboo.

If space allowed and unpublished data were available, many more important traits might be added. Moreover, the important orientation toward the Great Basin cultures has been completely omitted and only Pueblo and Plains acculturation stressed. If we strip away Pueblo and Plains traits, among all divisions, with the probable exception of Kiowa-Apache and possibly Lipan, we have a set of cultures which at least in economic dependence and material culture, most closely approximate those of the Great Basin area and parts of California. Though this outline is far from complete, it should at least afford the reader a grasp of the Southern Athapascans and make it clear that no special ethnological segregation of any one of their seven divisions should be attempted. Though to a varying degree all show marked acculturation from surrounding peoples, all share in certain basic traits which form the least common denominator of their cultural fabric, some of which they undoubtedly brought with them from the North.

Bibliography

Franciscan Fathers
   1910. An Ethnologic Dictionary of the Navajo Language. St. Michaels, Ariz.

Goodwin, Grenville
   1935. The Social Divisions and Economic Life of the Western Apache. American Anthropologist, Vol. 37, No. 1.
   1937. The Characteristics and Function of Clan in a Southern Athapascan Culture. American Anthropologist, Vol. 39, No. 3.
   1938. White Mountain Apache Religion. American Anthropologist, Vol. 40, No. 1.

Hill, W. W.
    1938.   Navajo Pottery Manufacture. Bulletin, University of New Mexico, Anthropological Series, 2, No. 3.

Hoijer, Harry
    1938.   The Southern Athapascan Languages, American Anthropologist, Vol. 40, No. 1.

McAllister, J. Gilbert
    1937.   Kiowa-Apache Social Organization. In Social Anthropology of North American Tribes. University of Chicago Press.

Opler, Morris E.
    1936.   A Summary of Jicarilla Apache Culture. American Anthropologist, Vol. 38, No. 2.
    1937.   An outline of Chiricahua Apache Social Organization. In Social Anthropology of North American Tribes. University of Chicago Press.

Reichard, Gladys
    1928.   Social Life of the Navajo Indians. Columbia University Contributions to Anthropology, Vol. VII.

Appendix B
Common and Species Names of Materials Used for Artifacts

Alan Ferg

Flora

Common Name	Species Name
Yellow Pine or Ponderosa Pine	*Pinus ponderosa*
Pinyon	*Pinus* spp.
Juniper (Cedar)	*Juniperus* spp.
Giant Reed ("cane")	*Arundo donax*
Common Reed or Carrizo ("cane")	*Phragmites australis*
Spike Muhly grass	*Muhlenbergia wrightii*
Vine-mesquite grass	*Panicum obtusum*
Jungle-rice grass	*Echinochla colonum*
Johnson Grass	*Sorghum halepense*
Yucca (Spanish-bayonet)	*Yucca* spp.
Bear Grass	*Nolina* spp.
Sotol	*Dasylirion wheeleri*
Agave or Mescal (Century-plant)	*Agave* spp.
Cottonwood	*Populus fremontii*
Willow	*Salix* spp.
Walnut	*Juglans major*
Gambel Oak	*Quercus gambelii*
Emory Oak	*Quercus emoryi*
Mulberry	*Morus microphylla*
Tansy-mustard	*Descurainia sophia*
Sycamore	*Platanus wrightii*
Mountain-mahogany	*Cercocarpus* spp.
Catclaw	*Acacia greggii*
Mesquite	*Prosopis juliflora*
Coral bean	*Erythrina flabelliformis*
Sumac ("squawberry")	*Rhus trilobata*
Tamarix	*Tamarix pentandra*
Saguaro	*Carnegiea gigantea*
Prickly Pear	*Opuntia* spp.
Cholla	*Opuntia* spp.
Ocotillo	*Fouquieria splendens*
Tobacco	*Nicotiana* spp.
Devil's claw (Unicorn-plant)	*Proboscidea* spp.
Bottle Gourd	*Lagenaria siceraria*
Cushaw Squash	*Cucurbita mixta*
Finger-leaf Gourd	*Cucurbita digitata*
Coyote Pumpkin	*Cucurbita palmata*
Batamote	*Baccharis glutinosa*
Arrow-weed	*Pluchea sericea*
Burro-brush	*Hymenoclea* spp.
Sunflower	*Helianthus* spp.
Corn	*Zea mays*

Fauna

Common Name	Species Name
Wood Ibis (Stork)	*Mycteria americana*
Golden Eagle	*Aquila chrysaetos*
Gambel's Quail	*Callipepla gambelii*
Common Turkey	*Meleagris gallopavo*

Common Name	Species Name	Common Name	Species Name
Band-tailed Pigeon	*Columba fasciata*	Packrat (Wood Rat)	*Neotoma* spp.
Great Horned Owl	*Bubo virginianus*	Porcupine	*Erethizon dorsatum*
Red-shafted Flicker	*Colaptes auratus*	Coyote	*Canis latrans*
Kingbird	*Tyrannus* spp.	Wolf	*Canis lupus*
Common Crow	*Corvus brachyrhynchos*	Gray Fox	*Urocyon cinereoargenteus*
Common Mockingbird	*Minus polyglottos*	Badger	*Taxidea taxus*
		Mountain Lion	*Felis concolor*
Hooded Oriole	*Icterus cucullatus*	Bobcat	*Lynx rufus*
Bullock's (Northern) Oriole	*Icterus galbula*	Peccary (Javelina)	*Pecari tajacu*
		Elk	*Cervus canadensis*
Rock Squirrel	*Citellus variegatus*	Black-tailed (Mule) Deer	*Odocoileus hemionus*
Abert's Squirrel	*Sciurus aberti*		
Beaver	*Castor canadensis*	Antelope (Pronghorn)	*Antilocapra americana*

Appendix C
Inventory of the Collections

Alan Ferg

The majority of the artifacts collected by Grenville Goodwin and Edgar and Minnie Guenther are now in the Arizona State Museum. The remainder of the Guenthers' Apache materials belong to their children, and some of those baskets were described by Tanner (1982: 135–141).

Neil Goodwin retains a few of the Apache items his father collected, including baskets and moccasins. Neil donated some items to the Taylor Museum of the Colorado Springs Fine Arts Center, including two *gaan* dancers' masks, one turkey feather cap, one pair of saddlebags, two bowl baskets, two burden baskets, three *tuses*, one animal-headed Jicarilla warclub, and nine Navajo, Paiute, or Ute bowl baskets. The Museum of New Mexico has six sherds from two Western Apache plain ware jars collected by Goodwin in 1937 near Globe (site survey collection for LA 2088). The Denver Art Museum received three unprovenienced Western Apache sherds from Goodwin in 1937, but they have been missing since 1969. The Arizona State Museum also has site survey boxes of sherds and miscellaneous material, and over fifty catalogued stone specimens from six sites in the Verde Valley collected by Goodwin and E. B. Sayles in 1937 that were originally housed at Gila Pueblo. Some of these materials are probably Apache, and others are undoubtedly prehistoric. Goodwin also recorded fifteen sites in Aravaipa Canyon in 1939 for the Arizona State Museum, some of which may be Apache, and collected samples of material from all of them (see Gilman and Richards 1975 for a recent discussion of some of these sites). Finally, the whereabouts of a few specimens listed in Goodwin's personal catalogue are unknown at this time. Of these, three would be of special interest for research concerned with Western Apache ceramics. Goodwin's No. 85 is an Apache pot found near Rice and purchased from a trader's store there. His No. 86 and No. 88 are two unfired pots made by Anna Price at Bylas in 1932. Apparently at the same time, she started a third pot base using a gourd scraper, both of which are now in the Museum collections (Fig. 5.26).

In the inventory that follows, the Goodwin and Guenther Western Apache materials have been integrated with one another and ordered as much as possible like the corresponding traits in *Navaho Material Culture* (Kluckhohn, Hill, and Kluckhohn 1971). This is essentially the same order of presentation as appears in Chapters 5 through 8, Subsistence, Clothing, Ritual, and Recreation. Where there are multiple examples of the same type of object, Goodwin materials are listed first, in order by Arizona State Museum catalogue numbers (either plain or preceded by an E–), and the Guenther materials follow, in order by EEG catalogue numbers.

Symbols indicate items that are currently missing (*), that are probably or possibly Western Apache but for which there are no positive identifications (#), and items that are illustrated in this volume but are either not from the Goodwin and Guenther collections or not among those donated to the Arizona State Museum (‡).

The few Chiricahua, Jicarilla, Lipan, Mescalero, Navajo, and miscellaneous items collected by Goodwin are listed at the end of the inventory, in order only by catalogue number.

The second column of the inventory indicates the figure number for those items illustrated in this volume, with figures of related scenes or materials in parentheses in the object column. In general, the date and location of collection for an object are usually the approximate date and location of manufacture. Goodwin consistently recorded makers' names and their band affiliation. In those cases where an item is of prehistoric manufacture, non-Apache manufacture, or is a natural object, the "Maker and Affiliation" columns are filled in with the name and affiliation of the person from whom it was collected, or the affiliation Goodwin assigned to it. The affiliation abbreviations are as follows.

WM	White Mountain group
EWM	Eastern White Mountain band of the White Mountain group
WWM	Western White Mountain band of the White Mountain group
SC	either the San Carlos group or band
Pinal	Pinal band of the San Carlos group
Arivaipa	Arivaipa band of the San Carlos group
AP	Apache Peaks band of the San Carlos group
Cibecue	either the Cibecue group or band
ST	Southern Tonto group
Chir.	Chiricahua Apache (not Western Apache)

The Western Apache term for a pitch-coated jar basket, *tus,* is used for convenience in the Jicarilla, Mescalero, and Navajo inventories, but should not be interpreted as a universal term for such containers.

Finally, this inventory serves only as a guide to the collections. The provenience information is often much more complex than what could be presented here. For the Chiricahua, Lipan, and Mescalero materials in particular there are questions as to affiliations and influences, because all three groups were living together on the Mescalero Reservation in New Mexico at the time Goodwin was in contact with them. For the Lipan materials, this difficulty is discussed in the Notes following the Inventory. Bowl basket E–43 is an example of the problem; it was collected at Mescalero and strongly resembles Mescalero basketry, but the woman who made it apparently said it was of an old Chiricahua type. For any specific research, the reader is directed to the full documentation on file at the Arizona State Museum.

NOTE. Goodwin used the spelling "Arivaipa" rather than "Aravaipa" that is in current use on maps. He published the term "Arivaipa band" in 1935 (see Chapter 4, Fig. 1), a spelling that has continued in use (Basso 1983: 488) and is used here. Also, as mentioned in the caption to Figure 1.4, the original town of San Carlos (Old San Carlos) was located at the confluence of the San Carlos and Gila rivers. With the construction of Coolidge Dam, Old San Carlos was abandoned and eventually submerged beneath San Carlos Lake. What had orginally been the town of Rice was renamed San Carlos in 1930. In his personal catalogue Goodwin refers to both "Rice" and "San Carlos" as the source for some of the things he collected. However, the waters of San Carlos Lake did not cover Old San Carlos immediately, and it was probably many years before local residents started routinely calling Rice by its new name. Because of this, when Goodwin refers to San Carlos, we cannot be certain whether he means Old San Carlos or New San Carlos (Rice). Under "Location Collected" below, either Rice or San Carlos is listed following whichever was used in Goodwin's catalogue. None of the items in the Guenther collection were collected at San Carlos.

Inventory

Arizona State Museum or E. E. Guenther (EEG) Catalogue No.	Fig. No.	Object (Figures of related scenes or materials are shown in parentheses)	Date collected	Location collected	Maker	Affiliation (See listing in text)
WESTERN APACHE						
Subsistence						
21442	5.5	Turkey tail decoy	1935	Bylas	Jewett Wright	EWM
EEG 234	5.49	Turkey feathers	1970s	Whiteriver		
21367	5.6	Deadfall trap sticks	1932	Bylas	Harvey Nashkine[1]	EWM
E–9242		Bow	1932	Nachez (Naches)	Sherman Curley	
E–9243		Bow	1930?	San Carlos		
#E–9244		Bow	1930s			
E–9245		Bow	1935	Bylas	Jewett Wright	EWM
21356	5.2	Bow, unfinished	1932	Bylas(?)	Palmer Valor	EWM
21357		Bow	1932	Nachez (Naches)	Sherman Curley	
EEG 45	5.2	Bow	1920s	E. Fork-Whiteriver		
21358–b		Arrow	1932	Nachez (Naches)	Sherman Curley	
21359–b–m	5.2–5.4	Arrows (12)	1930?	San Carlos		
21370	5.3	Arrow for birds	1932	Nachez (Naches)	Sherman Curley	
21437	5.3	Arrows (3)	1935	Bylas	Jewett Wright	EWM
26535	5.3	Arrows (13)	1932	Nachez (Naches)	Sherman Curley	
#E–9241		Arrows (16)	1930s			
21358–a		Quiver, peccary hide	1932	Nachez (Naches)	Sherman Curley	
21359–a	5.2	Quiver, coyote hide	1930?	San Carlos		
21443	5.4	Arrowshaft smoother-straightener (prehistoric?)	1935	Bylas	Andrew Stanley	
*21387		Arrowshaft smoother(?)	1932	Ash Flat		EWM
21438	5.4	Wrist guard for archer	1935	Bylas	Jewett Wright	EWM
21395	5.4	Arrow-poison lichen	1932	Geronimo		EWM
21373	5.8	Digging stick	1932	Bylas	Anna Price	EWM
#26531–x–3		Wooden peg(?)	1930s			
22273	5.8	Mescal knife, metal	1936	Bylas	Mrs. Francis Drake	EWM
GP 49410–x–1	5.23	Mescal knife, stone	1937	Near Rye		
21385	5.11	Mescal forming tray (Figs. 5.1, 5.9, 5.10)	1932	Bylas	Mrs. Jewett Wright	EWM
*21365		Mescal stalk, roasted	1932	Cottonwood Wash	Mrs. Richard Bylas	EWM
21421	5.12	Mescal head, trimmed	1931	Bylas(?)	Anna Price	EWM
21383	5.13	Prickly pear fruit tray and brush	1932	Bylas	Mrs. Jewett Wright	EWM
21362	5.13	Prickly pear fruit tongs	1932	Bylas	Mrs. Jewett Wright	EWM
21428		Yucca fruit, prepared	1931	Bylas	Mrs. Charlie Sego	EWM
21895	5.13	Saguaro fruit-pole	1932	Bylas	Mrs. Jewett Wright	EWM
21318	5.14	Seed beater	1930s			
21377	5.14	Seed beater	1932	Bylas	Anna Price	EWM

Arizona State Museum or E. E. Guenther (EEG) Catalogue No.	Fig. No.	Object (Figures of related scenes or materials are shown in parentheses)	Date collected	Location collected	Maker	Affiliation (See listing in text)
21399	5.14	Tansy-mustard seed	1932		G. Wright's children	EWM
21444	5.14	Seed-beating stick	1936	Bylas	Mrs. Jewett Wright	EWM
21427	5.14	Acorns	1931	Bylas	Mrs. Charlie Sego	EWM
21440	5.48	Storage bag, cloth	1935	Bylas	Mrs. Jewett Wright	EWM
21864		Burden basket	1934	Indian Springs	Anna Price	EWM
#23023		Burden basket(?) fragments	1930s			
#E–9256		Burden basket	1930s			
EEG 216	5.35	Burden basket	1975?	Whiteriver	Mrs. Taylor	
EEG 217	5.35	Burden basket (Fig. 5.37)	1919–1923	Carrizo		
EEG 218		Burden basket	1919–1923	Carrizo		
EEG 219	5.35	Burden basket (Fig. 5.36)	1911–1922	East Fork		
EEG 220	5.35	Burden basket (Fig. 5.47)	1911–1922	East Fork		
EEG 222	5.35	Burden basket	1911–1945	E. Fork-Whiteriver	Shima (B–3)	Chir.
‡1611	7.38	Burden basket (*daagodighá* movement?)	1916	Globe		
‡E–8466	7.39	Burden basket (*daagodighá* movement?)	1930s–1960s	Arizona		
21316	5.15a	Salt-drying tray	1936	Bylas	Mrs. Jewett Wright	EWM
21420	5.15b	Salt, prepared cake	1932	Bylas	Anna Price	EWM
21375		Gourd	1931	North Fork	Laban James	AP
21416	5.16	Corn, 6 ears	1931	North Fork	Laban James	AP
21422	5.16	Corn, 8 ears (Fig. 5.17)	1931	Bylas	Anna Price	EWM
#26531–x–1		Corn cob	1930s			
21871	5.49	"Turkey" basket	1932			
21317	5.7	Bird cage	1930s(?)	Bylas(?)	Anna Price(?)	EWM(?)
21407	5.44	Saddle for horse	1932	Bylas	Anna Price	EWM
21374	5.46a, b	Quirt, wood	1932	Bylas	Anna Price	EWM
EEG 57	5.46a	Quirt, horsehair	1912–1916(?)	East Fork	Silas John	
21413		Horse saddlebags, rawhide	1931	North Fork	Mrs. Laban James	AP
EEG 115	5.48	Horse saddlebags, rawhide	1918–1928	East Fork(?)	Alchesay household member	
21439		Horse saddlebags, canvas	1935	Bylas	Mrs. Jewett Wright	EWM
EEG 228		Horse saddlebags, cloth	1969(?)	Whiteriver	Clarinda B. Bonito(?)	
EEG 229	5.48	Horse saddlebags, cloth (Fig. 7.22)	1911–1961	E. Fork-Whiteriver		
EEG 114		Burro saddlebags, rawhide	1919–1924	Carrizo-E. Fork		
21406	5.45	Rawhide shoes for horse	1932	Bylas	Jewett Wright	EWM

Inventory

Arizona State Museum or E. E. Guenther (EEG) Catalogue No.	Fig. No.	Object (Figures of related scenes or materials are shown in parentheses)	Date collected	Location collected	Maker	Affiliation (See listing in text)
21441		Rawhide shoes for burro	1935	Bylas	Charley Denton	Chir.
21364	5.40	Rope twister	1932	Bylas	Jewett Wright	EWM
21389	5.30	Container, saguaro callus	1932	Bylas(?)	Anna Price	EWM
EEG 233	5.30	Container, metal cup	1919–1981	Canyon Day		
21863	5.30	Container, squash	1936	Bylas	Mrs. John Roberson	ST?
21435	5.30	Container, agave stalk	1935	Bylas	Mrs. John Roberson	ST?
21865	5.31	Basket splints, fine	1936	Near Kinishba		WWM
21866	5.31	Basket splints, coarse	1936	Near Kinishba		WWM
E–52	5.31	Sumac twigs	1938	Near Tucson		
21378	5.31	Brush for pitch	1932	Bylas	Anna Price	EWM
21862		*Tus*, unpitched				
E–9	5.33	*Tus*, bilobed	1932		Woman	EWM
E–9257	5.32	*Tus*	1931	North Fork	Daughter-in-law of Laban James	AP
#E–9258		*Tus*	1930s			
E–9259		*Tus*	1932	Bylas	Granddaughter of Harvey Nashkine	EWM
EEG 116	5.33	*Tus*, bowl-shaped	1960s	Whiteriver		
EEG 117	5.33	*Tus*, cylindrical	1965–1981	Whiteriver	Lassie Wright of Cibecue(?)	
EEG 197	5.30	*Tus*	1911–1922	East Fork	Mary Keyes	
EEG 199		*Tus*	1911–1981	E. Fork-Whiteriver	Nanabathan(?), B–88	
EEG 201	5.33	*Tus*	1965–1981	Whiteriver	Ruthena Dale Henry of Cibecue	
EEG 202	5.33	*Tus* (Fig. 5.29)	1911–1981	E. Fork-Whiteriver		
EEG 203	5.33	*Tus* (Fig. 5.34)	1911–1981	E. Fork-Whiteriver		
EEG 204	5.31	*Tus* (Fig. 5.34)	1911–1981	E. Fork-Whiteriver		
EEG 208	5.31	*Tus*, unpitched	1911–1922	East Fork		
EEG 209	5.31	*Tus*, unpitched	1911–1922	East Fork		
EEG 226	5.31	*Tus*(?), unpitched	1911–1981	E. Fork-Whiteriver		
*E–60		Mortar, stone (prehistoric?)	1936	Near Kinishba		WM
EEG 236–a	5.16	Mortar, stone (prehistoric)	1981	Whiteriver	Emma Cosay	
EEG 236–b	5.16	Pestle-mano, stone (prehistoric)	1981	Whiteriver	Emma Cosay	
*21898		Metate				SC
*E–59		Metate	1936	Bylas		
EEG 235–a	5.16	Metate (prehistoric)	1981	Whiteriver	Emma Cosay	

Arizona State Museum or E. E. Guenther (EEG) Catalogue No.	Fig. No.	Object (Figures of related scenes or materials are shown in parentheses)	Date collected	Location collected	Maker	Affiliation (See listing in text)
*21445		Mano	1936	Cedar Springs		
*21446		Mano	1936	Cedar Springs		
21899	5.16	Mano				SC
EEG 235–b	5.16	Mano (prehistoric)	1981	Whiteriver	Emma Cosay	
‡E-6815–x–4	5.16	Mano	1965	Spring Creek		Cibecue
EEG 104	7.3	Brush	1943	Whiteriver		
21363	5.27	Stirring sticks	1932	Bylas	Mrs. Jewett Wright	EWM
EEG 118	5.19	Fry-bread holder (Fig. 5.18)	1911–1945	E. Fork-Whiteriver	Shima (B–3)	Chir.
EEG 130		Fry-bread holder	1918(?)	East Fork	E. E. Guenther	
21382	5.21	Food strainer, bear grass	1932	Bylas(?)	Mrs. Jewett Wright	EWM
21867	5.21	Food strainer, metal	1936	Near Kinishba		WWM
‡79–95–1	5.20	Corn beer strainer	1960s	Carrizo		
21325	5.23	Chopper, stone	1936	Lower Pinal Creek		
21872		Chopper, stone	1936	Arivaipa Canyon		Arivaipa
21884		Chopper, stone		Near Kinishba		
21897	5.23	Chopper, stone				WM
21324	5.23	Knife, stone				WM
21423		Basketry splints	1932	Bylas	Mrs. Jewett Wright	EWM
21400	5.38	Unfinished basket	1932	Bylas(?)	Mrs. Jewett Wright	EWM
E–1	7.36	Bowl basket (daagodighá movement?) (Fig. 7.37)	1906?	Ft. Apache Res.		WM
E–4		Bowl basket	1930s			
EEG 30	5.38	Bowl basket	1912	East Fork		
EEG 66	5.38	Bowl basket	1911–1981	Cibecue		
EEG 67	5.49	Bowl basket	1911–1919	East Fork		
EEG 68	5.14	Bowl basket	1911–1919	East Fork		
EEG 69	5.14	Bowl basket	1911–1919	East Fork		
EEG 71	5.38	Bowl basket	1919–1981	Whiteriver		
EEG 73	5.38	Bowl basket	1922	Cedar Creek		
EEG 76	5.38	Bowl basket	1919–1981	Whiteriver		
‡EEG 80	7.37	Bowl basket (daagodighá movement?)	1911–1981	Carrizo-E. Fork-Whiteriver		
EEG 84	5.14	Bowl basket	1911–1919	East Fork		
EEG 89	5.38	Bowl basket	1911–1919	East Fork		
EEG 90	5.49	Bowl basket	1911–1919	East Fork		
EEG 103	7.3	Bowl basket	1943	Whiteriver		
EEG 91	5.38	Oval basket	1919–1923	Carrizo		
EEG 92	5.38	Plaque basket	1911–1919	East Fork		
EEG 170	6.31	Jar basket, twined	1980	Whiteriver		
EEG 93	5.38	Jar basket	1919–1924	Carrizo-E. Fork		
EEG 98	5.38	Jar basket	1930s	Florence Junction		
21384	5.22	Food preparation tray	1932	Bylas	Mrs. Jewett Wright	EWM
21397	5.25	Ladle, pottery		Dewey Flat		WWM

Inventory

Arizona State Museum or E. E. Guenther (EEG) Catalogue No.	Fig. No.	Object (Figures of related scenes or materials are shown in parentheses)	Date collected	Location collected	Maker	Affiliation (See listing in text)
21379		Spoon, yucca	1930(?)	Bylas	Anna Price	EWM
21380	5.24	Spoon, yucca	1932	Bylas	Anna Price	EWM
21419	5.26	Base of pottery jar	1932	Bylas	Anna Price	EWM
21877	5.26	Polishing stone for pottery		Near Kinishba		
21376	5.26	Pottery scraper, gourd	1932	Bylas	Anna Price	EWM
21861	5.30	Jar, pottery	1933	15 miles N of Rice		SC
21417		Jar, pottery (prehistoric?)	1932	Cave near Rice		SC
21430	5.26	Jar, pottery	1933	Near Tonto National Monument(?)		Pinal?
*21451–x–20		Sherd, unidentified	1931			WM
21873		Sherd (prehistoric?)	1936	Arivaipa Canyon		
21875		Sherd (prehistoric?)	1930s	Near Kinishba		
EEG 129	5.26	Jar, pottery	1919–1923	Carrizo area		
EEG 17	6.31	Napkin ring, beadwork	1920s	Whiteriver		
EEG 18	6.31	Napkin ring, beadwork	1920s	Whiteriver		
EEG 133	6.30	Woman's pin, miniature cradleboard	1965–1981	Whiteriver	Harry Tortice(?)	
EEG 147	6.30	Woman's pin, miniature *tus*	1918(?)	East Fork	Daughter of B–6	
EEG 148	6.30	Woman's pin, miniature *tus*	1919–1920	East Fork	Daughter of B–6	
EEG 134	6.31	Miniature cradleboards	1965–1981	Whiteriver	Harry Tortice(?)	
EEG 135	6.31	Miniature cradleboards	1965–1981	Whiteriver	Harry Tortice(?)	
EEG 171	6.31	Miniature burden basket, beadwork	1980(?)	Whiteriver		
EEG 187	6.31	Miniature doll, beadwork	1911–1981	E. Fork-Whiteriver		
EEG 119	6.31	Miniature moccasins	1965–1981	Whiteriver	Harry Tortice(?)	
EEG 120		Miniature moccasins	1965–1981	Whiteriver	Harry Tortice(?)	
EEG 121	6.31	Miniature moccasins	1965–1981	Whiteriver	Harry Tortice(?)	
EEG 122		Miniature moccasins	1965–1981	Whiteriver	Harry Tortice(?)	
EEG 123	6.31	Miniature moccasins	1965–1981	Whiteriver	Harry Tortice(?)	
EEG 247	7.12	Painting of *gaan* dancer (painted in 1979)	1981	Whiteriver	Curry Clawson of Cedar Creek	
E–53		Western Apache house model	1938			
*#23022		Strands of bark	1930s			
E–55		Western Apache house model	1938			
E–45		*Yucca bacata* leaf	1938	Near Tucson		
E–46		Yucca ties	1938	Near Tucson		
E–47		Bear grass	1938	Near Tucson		

Arizona State Museum or E. E. Guenther (EEG) Catalogue No.	Fig. No.	Object (Figures of related scenes or materials are shown in parentheses)	Date collected	Location collected	Maker	Affiliation (See listing in text)
E–48		Bata mota	1938	Near Tucson		
E–49		Johnson grass	1938	Tucson		
E–50		Mesquite limb	1938	Near Tucson		
E–51		Cottonwood limb	1938	Near Tucson		
19584	5.28	Firedrill with hearth	1930s	San Carlos Res.		
21366	5.28	Firedrill with hearth	1932	Bylas	Harvey Nashkine	EWM
21425	5.28	Torch, cedar bark	1932	East Fork	Samuel George	EWM
EEG 183	6.11	Knife, metal	1911–1922	East Fork		
*21447		Chipped stone, retouched flake(?)	1936	Cedar Springs		
*21448		Chipped stone, retouched flake(?)	1936	Cedar Springs		
21451–x–2		Chipped stone, biface	1931			WM
21878		Chipped stone, finely retouched flake	1930s	Near Kinishba		
21882		Chipped stone, biface	1930s	Near Kinishba		
21883		Chipped stone, finely retouched flake	1930s	Near Kinishba		
21884		Chipped stone, irregularly retouched flake	1930s	Near Kinishba		
21885		Chipped stone, scraper	1930s	Near Kinishba		
21886		Chipped stone, utilized flake	1930s	Near Kinishba		
21890		Chipped stone, irregularly retouched flake	1930s	Near Kinishba		
21900	5.49	Blanket, Zuni or Navajo	1931	Bylas	Charlie Sego	WWM
E–10	5.41	Cradleboard, temporary	1932	Bylas	Mrs. Jewett Wright	EWM
21414		Cradleboard	1932	Bylas	Harriet Nelson	EWM
EEG 127	5.43	Cradleboard and doll	1911–1919	East Fork		
EEG 128	5.42	Cradleboard	1912	East Fork	Mrs. Jack Keyes	
EEG 138	5.42	Cradleboard	1970	Whiteriver	June Beatty of of San Carlos	
EEG 248	5.42	Cradleboard	1981	Whiteriver	Melvina Bourke	
21319	5.40	Fleshing tool and whetstone (Fig. 5.39)	1936	Bylas	Mrs. Jewett Wright	EWM
21426	5.40	Rubbing stone for hides	1932	Bylas	Mrs. Jewett Wright	EWM
21891		Rubbing stone(?) fragment		Near Kinishba		
21402–b	6.11	Awl, wooden	1932	Bylas	Anna Price	EWM
Clothing						
21327	6.7	Child's carrying jacket	1936	Bylas	Mrs. Jewett Wright	EWM
21329–a, b	7.2	Puberty poncho and skirt, buckskin	1935	Bylas(?)	David Longstreet	EWM

Inventory

Arizona State Museum or E. E. Guenther (EEG) Catalogue No.	Fig. No.	Object (Figures of related scenes or materials are shown in parentheses)	Date collected	Location collected	Maker	Affiliation (See listing in text)
EEG 31	7.4	Puberty poncho, buckskin (Fig. 7.6)	ca. 1950	Whiteriver		
EEG 212		Puberty poncho, buckskin	1960s	Whiteriver	Daisey Johnson	
EEG 213		"Puberty" poncho, cloth	1970s	Whiteriver	Melvina Bourke	
EEG 214	6.24	Skirt, blouse, shawl, cloth (Figs. 6.20, 6.23)	1923–1924	East Fork		
EEG 215		Skirt, blouse, shawl, cloth	1934	Whiteriver		
#23020		Man's shirt, buckskin	1930s			
EEG 126	6.4	Man's shirt, buckskin (made in 1844?)	1919–1923	Carrizo		
EEG 211	7.40	Man's shirt, buckskin (Silas John movement; Mescalero?)[2]	1933(?)	Whiteriver		
21323	6.13	Girl's hair ornament	1932	Bylas	Daughter of Harvey Nashkine	EWM
EEG 19	6.13	Girl's hair ornament (Fig. 6.12)	ca. 1920	E. Fork-Whiteriver		
EEG 20	6.13	Girl's hair ornament	ca. 1920	E. Fork-Whiteriver		
EEG 21	6.13	Girl's hair ornament	1912–1913	East Fork	Kitty Savage (wife or daughter of B–6?)	
21410	7.21	Cap, buckskin (Type 1)	1930	Bylas		
#23019		Cap, buckskin (Type 1)	1930s			
#23029	7.20	Cap, buckskin (Type 1)	1930s			
EEG 36–a		Cap, buckskin (Type 1)	1920–1922	Whiteriver	Loco Jim	
EEG 39	7.20	Cap, buckskin (Type 1)	1920s	Carrizo-Cibecue	Medicine man, "M" tag band(?)	
EEG 40	7.20	Cap, buckskin (Type 1)	1914	Whiteriver	Coyote (H–2)	
21409	7.21	Cap, buckskin (Type 2) Made around 1898	1932	Bylas	Medicine man	EWM
19838		Cap (Type 4), turkey feather	1932	Bylas		
EEG 42	7.23, 7.25	Cap (Type 4), turkey feather	1916	East Fork	Loco Jim	
21432	7.23	Cap (Type 5), owl feather (Fig. 7.24)	1933	San Carlos		
21411	6.8	Baby's moccasins	1932	Bylas	Mrs. Jewett Wright	EWM
21328	6.9	Child's moccasins	1932	Bylas	Daughter-in-law of Palmer Valor	EWM

Arizona State Museum or E. E. Guenther (EEG) Catalogue No.	Fig. No.	Object (Figures of related scenes or materials are shown in parentheses)	Date collected	Location collected	Maker	Affiliation (See listing in text)
EEG 175	6.9	Child's moccasins	1919–1920	E. Fork-Whiteriver	Shima (B–3)	Chir.
EEG 176	6.9	Child's moccasins	1919–1920	E. Fork-Whiteriver	Shima (B–3)	Chir.
EEG 177	6.9	Child's moccasin	1911–1922	East Fork		
EEG 182	6.9	Child's moccasins	1912–1913	East Fork	Shima (B–3)	Chir.
21412	7.31	Moccasins, makeshift	1932	Bylas	Jewett Wright	EWM
#E–9248	6.10	Adult's moccasins (Figs. 6.1, 6.3)	1930s			
E–9249		Adult's moccasins	1935	Bylas	Mrs. George Buck	WM
#E–9250		Adult's moccasins	1930s			
#E–9251		Adult's moccasins	1930s			
EEG 173	8.8	Adult's moccasins	1919–1924	Carrizo-E. Fork	Johnson O'Hell (B–30)	
EEG 174	6.10	Adult's moccasins	1961–1969	Whiteriver		
EEG 178	6.10	Adult's moccasins	1911–1922	East Fork		
EEG 179	6.10	Adult's moccasins	1911–1922	East Fork		
EEG 180	6.10	Adult's moccasins	1911–1922	East Fork		
EEG 181		Adult's moccasins	1911–1922	East Fork		
#23021	6.14	Buckskin pouch	1930s			
21401	6.14	Buckskin pouch	1932	Bylas	Mrs. George Gray	EWM
21403	6.15	Buckskin pouch	1932	Bylas		
EEG 5	6.14	Buckskin pouch	1920s	E. Fork-Whiteriver		
EEG 6	6.14	Buckskin pouch	1920s	E. Fork-Whiteriver		
EEG 7	6.14	Buckskin pouch	1920s	E. Fork-Whiteriver		
EEG 9	6.15	Buckskin pouch	1919–1923	Carrizo		
EEG 10	6.15	Buckskin pouch	1919–1923	Carrizo		
EEG 11	6.15	Buckskin pouch	1919–1923	Carrizo		
EEG 12	6.15	Buckskin pouch	1919–1923	Carrizo		
EEG 13	6.15	Buckskin pouch	1919–1923	Carrizo		
EEG 26	6.31	Buckskin pouch	1965–1981	Whiteriver	Mrs. Nora Vlasquez Tortice(?)	
EEG 14	6.18	Buckskin purse	1911–1912	East Fork	Daughter of A–100	
EEG 15	6.18	Buckskin purse	1914	East Fork	Daughter of A–100	
EEG 16	6.18	Buckskin purse	1914	East Fork	Daughter of A–100	
EEG 27	6.30	Buckskin "wallet"	1965–1981	Whiteriver	Mrs. Nora Vlasquez Tortice(?)	
21402–a	6.11	Awl case	1932	Bylas	Anna Price	EWM
EEG 1	6.11	Awl case	1920s	E. Fork-Whiteriver		
EEG 2	6.11	Awl case	1920s	E. Fork-Whiteriver		
EEG 3	6.11	Awl case	1920s	E. Fork-Whiteriver		

Inventory

Arizona State Museum or E. E. Guenther (EEG) Catalogue No.	Fig. No.	Object (Figures of related scenes or materials are shown in parentheses)	Date collected	Location collected	Maker	Affiliation (See listing in text)
EEG 4	6.11	Awl case	1920s	E. Fork-Whiteriver	Nagaahoun(?), wife of Bezho (B–33)	
EEG 47	6.24	Walking cane (Fig. 6.23)	1911–1981	E. Fork-Whiteriver		
EEG 28	6.25	T–necklace (worn by Nora at her puberty ceremony, 14 July 1944)	1965–1981	Whiteriver	Mrs. Nora Vlasquez Tortice(?)	
EEG 29–a		T–necklace	ca. 1970	Whiteriver		
EEG 149	6.26	T–necklace	1911–1919	East Fork		
EEG 150	6.25	T–necklace (worn by Mary Keyes at her puberty ceremony, 1911)	1911	East Fork	Mary Keyes(?)	
EEG 151		T–necklace	1911–1981	E. Fork-Whiteriver		
EEG 152	6.26	T–necklace	1911–1922	East Fork		
EEG 153	6.25	T–necklace	1911–1922	East Fork		
EEG 154	6.25	T–necklace	1911–1922	East Fork		
EEG 155	6.25	T–necklace	1914(?)	East Fork		
EEG 156	6.26	T–necklace	1911–1981	E. Fork-Whiteriver		
EEG 157	6.26	T–necklace	ca. 1970	Whiteriver		
EEG 158	7.5	T–necklace (made before 1912)	1912–1916	East Fork		
EEG 159	6.26	T–necklace	1974	Whiteriver	Sylvania (Alchesay) Lee	
EEG 160	6.27	Shawl necklace	1920s	E. Fork-Whiteriver		
EEG 161		Shawl necklace	1920s	E. Fork-Whiteriver		
EEG 162	6.28	Shawl necklace	1911–1981	E. Fork-Whiteriver		
EEG 186	6.30	Rope necklace	1911–1981	E. Fork-Whiteriver		
EEG 210	6.30	Necklace, cedar berries	1911–1981	Carrizo-E. Fork-Whiteriver		
‡E–9885	6.30	Hair clip, beaded	1971	New San Carlos	Gloria Elgo	
EEG–124	6.30	Earrings, miniature burden baskets	1965–1981	Whiteriver	Harry Tortice(?)	
EEG 131		Earrings, miniature burden baskets	1965–1981	Whiteriver	Harry Tortice(?)	
EEG 132	6.30	Earrings, miniature moccasins	1965–1981	Whiteriver	Harry Tortice(?)	
EEG 184	6.30	Earring, beaded	1911–1981	E. Fork–Whiteriver		
‡74–68–1	6.30	Keyring, beaded buckskin	1974	Fort Apache area		
EEG 29–b, c		Belt and headband, beadwork	ca. 1970	Whiteriver		

Arizona State Museum or E. E. Guenther (EEG) Catalogue No.	Fig. No.	Object (Figures of related scenes or materials are shown in parentheses)	Date collected	Location collected	Maker	Affiliation (See listing in text)
EEG 188	6.29	Belt, beadwork	1911–1961	Carrizo-E. Fork-Whiteriver		
EEG 189	6.29	Belt, beadwork	1911–1961	Carrizo-E. Fork-Whiteriver		
EEG 190	6.29	Belt, beadwork	1911–1961	Carrizo-E. Fork-Whiteriver		
EEG 191	6.29	Belt, beadwork	1911–1961	Carrizo-E. Fork-Whiteriver		
EEG 192	6.29	Belt, beadwork	1911–1961	Carrizo-E. Fork-Whiteriver		
EEG 193	6.29	Belt, beaded	1919–1924(?)	Carrizo-E. Fork(?)		
EEG 194	6.29	Belt(?), beadwork	1911–1961	Carrizo-E. Fork-Whiteriver		
EEG 22	6.16	Watch fob, beadwork (Fig. 7.7)	1911–1919	East Fork		
EEG 23	6.16	Watch fob, beadwork	1911–1919	East Fork		
EEG 24	6.16	Watch fob, eagle claws	1918–1928	E. Fork-Whiteriver	Bertha Alchesay	
EEG 25	6.16	Watch fob, eagle claws	1918–1928	E. Fork-Whiteriver	Bertha Alchesay	
EEG 54	6.16	Watch fob, horsehair	1912–1916(?)	East Fork	Silas John	
EEG 55	6.21	Watch chain, horsehair	1912–1916(?)	East Fork	Silas John	
EEG 56	6.21	Watch chain, horsehair	1912–1916(?)	East Fork	Silas John	
EEG 58		Watch chain, horsehair	1912–1916(?)	East Fork	Silas John	
EEG 52	6.21	Hatband, horsehair (Fig. 6.22)	1912–1916(?)	East Fork	Silas John	
EEG 53	6.21	Hatband, horsehair	1912–1916(?)	East Fork	Silas John	
EEG 62	6.17	Finger ring, silver	1919–1924	Carrizo-E. Fork		
EEG 64	6.17	Buttons, metal (5)	1919–1924	Carrizo-E. Fork		
21876	6.17	Tweezers, cartridge		Near Kinishba		
*21394		Tweezers, cartridge	1932	Dewey Flat		WWM
EEG 109	6.17	Tweezers, cartridge	1919–1924	Carrizo-E. Fork		
EEG 110	6.17	Tweezers, cartridge	1919–1924	Carrizo-E. Fork		
E–11	6.17	Tweezers on necklace	1938		Chrysotile Charlie Nachu(?), A–19	SC
EEG 231	6.17	Comb, aluminum	1911–1981	E. Fork-Whiteriver		
21424		Yucca leaf bases for soap	1932	Bylas(?)	Anna Price	EWM
Ritual						
21396	7.10	Paint palette, stone	1929	Dewey Flat		WWM
21429	7.10	Paints, red, black, silvery	1932 and 1931	Bylas and Blue River		EWM and WWM
*21451–x–18		Paint, unidentified	1931			WM
*21451–x–19		Paint, unidentified	1931			WM
21892	7.10	Paint, red	1936	Rose Peak	Francis Drake	EWM
21893	7.10	Paint, white		Canyon Day		WM
21894	7.10	Paint, green				Cibecue

Inventory

Arizona State Museum or E. E. Guenther (EEG) Catalogue No.	Fig. No.	Object (Figures of related scenes or materials are shown in parentheses)	Date collected	Location collected	Maker	Affiliation (See listing in text)
21896	7.10	Paint, yellow				WM
21398		Puberty dance scratcher-drinking tube	1932	Bylas	David Longstreet	EWM
21869	7.3	Puberty dance scratcher-drinking tube	1936	Bylas	Mrs. Chris Adams	EWM
EEG 48	7.3	Puberty dance cane (Figs. 7.6, 7.7)	1919–1924	Carrizo–E. Fork		
EEG 49		Puberty dance cane fragment(?)	1911–1981	Carrizo-E. Fork-Whiteriver		
EEG 172	7.3	Puberty dance abalone pendant	1911–1981	Carrizo-E. Fork-Whiteriver		
EEG 232	5.49	Abalone shells (4)	1911–1981	E. Fork-Whiteriver		
EEG 105		Puberty dance cartoon by Reg Manning	1943	Whiteriver		
21870	7.15	Charm necklace for baby (Fig. 7.22)	1936	Bylas	Mrs. Jewett Wright	EWM
21326	7.18	Charm necklace for warrior	1935	Bylas	George Gray	EWM
21404	7.17	Charm, coral bean	1932	Bylas	Charlie Sego	WWM
EEG 185	6.31	Charm, coral bean	1911–1981	E. Fork-Whiteriver		
EEG 242	7.17	Charm, coral bean	1980	Whiteriver	Loretta Dazen	
‡74–61–1	7.17	Charm, coral bean	1970s	Whiteriver area		
EEG 230	7.17	Charm(?), coral beans (14)	1911–1981	E. Fork-Whiteriver		
EEG 36–b	7.14	Charm, buckskin	1920–1922	Whiteriver	Loco Jim	
EEG 43	7.14	Charm, buckskin	1914(?)	Whiteriver(?)	Coyote(?), H–2	
EEG 60	7.14	Charm, beads	1919–1924	Carrizo-E. Fork		
EEG 61	7.14	Charm, shell	1919–1924	Carrizo-E. Fork		
*21451–x–21		Charm(?), unidentified shell object	1931			WM
*21451–x–22		Charm(?), unidentified shell object	1931			WM
*21451–x–23		Charm(?), unidentified shell object	1931			WM
*21451–x–24		Charm(?), unidentified shell object	1931			WM
21433	7.35	Pollen sacks, *daagodighá* movement (made in 1906)	1933	Bylas	Mrs. Andrew Stanley	EWM
21453	7.34	Charm-insignia, *daagodighá* movement(?), made between 1903 and 1906? (Figs. 7.32, 7.33)	1931	Ash Flat		

Arizona State Museum or E. E. Guenther (EEG) Catalogue No.	Fig. No.	Object (Figures of related scenes or materials are shown in parentheses)	Date collected	Location collected	Maker	Affiliation (See listing in text)
EEG 59	7.14	Charm, Silas John movement	1920–1977	E. Fork-Whiteriver	Silas John	
21451–x–16		Crystal, calcite	1931			WM
*21451–x–17		Crystal, unidentified	1931			WM
21874	7.16	Crystal, quartz	1936		Francis Drake	EWM
21390	7.16	Chipped stone biface (prehistoric)	1932	North of Bylas		EWM
21450		Chipped stone point (prehistoric)	1936	Lower Pinal Creek		
21451–x–1		Chipped stone scraper (prehistoric)	1931			WM
21451–x–3		Chipped stone point (prehistoric)	1931			WM
21451–x–4		Chipped stone point (prehistoric)	1931			WM
21451–x–5		Chipped stone point (prehistoric)	1931			WM
21451–x–6		Chipped stone point (prehistoric)	1931			WM
21451–x–7		Chipped stone point (prehistoric)	1931			WM
21451–x–8		Chipped stone point (prehistoric)	1931			WM
21451–x–9		Chipped stone point (prehistoric)	1931			WM
21451–x–10		Chipped stone point (prehistoric)	1931			WM
21451–x–11		Chipped stone point (prehistoric)	1931			WM
21451–x–12		Chipped stone point (prehistoric)	1931			WM
21451–x–13		Chipped stone drill (prehistoric)	1931			WM
21451–x–14		Chipped stone point (prehistoric)	1931			WM
21451–x–15		Chipped stone point (prehistoric)	1931			WM
21879		Chipped stone point (prehistoric)	1930s	Near Kinishba		
21880		Chipped stone point preform or finished biface (prehistoric)	1930s	Near Kinishba		
21881		Chipped stone biface or point preform (prehistoric)	1930s	Near Kinishba		
21887		Chipped stone biface or point preform (prehistoric)	1930s	Near Kinishba		
21888		Chipped stone biface or point preform (prehistoric)	1930s	Near Kinishba		

Inventory

Arizona State Museum or E. E. Guenther (EEG) Catalogue No.	Fig. No.	Object (Figures of related scenes or materials are shown in parentheses)	Date collected	Location collected	Maker	Affiliation (See listing in text)
21889		Chipped stone biface or point preform (prehistoric)	1930s	Near Kinishba		
#26531–x–4		Chipped stone point (prehistoric)	1930s			
EEG 107	7.16	Prehistoric arrowshaft straightener and pipe (from "Blue Springs ruins")	1922–1923	Carrizo	V–50	
EEG 245	7.13	*Gaan* dancer dolls, set of 5	1981	Whiteriver	Ray Thompson of Canyon Day	
19839 through 19843	7.8	*Gaan* dancer's masks, set of 5 (Figs. 7.1, 7.9)	1932	Bylas	John Robinson	
EEG 163	7.10	*Gaan* dancer's mask, clown	1919–1924(?)	Carrizo-E. Fork(?)		
EEG 164		*Gaan* dancer's mask	1919–1924(?)	Carrizo-E. Fork(?)		
EEG 241		*Gaan* dancer's mask	ca. 1963	Carrizo		
EEG 243		*Gaan* dancer's mask fragment	ca. 1963	Carrizo		
21371		*Gaan* dancer's wands (pair)	1930	San Carlos		
21372	7.11	*Gaan* dancer's wands (pair)	1930	San Carlos		
EEG 50		*Gaan* dancer's wand	1911–1981	E. Fork-Whiteriver		
EEG 237		*Gaan* dancer's wands (pair)	1975	Whiteriver		
EEG 238		*Gaan* dancer's wands (pair)	1975	Whiteriver		
EEG 239		*Gaan* dancer's wands (pair)	1975	Whiteriver		
EEG 240		Wand or hoop segments (6)	1975	Whiteriver		
EEG 246		Wand or hoop segments (14)	ca. 1963	Carrizo		
EEG 244		Staffs, set(?) of 8	ca. 1963	Carrizo		
E–61		Reproduction by Goodwin of Western Apache painted ceremonial buckskin in Chicago Field Museum	1938			
EEG 140	8.13	Drum and drumstick (Fig. 7.7)	1961(?)	Whiteriver	Ted Bourke	
EEG 35	8.13	Drumstick	1911–1981	E. Fork-Whiteriver		
21361	8.12, 8.13	Flageolet, cane	1932	Bylas	Ambrose Swift	EWM
5871	8.13	Fiddle and bow	1931	Bylas(?)	Amos Gustina(?)[3]	
21431	8.13	Fiddle and bow	1933	Whiteriver	Old man	EWM

Arizona State Museum or E. E. Guenther (EEG) Catalogue No.	Fig. No.	Object (Figures of related scenes or materials are shown in parentheses)	Date collected	Location collected	Maker	Affiliation (See listing in text)
EEG 33	8.13	Fiddle and bow	1919–1924	Carrizo-E. Fork		
EEG 34	8.13	Fiddle and bows (2)	1919–1924	Carrizo-E. Fork		
21355	7.26	Lance	1932	Bylas	Anna Price	EWM
21452	7.30	Club, stone head	1931	Rice		
EEG 38	7.30	Club, stone head	1919–1924(?)	Carrizo-E. Fork(?)		
EEG 37	7.30	Club, solid wood	1920–1928	Whiteriver	Loco Jim	
21415	7.27	Shield (made in 1932)	1932	Bylas	Jewett Wright	EWM
EEG 125	7.27–7.29	Shield (made in 1800s)	1920	Carrizo	Tinilzay (V–18)	
Recreation						
21360	8.2	Set of hoop and poles (Figs. 8.1, 8.3)	1931	Tularosa R., N.M.	Charlie Sego	WWM
21405	8.7	Shinney ball	1931(?)	Bylas	Charlie Sego	WWM
21320	8.8	Hidden-ball game stick	1936	Bylas	Jewett Wright	EWM
21321	8.8	Hidden-ball game stick	1936	Bylas	Jewett Wright	EWM
21322	8.8	Ball for hidden-ball game	1936	Bylas	Jewett Wright	EWM
#26531–x–2		Yucca pith	1930s			
21434	8.8	Counters for hidden-ball game	1935	Calva		
21368	8.4	Set of staves for 3-stick game (Figs. 8.5, 8.6)	1931	Upper Black R.	Charlie Sego	WWM
21369	8.4	Set of staves for 4-stick game	1931	Bylas	Charlie Sego	WWM
21388	8.11	5 walnuts for five-stone-game	1932	Bylas	Mrs. Jewett Wright	EWM
EEG 63		Five-stone-game stones (2)	1911–1981	E. Fork-Whiteriver		
21868	8.11	Stone marbles (2)	1936	Bylas	Boys	EWM
EEG 44	8.11	Toy bow and arrows (2)	1920s–1930s	Whiteriver		
EEG 112	8.11	Toy saddlebags, rawhide	1918–1928	E. Fork-Whiteriver	Alchesay household member	
EEG 113		Toy saddlebags, rawhide	1918–1928	E. Fork-Whiteriver	Alchesay household member	
EEG 227		Toy saddlebags, cloth	1950s–1960s	Whiteriver		
EEG 136		Toy cradleboard	1911–1922	East Fork		
EEG 141	8.10	Toy cradleboard	1911–1922	East Fork		
EEG 142	8.10	Toy cradleboard	1911–1922	East Fork		
EEG 143	8.10	Toy cradleboard	1911–1922	East Fork		
EEG 144	8.10	Toy cradleboard	1911–1922	East Fork		
EEG 145	8.10	Toy cradleboard	1911–1922	East Fork		
EEG 146	8.10	Toy cradleboard	1911–1922	East Fork		
21418		Toy bilobed *tus* of clay	1932	Bylas(?)	Anna Price	EWM
21386	8.11	Doll, female, clay	1932	Bylas(?)	Anna Price	EWM

Inventory

Arizona State Museum or E. E. Guenther (EEG) Catalogue No.	Fig. No.	Object (Figures of related scenes or materials are shown in parentheses)	Date collected	Location collected	Maker	Affiliation (See listing in text)
EEG 223	8.11	Doll, female, buckskin (made in 1877)	1919–1923	Carrizo		
EEG 224		Doll, female, buckskin (made in 1923)	1923	Carrizo-E. Fork		
EEG 225		Doll, female, buckskin (made in 1927)	1927(?)	E. Fork-Whiteriver		
21408	6.2	Doll, female, cloth	1932	Bylas	Mrs. Jewett Wright	EWM
21436	6.2	Doll, male, cloth (Fig. 6.3)	1935	Bylas	Mrs. Jewett Wright	EWM
EEG 165	8.9	Doll, female, cloth	1913–1914	East Fork	Shima (B–3)	Chir.
‡EEG 166	8.9	Doll, female, cloth	1960s(?)	Whiteriver(?)		
EEG 167	8.9	Doll, female, cloth	1960s(?)	Whiteriver		
EEG 168	8.9	Doll, female, cloth	1960s	Whiteriver		
EEG 169	6.19	Dolls, male and female, cloth (Fig. 6.20)	1950s(?)	Whiteriver	Mrs. Joe Crocker	
EEG 8	8.11	Toy buckskin pouch	1912–1954(?)	E. Fork-Whiteriver		
21381	7.19	Corn husks used in rolling cigarettes	1932	Bylas	Anna Price	EWM
21391	7.19	Pipe, yucca	1932	Cochise Stronghold	Charlie Sego	WWM
21392	7.19	Pipe, clay	1932	Bylas	Palmer Valor	EWM
21393	7.19	Pipe, clay	1930	Whiteriver		
CHIRICAHUA						
E–12		Arrow	1938	Mescalero Res.	Fatty	Chir.(?)
E–32	3.4	Rope, rawhide	1930	Chihuahua		Chir.
E–33	3.4	Container, rawhide	1930	Chihuahua		Chir.
E–34		Rope twister	1930	Chihuahua		Chir.
E–35	3.4	Container, calf skin sack	1930	Chihuahua		Chir.
E–36		Lashing, rawhide	1930	Chihuahua		Chir.
E–43		Bowl basket	1938	Mescalero Res.	Mrs. Marie Chatto	Chir.(?)
E–58	3.4	Saddlebags, semi-tanned cowhide	1930	Chihuahua		Chir.
JICARILLA						
E–2		Bowl basket	1932			Jicarilla
E–5		Bowl basket	1931			Jicarilla
E–15		Arrow	1938	Jicarilla Res.		Jicarilla
E–16		Bow	1938	Jicarilla Res.		Jicarilla
E–17		Snowshoes (pair)	1938	Jicarilla Res.		Jicarilla
E–18		Container, parfleche	1936	Taos[4]		Jicarilla
E–19		Sherds, micaceous plain ware jar rim	1938	old camp near Horse Lake on Jicarilla Res.		Jicarilla
E–20		Pitcher, pottery, micaceous plain ware	1938	Jicarilla Res.		Jicarilla
E–21		Adult's moccasins	1931	Jicarilla Res.		Jicarilla
E–22	AA.5	Doll, male, buckskin	1938	Jicarilla Res.		Jicarilla

Arizona State Museum or E. E. Guenther (EEG) Catalogue No.	Fig. No.	Object (Figures of related scenes or materials are shown in parentheses)	Date collected	Location collected	Maker	Affiliation (See listing in text)
E–23	AA.5	Doll, female, buckskin	1938	Jicarilla Res.		Jicarilla
E–24		Cradleboard	1938	Jicarilla Res.		Jicarilla
E–25		*Tus*	1931	Jicarilla Res.		Jicarilla
E–44		Bowl basket	1930	Jicarilla Res.		Jicarilla
E–54		Jicarilla Apache tipi model	1938	Jicarilla Res.		
E–9252		Adult's moccasins	1930s			Jicarilla[5]
Lipan						
E–29	AA.7	Doll, male, buckskin	1938	Mescalero Res.	Augustina Zwazwa	Lipan[6]
E–30	AA.7	Doll, female, buckskin	1938	Mescalero Res.	Augustina Zwazwa	Lipan
E–31		Cradleboard	1938	Mescalero Res.	Augustina Zwazwa	Lipan
Mescalero						
E–6		Bowl basket	1931	New Mexico		Mescalero
E–13		Arrow	1938	Mescalero Res.		Mescalero
E–14		Arrow	1938	Mescalero Res.		Mescalero
E–26		Adult's moccasins	1938	Mescalero Res.		Mescalero
E–27	AA.6	Doll, male, buckskin	1938	Mescalero Res.		Mescalero
E–28	AA.6	Doll, female, buckskin	1938	Mescalero Res.		Mescalero
E–9260		*Tus* (made ca. 1860)[7]	1930s			Mescalero
Navajo						
E–37		Hobble for horse, rawhide	1927	Walpi[8]		
E–38		Mold for silver jewelry, stone	1930	Monument Valley		Navajo
E–39		Weaving tool, wood	1930	Monument Valley		Navajo
E–40		Weaving batten, wood	1930	Monument Valley		Navajo
E–41		Bullroarer	1930	Manuelito		Navajo
E–42		Drumstick	1930	Manuelito		Navajo
E–56	8.13	Drum, pot with buckskin head	1930	Manuelito		Navajo
E–57		*Tus*	1896	Chicago World's Fair[9]		
E–9246		Saddle, wood and leather	1938			Navajo[10]
Miscellaneous						
E–9239		Gun case, buckskin	1930s			Apachean
E–9240	5.2	Quiver with attached bowcase	1930s			Apachean
E–9247		Vest, beaded cloth	1930s			Sioux(?)[11]
E–9253		Leggings, beaded buckskin	1930s			Arapaho(?), Mescalero(?)[12]
E–9254		Belt, beaded with silver concho	1930s			Ute(?), Jicarilla(?)[13]
E–9255		Snowshoes, wood and rawhide	1930s			Taos(?)[14]

Inventory

* Currently missing.

\# Possibly or probably Western Apache, but no definitive documentation in Museum or Goodwin notes.

‡ Specimen is either not from the Goodwin or Guenther Collections or not among those donated to the ASM.

1. Actually made by Goodwin, but under Nashkine's instruction.

2. Although this shirt presumably was obtained by Silas John from Mescalero (see Fig. 7.40), the Mescaleros could have obtained it from the Jicarilla. Initial impressions of several experts are mixed: Morris Opler and Richard Conn feel it is probably of Jicarilla manufacture, and Jonathan Batkin feels it is probably Mescalero.

3. Although Goodwin did not record the maker's name, this fiddle almost certainly was made by Amos Gustina, who is known to have made large, elaborately painted, two-string fiddles such as this (see Ferg 1981).

4. Although he purchased it at Taos (town or pueblo?), Goodwin identified this parfleche as Jicarilla and remarked that it was old and an excellent example of Jicarilla decoration (see Tiller 1983, Fig. 4). Comparisons with other parfleches attributed to the Jicarilla leave little question that Goodwin was correct. Its large size (87 cm by 43 cm when folded), painting inside the flaps, the hourglass-shaped layout of the design, and the numerous small triangular "fringe" elements are all considered typical of Jicarilla parfleches even though other examples were, like Goodwin's, not collected from the Jicarilla themselves but at Taos and Santa Clara pueblos (Batkin 1986:77; Morrow 1975:59, 85, 86; Torrence 1994:152, 153, Plate 57).

5. No provenience information accompanied this pair of moccasins, but there is little doubt that it is of Jicarilla manufacture. Morris Opler and Jonathan Batkin agree, and Batkin (letter of 30 October 1985) further suggests they are men's moccasins: "Typical of Jicarilla men's moccasins is the cut used . . . with a triangular insert in the upper, often in combination with a style of beadwork that is very handsome, sometimes resembling Cheyenne beadwork. Wissler [1910: 140, Fig. 88] attributed this cut to the Apaches, but not specifically the Jicarillas. . . . I have shown moccasins of both types to about a half dozen Jicarillas. . . . All agreed that the type with rounded toe, insert and beadwork, like your [ASM] E–9252, were Jicarilla."

6. The maker's name is given in a letter from Goodwin to Morris Opler (Opler 1973: 87–90) in which Goodwin is inquiring as to whether the details of the dolls' costumes are correct for Lipan. Augustina Zwazwa was a relatively young woman, apparently had no first-hand knowledge of old Lipan dress, and may have unintentionally incorporated Mescalero elements into these dolls, living as she was among the Mescalero.

7. There is no record of when or where Goodwin acquired this *tus;* however, pasted to its side is a paper with the following inscription written in Spanish: "This jar was taken from the Mescalero Indians in the Guadalupe Mountains, Texas, in the year of 1860 by Crecencio Roybal of San Elizario, Texas."

8. This hobble was collected at Walpi. The catalogue card refers to it as "Type used by Navajo," but it appears that this hobble may have been Hopi-made and may never have been used by Navajos. Nevertheless, it is of the type made and used by Navajos (Kluckhohn, Hill, and Kluckhohn 1971: 90–91), and it has been included with the Navajo items here, as Goodwin classified it. Three very similar hobbles can be found in other museum collections. At the American Museum of Natural History there is a hobble of this type collected on the Navajo Reservation in Arizona in 1910 by Pliny Earle Goddard (AMNH Cat. 50/9221). At the Southwest Museum there are two such hobbles. One is identified only as Hopi (Cat. 421-G-1147), while the other was collected by M. R. Harrington at Oraibi in 1929 (Cat. 491-G-108). But these new examples shed no additional light on whether both the Navajo and the Hopi were making this simple type of hobble, each for their own use, or whether the Navajo were making them and trading them to the Hopi, or vice versa.

9. When and where Goodwin acquired this pitched basketry water bottle is not recorded, but he noted that it had originally been purchased from Navajos at the 1896 Chicago World's Fair and that it might possibly be of Southern Paiute origin.

10. Goodwin left no notes identifying this saddle. In a letter to Emil Haury on 17 September 1938 (in ASM Accessions File No. 2021), he notes having obtained a Navajo saddle, but does not elaborate. This and an old-style Western Apache saddle (Fig. 5.44) are the only saddles Goodwin is known to have collected. Based on that and the saddle's resemblance to known Navajo saddles, it has been identified here as Navajo.

11. This beaded vest had no provenience information with it but is almost certainly Sioux in origin. With American flags depicted on both sides of the front, it is typical of the innumerable flag-decorated Sioux vests made primarily in the 1880s and 1890s, and on into the 1920s (Pohrt 1975: 8–10). Based on an examination of black-and-white photographs of this specimen, Pohrt agrees. See Pohrt (1975) for photographs of a variety of American-flag-decorated Sioux items, including fifteen beaded or porcupine quillwork vests.

12. Morris Opler suggests these unprovenienced leggings may be Mescalero, while Jonathan Batkin

indicates they are a type of women's legging worn by both Cheyenne and Arapaho and that this pair is almost certainly Arapaho. Richard Conn agrees that they are Arapaho.

13. Goodwin left no notes identifying this belt, but Thomas Bahti identified it as either Ute or Jicarilla, manufactured around the turn of the century. This is not one of the extremely wide belts typical of the Jicarilla (Tiller 1983, Figs. 6, 7); it is only 5.5 cm wide and is decorated in beadwork and a single silver concho on a leather backing. Jonathan Batkin (letter of 30 October 1985) agrees with Bahti's assessment that this belt ". . . is probably Ute. Belts in this style were worn by several tribes of the northern Plains and Plateau, but the conchas on this one sure suggest a Ute origin. It is even possible that the Jicarillas wore these, but I have not seen any documented examples. . . . it is probably a woman's belt. . . ." A similar belt (but without a concho) is in the Smithsonian Institution (Cat. 380174), collected in either Arizona or New Mexico, accessioned in 1939 and identified as "Apache(?)."

14. Goodwin collected one pair of Jicarilla teardrop-shaped snowshoes (E–17, illustrated in Tiller 1983, Fig. 3); however, this pair (E–9255) has no documentation. In their circular hoop and leather netting they most closely resemble Taos snowshoes (see Fox 1980). They do not resemble the teardrop-shaped Jicarilla pair, or Navajo snowshoes, which are consistently made with wooden crosspieces rather than netting (Kluckhohn, Hill, and Kluckhohn 1971: 292–294), hence the tentative identification here as from Taos.

References and Suggested Readings

The Arizona Daily Star
   1950   Apache Indians witness historic events of forefathers' lives in motion picture. 9 July.

Arizona Highways
  *1962   July, 37(7).
  *1977   July, 53(7).

Baldwin, Gordon C.
  *1965   *The Warrior Apaches: A Story of the Chiricahua and Western Apache.* Tucson: Dale Stuart King, Six Shooter Gulch Press.

Basso, Keith H.
   1966   The Gift of Changing Woman. *Anthropological Papers 76, Bureau of American Ethnology Bulletin* 196. Washington: Smithsonian Institution.
   1969   Western Apache Witchcraft. *Anthropologi-cal Papers of the University of Arizona* 15. Tucson: University of Arizona Press.
  *1970   *The Cibecue Apache.* New York: Holt, Rinehart and Winston.
  *1971   (Editor) *Western Apache Raiding and Warfare: From the Notes of Grenville Goodwin.* Tucson: University of Arizona Press.

   1977   History: In Pursuit of the Apaches. *Arizona Highways,* July, 53(7): 2–9, 39–48.
  *1983   Western Apache. In *Handbook of North American Indians, Southwest,* edited by Alfonso Ortiz, Vol. 10, pp. 462–488. Washington: Smithsonian Institution.

Basso, Keith H., and Ned Anderson
   1973   A Western Apache Writing System: The Symbols of Silas John. *Science* 180(4090): 1013–1022.

Batkin, Jonathan
   1986   The Taylor Museum: A Tribute to Folk Culture. In *Colorado Springs Fine Arts Center: A History and Selections from the Permanent Collections.* Colorado Springs: Williams Printing, Inc.

Board of Education
   1947   *Our Synod and Its Work.* Milwaukee: Northwestern Publishing House.

Bourke, John G.
   1886   *An Apache Campaign in the Sierra Madre; an Account of the Expedition in Pursuit of the Hostile Chiricahua Apaches in the Spring of 1883.* New York: Charles Scribner's Sons.

---

*Suggested readings

*1891   *On the Border with Crook*. New York: Charles Scribner's Sons.

1892   The Medicine-men of the Apache. In *9th Annual Report of the Bureau of American Ethnology for the Years 1887–1888,* pp. 443–595. Washington: Smithsonian Institution.

Brandt, Elizabeth A., Bonnie Lavender-Lewis, and Philip J. Greenfeld
   1994   Foreword. In *Myths and Tales of the White Mountain Apache*, by Grenville Goodwin. Tucson and London: University of Arizona Press.

Brown, Lenard E.
   1963   The Arizona Apaches and Christianization: A Study of Lutheran Missionary Activity, 1893–1943. MS, Master's thesis, University of Arizona, Tucson.

Bullis, John L.
   1888   Report of San Carlos Agency. In *Fifty-seventh Annual Report of the Commissioner of Indian Affairs to the Secretary of the Interior,* pp. 121–123. Washington.

Clark, LaVerne Harrell
   1963   Early Horse Trappings of the Navajo and Apache Indians. *Arizona and the West* 5(3): 233–248.

Clum, John P.
   1875   Office of United States Indian Agent, San Carlos, Arizona, September 1, 1875. In *Annual Report of the Commissioner of Indian Affairs to the Secretary of the Interior for the Year 1875,* pp. 215–220. Washington.

Cole, Fay-Cooper
   1941   Grenville Goodwin. *American Anthropologist* 43(1): 135.

Cole, Fay-Cooper, Fred Eggan, Harry Hoijer, and Edward Spicer
   1942   Introduction. In *The Social Organization of the Western Apache,* by Grenville Goodwin, pp. xiii–xvi. Chicago: Univeristy of Chicago Press.

Colorado Springs Fine Arts Center
   1986   *Colorado Springs Fine Arts Center; a History and Selections from the Permanent Collections.* Colorado Springs: Williams Printing, Inc.

Corbusier, William H.
   1886   The Apache-Yumas and Apache-Mojaves. *The American Antiquarian* 8(5): 276–284 and 8(6): 325–339.

Cosner, Aaron J.
   1951   Arrowshaft-straightening with a Grooved Stone. *American Antiquity* 17(2): 147–148.

Culin, Stewart
   1907   Games of the North American Indians. In *24th Annual Report of the Bureau of American Ethnology for the Years 1902–1903,* pp. 1–846. Washington: Smithsonian Institution.

Curtis, Edward S.
   1907–1930   *The North American Indian: Being a Series of Volumes Picturing and Describing the Indians of the United States, and Alaska,* edited by Frederick W. Hodge, 20 vols. Norwood, Mass.: Plimpton Press.

Dittemore, Diane Dean
   1978   A Comparison of Seri and Western Apache One-string Fiddles. MS, Master's thesis, University of Denver, Colorado.

Driver, Harold E., John M. Cooper, Paul Kirchhoff, Dorothy Rainier Libby, William C. Massey, and Leslie Spier
   1953   Indian Tribes of North America. *Supplement to International Journal of American Linguistics* 19(3), *Indiana University Publications in Anthropology and Linguistics Memoir* 9. Baltimore: Waverly Press.

Dutton, Bertha P.
   1980   Cultural gaps and a construct. In "Collected Papers in Honor of Helen Greene Blumenschein," edited by Albert H. Schroeder, pp. 211–219. *Papers of the Archaeological Society of New Mexico* 5. Albuquerque: Albuquerque Archaeological Society Press.

References

Fairchild, Dean
   1961   Apaches rally to benefactor. *The Arizona Daily Star*, February 23, Section B.

Farrer, Claire R., and Bernard Second
   1981   Living the sky: aspects of Mescalero Apache ethnoastronomy. In "Archaeoastronomy in the Americas," edited by Ray A. Williamson, pp. 137–150. *Ballena Press Anthropological Papers* 22. Los Altos, California and College Park, Maryland: Ballena Press and the Center for Archaeoastronomy.

Ferg, Alan
   1981   Amos Gustina, Apache Fiddle Maker. *American Indian Art Magazine* 6(3): 28–35.

Fontana, Bernard L.
   1979   *The Material World of the Tarahumara*. Tucson: Arizona State Museum, University of Arizona.

Forde, C. Daryll
   1931   Ethnography of the Yuma Indians. *University of California Publications in American Archaeology and Ethnology* 28(4). Berkeley: University of California Press.

Fort Apache Scout
   1967   America's 1967 'Mother' Comes Home. *Fort Apache Scout* 6(12): 1–2, Official Newspaper, White Mountain Apache Tribe.

Fox, Nancy
   1980   Snowshoes from Taos Pueblo. In "Collected Papers in Honor of Helen Greene Blumenschein," edited by Albert H. Schroeder, pp. 171–178. *Papers of the Archaeological Society of New Mexico* 5. Albuquerque: Albuquerque Archaeological Society Press.

Franciscan Fathers
   1910   *An Ethnologic Dictionary of the Navaho Language*. St. Michaels, Arizona: St. Michael's Press.

Frank, Larry, and Millard J. Holbrook III
   1978   *Indian Silver Jewelry of the Southwest 1868–1930*. Boston: New York Graphic Society.

Gardner, Erle Stanley
   1952   Murder on the Apache Trail. *Argosy*, December, pp. 34–35, 72–75.

Gay, Dorothy Frances
   1933   Apache Art. MS, Master's thesis, University of Arizona, Tucson.

Gifford, E. W.
   1932   The Southeastern Yavapai. *University of California Publications in American Archaeology and Ethnology* 29(3). Berkeley: University of California Press.
   1940   Culture Element Distributions: XII Apache-Pueblo. *University of California Anthropological Records* 4(1). Berkeley: University of California Press.

Gifford, James C.
   1980   Archaeological Explorations in Caves of the Point of Pines Region, Arizona. *Anthropological Papers of the University of Arizona* 36. Tucson: University of Arizona Press.

Gilman, Patricia, and Barry Richards
   1975   An Archaeological Survey in Aravaipa Canyon Primitive Area. *Arizona State Museum Archaeological Series* 77. Tucson: Arizona State Museum, University of Arizona.

Glances at Greater Arizona
   1968   Minnie Guenther American Mother of the Year. *Glances at Greater Arizona* 5(1): 5. Greater Arizona Savings and Loan Association.

Goddard, Pliny Earle
   1916   The Masked Dancers of the Apache. In *Holmes Anniversary Volume: Anthropological essays presented to William Henry Holmes in honor of his seventieth birthday, December 1, 1916,* edited by Frederick W. Hodge, pp. 132–136. Washington: James William Bryan Press.
   1918   Myths and Tales from the San Carlos Apache. *Anthropological Papers of the American Museum of Natural History* 24(1). New York: American Museum Press.

*1919 Myths and Tales from the White Mountain Apache. *Anthropological Papers of the American Museum of Natural History* 24(2). New York: American Museum Press.

Goodwin, Grenville
- 1933 Clans of the Western Apache. *New Mexico Historical Review* 8(3): 176–182.
- 1935 The Social Divisions and Economic Life of the Western Apache. *American Anthropologist* 37(1): 55–64.
- 1936 Experiences of an Indian Scout: Excerpts from the Life of John Rope, an Old-Timer of the White Mountain Apaches. *Arizona Historical Review* 7(1): 31–68 and 7(2): 31–73.
- 1937 The Characteristics and Function of Clan in a Southern Athapascan Culture. *American Anthropologist* 39(3): 394–407.
- 1938a The Southern Athapascans. *The Kiva* 4(2): 5–10.
- *1938b White Mountain Apache Religion. *American Anthropologist* 40(1): 24–37.
- *1939 Myths and Tales of the White Mountain Apache. *Memoirs of the American Folk-Lore Society* 33.
- 1942 *The Social Organization of the Western Apache.* Chicago: University of Chicago Press.
- 1945 A Comparison of Navaho and White Mountain Ceremonial Forms and Categories, edited by Clyde Kluckhohn and Leland C. Wyman. *Southwestern Journal of Anthropology* 1(4): 498–506.

Goodwin, Grenville, Archival Material

The Goodwin archives, cited throughout the text as A–56 through A–79, A–1087, AA–1, and AA–4 through AA–6, have been recatalogued. All of these notes (except MS 298 at the Arizona Historical Society) are now part of Manuscript Series 17 (MS 17) at the Arizona State Museum Archives, University of Arizona, Tucson. Citation of these materials should henceforth refer to MS 17 and the appropriate Folder number. The preparation of most of these documents spanned many years, and can only be dated as sometime between 1927 and 1940, except where specifically noted otherwise.

In the ten years that have passed since this book was prepared, several significant pieces of Grenville Goodwin's research have surfaced which were previously unknown to the editor. Copies are now reunited with Goodwin's other materials at the Arizona State Museum, and are listed below as Folders 81 through 102.

- A–56 Place Names in the Coyotero Area. Folder 26, 1932.
- A–57 Place Names in the Territory of the Arivaipa, Pinal, San Carlos, and Peaks Bands. Folder 27, 1932.
- A–58 Place Names in the Territory of the Carrizo, Cibicu, and Canyon Creek Bands. Folder 28, 1932.
- A–59 Place Names in the Territory of the Southern Tonto. Folder 29, 1932.
- A–60 Place Names in the Territory of the Northern Tonto. Folder 30, 1932.
- A–61 Place Names in the Territory of the Chiricahua, Mogollon, and Mimbres. Folder 31, 1932.
- A–62 Field Notes Arranged by Informant. Folder 32, 1932.
- A–63 Field Notes Arranged by Informant. Folder 33, 1932.
- A–64 Field Notes Arranged by Informant. Folder 34, 1932.
- A–65 Field Notes Arranged by Informant. Folder 35, 1932.
- A–66 Early Dress, Body Painting, Pottery, Baskets, Utensils. Folders 40–41.
- A–67 Weapons, Raids, and Warfare. Folders 42–45.
- A–68 Hunting, Food Gathering, Foods, and Cooking. Folders 46–48.
- A–69 Games, Dancing, and Singing. Folders 49–50.
- A–70 Agriculture, Cattle, and Domestic Animals. Folders 51–53.
- A–71 Dwellings of the White Mountain Apache, Artifacts, Fire, and Tobacco. Folders 54–55.
- A–72 Concepts of Life, Bodily Functions, and Superstitions. Folders 56–58.
- A–73 Mrs. Andrew Stanley, Anna Price, and Sherman Curley. Folders 72–74.

References

A–74 Palmer Valor, David Longstreet, and Joseph Hoffman. Folders 75–77.

A–75 Reminiscences of John Rope. Folder 78.

A–76 Miscellaneous Notes–Addenda and Stories and Story-telling. Folders 60–71.

A–77 Watercolors of Navajo and Apache artifacts. Folder 39. See also Folder 82.

A–78 Apache Linguistic Constructions. Folder 25.

A–79 Sketches of Western Apache camp layouts, games, artifacts, and designs. Folder 38.

A–1087 Catalogue of the Articles Collected from the Western Apache in Arizona. Folder 79.

AA–1 Notebooks on Western Apache. Phonology, Word Lists, Conjugations. Folders 1–23, 1932.

AA–4 Apache Notebooks—Original Copies of Biographies. Folder 37.

AA–5 Apache Notebooks—Warfare. Informant, John Rope. Folder 36.

AA–6 Apache Linguistic Constructions. Folder 24, 1931.

MS 17 Goodwin and Sayles' archaeological survey from Montezuma's Well to Payson, 1937; additional notes on Chiricahua traits by Morris E. Opler. Folder 59.

MS 17 Report on the San Carlos Indian Reservation. Report submitted to the United States Department of the Interior, Office of Indian Affairs, File No. 8962, 1943, San Carlos, 042. Folder 80.

MS 17 Biographical Notes and Correspondence with Apache Friends. Folder 81.

MS 17 Black-and-white copies of watercolors of Navajo and Apache artifacts, mounted four to a page (not identical to Folder 39). Folder 82.

MS 17 Notes on the Sierra Madre Chiricahua. Folder 83.

MS 17 Notes on Various Topics: Clothing, Ornaments, Hair, Divining Power, Learning Power, Deer Power Dream, Hawk Power and Curing Ceremonies, Lightning Power and Curing. Folder 84.

MS 17 Concepts of Earth, Nature, Universe. Folder 85.

MS 17 Various Sicknesses and Cures, Learning Curing Power. Folder 86.

MS 17 *Gaan* Masks. Folder 87.

MS 17 *Gaan* Dance. Folder 88.

MS 17 Notes on Various Topics: Songs, Prayers, Cardinal Points, Caps, Causes of Various Sicknesses, Silas John, Love Power, Pollen-Giving Dance 1932, Cosmology, Concepts of Love. Folder 89.

MS 17 Girl's Puberty Ceremony. Folder 90.

MS 17 Various Curing Ceremonies. Folder 91.

MS 17 Origin of Curing Ceremonies. Folders 92–93.

MS 17 Copy of manuscript on Silas John Edwards, written by Jules Henry. No date. Folders 94–95.

MS 17 "Apache Ethnobotany Manuscript" comprised of Goodwin's notes with additional materials by Alfred E. Whiting. On file at the Museum of Northern Arizona, Flagstaff. Copy in Folders 96–97.

MS 17 "Selected Items from Grenville Goodwin's Unpublished Notes." On file at the Laboratory of Anthropology, Museum of New Mexico, Santa Fe. Copy in Folders 98–102.

AHS 298 Grenville Goodwin Papers. Correspondence and the original typescript of Goodwin 1936. MS 298, Arizona Historical Society, Tucson, Arizona.

Goodwin, Grenville, and Charles R. Kaut
1954 A Native Religious Movement Among the White Mountain and Cibecue Apache. *Southwestern Journal of Anthropology* 10(4): 385–404.

Gregory, David A.
*1981 Western Apache archaeology: problems and approaches. In "The Protohistoric Period in the North American Southwest, A.D. 1450–1700," edited by David R. Wilcox and W. Bruce Masse, pp. 257–274. *Arizona State University Anthropological Research Papers* 24. Tempe: Arizona State University.

Griffen, William B.
1983 Southern Periphery: East. In *Handbook of North American Indians, Southwest,* edited by Alfonso Ortiz, Vol. 10, pp. 329–342. Washington: Smithsonian Insitution.

Guenther, Arthur Alchesay
- 1972 50 Years in Apacheland. *White Mountains of Arizona*. Mesa, Arizona: Norm's Publishing House.

Guenther, E. Edgar
- 1920 Report on the Evangelical Lutheran Missionary Activities, Fort Apache Indian Reservation. Report on file with William B. Kessel.
- 1923 Items of Interest. *The Apache Scout* 1(1): 8.
- 1928a Chief Alchesay. *The Apache Scout* 6(5): 2–3.
- 1928b *The Apache Scout* 5(8): 7.
- 1939 Whiteriver Rededication. *The Apache Scout* 17(11): 87–88.
- 1945 Shimah. *The Apache Scout* 23(6): 608–609.
- 1949a Y–24 (Arthur Garland). *The Apache Scout* 27(2): 293.
- 1949b Mission Superintendent E. E. Guenther's Report to Wisconsin Lutheran Synod. Report on file with William B. Kessel.
- 1956 Autobiography of E. Edgar Guenther, '08. *Black and Red*. Watertown: Northwestern Lutheran College.
- 1957 Autobiography of E. Edgar Guenther, '08. *Black and Red*. Watertown: Northwestern Lutheran College.

Guenther, Minnie
- 1911 Diary. On file with William B. Kessel. Entries for July 23, August 9, and August 25.
- 1928 Loco Jim. *The Apache Scout* 5(9): 3–5.
- 1929 Extracts from the Diary of a Missionary's Wife. *Walther League Messenger*, November, pp. 142–143 and 186–187.
- 1935 Shi-Mah. *The Apache Scout* 13(7): 413–414.
- 1956 Apache Anecdotes. *This Day*, February, p. 40. St. Louis: Concordia Publishing House.

Guy, Hubert
- 1977 Arts and Crafts: Baskets, Beads and Buckskin. *Arizona Highways*, July, 53(7): 10–19.

Herbert, Lucile, and Charles Herbert
- 1962 Rev. Edgar Guenther. *Arizona Highways*, July, 37(7): 40–43.

Hess, Bill
- *1980 The White Mountain Apache, Seeking the Best of Two Worlds. *National Geographic* 157(2): 272–290.

Hildburgh, W. L.
- 1919 On the Flint Implements Attached to Some Apache "Medicine Cords." *Man* 19: 81–87. Royal Anthropological Institute of Great Britain and Ireland.

Hill, W. W.
- 1940 Navajo Salt Gathering. *The University of New Mexico Bulletin, Anthropological Series* 3(4): 3–25. Albuquerque: University of New Mexico Press.

Hinton, Thomas
- 1983 Southern Periphery: West. In *Handbook of North American Indians, Southwest*, edited by Alfonso Ortiz, Vol. 10, pp. 315–328. Washington: Smithsonian Institution.

Hrdlička, Aleš
- 1904 Method of Preparing Tesvino Among the White River Apaches. *American Anthropologist* 6(1): 190–191.
- 1908 Physiological and Medical Observations Among the Indians of Southwestern United States and Northern Mexico. *Bureau of American Ethnology Bulletin* 34. Washington: Smithsonian Institution.

Iverson, Peter
- 1982 *Carlos Montezuma and the Changing World of American Indians*. Albuquerque: University of New Mexico Press.

Johnson, Lewis
- 1892 Report of San Carlos Agency. In *Sixty-First Annual Report of the Commissioner of Indian Affairs to the Secretary of the Interior*, pp. 219–223. Washington.

Kennedy, John G.
- 1963 Tesguino Complex: the Role of Beer in Tarahumara Culture. *American Anthropologist* 65(3, pt. 1): 620–640.

References

Kessel, William B.
*1974 The Battle of Cibecue and Its Aftermath: A White Mountain Apache's Account. *Ethnohistory* 21(2): 123–134.
1976 White Mountain Apache Religious Cult Movements: A Study in Ethnohistory. MS, Doctoral dissertation, University of Arizona, Tucson.

Kluckhohn, Clyde, W. W. Hill, and
Lucy Wales Kluckhohn
1971 *Navaho Material Culture*. Cambridge: Belknap Press of Harvard University Press.

Knoop, Karl
1981 Letter to William B. Kessel, June 4. On file with William B. Kessel.

Koehler, John Philipp
1970 *The History of the Wisconsin Synod*. St. Cloud, Wisconsin: Sentinel Publishing.

Lamb, Frank W.
1972 *Indian Baskets of North America*. La Pine, Oregon: Rubidoux Publishing.

Mahoney, Ralph
1954 Spirit of Christmas is Exemplified in Missionary's 43 Years of Service. "Arizona Days and Ways," *The Arizona Republic*, July 4, pp. 3–5.
1956 Apache Mission. *This Day*, February, pp. 37–39. St. Louis: Concordia Publishing House.

Mails, Thomas E.
*1974 *The People Called Apache*. Englewood Cliffs, New Jersey: Prentice-Hall.

Mason, Otis Tufton
1904 Aboriginal American Basketry: Studies in a Textile Art Without Machinery. In *Annual Report of the Smithsonian Institution for 1902*, pp. 171–548. Washington.

McCoy, Ronald
1984 Circles of Power. *Plateau* 55(4): 1–32.
1985 Gan: Mountain Spirit Masks of the Apache. *American Indian Art Magazine* 10(3): 52–58.

Meader, Forrest W., Jr.
1967 N¹*ailde*¹: The Ghost Dance of the White Mountain Apache. *The Kiva* 33(1): 15–24.

Merrill, William L.
1977 An Investigation of Ethnographic and Archaeological Specimens of Mescalbeans (*Sophora secundiflora*) in American Museums. *Technical Reports* 6. Ann Arbor: Museum of Anthropology, University of Michigan.
1983 Tarahumara Social Organization, Political Organization, and Religion. In *Handbook of North American Indians, Southwest*, edited by Alfonso Ortiz, Vol. 10, pp. 290–305. Washington: Smithsonian Institution.

Morrow, Mable
1975 *Indian Rawhide: An American Folk Art*. Norman: University of Oklahoma Press.

Newcomb, Franc J., and Gladys A. Reichard
1937 *Sandpaintings of the Navajo Shooting Chant*. New York: J. J. Augustin.

Nicholson, Philip
1984 A New Apache Presence: The Art of Nah-ih-es. *Art West* 7(6): 76–82, 84, 120 and 8(1): 66–71.

Olsen, Stanley J.
1963 Dating Early Plain Buttons by Their Form. *American Antiquity* 28(4): 551–554.

Opler, Morris E.
1941 *An Apache Life-way: The Economic, Social, and Religious Institutions of the Chiricahua Indians*. Chicago: University of Chicago Press.
1969 *Apache Odyssey: A Journey Between Two Worlds*. New York: Holt, Rinehart and Winston.
1973 (Editor) *Grenville Goodwin Among the Western Apache: Letters from the Field*. Tucson: University of Arizona Press.
*1983 The Apachean Culture Pattern and Its Origins. In *Handbook of North American Indians, Southwest*, edited by Alfonso Ortiz, Vol. 10, pp. 368–392. Washington: Smithsonian Institution.

Otto, R.
   1936   A Twenty-Fifth Anniversary Celebration. *The Apache Scout* 14(6): 486.

Pardue, Diana Flynn
   1982   Western Apache Beadwork. MS, Master's thesis, Arizona State University, Tempe.

Pennington, Campbell W.
   1963   *The Tarahumar of Mexico: Their Environment and Material Culture.* Salt Lake City: University of Utah Press.

Perry, Edgar, Canyon Z. Quintero, Sr., Catherine D. Davenport, and Corrine B. Perry
   1972   *Western Apache Dictionary.* Fort Apache, Arizona: White Mountain Apache Tribe.

Pierce, F. E.
   1886   San Carlos Agency, Arizona, August 31, 1886. In *Annual Report of the Commissioner of Indian Affairs to the Secretary of the Interior for the Year 1886,* pp. 39–41. Washington.

Pohrt, Richard A.
   1975   *The American Indian/The American Flag.* Flint, Michigan: Flint Institute of Arts.

Quintero, Nita
   1980   Coming of Age the Apache Way. *National Geographic* 157(2): 262–271.

Reagan, Albert B.
   1929   Plants Used by the White Mountain Apache Indians of Arizona. *The Wisconsin Archaeologist* 8(4): 143–161.
   1930   Notes on the Indians of the Fort Apache Region. *Anthropological Papers of the American Museum of Natural History* 31(5). New York: American Museum Press.

Roberts, Helen H.
   1929   Basketry of the San Carlos Apache. *Anthropological Papers of the American Museum of Natural History* 31(2). New York: American Museum Press.

Rosnek, Carl, and Joseph Stacey
   1976   *Skystone and Silver: The Collector's Book of Southwest Indian Jewelry.* Englewood Cliffs, New Jersey: Prentice-Hall.

Schaafsma, Polly
   1980   *Indian Rock Art of the Southwest.* Santa Fe and Albuquerque: School of American Research and University of New Mexico Press.

South, Stanley
   1964   Analysis of the Buttons from Brunswick Town and Fort Fisher. *The Florida Anthropologist* 17(2): 113–133.

Spicer, Edward H.
   1971   Grenville Goodwin: A Biographical Note. In *Western Apache Raiding and Warfare: From the Notes of Grenville Goodwin,* edited by Keith H. Basso, pp. 3–7. Tucson: University of Arizona Press.

Stewart, Kenneth M.
   1983   Mohave. In *Handbook of North American Indians, Southwest,* edited by Alfonso Ortiz, Vol. 10, pp. 55–70. Washington: Smithsonian Institution.

Tai, Pauline
   1980   Car Seats that Care for Kids. *Money Magazine* 9(12): 115.

Tanner, Clara Lee
   1960   Crafts of Arizona Indians. *Arizona Highways,* July, 36(7): 8–35.
   1968   *Southwest Indian Craft Arts.* Tucson: University of Arizona Press.
   1973   *Southwest Indian Painting; A Changing Art.* Second Edition. Tucson: University of Arizona Press.
  *1982   *Apache Indian Baskets.* Tucson: University of Arizona Press.
   1983   *Indian Baskets of the Southwest.* Tucson: University of Arizona Press.

Teleki, Gloria Roth
   1975   *The Baskets of Rural America.* New York: E. P. Dutton.

Thrapp, Dan L.
   1967   *The Conquest of Apacheria.* Norman: University of Oklahoma Press.

Tiller, Veronica E.
1983 Jicarilla Apache. In *Handbook of North American Indians, Southwest,* edited by Alfonso Ortiz, Vol. 10, pp. 440–461. Washington: Smithsonian Institution.

Torrence, Gaylord
1994 *The American Indian Parfleche: A Tradition of Abstract Painting.* Seattle: University of Washington Press.

Treutlein, Theodore E., Translator
1949 *Ignaz Pfefferkorn: Sonora, A Description of the Province.* Albuquerque: University of New Mexico Press.

U.S. Army Census
1900 Census of the White Mountain Apache Indians of Fort Apache Agency Arizona. Taken by A. A. Armstrong, U S Indian Agent, June 30, 1900. MS on file with William B. Kessel.
1906 Census of the White Mountain Apache Indians of Fort Apache Indian Agency, Arizona. Taken by C. W. Crouse Supt & Special Disbursing Agent, June 30, 1906. MS on file with William B. Kessel.

Utley, Robert M.
1977 *A Clash of Cultures; Fort Bowie and the Chiricahua Apaches.* Washington: National Park Service.

Wehausen, M. J.
1923 Our Apache Orphans. *The Apache Scout* 1(1): 1–4.

Wilcox, David R.
*1981 The entry of Athapaskans into the American Southwest: the problem today. In "The Protohistoric Period in the American Southwest, A.D. 1450–1700," edited by David R. Wilcox and W. Bruce Masse, pp. 213–256. *Arizona State University Anthropological Research Papers* 24. Tempe: Arizona State University.

Williams, Anita Alvarez de
1983 Cocopa. In *Handbook of North American Indians, Southwest,* edited by Alfonso Ortiz, Vol. 10, pp. 99–112. Washington: Smithsonian Institution.

Wissler, Clark
1910 Material Culture of the Blackfoot Indians. *Anthropological Papers of the American Museum of Natural History* 5(1). New York: American Museum Press.

Woodward, Arthur
1943 John G. Bourke on the Arizona Apache, 1874. *Plateau* 16(2): 33–44.

Wright, Barton
1976 *Pueblo Shields from the Fred Harvey Fine Arts Collection.* Flagstaff: Northland Press.

Wyman, Leland C.
1983 *Southwest Indian Drypainting.* Santa Fe and Albuquerque: School of American Research and University of New Mexico Press.

Index

A–19. *See* Nachu
A–100, Chief, daughter of, 100, 186
Abalone shell, 86, 108, 113, 126, 189
Acorns, 32, 46, 47, 59, 61, 83, 170, 180
Adams, Mrs. Chris, 189
Adhesive tape, 125
Agave (Century-plant, Maguey, Mescal), 63, 69, 107, 158, 161, 162, 175, 181. *See also* Mescal
Agriculture. *See* Plants and planting
Alchesay, Bertha, 99, 188
Alchesay, Chief, 15–17, 20, 22, 83, 88, 99, 160
Alchesay household member, 83, 160, 180, 192
Alchesay Lee, Sylvania. *See* Lee, Sylvania Alchesay
American Folklore Society, Memoirs of, 36
American Museum of Natural History, 107, 126, 146, 195 n. 8
Anglos, 8, 44, 63, 77, 86, 129, 132, 144, 161; clothes of, 90, 91, 103, 116; and Yoohn, 99, 152
Antelope (Pronghorn), 45, 96, 168, 176
Anthropology and anthropologists, 4, 5, 7, 31
Apache Scout, The, 21
Apache Scouts. *See* Scouts, Apache
Apache Tribal Council, 25
Apaches Mansos band, 41
Arapaho leggings, 194, 195 n. 12
Archaeologists, 27, 31, 32
Argillite bead, 127

Arizona Historical Society, 138
Arizona Republic, The, 113
Arizona State Museum, 2, 117, 160, 178; Apache collections, 3, 4, 5, 7, 33, 67, 77, 148, 177, 195
Army. *See* United States Army
Arrows, 50–52, 179, 192, 193, 194; in caves, 28; for children, 160, 161; fletching, 86; points, 50–52, 85, 89, 91, 92, 131, 190–91; poison, 52, 179; Southern Athapaskan, 172; traded for tobacco, 132
Arrowshafts, 34, 35, 52; smoothers, 52, 85, 128, 179, 191
Arrow weed, 52, 71, 175
Arts and crafts, revitalization, 25
Ash Flat, Ariz., 145–46, 179, 189
Awls, 95, 111, 184; cases, 186, 187
Ax, 78

B–3. *See* Shima
B–6, 107, 183, 185
B–18. *See* Santa Cruz
B–30. *See* O'Hell, Johnson
B–33. *See* Bezho
B–88. *See* Nanabathan
Babies, 20, 78–80, 92, 127, 170, 185, 189
Badgers, 132, 176
Bags, 82–84, 120, 132, 180; cement, 120, 121. *See also* Pouches; Purses; Sacks; Saddlebags

Baha, Chief, 22, 87–88, 99
Bahti, Thomas, 195 n. 13
Baking powder cans, 115
Balls and ball games, 158–59, 192
Banashley, Rodney, 125
Bands, of Western Apache, 41–45, 46, 47 n. 3, 85, 172
Baptisms, 20, 21
Bark, tree, 67, 71, 73, 78, 81, 183
Barrel hoops, 95
Baskets and basketry, 5, 8, 19, 26, 46, 47, 66, 177, 178, 182; awl, 95; cages, 52, 55, 86; coiled, 2, 71, 77, 170; commercial, 108; *daagodigha*, 145, 148–149, 180, 182; Mescalero, 178, 193; puberty ceremony, 112, 113, 116; seed beaters, 58–59; trade, 85–86, 96. *See also* Burden baskets; Trays; *Tuses*
Basso, Keith H., 36, 97
Batamote, 156, 175, 184
Batkin, Jonathan, 40 n. 3, 195 nn. 2, 5, 12, 196 n. 13
Bats, 140, 142
Beads and beadwork, 5, 28; awl cases, 95; barrettes, 107; baskets, 108, 183; belts, 106–07, 187–88, 194, 196 n. 13; bracelets, 68, 88, 89; caps, 133, 135; carrying-jacket, 91, 92; charms, 126, 127, 129, 136; commercials items, 107, 108; cradle, 80, 160; *daagodigha* emblems, 148; dolls and toys, 88, 89, 101, 159–60; dresses, 111; earrings, 88, 89, 107, 187; fobs, 99, 117, 188; game hoop, 154; hair ornaments, 96, 107, 187; keyring, 107, 187; leggings, 194, 195 n. 12; moccasins, 93, 95, 107, 195 n. 5; necklaces, 68, 88, 89, 99, 105, 106, 107, 117; pollen sack, 145; poncho, 113–15; pouches, 97, 108; purses, 100–101; quiver, 50; shirts, 90, 150; trade, 86; vest, 194, 195 n. 11; wallet, 107
Beans, 46, 108, 129, 130, 170. *See also* Coral beans; Mesquite: beans
Bears, 45, 50, 99
Beatty, June, 79, 184
Beaty, B., 125
Beavers, 81, 132, 176
Beer. *See* Corn: beer
Bells, commercial, 106, 113–115
Belts, 71, 91, 125, 156; beaded, 106–107, 187, 188; dolls, 89, 101, 159; Jicarilla, 171, 194, 196 n. 13; rattlesnake skin, 99, 147, 152
Bezho (B-33), 95, 187
Big John (medicine man), 145, 146

Birds, 45, 52, 138, 141, 179; cages, 52, 54–55, 86, 180; nests, 131. *See also names of individual birds*
Black (color): on arrows, 52; basket designs, 71, 73, 77, 148; beads, 135, 145, 148, 160; on caps, 133, 135, 137; cardinal direction (East), 127, 135, 140–41; charms, 92, 127, 131; clan symbols, 71; cloth, 83, 84, 88, 89, 96, 120, 133, 137; *daagodigha* items, 145, 148, 149; on *gaan* items, 120, 125; game staves, 156; horsehair, 82, 99, 102; paint, 52, 123, 125, 140, 141, 156, 188; ribbon, 113; on shields, 140, 141, 142; stone, 91, 92, 127; wool, 86
Black Mountain, Ariz., 27
Black River, Ariz., 2
Black River Crossing, Ariz., 11
Blankets, 85, 86, 89, 116, 132, 136, 165, 170, 172, 184
Blouses, 101, 103, 104, 185; charms on, 126, 146
Blue (color): on basket, 73; beads, 99, 135, 150, 160; cardinal direction (South), 115, 127, 135, 140–41; charm, 127; cloth, 84, 104, 148; on *daagodigha* items, 135, 148; on game poles, 154; on medicine shirt, 150; on moccasin, 93; paint, 73, 93, 135, 140, 141, 154; on puberty poncho, 115; on saddlebags, 84, 160; on shields, 140, 141, 142; on war caps, 135
Blue River, Ariz., 123, 188
Blue Springs ruins, Ariz., 191
Boarding schools, 12, 18, 19, 21
Bobbydoklinny (medicine man), 144
Bobcats, 50, 176
Bones, animal, 65; items made from, 78, 97, 138, 158, 159
Bonito, Clarinda B., 180
"Born from Water" (culture hero), 121, 142, 173
Bottles: cap, 108; pitched basketry, 66, 73, 159; rawhide, 32; saguaro "boot," 69
Bourke, Melvina, 79, 184, 185
Bourke, Ted, 162, 191
Bowie, Ariz., 11
Bows (archery), 45, 50–51, 85, 160, 172, 179, 192, 193
Bows (musical), 163, 191–192
Boys: cradleboards, 79; hunting, 45, 68; marbles, 160, 192; pouch, 160; raiding paraphernalia, 113, 133
Bracelets, 68, 88, 89, 99, 113, 127
Braids and braiding, 82, 99, 170, 171, 172
Bread. *See* Fry-bread and holders
Breechclouts, 88, 89, 103, 116, 140, 171
Broadmoor Art Academy, 39 n. 3
"Broken Arrow" (movie), 116–17

Index

Brushes, 56, 71, 179, 181, 182. *See also* Hairbrushes
Buck, Mrs. George, 186
Buck, Neil, 55, 146, 148
Buckskin, 31, 191; awl cases, 95, 156, 194; ball, 158; on baskets, 73, 75, 82, 148, 149; caps, 5, 86, 113, 132–35, 136, 137, 185; carrying-jacket, 92; charms, 126, 127, 129, 130, 136, 146, 189; clothing, 103, 110–11, 145, 170, 172; commercial items, 107, 108; on cradleboards, 78, 79, 80; on decoy, 52; dog boots, 81; on drums, 117, 162, 194; for fobs, 99; in *gaan* masks, 120; on game hoop, 154; in hair ornaments, 96; on hide scraper, 78; for keyring, 107, 187; leggings, 194; moccasins, 75, 82, 88, 89, 92–95, 103, 108, 143, 154; pollen sacks, 146; ponchos, 113–115, 184–185; pouches and purses, 97, 100, 186, 193; on quirt, 82; quiver, 50; in saddles and saddlebags, 81, 84; shield covers, 140; shirts, 35, 90–91, 150, 185; skirt, 111, 184; and toys, 88, 89, 160, 161, 193, 194; for trade, 85, 132; on wands, 125; on wrist guard, 52–53
Buffalo, 85, 168, 170
Bullroarers, 125, 194
Burden baskets, 5, 22, 31, 47, 59, 73–75, 82, 177, 180; *daagodigha*, 145, 148–49, 180; miniature, 107, 108, 183, 187; for trade, 85
Bureau of Indian Affairs, 63, 78, 151
Burial rituals, 173. *See also* Death and the dead
Burns, Barney T., 38–39 n. 2
Burro brush, 56, 175
Burros, 45, 81, 84, 180, 181
Butterfly designs, 106, 162
Buttons: on caps, 133, 135, 136, 137, 138; Horstmann, 100; metal, 99, 100, 188; on poncho, 115; for pouches, 97, 108; on shirt, 90
Bylas, Ariz., 7, 28, 31, 35, 50, 77, 78, 128
Bylas, Mrs. Richard, 179

Caches and caching: food, 46, 66, 73; game items, 159; religious items, 121, 140; tobacco, 132
Cactus, 56–57, 69, 73, 139. *See also names of individual cacti*
Calfskin sack, 32, 193
Calva, Ariz., 159, 192
Camps, 17, 68, 73, 82, 86; Ash Flat, 145–46; Bylas, 54, 55; Dewey Flat, 65, 123; Jicarilla, 168–69; near Kinishba, 67, 71, 128; in Mexico, 29, 30, 32, 38–39 n. 2

Camp Verde, Ariz., 47 n. 1, 128
Cane, 175; arrowshafts, 52, 132, 160, 172; drinking tube, 113; flutes, 162, 191; puberty dance, 111, 113, 116, 117, 189; walking, 104, 113, 187
Cans, 39 n. 2, 62, 63, 111, 115, 162
Canteens, 73
Canyon Day, Ariz., 18, 21, 22
Caps, 5, 19, 86, 113, 126, 131, 132–138, 172, 177, 185
Captives, 86, 122
Carrizo, Ariz., 7, 19, 122, 128
Carrizo cane. *See* Cane
Carrizo Creek, Ariz., 19, 122
Carrying-jackets, 79, 89, 91–92, 184
Carrying straps, 56, 69, 78, 80. *See also* Tumplines
Cartridges, 99, 188. *See also* Guns and gun cases
Carvers and carving, 82, 121, 125
Cases, 95, 111, 129, 156, 186–187, 194
Catalogue, Goodwin's personal, 3–5, 52, 177, 178
Catclaw, 55, 175
Cattail, 144
Cattle. *See* Cows; Livestock
Cavalry. *See* United States Army
Caves and rock shelters, 28, 46, 52, 132, 183
"Cave Springs," Chinle Valley, Ariz., 168
Cedar, 184, 187. *See also* Juniper
Cedar Creek, Ariz., 23, 77, 125, 146, 182, 183
Cedar Springs, Ariz., 182, 184
Census (1900), 116, 140
Century-plant. *See* Agave; Mescal
C. G. 10, 135
Changing Woman, 113, 146
Charcoal, 123, 159
Charms (amulets), 189; arrow points, 50, 89, 131; for babies and children, 89, 91–92, 127; on caps, 132; cross-shaped, 136; *daagodigha*, 126–27, 146, 189; metal jewelry, 99; puberty ceremony, 113; with "serpent lightning," 121; shell, 126, 127; Silas John movement, 127, 190; war, 89, 130–31. *See also* Coral beans
Chatto, Mrs. Marie, 193
Cheyenne tribe, 195 n. 12
Chicago Field Museum, 157, 191
Chicago World's Fair, 194
Chiefs, 43, 44, 144, 172. *See also* A–100; Alchesay; Baha; Diablo; Eskiole; Y–1
Chihuahua, Mexico, 29, 30, 32, 38–39 n. 2, 167, 193
"Child of the Water." *See* "Born from Water"

Children: charms, 89; clothes, 89, 91–93, 136; cradleboards, 75, 78, 79, 80–81; with deformities, 20, 25; first born, 96; responsibilities, 44; toys, 159–61; twins, 20. *See also* Babies; Boys; Girls
Chinle Valley, Ariz., 168
Chipmunks, 55
Chipped stone tools, 39 n. 2, 65, 127, 128, 130, 177, 182, 184, 190–91
Chiricahua Apache tribe, 1, 2, 3, 14, 165, 167; basketry, 178, 180; cap, 132; in Chihuahua, 28–31, 32, 193; coral beans, 129; corn beer, 63; doll, 193; in Florida, 122; foods, 168, 170; 4-stick game, 156; fry-bread holder, 182; *gaan* masks, 121; material culture, 170, 172; moccasins, 94, 186; quivers, 50; raiding, 170; religion, 173; rock art, 122; social organization, 36, 172; and U.S. Army, 116; and Western Apache, 41. *See also* Shima
Cholla, 45, 127, 175
Christianity, 12, 144. *See also* Lutheran missions
Chrysotile Charlie, 99, 188
Cibecue, Ariz., 73, 97, 144, 181
Cibecue Apache group, 1, 2, 35, 41, 46, 167
"Cibecue Massacre," 144
Cigarettes, 132, 193
Circle designs, 120, 140, 141
Clans, 35, 43–44, 46, 71, 73, 99, 172
Claws: bear, 99; eagle, 99, 188
Clawson, Curry, 124–25, 183
Clay, 66, 67, 123, 132, 161, 192, 193
Cloth, 28, 85, 170; burlap, 69; calico, 68, 75, 88; canvas, 69, 168, 180; flannel, 50
Clothes and clothing, 19, 47, 127, 195 nn. 2, 11; Anglo, 103, 154; bandanna, 101; change from buckskin, 103; cult movements, 144, 145; dolls, 101, 159; influences on, 90, 91; jeans, 103; Southern Athapaskan, 170–71. *See also names of individual types of clothing*
Clowns, 120, 123, 125
Clubs (weapons), 26, 143, 172, 177, 192
Cochise, 116
Cochise Stronghold, Ariz., 193
Cocopa tribe, 106
Coffee, 62, 115, 140
Coins, 99, 100, 135, 146
Colorado River tribes, 106
Colorado Springs, Colo., 35, 39 n. 3
Colorado Springs Fine Arts Center, 39–40 n. 3, 177

Colors, 123, 127, 135, 140, 160; and cardinal directions, 115, 127, 135, 140–41. *See also names of individual colors*
Comb, aluminum, 99, 188. *See also* Hairbrushes
Coming-out dance. *See* Puberty ceremonies and dances
Commercialization, 73, 79, 108
Conchos, 99, 100, 105, 146, 194, 196 n. 13
Cones. *See* Tinklers
Conn, Richard, 195 nn. 2, 12
Cooking, 44, 64, 67
Coolidge Dam, 7, 178
Coral beans, 108, 129, 130, 175, 189
Corn, 28, 46, 61, 144, 170, 175, 180; beer, 62–63, 66, 162, 182; on charm, 127; gathering and preparation, 59–61, 66, 75, 95; husks, 132, 193; pollen, 144; pudding, 64; storage, 66; from Yavapai, 86
Cosay, Emma, 59, 61, 181, 182
Cosay, Yale, 61
Cosmology, Mescalero, 146
Cotton, 47, 104
Cottonwood, 78, 175, 184; bark for tinder, 67; for basketry, 77; drums, 162; leaves for roasting, 55; shoots for beater, 59
Cottonwood Wash, Ariz., 179
Courting, 35, 59, 123, 162
Cows, 111; bone, 159; hide, 32, 81, 82, 84, 95, 140, 193; horns, 69; rib, 78; tail, 139, 143. *See also* Livestock
Coyote (H–2), 126, 135, 136, 185, 189
Coyotes, 50, 132, 176, 179
Cradleboards, 5, 8, 25, 75, 78–81, 82, 91, 92, 184; charms, 131; drying of frames, 59; Jicarilla, 194; miniature, 107, 108, 183; toy, 160, 192
Crafts and craft items, 8, 71, 108, 111, 125, 129; and Goodwin, 31; and Guenthers, 5, 25; sold to soldiers, 99
Crayons, 123
Crescent designs, 140, 141, 149. *See also* Cross-and-crescent emblems
Crocker, Mrs. Joe, 101, 193
Crook, General George, 15
Cross-and-crescent emblems, 126, 127, 133, 135, 136, 144–49. *See also* Crescent designs
Crosses: and charms, 126, 127; on *daagodigha* items, 146, 148, 149; at "holy ground," 144, 146; on masks, 120, 121, 142; on shield, 140, 142; and Silas John's religion, 144. *See also* Cross-and-crescent emblems

Index

Crown dancers. *See Gaan* dances and dancers
Crows, 140, 176
Crystals, 89, 91, 92, 126, 127, 128, 190
Cummings, Byron, 27, 28, 31, 32, 36
Cups, 69, 181
Curing and curing ceremonies, 173; caps, 132; charms, 126, 128; prehistoric items, 128; puberty ceremonies, 110, 111; Silas John, 21, 121–22, 127
Curley, Sherman, 50, 179
Curtis, Bill, 28, 29, 32, 38 n. 2
Cutter, Ariz., 7

Daagodigha (*Da-xo-di-ya*) religious movement, 127, 133, 135, 144, 145–49; inventory items, 180, 182, 189. *See also* Cross-and-crescent emblems
Dances and dancing, 173; caps, 137; puberty ceremonies, 116, 189; religious movements, 144, 145, 151; with snakes, 145; songs, 162; war and victory, 137, 172. *See also Gaan* dances and dancers; *and individual ceremonies and dances*
Daslahdn (medicine man), 144
Dazen, Loretta, 129, 189
Death and the dead, 14, 19, 133, 144, 173
Decoy, turkey tail, 52–53, 179
Deer, 45, 168, 176; antler, 95; bones, 78, 95; hoofs, 111; jaw, 35; power, 152; skins, 32, 50, 84, 111, 132. *See also* Buckskin
Denton, Charley, 181
Denver Art Museum, 177
Designs. *See* Symbols; *and names of individual designs*
Devil dancers. *See Gaan* dances and dancers
Devil's claw, 71, 73, 77, 175
Dewey Flat, Ariz., 65, 123, 182, 188
Diablo, Chief, 144
Diapers, 80–81
Digging sticks, 46, 54–55, 179
Directions (cardinal), 113, 115, 127, 135, 140, 141, 142, 146
"Dirt Hill Night Ball," 158–59
Disease and illness, 63, 92, 111, 113, 127, 133, 140. *See also* Epidemics; Tuberculosis
Divination rites, 128, 173
Documentation, of collections, 3–5, 7, 8, 120
Dodzondiski (M–2), 90
Dogs, 75, 170; buckskin boots, 81
Dolls, 5, 19, 25; buckskin, 160–61, 193, 194; clay, 161, 192; cloth, 80, 108, 159–60, 183, 184, 193; clothing, 88–89, 101; *Gaan* dancer, 125, 191; Southern Athapaskan, 4, 171, 194, 195 n. 6; for trade, 19
Dot designs, 120, 122, 140, 142
Douglas, Ariz., 28, 38 n. 2
Doves, 55
Dowahongva, Vincent, 125
Drake, Francis, 188, 190
Drake, Mrs. Francis, 55, 179
Drawings, by Goodwin, 3, 27, 29, 34–35
Drawstrings, 83, 97
Dresses, 68, 101, 102, 104, 107, 110–11, 117, 170, 172
Drills and drilling, 67, 113
Drinking tubes, 89, 113, 189
Drums and drumsticks, 8, 66, 117, 162, 163, 191, 194
Dwellings, 47, 165, 170. *See also* Hogans; Models; Tipis; Wickiups
Dyes and dyeing, 78, 86, 120

Eagles, 99, 105, 175; claws, 99, 188; feathers, 89, 113, 117, 120, 130–31, 132–33, 135, 137, 138, 140
Ears and earrings, 88, 89, 107, 187
East (cardinal direction), 127, 146
East Fork, Ariz., 5, 7, 11, 16, 20, 21; church at, 11, 15, 135; orphanage, 7, 20, 21, 26n; photos at or near, by Guenther, 14, 15, 62, 102, 103, 116, 136, 151–52; photos at or near, by Mayerhoff, 61, 68, 75, 82–83, 88, 96, 154, 155, 157
Eden, Ariz., 110
Edwards, Silas John (medicine man), 121–22, 146, 150–52, 190, 195 n. 2; and the Guenthers, 7, 21, 82, 99, 102, 144–45, 151; horsehair items by, 82, 99, 102, 152, 180, 188
Eggan, Fred, 36
Elderly. *See* Old people
Elgo, Gloria, 107, 187
Elk, 45, 84, 176
Embroidery, 149
Enamelware dishes, 62, 69, 78
Epidemics, 11, 13, 16–17, 19. *See also* Disease and illness; Tuberculosis
Eskiaga, 88
Eskiole, Chief, 144
Exhibits, comparative, 2, 3, 4

Face painting, 35, 123
Families and family groups, 43, 44–45, 46, 136, 172. *See also* Bands, of Western Apache

Farms and farming. *See* Plants and planting
Fatty, arrow made by, 193
Feathers: on arrows, 85, 160; on caps, 132–33, 135, 136, 137–38, 177, 185; as charms, 89, 91–92, 127, 131; on doll, 89; on dress, 117; on *gaan* dancers, 120, 125; for puberty ceremony, 113, 117; on shields, 140
Ferg, Alan, 4, 7, 38 n. 1, 40 nn. 3, 4, 165
Fiddles, 162–63, 191–92, 195 n. 3
Field Columbian Museum. *See* Chicago Field Museum
Fire, 68, 103, 159
Firedrills, 8, 67, 184
Flags, American, 105, 195 n. 11
Fleshing tools, 78, 184
Flickers, Red-shafted, 89, 91, 92, 176
Floods, 121
Florence Junction, Ariz., 77, 182
Flour sacks. *See* Sacks: flour
Flowers, in mineral paints, 123
Flu epidemic of 1918–19, 16–18
Flutes and flageolets, 162–63, 191
Food, 45, 47, 50; caching, 46, 66, 73; gathering, 43, 73, 75, 82; preparation, 59, 64; of Southern Athapaskans, 168, 170; strainers, 64, 182; trading, 90, 128
Forestdale, Ariz., 59
Fort Apache, Ariz., 86, 99, 107, 125, 187; ceremonies near, 117, 137; Guenthers at, 8, 13–14, 18, 20–21, 23
Fort Apache Indian Reservation, Ariz., 1; baskets, 77, 148, 182; Guenthers at, 5, 19, 21, 22, 77; religious cults, 144–45
Fort Huachuca, Ariz., 139
Fort Marion, Florida, 122
Fort McDowell Indian Reservation, Ariz., 145
Foxes, 50, 132, 176
Frankfort Arsenal, 99
Friday, Tom, 75
Fringes, 73, 97, 108, 111, 115, 127, 150, 161, 195 n. 4
Fry-bread and holders, 62, 63, 182

Gaan, 8, 110; motif, 5, 105, 108, 125, 141
Gaan dances and dancers, 5, 105, 110, 111, 122, 124–25, 183, 191. *See also* Wands, for *gaan* dance
Gaan masks, 110, 123, 125, 140, 162, 177; by John Robinson, 35, 117–22, 142, 191

Galena, 127, 140. *See also* Lead
Game animals, 45, 46, 47. *See also names of individual game animals*
Games and game paraphernalia, 12, 154–59, 161, 192
Gass, Carl, 103
Gathering, 8, 46, 47, 56, 61, 73, 75, 82–83
Gatliffe, Leslie, 28
Gavilando brothers, 39 n. 2
Gay, Dorothy Francis, 120
Gee-strings, 103. *See also* Breechclouts
George, Samuel, 184
Geronimo, 14, 63, 116
Geronimo, Ariz., 179
Getty, Harry, 4
Ghosts, 133
Giants, 121
Gila Pueblo Archaeological Foundation, 177
Gila River, 2, 7, 128, 178
Gila Valley Mills, 120, 121
Girls: and beadwork, 105, 106, 136; cradleboards, 75, 79; crafts, 108; and flutes, 162; games and toys, 160, 161; hair ornaments, 96, 185; hunting and gathering, 46, 68; pendants, 86; water carrying, 68. *See also* Puberty ceremonies and dances
"Giver of Life" (Holy Being), 142
Glass, 39 n. 2, 50, 89; beads, 80, 91, 99, 107, 160
Globe, Ariz., 11, 67, 137, 148, 177, 180
Glue, 120, 125
Goats, 45, 170
Goddard, Pliny Earle, 126, 127, 146, 168, 195 n. 8
Gong, alarm, 39 n. 2
Goodwin, Elizabeth Sage, 39–40 n. 3
Goodwin, Grenville: and Apache culture, 28, 31–35, 40 n. 3; definition of Western Apache, 1, 41; education, 27, 36, 38 n. 1; field documentation, 2–5, 8, 29, 35–36, 38–39 n. 2, 177; in Mexico, 28–31, 32, 38–39 n. 2; Opler's impressions of, 36–38; trap sticks made by, 52, 195 n. 1; University of Arizona, 27, 32, 36, 38 n. 1, 40 n. 4, 47 n. 1. *See also* Goodwin Collection
Goodwin, Janice, 36, 40 n. 3
Goodwin, Neil, 4, 29, 38 n. 2, 40 n. 3, 177
Goodwin, Sage, 35, 40 n. 3
Goodwin Collection, 2–5, 8, 31, 33, 177–78, 195
Gourds, 69, 158, 170, 175; scrapers, 67, 177, 183
Grainers, hide, 78

Index

Grass and grasses, 73, 155; bear, 56, 64, 65, 67, 78, 103, 175, 182, 183; Johnson, 81, 175, 184; jungle-rice, 78, 175; Spike Muhly, 113, 175; vine-mesquite, 56, 175

Gray, George, 130, 189

Gray, Mrs. George, 97, 186

Green (color): bead, 91; on cap, 135; cardinal direction (South), 113, 115, 127, 141; charms, 91, 127; cloth, 84, 160; paint, 123, 125, 135, 140, 141, 160, 188; plastic, 115; ribbons, 113; on saddlebags, 84; on shields, 140, 141, 142; on toys, 160

Ground stone tools: handstone, 59, 61; manos and metates, 39 n. 2, 59–61, 181, 182; mortars and pestles, 59–61, 181; palette, paint, 123, 188; polishing stone, 67, 183; tabular knife, 65; whetstone, 78

Groups, 47 nn. 2, 3. *See also* Bands, of Western Apache; Families and family groups; Local groups

Guadalupe Mountains, Tex., 195 n. 7

Guenther, Arthur Alchesay, 17, 23, 25, 63

Guenther, E. Edgar, and Minnie Knoop Guenther: Apache arts and crafts, 5, 25, 108; and Apache culture, 5, 12; awards to, 9, 23, 25; camp calls, 12, 13, 17, 19, 21, 23; children, 7, 9, 15, 17; and epidemics, 13, 16–17, 19; Lutheran ministry, 9–10, 11, 12, 18, 19, 21, 23; marriage, 9, 10, 11, 23; and orphanage, 9, 20, 21, 26; photographs of, 13, 14, 22, 24; photography by, 7; and puberty ceremony, 116; and schools, 12, 15, 17, 18, 19, 21; and Silas John, 7, 21; and White Mountain Apache Tribe, 9, 21–22, 23. *See also* Guenther Collection; Lutheran missions

Guenther, Edgar, Jr., 93

Guenther, Emma, 100, 101

Guenther, Gloria, 107

Guenther, Wenonah, 15, 19, 80, 93, 159

Guenther Collection, 5, 8, 25, 26, 77, 133, 148, 177–78, 195; and Knoops, 7, 19

Guns and gun cases, 9, 14, 19, 85, 194

Gustina, Amos, 163, 191, 195 n. 3

H–2. *See* Coyote

Hail, 121

Hair: clip, 107, 187; facial, 99, 113; hair styles, 96, 103, 154, 159, 160; ornaments, 88, 96, 113, 160, 161, 185; of Southern Athapascans, 170, 171, 172

Hairbrushes, 89, 113

Handles, 55, 59, 62, 65, 69, 71, 78, 82, 95

Hands, E. J., 32

Hanna, Forman G., 110

Hare, Meredith, 40 n. 3

Hare, Mrs. Meredith. *See* Goodwin, Elizabeth Sage

Harrington, M. R., 195 n. 8

Harvesting, 44, 46, 132. *See also* Gathering

Hastings, Cain, 125

Hats and hatbands, 52, 101, 102, 103. *See also* Caps

Haury, Emil W., 2, 31, 36, 40 n. 4, 195 n. 10

Hawks and hawk feathers, 99, 140

Headbands, 88, 89, 107, 154, 170, 187

Healing and health, 127, 129, 132, 144, 145

Hearths, firedrill, 67, 184

Hematite, 71, 123, 127, 137, 140

Henry, Ruthena Dale, 73, 181

Heroes, culture, 121, 141, 142, 173

Hides, 77–78, 85, 95, 96, 132, 168, 184

Hobbles, for horses, 194, 195 n. 8

Hoes, 85

Hoffman, Mr., 28

Hogans, 168, 170

Hoijer, Harry, 35, 36

Holbrook, Ariz., 11

Holy grounds, 144, 146, 151

Hook-and-eyes, 106, 107

Hoop segments, 191

Hopi tribe, 3, 50, 85, 125, 172, 195 n. 8

Horsehair: on dolls, 88, 89; handles, 71; hatbands, 102, 103, 188; items made by Silas John or Yoohn, 82, 99, 102, 152, 180, 188; quirts, 82, 180; rope, 78; strings on fiddles, 162; watch chains and fobs, 99, 102, 188

Horse Lake, N.Mex., 193

Horses, 11–12, 45, 47, 170; in *aaghode* prophecy, 144; and *daagodigha* dance, 145; harness, 71, 136, 140; hide, 50, 81, 140; horseshoes, 81; and *na'ilde'*, 144; for packing, 61, 82; as payment, 111; for pulling, 146; rib, 78; saddlebags, 82–84, 180; saddles, 81; for trade, 85, 132; whips, 82

Hospital, Whiteriver, 22

Hourglass shape design, 96, 195 n. 4

Houses, models of, 183

Hubbard, Joseph, 32

Hummingbirds, 120, 121, 133, 135, 141–42

Hunt, George W. P., 148

Hunting, 8, 23, 44, 45, 46, 97; by Athapaskans, 168; deer, 52, 132; rites, 173; by torch light, 68, 73

Ibis, Wood, 132, 175
Inashoot ndezen, 17
"In Charge of Life" (Holy Being), 142
Indian Agency, in Whiteriver, 18
Indian Arts Fund (Santa Fe), 40n. 3
Indian Springs, Ariz., 180
Informants, relationship with Goodwin, 2, 5
Inks, 88, 89, 123
Installment plans, 104
Interpreters, 21, 120
Irrigation, 46, 170

Jackets, 89, 91–92, 103. *See also* Carrying-jackets
James, Laban, 61, 71, 180, 181
James, Mrs. Laban, 180
Jars and jar forms: basketry, 69, 71, 77, 182; pottery, 66–67, 69, 177, 183, 193
Javelina. *See* Peccary
Jeffords, Tom, 116
Jernigan, Wesley, 151
Jet (stone), 127
Jewels and jewelry, 98, 99–100, 107, 115, 127, 183, 194. *See also* Beads and beadwork; Pendants
Jicarilla Apache tribe, 1, 150–51, 165, 167, 168, 170–73; inventory items, 178, 193–94, 195 nn. 2, 4, 196 nn. 13, 14; reservation, 193, 194
John, Silas. *See* Edwards, Silas John
Johnnie Yuma. *See* Yoohn
Johnson, Daisey, 185
Juniper, 45, 136, 175; bark, 67, 73, 81, 184; berries, 46, 59, 107, 168, 187; bow and arrows of, 160; game staves, 156; leaves, as caulking, 71; warclub, 143; in wickiups, 146

Kachinas, 173
Kaut, Charles, 36
Kennedy, John F., 137
Kessel, Ruth Guenther, 25
Kessel, William B., 7, 19, 142
Keyes, Jack, 105
Keyes, Mrs. Jack, 15, 80, 184
Keyes, Mary, 69, 105, 115, 181, 187
Keyring, 107, 187
Kidder, A. V., 168
Kingbird, 55, 176
Kinishba, Ariz., 28, 64, 67, 71, 128
Kiowa-Apache tribe, 1, 165, 167, 168, 170, 172, 173

Knives, 156; ceremonial, 128; drawknife, 78; for mescal, 54–55, 65, 86, 179; metal, 52, 67, 78, 95, 179, 184; sheaths for, 19; stone, 65, 91, 92, 179, 182
Knoch-e-da-klinne (medicine man), 144
Knoop, Arnold and Frieda, 7, 19–20
Knoop, Minnie. *See* Guenther, E. Edgar, and Minnie Knoop Guenther
Knot, quirt, 82

Ladles, 65, 69, 182
Lances, 139, 172, 192
Languages and linguistics, 3, 8, 11, 36, 165, 166, 167
Lard pails, 63
Laveen, Ariz., 145
Lazy stitch, 90, 150
Lead, 85, 127. *See also* Galena
Leatherwork: belts, 50, 71, 89; netting, 196 n. 14; in quirt, 82; saddle, 194; on shields, 140, 142; on toys, 160; on warclub, 143; for wrist guards, 52
Lee, Sylvania Alchesay, 105, 187
Leggings, 170, 171, 194, 195 n. 12
Lichen, 52, 179
Lightning, 120, 121, 122, 142; charms, 89, 92, 128, 131; "lightning power," 144, 152
Limonite, 123
Lipan tribe, 1, 165, 167, 168, 170, 171, 172, 173; material collected by Goodwin, 178, 194, 195 n. 6
Livestock, 45, 47, 170, 172. *See also* Cows; Horses; Sheep
Lizards, 77, 121
Local groups, 43, 44, 45, 172
Loco Jim, 126, 127, 137, 143, 185, 189, 192
Loe, Fred, 17
Longstreet, David, 5, 111, 113, 189
Looms, 105, 170
Lower Pinal Creek, Ariz., 182, 190
Lupe, Nelson, Sr., 22
Lupe, Ronnie, 25
Lutheran missions, 1, 5, 9, 10, 11, 12, 15, 19–21, 23, 135

M-2. *See* Dodzondiski
Maguey. *See* Agave
Mahogany. *See* Mountain-mahogany
Malachite, 123
Manganese oxide, 123
Manning, Reg, 113, 189

Index

Manson, James W., 149
Mansos. *See* Apaches Mansos band
Manuelito, N.Mex., 125, 194
Marbles, 160, 192
Marriage and marriages, 43, 44, 96, 111, 172
Masks. *See Gaan* masks
Masonite, 125
Material culture studies, 7–8, 31, 170–72
Maverick, Ariz., 23
Mayerhoff, Paul, 7, 11, 19, 88, 154, 157
Mazatzal band, 46
McCormack, Mrs. Frances J., 67, 137
McKee, Charles, 32
McNary, Ariz., 23
Meat, 45, 47, 65, 66, 168
"Medicine beans," 108, 129
Medicine caps, 140, 145, 146
Medicine charms, 126; cords for, 89, 136; designs on shields, 140
Medicine men (shamans), 21, 142, 143, 144, 145, 146, 173; and caps, 132, 133, 135, 136, 185; and cults, 144, 145; and masks, 120, 121, 122
Medicine shirts, 35, 150–51
Meem, John Gaw, 40 n. 3
Men: caps, 132–38; clothing, 89–91, 103, 170–72, 185; courting by, 162; dolls of, 101, 193, 194; face paints, 123; games, 156, 158; moccasins, 94, 194, 195 n. 5; necklaces, 130; older, 131, 132, 133, 158; pouches, 97; recreation, 154–55; responsibilities, 44; shields, 140; spoons, 65; and tobacco, 131; tump ropes, 68
Mesa, Ariz., 69
Mesa Ranch School, Ariz., 27
Mescal, 46, 47, 55; heads, 56, 57, 73, 179; juice, 73; knives, 54–55, 65, 86, 179; preparation and roasting, 50, 54–56, 176; and Southern Athapaskans, 168, 170; trade, 85. *See also* Agave
Mescal beans, 129
Mescalero Apache tribe, 1, 165, 167, 171, 172, 173; carver from, 125; cosmology, 146; foods, 168, 170; items in Goodwin Collection, 178, 194, 195; medicine shirt, 150, 185, 195 n. 2; reservation, 145, 170, 178, 194
Mesquite, 45, 55, 56, 78, 175, 184; beans, 46, 61, 168, 170; game sticks, 158, 159
Metal: aluminum: 99, 188; bells, 113, 115; brass, 86, 88, 89, 90, 96, 99, 106; buttons, 97, 99–100, 188; commercial items, 107; copper wire and rivets, 71, 140, 142; cup, 69; *daagodigha* emblem, 146; file, 65; iron, 55, 85, 123, 139, 146, 147, 162; jewelry, 98, 99–100; knives, 52, 67, 95, 179, 184; nickel, crosses of, 148; pan, 68; scarcity of, 65; at Sierra Azul camp, 39 n. 2; steel, 95, 100; strainer, 64, 182; tacks, 133, 135, 137; tinklers, 73, 88, 93, 97, 107, 111, 115, 160
Mexicans, 63, 82, 86, 90, 91
Mexico, 28–31, 32, 38, 91, 111, 137; raiding of, 45, 170; ranches in, 39 n. 2, 47
Miller, Carl F., 32
Mills, 23, 69, 120, 121
Miniatures, 107, 108, 183, 187
Mirrors, 35, 68, 89
Missionaries, 1. *See also* Guenther, E. Edgar and Minnie Knoop; Mayerhoff, Paul
Moccasins, 5, 15, 19, 140, 154, 177; adult's, 94–95, 103, 159, 186, 193, 194; baby's, 92, 185; children's, 93, 185–86; on doll, 88, 89, 159, 160; and hidden-ball game, 159; Jicarilla, 194, 195 n. 5; makeshift, 143, 186; Mescalero, 194; miniature, 107, 108, 183; with "noses," 5, 68, 75, 82, 88, 89, 94–95, 159; for Southern Athapaskans, 170, 171, 172
Mockingbirds, 55, 176
Models: of drying tray, 59; of house, 183; of shield, 140; of tipi, 194
Model-T Ford, 18, 80
Mohave tribe, 3, 106, 107
Money. *See* Coins
Monsters, 141
Monument Valley, Ariz., 194
Moon, 141, 146
Mother-of-pearl, 97, 137
Mothers, 79, 92, 121, 144
Mountain lions, 50, 176
Mountain-mahogany, 139, 158, 175
Mountain Spirits. *See Gaan*
Movies: "Broken Arrow," 116–17
Mulberry, 50, 77, 175
Mules, 45
Museum of New Mexico, 177
Museums, 31. *See also names of individual museums*
Musical instruments, 8, 162–63. *See also names of individual musical instruments*
Myths and mythology, 36, 50, 67, 86, 121, 122, 162, 173

Na ih es. See Puberty ceremonies and dances
Naches (Nachez), Ariz., 179
Nachu (A–19), 99, 188
Nagaahoun, 95, 187
Nails, 62, 95, 120
Nanabathan (B–88), 181
Napkin rings, 108, 183
Nashkine, Harvey, 5, 52, 91, 156, 179, 181, 184, 195 n. 1; daughter of, 96, 185
Nativistic movements. *See* Religious movements
Navaho Material Culture (Kluckhohn et al.), 7, 8, 177
Navajo tribe, 1, 47, 165; agriculture, 168, 170; arrows, 52; baskets, 177; Big Snake, 122; blankets, 85, 86, 89, 184; braiding, 82; bullroarer, 194; compared to Apache, 8, 167, 170; drum and drumstick, 162, 163, 194; and Grenville Goodwin, 27, 178, 195 nn. 8, 9, 10, 196 n. 14; hogans, 168, 170; livestock, 45, 165, 168, 170; material culture, 8, 172; needle case, 111; pottery making, 170; raids on, 45; religion, 173; reservation, 27–28, 195 n. 8; saddle, 194, 195 n. 10; salt gathering, 59; shinney sticks, 158; silverwork, 102, 194; social organization, 172; stirring sticks, 67; trade with Apache, 50, 85, 86, 95, 99; trade with Hopi, 195 n. 8; weaving tools, 194
Naylor, Thomas H., 38 n. 2
Necklaces: baby's charm, 127, 189; of beads and mirrors, 68; choker-type, 88, 89; commercial, 107, 187; on Coyote and family, 136; on dolls, 101, 160; for puberty ceremony, 113; with tweezers, 99, 188; war charm, 130, 189. *See also* Shawl necklaces; T–necklaces
Needle case, Navajo, 111
Nelson, Harriet, 184
New San Carlos, Ariz. *See* Rice, Arizona
Noch-ay-del-klinne (medicine man), 144
North (cardinal direction), 127, 146
Northern Tonto group, 1, 2, 35, 41, 46, 47 n. 3, 167
North Fork, Ariz., 15, 19, 61, 79, 180, 181

Oak trees, 45, 77; boles, 69; Emory oak, 59, 170, 175; Gambel oak, 154, 156, 175. *See also* Acorns
Obsidian, 89, 127, 130, 131
Ocher, yellow, 50, 79, 88, 90, 92, 95, 113, 115, 127, 137
Ocotillo, 55, 175
O'Hell, Johnson (B–30), 116, 186
Old people, 78, 103, 133, 158, 191

Old San Carlos, Ariz., 7, 178
Oliver, Lester, 137
Opata tribe, 63
Opler, Morris E., 35, 121, 195 nn. 2, 5, 6, 12
Oraibi, Ariz., 195 n. 8
Orange (color), 52, 80, 89, 127, 135, 154, 156
Orioles, 113, 131, 133, 176
Ornamentation and ornaments: buckskin caps, 133, 137; buckskin dresses, 111; burden baskets, 73; *daagodigha* movement, 145; medicine shirt, 150; pouch, 97; saddle, 100; on toys, 88–89, 160–61. *See also* Beads and beadwork; Hair: ornaments; Silverwork
Orphanage, 9, 20, 21, 26
Osborne's store, Bylas, Ariz., 86, 97, 143
Owls and owl feathers, 113, 133, 137, 138, 176
Oxhide, 81

P–1 (medicine man), 144
Packrats, 45, 52, 176
Packs and packing, 69, 75, 81, 82, 170
Pails, lard, 63
Paints and painting, 35, 123, 127, 143, 160, 188–89; on buckskin, 111, 135, 137, 140, 191; with cactus juice, 139; enamel paint, 123; of *gaan* mask, 120; oil paintings, 5, 124–25, 183; on shields and covers, 140–42; on wands, 125; water colors, 3, 35, 123, 125. *See also* Ocher, yellow
Paiute tribe, 177
Papago (Tohono O'Odham) tribe, 170
Parfleche, 193, 195 n. 4
Payson, Ariz., 1, 47 n. 1
Peccary, 50, 176, 179
Pencil lines, 101, 123
Pendants, 86, 107, 113, 126, 127, 135, 189
Penrose, Julie, 39 n. 3
Peridot, Ariz., 7
Petroglyphs, 28, 29. *See also* Pictographs
Pets, 55, 86
Peyote rites, 173
Peyote stitch, 105, 115
Phoenix, Ariz., 69, 138
Photography: by Goodwin, 3, 29, 38–39 n. 2; by Guenther and Mayerhoff, 7
Pictographs, of snakes, 122. *See also* Petroglyphs
Picuris Pueblo, N.Mex., 170
Pigeons, 55, 176

Index

Pima and Piman peoples, 1, 3, 170
Pine trees (Piñon, Pinyon, Ponderosa, Yellow), 45, 77, 91, 92, 146, 155, 175; nuts, 46, 168; pitch, 69, 71
Piñon, Ariz., trading post at, 27–28
Pipes, 5, 128, 132, 191, 193
Pitch, 35, 52, 64, 66, 69, 73; brush for, 71, 181. *See also Tuses*
Pits: for games, 159; for roasting, 55, 56
Plains Indians and tribes, 100, 105, 140, 167, 168, 170, 172, 173. *See also names of individual tribes*
Plants and planting, 8, 43, 45–47, 55, 106, 123, 131–32, 152, 170, 177
Plastic "jewels," 115
Poisons, for arrows, 52, 179
Poles, 56, 77–78, 146, 179. *See also* Games and game peraphernalia
Pollen, 77, 89, 113, 116, 126, 129, 144. *See also* Sacks: pollen
Ponchos, 88, 89, 111, 113–15, 116, 160, 172, 184–85
Porcupines, 121, 176, 195 n. 11
Pottery and pots, 5, 8, 39 n. 2, 47, 69, 71, 132, 170, 193; by Anna Price, 67, 177, 183, 192; drums, 8, 66, 162; ladle, 65, 182; making of, 66–67, 162; scrapers for, 67, 183; sherds, 65, 177, 183, 193
Pouches, 97, 108, 126–27, 186; for dolls, 89, 159; toy, 160, 193
Power: "bat," 142; in buckskin caps, 135; "enemies-against," 140, 141; and games, 154, 156; of medicine men, 121, 122; of shields, 140; of Silas John, 144, 152
Prayers, 132, 140, 144
Prehistoric artifacts, reuse of, 177, 178; arrowpoints, 50, 190–91; arrowshaft tools, 52, 128, 179, 191; as charms, 50, 89, 113, 127, 128, 131, 189, 190, 191; knives, 128; metates and manos, 59, 181, 182; mortars and pestles, 59, 61, 181; pots and sherds, 65, 182, 183; shell, 113, 127, 189; stone pipes, 128, 132, 191
Price, Anna, 5, 103; awl and case, 95, 184, 186; basket, 180; bird cage, 52, 180; brush, 181; clay doll, 161, 192; corn from, 61, 180; corn husk cigarettes, 132, 193; cradleboard, 78; digging stick, 55, 179; 4–stick game, 156; lance, 139, 192; mescal head, 56, 179; pots, 67, 177, 183, 192; quirt, 82, 180; saddle, 81, 180; saguaro container, 69, 181; salt cake, 59, 180; scraper, 183; seed beater, 59, 179; spoons, 65, 183; tump ropes, 68; turkey baskets, 86; yucca soap, 188

Prickly pear, 46, 168, 175, 179
Prisons, 99, 145, 151, 152
Prophets and prophecies, 144, 145
Puberty ceremonies and dances (*na ih es*), 8, 62, 77, 122, 173, 189; clothing, 110–11, 113–15, 116–17, 184–85; necklaces, 105, 106, 115, 187, 189; paraphernalia, 86, 89, 112–13, 189
Pueblo Indians and Puebloan peoples, 1, 140, 162, 165, 167, 170, 172, 173, 195 nn. 4, 8
Purses, 100–101, 186
Puttees, 172

Quail, 55, 91, 92, 133, 175; hunting, 68, 73
Quartz crystal, 89, 91, 92, 126, 127, 128, 190
Quillwork, 195 n. 11
Quirts, 82, 180
Quivers, 50–51, 67, 179, 194

Rabbits, 45, 81
Raids and raiding, 8, 39 n. 2, 43, 45, 46, 97; by boys, 89, 113, 133; caps, 132, 133–35, 137; horseshoes used on, 81; knives obtained on, 95; into Mexico, 94, 111, 129, 162; moccasins, 143; necklaces, 130; by Southern Athapaskans, 170, 172. *See also* Warfare
Rain, 46, 111, 121, 142, 173
Ranches and ranchers, 11, 39 n. 2, 45, 47, 103
Rattlesnakes, 99, 121, 122, 144, 152
Rau, Mrs. Augusta, 100, 101
Rawhide: on basket, 148; bottle, 32, 193; on drum, 162; in hair ornament, 88, 96; hobble, 194; on lance, 139; lashing, 193; on moccasins, 92, 143; on quirt, 82; on quiver, 50; rope, 32, 78, 193; saddle and saddlebags, 81, 82, 83, 84, 180; shields, 140; shoes for animals, 81, 180, 181; snowshoes, 194; on warclub, 143
Red (color): on arrows, 35, 52; on bag, 83; on baskets, 71, 73, 77; on caps, 133; cardinal direction (West), 115, 127, 140; on carved dancers, 125; on charm, 127; cloth, 84, 104, 115, 125; on dress, 104; on fiddle, 163; on *gaan* masks, 120; on medicine shirt, 150; on moccasins, 93; paint, 73, 123, 188; plastic, 115; on poles, 154; on poncho, 115; on saddlebags, 84; on shields, 140; on toys, 88, 89, 160
Red Knolls Amphitheater, Ariz., 110
Reeds. *See* Cane
Religious movements, 1, 115, 127, 133, 144–52. *See also Daagodigha*

Religious symbols and motifs, 121–22
Reservations and reservation life, 1, 55, 111, 116. *See also names of individual reservations; and under names of individual tribes*
Ribbons, 113
Rice (New San Carlos), Ariz., 7, 52, 69, 177, 178, 183, 187, 192
Rick-rack, on cradle boards, 79, 80
Riding, horseback, 82, 83, 170
Riley, John, 115
Rings, 99, 108, 183, 188
Rio Grande River Valley, 167, 170
Rituals, 8, 99, 111, 128, 132, 165, 173. *See also* Puberty ceremonies and dances
Rivets, on shield, 140, 142
Roberson, Mrs. John, 69, 181
Robinson, John, 35, 117–20, 121, 122, 142, 191
Robison, John. *See* Robinson, John
Rock art. *See* Petroglyphs; Pictographs
Rock shelters. *See* Caves and rock shelters
Rope, John, 5, 52, 55, 91, 123, 140, 143
Rope and rope twisters, 32, 68, 73, 78, 82, 83, 136, 181, 193
Rose Peak, 123, 188
Rothrock, G. H., 138
Roybal, Crecencio, 195 n. 7
"Rules over Life" (Holy Being), 142
Rye, Ariz., 179

Sacks, 32, 193; flour, 69, 120, 160; pollen, 89, 126, 145, 146–48, 189. *See also* Bags; Saddlebags
Saddlebags, 31, 32, 82–84, 136, 177, 180, 193; toy, 160, 192
Saddles, 81, 82, 92, 100, 136, 180; Mexican, 81; Navajo, 194, 195 n. 10
Safety pins, 107, 127
Safford, Ariz., 69, 120, 121
Saguaro, 45, 175; callus ("boot"), 69, 181; fruit and pickers, 46, 56, 85, 86, 170, 179
Salesmen, traveling, 104
Salt and salt-drying, 58, 59, 140, 180
San Carlos, Ariz., 7, 8, 78, 99, 122, 178. *See also* Old San Carlos; Rice, Ariz.
San Carlos Apache tribe, 1, 2, 41, 167; bands, 42; farming, 46; *gaan* masks, 121; group or band, 35, 42, 67, 133, 178; hidden-ball, 159; metate and mano, 181, 182; pottery jars, 183; wands, 125, 191

San Carlos Indian Reservation, Ariz., 1, 7, 19, 28, 45, 47 n. 1; dances, 151; epidemic at, 16–17; religious cult movement, 144–45; wickiup on, 168; Yuman tribes on, 106
Sand paintings, 8, 122, 173
Santa Clara Pueblo, N.Mex., 195 n. 4
Santa Cruz (B–18), 103
Sashes, 85
Savage, Kitty, 96, 185
Sayles, E. B., 4, 177
Scalping, 172
Scavenging from prehistoric sites, 52, 59, 61, 65
Scent, added to mineral paints, 123
Schools. *See* Boarding schools; *and under* Guenther, E. Edgar and Minnie Knoop
Schraeder, Art, 29
Scoria, red, 123
Scouts, Apache, 14, 15, 18, 133, 137, 138, 139, 144, 152
Scratchers. *See* Sticks: scratching
Screen, window, 64
Seasons, 45, 46, 142
Seed beaters, 58–59, 179, 180
Seeds, 59, 66, 73, 107, 129, 132, 180; storage of, 32, 83; for trade, 85
Sego, Charlie, 86, 129, 132, 154, 156, 158; inventory items, 189, 192, 193
Sego, Mrs. Charlie, 179
Semi-bands, 41–43, 44, 45, 46
Sequins, 101, 113, 115
Sewing and sewing machines, 83, 84, 101, 104, 159
Shawl necklaces, 106, 107, 187
Shawls, 102, 103, 104, 159, 185
Sheep, 45, 85, 165, 168, 170. *See also* Wool
Sheet metal, 50, 78, 146
Shells, 86, 108, 113, 133; charms made from, 91–92, 126, 127, 132, 189
Shields, 5, 140–42, 172, 192
Shima (B–3), 14–15, 62, 73, 93, 159, 180, 182, 186, 193
Shinney ball and sticks, 158, 192
Shirts, 5, 89, 129; charms on, 126, 146; men's buckskin, 90–91, 185; of Silas John, 150–51, 185, 195 n. 2; for Southern Athapaskan men, 170
Shoes, 52, 101, 103; for animals, 81, 180, 181. *See also* Moccasins
Shovel blades, 55, 86

Index

Sierra Azul Mountains, Mexico, 38–39 n. 2
Sierra Madres, Mexico, 28, 31, 32, 39 n. 2
Silas John. *See* Edwards, Silas John
Silver (color): paint, 123, 188
Silverwork, 8, 165; on cap, 132, 135, 136; in charms, 99, 126, 127, 146; *daagodigha* ornaments, 145–48; jewelry, 88, 89, 97, 99, 102, 105, 135, 36, 188, 194, 196 n. 13
Sinew, 32, 50, 52, 67, 90, 120, 127, 130, 133, 143, 154, 160, 162, 172
Sioux tribe, 194, 195 n. 11
Skilskoy. See Y–1
Skins, animal, 47, 50, 85
Skirts: buckskin, 111, 160, 172, 184; cloth, 88, 102, 103, 104, 116, 185
Skunks, 13, 121
"Slayer of Monsters" (culture hero), 141, 142, 173
Smith, Misse, 38–39 n. 2
Smithsonian Institution, 32, 35, 196 n. 13
Smoking, 128, 131–32
Snakes: in curing ceremonies, 122; designs on *gaan* masks, 120–22; and Silas John, 144–45, 146; "snake power," 122, 144, 152; supernatural, 121, 122
Snow and snowshoes, 146, 159, 193, 194, 196 n. 14
Soap, 188
Sobaipuri tribe, 3
Social Organization of the Western Apache (Goodwin), 36
Solder, 135, 146
Songs, ceremonial, 162
Sonora, Mexico, 28, 38 n. 2, 47
Sotol, 56, 59, 67, 82, 103, 120, 125, 139, 175
South (cardinal direction), 127, 146
Southeastern Yavapai tribe, 3, 111
Southern Paiute tribe, 170
Southern Tonto group, 1, 2, 35, 41, 43, 46, 167
Southwest Forest Industries, 23
Southwest Museum, Los Angeles, 195 n. 8
Spanish, 63, 81, 139, 165, 170
Spicer, Edward, 35
Spier, Leslie, 35
Spoons, 65, 183
Spring Creek, Ariz., 182
Squash, 46, 69, 170, 175, 181
Squawberry. *See* Sumac
Squirrels, 45, 55, 81, 88, 92, 132, 176
Staffs, 103, 113, 191
Stanley, Andrew, 179

Stanley, Mrs. Andrew, 5, 59, 146, 189
Stars, 126, 140–41
Stevens, Bill, 125
Sticks: for beating tobacco, 132; in burden baskets, 73, 75, 82, 149; for digging, 54, 55, 179; for games, 156, 158, 159, 192; scratching, 89, 113, 189; stirring, 66, 67, 182; for traps, 52, 53, 179. *See also* Twigs
Stitches. *See* Lazy stitch; Peyote stitch
Stone, Lambert, 116
Stone, Sadie, 62, 77, 116
Stone and stones: from archaeological sites, 177, 184; basalt (lava), 52, 60, 61, 78; calcite, 123, 190; calcium carbonate, 123; chalcedony, 89, 128, 130; charms, 130; concretions, 160; deadfall trap, 53; feldspar, 123; for games, 156–57, 161, 192; gneiss, 78; for hammer, 55; with lichen for poison, 52; for marbles, 160, 192; to melt pitch, 71; Navajo silver mold, 194; quartzite, 61; shale, 127; steatite, 89, 127, 128; in warclub, 143, 192. *See also* Chipped stone tools; Ground stone tools
Storage and storing, 66, 69, 73, 82, 83, 132, 140
Strainers, 62–63, 64, 182
Strings (twine), 52, 104, 120, 127, 133, 143, 154, 162–63
Sumac, 71, 175, 181
Sun, 120, 121, 142, 146
Sun (culture hero), 120, 141, 142, 146
Sun-dance, 173
Sunflowers, 46, 59, 85, 175
Sunrise dance. *See* Puberty ceremonies and dances
Swift, Ambrose, 162, 191
Swords and sabres, 139
Sycamore, 103, 175
Symbols, 71, 113, 120, 121, 146. *See also names of individual symbols*

Tacks, metal or brass, 86, 133, 135, 137
Tag-band numbers, 95, 99, 135, 140
Tamarix (Tamarisk) tree, 59, 67, 78, 159, 175
Tanning and tanning tools, 44, 78
Tansy-mustard, 59, 175, 180
Taos Pueblo, N.Mex., 170, 193, 194, 195 n. 4, 196 n. 14
Tarahumara tribe, 63
Taylor, Alice Bemis, 39 n. 3
Taylor, Gracie S., 78
Taylor, Mrs., of Whiteriver, 73, 180

Taylor Museum of the Colorado Springs Fine Arts Center, 39–40 n. 3, 177
Thompson, Ray, 125, 191
Thongs, 97, 108, 120, 126, 127
Thread, commercial, 90, 129
Thunder, 120, 142; "thunder knife," 92
Tinilzay (V–18), 140, 192
Tinklers (cones), 73, 88, 93, 97, 107, 111, 115, 160
Tipis, 168, 170, 194
Tiswin. See Corn: beer
Titla, Philip, 125
T–necklaces, 105, 106, 115, 117, 160, 187
Tobacco, 66, 89, 131–32, 175
Toe tabs ("noses"). See Moccasins: with "noses"
Tohono O'Odham tribe, 170
Tonay, Bart, 62
Tongs, 56, 179
Tonto Apache Indian Reservation, Ariz., 1
Tonto group: medicine men, 122. *See also* Northern Tonto group; Southern Tonto group
Tonto National Monument, 66, 183
Torches, 67–68, 73, 89, 184
Tortice, Harry, 107, 108, 183, 187
Tortice, Nora Vlasquez, 105, 107, 108, 186, 187
Tortoise-shell, false, 101
Tourist trade and tourists, 79, 84, 111, 129, 159
Toys, 5, 84, 159–61, 192, 193. *See also names of individual toys*
Trade and trading, 45, 85–86, 90, 100, 132, 195 n. 8; with Hopi, 50, 85; with Navajo, 50, 85–86, 95, 99; with traders, 19, 27–28, 31, 33, 128, 135, 140, 177; with Yavapai, 85–86; with Zuni, 50, 52, 78, 85–86, 96
Trap sticks, deadfall, 52–53, 179, 195 n. 1
Travois, 170
Trays, 64; coiled basketry, 31, 76–77, 170; for mescal, 50, 54–56, 179; for salt, 58, 59, 180
Triangles: on cap, 135; on shield, 140, 141, 142
Tuberculosis, 12, 39 n. 3
Tucson, Ariz., 23, 25, 28, 36, 38 n. 2, 67, 69, 129, 167; and Apaches Mansos, 41; inventory items, 183–84
Tularosa River, N.Mex., 192
Tulpai. See Corn: beer
Tumplines, 68, 75. *See also* Carrying straps
Turkey Creek, Ariz., 144
Turkey Hill Pueblo, Ariz., 32, 38 n. 1

Turkeys, 23, 52–53, 65, 85, 86, 175, 179, 180; feathers, 52, 85, 132, 133, 137, 138, 160, 177, 179, 185
Turquoise, 86, 113, 126, 127, 132, 135
Tuses, 25, 35, 68, 69, 71–73, 82, 145, 177; inventory items, 181, 183, 192, 194, 195 nn. 7, 9; for trade or for sale, 73, 85, 107; use of term, 8, 178
Tweezers, 89, 99, 136, 138, 188
Twigs, 71, 89, 91, 92

Underwear and underclothing, 101, 103, 159, 160
Underworld, 173
United States Army, 11, 44, 63, 90, 99, 111, 116, 139, 144. *See also* Scouts, Apache
University of Arizona, 2, 23, 27, 47 n. 1; Department of Anthropology students, 4, 38 n. 2, 120; excavations by, 32; Goodwin at, 36, 38 n. 1, 40 n. 4
University of Chicago, 2, 36
Upper Black River, Ariz., 192
Upper worlds, 120
Ute tribe, 170, 177, 194, 196 n. 13

V–18. *See* Tinilzay
V–50, 128, 191
Valor, Palmer, 5, 50, 93, 111, 132, 139, 185, 193
Venuio, Tofilo, 168
Verde Valley, Ariz., 177
Vest, beaded, 194, 195 n. 11
Victory dance, 172
Villa, Pancho, 137

Wallet, buckskin, 107, 186
Walnut trees, 77, 175; nuts from, 61, 120, 161, 192
Walpi, Ariz., 194, 195 n. 8
Wands, for *gaan* dance, 124–25, 162, 191
War bonnets and caps, 5, 132, 133–135, 172
Warfare, 1, 35, 44, 52, 91, 130, 143; charms, 89; dances, 137, 172; "war power," 140, 141. *See also* Clubs; Raids and raiding; Shields
Watch chains and fobs, 98–99, 102, 117, 188
Water: carrying of, 68, 69, 73, 123; containers for, 31, 66, 69, 73, 170; depictions of, 121, 122
Weaving, 8, 47, 170, 194
Wedel, Waldo, 32
Wehausen, M. J., 18, 20
West (cardinal direction), 127, 146
Western Apache Dictionary (Perry et al.), 8

Index

Western Apache tribe, 1–3, 41–47, 165, 167, 168–73. *See also names of individual groups and bands*
Western Archeological Center, Tucson, Ariz., 67
Western White Mountain band, 133
Wheat, 46, 120, 160
Whiskey Flat, Ariz., 61
White, William. See Y–1
White (color): in *aaghode* prophecy, 144; arrow points, 50, 91, 92; in blanket, 86; on caps, 135; cardinal direction (North), 127, 135, 140–41; in charms, 91, 92, 127, 129, 130; on *daagodigha* paraphernalia, 145, 148; on dress, 104; on *gaan* paraphernalia, 120, 125; on horsehair items, 82, 99, 102; on medicine shirt, 150; paint, 123, 188; on saddlebags, 84; on shields, 140, 141; on toys, 88, 89, 160
White Mountain Apache tribe: agriculture, 46; bands, 42; in "Broken Arrow," 116; charm, 126; clans, 99; cradleboards, 79; defined, 1, 2, 35, 41–42, 167; drum, 162; and flu, 17; and Guenther, 22, 23; hidden-ball game, 159; as informants, 5; inventory items, 178, 181–84, 186, 188, 189–90; necklace, 107; 3–stick game, 157; and turkeys, 86
White Mountain Indian Reservation, Ariz., 45, 47 n. 1. *See also* Fort Apache Indian Reservation, Ariz.
Whiteriver, Ariz., 50, 61, 137; church at, 20; coral beans and, 108, 129, 189; Emma Cosay of, 59; and flu, 17; and Guenthers, 5, 7, 12, 18–25; hospital, 22; Lutheran mission in, 18
White-Shell-Woman, 113
Wickiups and domed dwellings, 29, 47, 67, 136, 148, 168, 170; for *daagodigha*, 145–146
Widows and widowers, 44, 90
Wild plant foods, 45–47, 170
Willow, 59, 77, 86, 103, 175
Wire, 55, 62, 71
Wisconsin, 9, 10, 11
Wisconsin Evangelical Lutheran Synod, 9, 10, 11
Wisdom, Charles, 32
Witches and witchcraft, 129, 130
Wolf, 50, 176
Women, 45; charms, 136, 146; as chief, 43; clothing, 68, 88, 101, 102, 170–72, 195 n. 12; and flute playing, 162; games, 154, 156, 157, 158, 161; gathering, 43, 46, 75; hide preparation, 77–78; mescal roasting, 50, 55–56; moccasins, 68, 94; packing on horseback, 82; pouches, 97; responsibilities, 44; spoons, 65; tump ropes, 68. *See also* Girls

Wood rats. *See* Packrats
Wool, 47, 86, 170. *See also* Sheep
Wright, George, children of, 59, 180
Wright, Jewett, 52, 78, 81, 128, 140, 143, 159; inventory items, 179, 180, 181, 186, 192
Wright, Mrs. Jewett, 5; bag, 83, 180; baskets, 59, 73, 77, 182; cradleboard, 78, 184; dolls, 88, 193; "Five Stone Game" walnuts, 161, 192; inventory items, 179, 180, 182, 184, 185, 189, 192, 193; items for babies, 91, 92, 127, 184, 185, 189; mescal preparation, 50, 55, 56; seed beaters, 59, 180; stirring sticks, 67, 182; strainer, 64, 182; tanning tools, 78, 184; trays, 56, 179, 180, 182
Wright, Lassie, 73, 181
Wrist guards, 52, 179

Y–1, Chief, 77, 116
Yarn, 80, 86, 159
Ya-Va-Ki-Shi (Apache Scout), 138
Yavapai tribe, 3, 47 n. 3, 85, 86, 106, 111, 122, 138
Yellow (color): on bag, 83; on burden baskets, 73; on caps, 135, 137; cardinal direction (West), 115, 127, 135, 140, 141; on carrying-jacket, 92; on charms, 127, 131; on cradleboards, 79; on doll's clothing, 88; on dress, 104; on hide scraper, 78; on moccasins, 93, 95; paint, 123, 189; on puberty ceremony paraphernalia, 111, 113, 115; on quivers, 50; on shields, 140–41; on shirts, 90, 150
Yoohn (medicine man), 99, 151–52
Yucca (Spanish bayonet), 45, 46, 123, 175, 192; bird cage, 52, 180; brush for pitch, 71, 181; in cradleboard, 79; fruit, 168, 179; in *gaan* paraphernalia, 120, 125; game paraphernalia, 159, 192; juice, 90, 123; leaves, 35, 65, 71, 132, 183, 188; pipe, 132, 193; spoons of, 65, 183; staff of, 103; strips and ties of, 56, 59, 61, 64, 65, 67, 71, 81, 183; in trays, 56, 59, 64
Yuma, Johnnie. *See* Yoohn
Yuma (Quechan) and Yuman peoples, 1, 3, 106
Yuma Territorial Prison, 99

Zigzag designs, on shield, 140, 142
Zuni Salt Lake, New Mexico, 59
Zuni tribe, 3, 125, 172, 184; trade with, 50, 52, 78, 85, 86, 96
Zwazwa, Augustina, 194, 195 n. 6

Contributors

ALAN FERG holds a Master's degree in anthropology from the University of Arizona, and is presently an Assistant Curator at the Arizona State Museum. He has participated in archaeological projects in Arizona and New Mexico, catalogued ethnographic collections from Arizona and northern Mexico, and conducted archaeological and ethnographic research using museum collections and archival materials. His research interests include ceramics, rock art, and general material culture studies of the late prehistoric and early historic periods in the American Southwest. He has written numerous articles on these and related subjects and has contributed extensively to several archaeological volumes published by the Arizona State Museum.

WILLIAM B. KESSEL holds a doctorate in anthropology from the University of Arizona, and a Master of Divinity in theology from Bethany Lutheran Seminary in Mankato, Minnesota. He is now Dean of Academic Affairs at Bethany Lutheran College. He has conducted archaeological and ethnographic fieldwork on the Fort Apache Indian Reservation, taught anthropology at the University of Arizona and Northern Arizona University, and served as Mission Organizer for several congregations in Arizona and California. He was an editorial assistant for the journal *Ethnohistory* and for a published volume of Grenville Goodwin's notes, *Western Apache Raiding and Warfare*. Kessel continues to research and write on a variety of ethnographic and theological topics, including the genesis of religious cults.

MORRIS E. OPLER has devoted much of his long professional career to research dealing with the seven Apachean-speaking tribes of the American Southwest and southern Plains. Holder of a doctorate in anthropology from the University of Chicago, Opler is well known for his numerous books, monographs, and journal articles dealing with anthropological theory and ethnographic work, and he recently contributed four chapters dealing with Apache groups for the Smithsonian *Handbook of North American Indians*. He has received many awards and honors and has served as president of the American Anthropological Association. Professor Emeritus of Cornell University and the University of Oklahoma, he continues to pursue his research at his home in Norman, Oklahoma.

JAN BELL is Curator of Collections at the Arizona State Museum. She holds a Master's degree in anthropology from the University of Arizona, where she has taught museum studies and anthropology. She has written papers on various logistical and ethical aspects of collecting by museums and on curation of archaeological and ethnographic materials in the Southwest. She currently is researching contemporary Navajo pottery, Tohono O'odham (Papago) wire baskets, and their makers.